Pitt Series in Policy and Institutional Studies

Executive Leadership in Anglo-American Systems

COLIN CAMPBELL, S.J., AND
MARGARET JANE WYSZOMIRSKI,

EDITORS

University of Pittsburgh Press

Published by the University of Pittsburgh Press, Pittsburgh, Pa., 15260
Copyright © 1991, University of Pittsburgh Press
All rights reserved
Eurospan, London
Manufactured in the United States of America

Library of Congress Cataloging-in-Publication Data

Executive leadership in Anglo-American systems / Colin Campbell and
Margaret Jane Wyszomirski, editors.
  p.   cm.—(Pitt series in policy and institutional studies)
ISBN 0-8229-3677-1
  1. Presidents—United States.   2. Presidents—United States—
Staff.   3. Executive departments—United States.   4. Cabinet
system—Great Britain.   5. Cabinet system—Canada.   6. Comparative
government.   I. Campbell, Colin, 1943– .   II. Wyszomirski,
Margaret Jane.   III. Series.
JK516.E94   1991
353.03—dc20   90-25483
                                                                           CIP

A CIP catalogue record for this book is available from the British Library.

To the memory of
Marver H. Bernstein and Charles H. Levine

Contents

Acknowledgments   ix

1 Introduction   3
Colin Campbell, S.J., and Margaret Jane Wyszomirski

PART I   EXECUTIVE LEADERSHIP:
WHY THE SENSE OF MALAISE?

2 The Leadership Question: Is There an Answer?   35
Bert A. Rockman

3 Executive Leadership in an Age of Overload
and Retrenchment   57
B. Guy Peters

4 The Discontinuous Institutional Presidency   85
Margaret Jane Wyszomirski

PART II   CABINET GOVERNMENT:
A CLEAN BILL OF HEALTH?

5 Presidentialization in a Parliamentary System?   111
George W. Jones

6 Cabinet Government in Canada: Corporate
Management of a Confederal Executive   139
Peter Aucoin

7 A View from the Cabinet in Canada   161
Thomas Hockin

PART III   ADVICE TO PRESIDENTS AND
PRIME MINISTERS ON DOMESTIC AND
ECONOMIC POLICY

8 The Council of Economic Advisers   171
Roger B. Porter

9 OMB: Professionalism, Politicization, and the Presidency   195
   James P. Pfiffner

10 Providing Countervailing Analysis and Advice in a
   Career-Dominated Bureaucratic System: The British
   Experience, 1916–1988   219
   William Plowden

11 Executive Office Agencies and Advisory Policy Units   249
   Stuart E. Eizenstat

          PART IV   ADVICE TO PRESIDENTS AND
          PRIME MINISTERS ON FOREIGN AND
                    DEFENSE POLICY

12 The National Security Adviser: A Presidential Perspective   259
   Kevin V. Mulcahy and Harold F. Kendrick

13 National Security Affairs: A Defense Department
   Perspective   281
   Lawrence J. Korb

14 The Whitehall Model: Career Staff Support for Cabinet
   in Foreign Affairs   295
   Peter Hennessy

          PART V   PERSONAL STAFF FOR PRESIDENTS
                    AND PRIME MINISTERS

15 White House Staffing: Salvation, Damnation,
   and Uncertainty   319
   Joseph A. Pika

16 New and Old Lessons on White House Management   341
   Samuel Kernell

17 Support for Prime Ministers: A Comparative Perspective   361
   Patrick Weller

18 The Role of Press Secretaries on Chief Executive Staffs
   in Anglo-American Systems   381
   Colin Seymour-Ure

   Notes on Contributors   413

Acknowledgments

This book is the product of a conference entitled "The Executive Establishment and Executive Leadership: A Comparative Perspective" which was held on September 5–7, 1988. This conference was the inaugural event of Georgetown University's Bicentennial Program. We owe our greatest debt of gratitude to Charles L. Currie, S.J.—the Bicentennial director and Kathleen Lesko of the Bicentennial office for their tremendous help with the organization and support of the conference. We are also grateful to Timothy S. Healy, S.J.—at that time president of Georgetown—and J. Donald Freeze, S.J.—the provost—for their support of the conference.

An exceedingly distinguished group of scholars and practitioners contributed immensely to the conference proceedings and deserve mention even though they have not written chapters for this book. In order of appearance, these are: John Gardner, Marver H. Bernstein, Norman C. Thomas, Gillian Peele, Charles H. Levine, Allan Fatheringham, David Gergen, Michael Robinson, Anthony King, Charles Shultze, Brent Scowcroft, Brian Fall, Jack Watson, Thomas Hockin, Richard Rose, Arch Dotson, John Hart, Arturo Valenzuela, Renate Mayntz, Hans-Ulrich Derlien, Harvey Feigenbaum, Ulrich Kloti, Metin Heper, George J. Szablowski and John Power.

We had excellent staff support for the conference at Georgetown. John Crapo—the administrative officer of the Graduate Public Policy Program—did an excellent job with arrangements and Jenefer Ellingston—Colin Campbell's former assistant—worked superbly as ringmaster for bringing together this volume. In addition, several student assistants helped us. These include: Kelly Sweeney, Janet Kim, Marion Gray, and Connor O'Brien.

As usual, Jane Flanders, editor of the Pitt Series in Policy and Institutional Studies, made the process of turning our manuscript into a book an exceedingly pleasant experience.

We have dedicated this volume to two participants who have passed away since the conference. Marver H. Bernstein was a university professor in the Government Department at Georgetown University. He previously had been president of Brandeis University and dean of the Woodrow Wilson School of Public and International Affairs. We remember him especially for his tireless efforts on behalf of the Georgetown Graduate Public Policy Program, which is a co-sponsor of this volume. Charles H. Levine was distinguished professor of government and public administration at the American University. He had held prior posts with the Congressional Research Service, the Brookings Institution, the University of Kansas, the University of Maryland, and Syracuse University. We honor in particular his dedication to the work and ideals of the International Political Science Association Research Committee on the Structure and Organization of Government, which also served as a co-sponsor of this volume.

Executive Leadership
in Anglo-American Systems

1

Introduction

COLIN CAMPBELL, S.J., AND
MARGARET JANE WYSZOMIRSKI

> The president was playing badminton in Aspen the day vast hordes of
> barbaric Huns invaded Chicago. . . . Mr. Bush, though caught off
> guard by news of the invasion, said, "We're following the whole Hun
> situation very closely, and right now it looks encouraging." Over the
> next three days, additional hordes . . . swarmed into the Windy City
> [and] Mr. Bush was said to be conferring with John Sununu [the
> White House chief of staff]; then in came Robert Teeter [the leading
> Republican political strategist] with a poll that showed that 70 per-
> cent of the American people thought the president was doing an
> excellent job with the barbarians.
> —*Garrison Keillor (1989)*

Thus far into a prolonged period of Republican control of the White
House, it seems scarcely believable that Americans actually tossed a
president—Jimmy Carter—out of office in the 1980 election. The
public had, it appeared, punished Carter for being president at a
time when stagflation paralyzed most advanced economies and
religious extremists humiliated the United States through the protracted Iranian hostage incident.

A lot of water has passed under the bridge since Carter's departure from the White House. During Reagan's first two years, the
U.S. economy slipped into its deepest decline since the Depression.
Through the period of recovery, the deficit bloated to unprecedented proportions—helping the United States become the greatest
debtor nation in the world. Throughout the Reagan years, the
United States stood by powerlessly as the nation's citizens—
Marines garrisoned in Beirut and airline passengers alike—became
subject to horrific terrorist actions.

Observers coined the phrase *sleaze factor* to underscore the degree
to which Republican appointees had appeared to surpass all previ-

ous benchmarks in their abuse of public office for personal gain. By 1986, it became clear that the administration had mired itself in a sordid arrangement whereby profits from arms sold illegally to Iran had found their way into the coffers of the Nicaraguan contras. The U.S. public divided between those who thought the president had not approved the scheme (the minority) and those who believed he was too senile to recognize the implications if he had given his approval (the majority). The nation had also turned off politics— except when Colonel Oliver North rendered his stirring self- defense—so it did not matter what the Congress, the media, and others who fussed about the Iran-contra affair came up with. For most people, the bottom line—more disposable income coated in eye-watering patriotism—said, "Have a nice day."

We live in an age in which minimalism governs U.S. citizens' expectations for the performance of their presidents. Assuming economic growth and the right mix of diplomatic spear-rattling and accommodation, Americans want their presidents to leave them alone—"Just say 'Yes' or 'No'; don't muck around with making sure that things actually happen." These are trying times for the Garrison Keillors of the world who grew up during a period when even the eminently likable Dwight Eisenhower—the mightiest and most popular general in World War II—drew heavy fire while president for not seeming to work at the job.

This collection of eighteen essays juxtaposes the current mini- malist era with a more vigorous one in which the nation expected a great deal more of presidents. These essays were originally pre- sented at a conference entitled "The Executive Establishment and Executive Leadership" that formed part of the bicentennial celebra- tions at Georgetown University in 1988–89.

The Georgetown conference sought to achieve two things. First, it chose to mark in a special way the fiftieth anniversary of the passage of the Reorganization Act of 1939. This legislation— which was key to the development of the White House Office and the Executive Office of the President—stemmed from the Brown- low Committee report of 1937. Franklin D. Roosevelt had assem- bled this panel of three eminent students of public administration to advise him on how he might enhance the ability of presidents to give the executive branch greater coherence.

In the spirit of the age, the committee handed down a set of prescriptions that fit the bill for an activist president. Further, it

tried to address the requirements of executive-branch coordination in an era in which both the government's role and citizens'
expectations for it had expanded exponentially with the immense
challenge of helping the country to recover from the Depression.[1]

The 1939 legislation did not respond fully to the committee
report. However, it went far toward legitimizing the process
whereby the White House Office and the Executive Office of the
President would become highly differentiated and entrenched fix-
tures within the "institutional presidency." The White House has
seen the steady accretion of units under assistants to the president
for every dimension of the president's affairs—including national
security, domestic policy, legislative affairs, communications, and
many more fields. The Executive Office of the President—which
began as the umbrella organization for the old Bureau of the
Budget and three other agencies—now takes in several major
presidential agencies including the National Security Council
Staff, the Office of Management and Budget, the Council of Economic Advisers, and the Office of the U.S. Trade Representative.

By using the 1939 Reorganization Act as a point of reference,
the Georgetown conference set out to take stock of how exactly
the institutional presidency has adapted over the intervening years
to changes in the expectations and management styles of incumbents. In this regard, it took special pains to assess the organizational consequences of the past decade in which Ronald Reagan
and George Bush have responded to public pressures to reduce the
role of government.

In addition to tracing the emergence—and, recently, the decline—of the institutional presidency since 1939, the Georgetown
conference sought to inform discussion about executive leadership
in the United States by comparison with the organization of central control and coordination in other political systems. Four papers, on West Germany (by Renate Mayntz and Hans-Ulrich
Derlien), France (Harvey Feigenbaum), Switzerland (Ulrich Klöti)
and Turkey (Metin Heper), have subsequently been published in
the October 1989 and July 1990 issues of *Governance: An International Journal of Policy and Administration*.

Those papers from the Georgetown conference that were concerned with the institutional dimensions of executive leadership
in the United Kingdom, Canada, and Australia have all found
their way into this volume. These contributions from the "West-

minster" systems have proven especially useful in two respects. First, no matter how much we consider the United States—with its separation of powers—as unique, we still can derive much from a knowledge about other countries. Some difficulties with executive leadership in our current era seem to be independent of substantial differences between political systems. Second, we can see that the personalities of presidents and prime ministers alike can significantly influence how executive institutions actually operate. With these considerations in mind, let us examine in greater detail the implications of the minimalist era for the U.S. presidency.

The Presidency in an Age of the Modest Job Description

Few would dispute the assertion that the U.S. presidency has dominated the skyline of high political office in advanced democracies at least since World War II. U.S. presidents lead the most powerful nation in the West. As if this were not enough, they enjoy a level of prestige not enjoyed by heads of government in other systems. That is, by virtue of being head of state, they are symbols of national integrity and unity. Only the French president even comes close to rivaling his U.S. counterpart in being both the chief executive and the high priest of the national liturgy. And, as we saw during the period of cohabitation in France from 1986 to 1988, the control of the French Parliament by a party other than the president's can greatly diminish his power.

The generosity of the American Constitution toward the president falls short of unambiguous affirmation. By separating the powers of the executive and legislative branches, the Founding Fathers made it difficult for presidents to achieve unity of purpose between their administrations and Congress. The increasingly recurrent tendency of American voters to split their support so as to give one party the presidency and the other control of one or both of the houses of Congress has deepened this ambiguity. With dismay bordering on alarm, some scholars have pointed up the dysfunctions of such "divided government."[2] In some quarters, the belief has emerged that only a series of constitutional amendments can revive the presidency to the point where incumbents can actually reestablish national purpose and direction.

Such views run head-on into contrasting ideas about the presidency that have held increasing sway over the past two decades. Indeed, the dominant views of the current state of the presidency range from counsel to leave-well-enough-alone to outright celebrations of the genius of the institution. Most observers argue that, above all, we should avoid experimentalism regarding the presidency, observing that the strength of the presidency waxes and wanes according to the character of the incumbent and the circumstances of the moment. Therefore, we should avoid tinkering—not to mention making major constitutional changes. All too often, this view maintains, reformists tend to overreact to transitory problems. For instance, advocates of the status quo note that reformists bemoaned the weakness of the presidency as an institution at the end of the Carter administration and then turned around and registered alarm about the impotence of Congress during the early years of the Reagan administration.

Holding that Americans reveal at their core a strong monarchical tendency, those opposing experimentalism point to Dwight D. Eisenhower and Richard M. Nixon as exemplifying presidents who abused their prerogatives in opposite directions.[3] Eisenhower exploited the prestige of office—which his illustrious military career strongly reinforced—by avoiding situations and commitments that would place his standing at risk. Nixon's imperial presidency, on the other hand, so depleted the public's willingness to suspend disbelief that he left the office close to bankrupt.

More recent studies of Eisenhower have even absolved him from the charge that he hid behind the trappings of office. According to this view, a president's dual role as head of both government and of state requires him to balance astutely the inspirational and operational dimensions of the office.[4] This allows for immense latitude in the degree to which a president assumes an active or reactive mode of leadership. Eisenhower often chose to disguise his effectiveness as a political leader in order to maintain the generality of his appeal. The Watergate debacle preordained that those taking an indulgent attitude toward Richard Nixon will have to wait some time for a revisionist view of his exercise of presidential prerogatives.

Just as the revisionist view of Eisenhower was winning credence among political scientists, Ronald Reagan emerged as a president who seemed self-consciously to emphasize inspiration over executive leadership. Here again, political scientists are of two minds about the significance of Reagan's appeal. Some have traced a gradual drift in the presidency away from executive leadership—with its emphasis on developing and nurturing bargaining relationships with Congress, the bureaucracy, and outside interests. Instead, presidents have tilted in favor of going public— that is, making direct appeals to the electorate over the heads of institutionalized participants in the policy arena.[5]

A president who leans too far in favor of going public runs the risk of making his administration a permanent campaign. This ultimately undermines the capacity of the president and Congress to grapple with the real-life issues facing the nation.[6] Some observers, however, underscore the inherent risks and limitations of going public and conclude that—even under Reagan—the approach did not work the wonders that scholars have attributed to it.[7]

Ronald Reagan's election in 1980 posed a serious challenge to those arguing that an administration's success rests substantially on a president's capacity to manage the executive branch. Unlike Jimmy Carter, Reagan had—even while governor of California— proven veritably immune to concern with factual and administration detail.[8] If anything, Reagan applied himself less rigorously to micromanagement of the presidency. However, he won a landslide victory in his 1984 reelection bid. It became clear that the nation would absolve Reagan of his detached management style—especially since the recovery of the economy began to match his upbeat rhetoric.[9]

During 1986 and 1987, the mounting evidence of the Iran-contra inquiries pointed (at least) to negligence on Reagan's part in his constitutional duty to oversee the activities of his cabinet secretaries and aides. However, after a precipitous fall from approval levels approaching canonization (from over 68 percent), Reagan's ratings during 1987 rarely dipped below 50 percent.[10] Analysis of the 1988 election suggests in fact that public approval of Reagan—his persona if not his approach to administration— helped turn the vote partially into a referendum on his policies.[11]

Some political scientists have called for a radical alteration of our criteria for evaluating presidential performance in light of Reagan's success. Some have even promoted the argument that the Reagan administration was not an aberration.[12] They subscribe to the view that recent presidents gradually have eroded the institutionalized features of the presidency. Ironically, the effect has been to abandon the emphasis on institutional management and replace it with a personal control imperative even as the federal government's role has expanded. Some have noted that Richard Nixon's dramatic increase in the number of political appointees in the previously career-oriented Office of Management and Budget was an example of this process. For instance, Terry Moe maintains that it

[fit] into a larger pattern of institutional development; and . . . [extended] that pattern in ways that, while sometimes excessive and politically unwise, were consistent with both its historical trajectory and the institutional forces behind it.[13]

At the heart of such analyses are deep reservations about whether a president can enhance his performance by improving his ability to tap the *neutral competence* of the state apparatus. In recent decades, several political scientists have asserted that presidents could improve their effectiveness by regularizing cabinet-level consultations and using more permanent officials as staff support for such coordinative councils.[14] On the other hand, those arguing for deinstitutionalization assume that incumbents only vaguely want such devices and resources.[15] What they really strive for is *responsive competence*. Presidents' institutional strategies will thus focus on centralizing decisions in the White House and politicizing the bureaucracy. Both tracks bolster their ability to circumvent established organizations and vested interests, or—to use Kernell's phrase—go public.

Scholars whose work preceded analyses based on the deinstitutionalization thesis had detected recent presidents' focus on responsive competence and warned of its dangers. They underscored, for instance, the fact that presidents cannot override permanent officialdom by fiat alone.[16] Bureaucracy by its nature serves up "complexity, diversity, jurisdictional dispute, and recalcitrance." True executive leadership masters and redirects these factors.

Some scholars have, in fact, called for blending the use of the state apparatus with attention to political appeal in what they term *policy competence*.[17] Responsive competence should not overshadow neutral competence so much that the president cannot gauge the effects of policies in light of a long-term perspective. Too much emphasis on responsive competence makes it appear that the presidency is less concerned with policies in the national interest than with opportunistic moves designed to gain short-term political support.

Stephen Hess recently has taken this critique of the deinstitutionalists a step further by attacking the centralization of power in the White House and the politicization of the bureaucracy as "the managerial presidency."[18] Hess charges that this has led to bloating the White House staff at the cost of making cabinet secretaries and career civil servants marginal within the policy process. In Hess's view, the fact that centralization exacerbates bureaucratization is especially paradoxical. Similarly, Richard Rose has recently asserted that—even in the age of going public—competent presidents provide a mix of public responsiveness and effective handling of policies:

Responsiveness to the electorate is necessary if the authority of a President is to rest on the consent of the governed. . . . A President must be judged by the actual impact of his policies as well as by what he would like to do. Effectiveness is necessary if a nation's leader is to do more than declare good intentions.[19]

The Importance of a Comparative Perspective on Executive Leadership

All too often, commentators characterize the U.S. trend toward the minimalist and deinstitutionalized presidency as uniquely American. A closer examination of other systems, however, reveals similar shifts in executive leadership from an emphasis on policy to responsive competence. In no small part, these developments relate to sharply declining expectations among the electorates of advanced democracies and less support for government involvement in their lives.

In 1978, Richard Rose and B. Guy Peters anticipated a backlash against government intervention.[20] Although voters had supported the rapid expansion of government programs in the postwar years because their net impact increased average disposable income, in the 1970s, governments were approaching the point at which funding additional programs would actually bite into disposable income.

To add to this problem, the two major energy shocks of 1973 and 1979 deeply impaired economic growth during the decade.

Sluggish economies laboring simultaneously under both high unemployment and inflation prevented governments from expanding their roles. In addition, neoconservative and neoliberal leaders began to rally support for the view that the size and pervasiveness of government had become millstones around the necks of national economies.

In *The President as Prisoner,* William F. Grover argues that presidents have become prisoners of the market—ever fearful that any proposals to address problems with additional funds will result in a decline of "business confidence."[21] In the minds of the electorate, small government has become beautiful.

During the 1980s, prime ministers, as much as presidents, abandoned expansive views of government and—by extension—their own roles. In the United States and the three Westminster systems examined in this book, each party that controlled the executive branch at the beginning of 1979 had lost power by 1983—with the reins turning over in the United Kingdom and Canada in 1979, in the United States in 1980, and in Australia in 1983. Of course, Canada's Liberal party regained power in 1980 only to lose it to the Progressive Conservatives in 1984. We would be hard pressed indeed to find in this century another seven-year period during which the governments of all four countries remained the same.

Scholars characterize such periods as realignments. However, they associate these occurrences with "critical elections" in which cathartic or epochal experiences cause voters to shift allegiance from one party to another.[22] We can see, for instance, why the Great Depression effected a realignment from the Republicans to the Democrats in the United States. The economic catastrophe put the nation under siege. The public embraced the interventionist politics of the New Deal because dire circumstances seemed to warrant radical action.

The resilience of the parties that took power in our four nations between 1979 and 1984 is undoubtedly largely owing to the trauma through which their citizens passed during the economic stagnation of the late 1970s and early 1980s. While in all four nations economic decline fell short of a depression, voters apparently believed that they missed one by just a hair. As we saw in March 1990, Australians will not abandon a Labor government even in favor of the Conservative coalition, which still evokes too many memories of the economic crisis of the early 1980s. Meanwhile, in an astute reading of the times, the center-left Australian Labor party has wrapped itself in precisely the neoliberal, market-oriented, limited-government rhetoric that has proven so successful in the United States, United Kingdom, and Canada.

Concerns about the personalization of executive leadership, the deinstitutionalization of cabinet and bureaucratic systems, and the emphasis on *responsive,* at the expense of *policy,* competence also loom large in the United Kingdom, Canada, and Australia—not just in the United States. While these problems differ greatly across systems, the presence of cabinet government versus presidential leadership, permanent versus appointive bureaucracies, and—in the case of Australia—left-center versus right-center parties does not immunize Westminster systems from detached executive styles. These approaches by prime ministers—whatever the dysfunctions—respond to the prevailing public mood about government. They also exploit the electronic technologies that allow presidents and prime ministers alike to go over the heads of their institutional antagonists and short-circuit standing operating procedures.

A Sense of Malaise About Executive Leadership?

This book is divided into five parts. The first probes the origins of the sense of malaise which seems to enshroud contemporary studies of executive leadership in the United States, the United Kindgom, Canada, and Australia. Bert Rockman, leading off this section, asserts that a great deal of unease among some attentive observers about the state of executive leadership stems from a shift in our political cultures from a collectivist to an individualistic or entrepreneurial age. The former system favored the "insider politics" that gave a high degree of salience to cabinet members, the standing bureaucracy, institutionalized support systems for presidents and prime ministers, and, in the case of the United States, the congressional leadership.

The rise of an individualistic or entrepreneurial spirit, on the other hand, has ushered in an era of "outsider politics" that places a premium on presidents and prime ministers who operate in bold strokes. These styles—marked by what Rockman terms "decisive and clear-cut direction"—expressly discount consultative and consensual ways of making decisions. Hence, Margaret Thatcher projected herself as a conviction politician bent on stamping out all "consensus mongering."

On the other hand, George Bush—especially, following upon the heels of Reagan—appears to be a throwback to insider politics. This observation leads to the very important point that the trend from insider toward outsider politics has occurred at a different rate in various systems. Americans, however, persist in believing that Westminster systems are less subject to the trend than the United States because of the tradition in London, Ottawa, and Canberra whereby prime ministers tend to work their way up through various cabinet posts before assuming party leadership.

This pattern might hold up in Britain—Mrs. Thatcher at least held one cabinet portfolio, though a minor one, before becoming the leader of her party. John Major, although relatively new to cabinet, had held three key posts before he became prime minister. However, Neil Kinnock—the Labour leader—has never served in cabinet. Nor had Brian Mulroney or Bob Hawke served in the cabinet before becoming Canadian and Australian prime minister, respectively. In fact, Mulroney first won election to the House of Commons one year before he became prime minister, while Hawke first won his seat in the House of Representatives only three years before becoming prime minister. The careers of Kinnock, Mulroney, and Hawke suggest, therefore, that outsider politics has become more significant in Westminster systems than American commentators realize. In this company, Bush comes out as relatively experienced!

B. Guy Peters's chapter examines changes in the styles of executive leadership as related to government overload and retrenchment. Peters finds that the most successful leaders have run against "government as usual." But this does not suggest that they have provided an alternative ideology about government that includes an integrated and coherent vision of the state. They have, in fact, only proffered a series of beliefs about government that resonate with voters' disenchantment. Increasingly, the political debates center on slogans such as Mrs. Thatcher's "enterprise culture" that appeal to voters who have written off government's ability to solve problems.

In the process, Peters notes, rationality has fallen out of favor. Executives do not seek—either from their cabinet colleagues or from the public service—detailed information about alternatives. They want to get on with the job of governing without canvassing all of the ambiguities and potential pitfalls. This perhaps works well in clearly defined areas—such as cutting social services or privatizing public enterprises—in which government arguably has taken on more than it should have. However, it presents clear problems in areas in which the government has yet to define a role. That is, some problems are "too massive and/or too inadequately understood" for the type of intuitive decision making that has become the hallmark of personalized executive leadership. Minimalist leadership seems to operate from the assumption that the number of issues on government's platter will continue to shrink indefinitely. However, the real world continues to provide an endless supply of new and seemingly insoluble problems. These more than cover the slack left by the government's declining attention to agenda items left over from the 1960s and 1970s.

Margaret Jane Wyszomirski focuses our attention more expressly on the U.S. presidency. She begins by tracing the origins of the institutional presidency in the plea made by the Brownlow Committee report for increased managerial and staff support. These would allow the chief executive to pursue his tasks with "energy, direction, and administrative management." Wyszomirski observes that, notwithstanding its widespread use, the concept "institutionalized presidency" is unclear. For instance, scholars disagree on the exact shape that such institutionalization would take. To name just a few perspectives: some see it as the expansion of career-based agencies serving the president; others view it as the development of specialized appointee-based offices that look after the various dimensions of the president's political well-being; still others construe it as routinizing presidential decision making through greater use of such coordinative devices as cabinet councils.

For Wyszomirski, this seeming confusion simply highlights the multidimensionality of institutionalization. For example, she asserts that we should consider bureaucratization as contributing to a continuous process rather than an indication of the actual degree of institutionalization. As well, Wyszomirski questions the common assumption that the career civil service stands for neutral competence whereas appointees tend to politicize presidential institutions. She argues that all potential pools of neutral competence—

including the permanent bureaucracy—are politicized in their own peculiar ways.

Regarding the politicization of the career bureaucracy, authors have begun to question the validity of the view that political executives and appointive officials concern themselves with policy while career civil servants focus only on administration.[23] To be sure, career officials—even in the United States where they work under ever increasing layers of partisan appointees—maintain some detachment from the political fray. The evidence from numerous empirical studies suggests that, however privately and discreetly, career officials pursue relatively defined agendas and thrive on behind-the-scenes gamesmanship.[24]

Thus, Wyszomirski's observation serves as a caution for those who decry the deinstitutionalization of the presidency. Their critique might simply be a lament for a neutrally competent presidential branch that never existed—one in which officials offered their advice and conducted the affairs of state without any personal commitments of a partisan or political nature. In other words, observers should be more precise in defining what exactly career officials contribute to policy making.

A distinction between Carter's and Reagan's posture toward the career civil service perhaps best conveys the point we have made here. Carter gave due obeisance to the input of the career civil service through his insatiable appetite for detail and his firm belief that enough analysis would yield the right answer. However, he often scuttled his laborious consultative processes when political exigencies forced him to make a decision or abandon an initiative. Reagan and his advisers, on the other hand, did everything they could to keep the permanent bureaucracy out of the policy-making loop.

Neither president, thus, knew how to engage the standing civil service creatively in cases in which expertise and institutional memory could have made—notwithstanding the inevitable bias of any interested and engaged party—the difference between good and bad actions and decisions. A neutrally competent public service has earned its title not because it is utterly devoid of political conviction and design. Rather, its legitimacy is based on its relative preparedness to change clients each time the executive branch passes from one party to the other. Presidents and other members of administrations who use this resource maladroitly, ignore it, or try to suppress it, deny themselves and the nation an essential device for achieving policy competence.

Does Cabinet Government Always Get a Clean Bill of Health?

Part II includes three chapters, each of which looks at the state of health of cabinet government. George Jones focuses on the United Kingdom, while two, Peter Aucoin and Thomas Hockin look at Canada. We can derive a great deal from a close examination of how cabinet government actually works. American scholars and political leaders alike often look longingly at Westminster systems. From afar, cabinet government seems to have avoided the dysfunctions of the U.S. system. In Westminster systems, the constitutional convention of collective cabinet responsibility constrains, it is believed, prime ministers from acting without adequate consultation of their colleagues. Moreover, these systems' bureaucracies still run overwhelmingly under the direction of permanent civil servants who, theoretically, remain indifferent as to which party holds power and precisely which policy options will hold sway.

George Jones and Patrick Weller have been waging a debate for some years now on whether the idealized view of cabinet government still pertains or, instead, prime ministers so exert their prerogatives that collective decision making has greatly diminished.[25] Jones adopts the former view, whereas Weller has taken the latter stance. In this volume, Jones's chapter has focused on Mrs. Thatcher's relations with cabinet and Parliament while Weller's relates more to prime ministers' use of personal staffs and secretariats. We will, thus, discuss Weller's piece when we come to the section on the personal staffs of presidents and prime ministers.

Jones's chapter continues along the lines of his previous work. However, it relates his argument more directly to the hypothesis that prime ministers have begun to behave in a "presidential" way. Jones maintains that prime ministers can never become thoroughly presidential. The very character of Westminster systems requires that they function within the confines of the support they can muster in cabinet. In turn, cabinet cannot operate as a viable government unless it maintains the support of Parliament.

This line of attack might surprise Americans. It stands in direct variance with the dominant diagnosis about what is wrong with the U.S. presidency. This maintains that parliamentary systems—in which the discipline of collective responsibility prevails—allow for greater potential than provided in the United States "for concentrated power [especially] if a prime minister has a firm majority in the legislature and surrounds him (or her) self with weak and compliant ministers."[26] That is, American observers frequently allow greater latitude for strong personal direction to prime ministers than they would to presidents.

Nonetheless, Jones sticks to his guns. In a thoroughgoing assessment of Margaret Thatcher's approach to the prime ministership, he concludes that she stretched but did not break the normal parameters of cabinet government. That is, the "constitutional structures and political pressures" of the system kept her from personalizing British executive leadership. We would expect Jones to affirm this even in the face of the dramatic decline in Mrs. Thatcher's support that resulted in her resignation in 1990. In other words, he would see the resignation as validating his assertion that the system will only allow so much deviation from the accepted parameters before a prime minister must pay a price for overstepping his or her prerogatives.

Peter Aucoin pursues many of the issues raised by Jones and Weller in his study of the Canadian cabinet system. With some forty members, Canada's cabinet far exceeds in size both Britain's and Australia's. Campbell has attributed the bloated size of Canada's cabinet to the difficulties associated with imposing party discipline in a highly fragmented federal political system. Under the pressures of myriad unresolved "representational imperatives," cabinet increasingly acts as a surrogate legislature.[27] Aucoin adds the important point that the fragmented nature of program delivery and regulation in Canada—requiring a great deal of fine-tuning on a regional basis—greatly exacerbates the tendency for cabinet to mirror the diversity of the nation.

Recent prime ministers have tried in vain to achieve greater programmatic rationality—notwithstanding the unwieldiness of cabinet. In all cases, their strategies have impinged—in some important respects—upon the collective nature of cabinet decision making. Most recently, Brian Mulroney has employed a hierarchical model. Under this approach, full cabinet meets relatively rarely. As well, the prime minister does not always preside at meetings of the executive committee of cabinet—namely, Priorities and Planning. Two much less formalized bodies—the Operations Committee (Ops) and, since January 1989, the Expenditure Review Committee—resolve most of the higher-level decisions about policy priorities and the allocation of resources. Both groups incorporate only the most trusted inner circle of ministers and officials. In this sense, they have become strongly personalistic.

Thomas A. Hockin—a noted authority on prime ministerial leadership in Canada[28] who has entered politics—contributes to this section his reflections as a cabinet minister in the federal government. Hockin asserts that whereas the presidency has taken full-blown institutional shape, we cannot say the same for the prime ministership. No matter how much the prime minister tests and exerts his prerogatives, he still works within the institutional framework of cabinet government. Adding an especially Canadian note, which also enjoys considerable Australian validity, Hockin reminds us that Canadian prime ministers carry the added burden of participating in weekly meetings of their party's parliamentary caucus. British prime ministers face their caucus only sporadically. The Canadian and Australian practices certainly make it more difficult for prime ministers in these countries to lose touch with their power base in Parliament.

Domestic and Economic Policy Advice: The Trade-Offs Between Responsiveness and Neutral Competence

Three of the four authors in part III offer, like Hockin, practitioners' views. These are Roger Porter, who has served in the Ford, Reagan, and Bush White Houses (currently he is assistant to President Bush for economic and domestic policy) as well as holding down an academic post at Harvard University; William Plowden, a former British career civil servant; and Stuart E. Eizenstat, a Washington lawyer who occupied a position similar to Porter's during the Carter administration.

The four chapters in this section address the issue of how best to provide economic and domestic policy advice to presidents and prime ministers. One important issue that emerges from any assessment of this area concerns whether the organizations set up to advise chief executives enjoy some sort of statutory base. This consideration came to the fore early in 1985 when Ronald Reagan asked his advisers if he could abolish the Council of Economic Advisers (CEA) by executive order. He found that abolition of the CEA would require legislation revoking sections of the 1946 Employment Act, which authorized the creation of the agency. Of the organizations considered in this section, CEA and the Office of Management and Budget enjoy statutory mandates. On the other hand, Britain's Central Policy Review Staff—which Plowden examines—owned no such lease on life. Thus, it met a quick demise when Mrs. Thatcher decided that she could do without it.

Porter's chapter on the CEA serves almost as a "how-to" guide. That is, it makes some very sage observations about how a presidential advisory agency with a statutory base might achieve the optimal mix between responsiveness to the preferences of each incumbent and provision of reputable analysis. Porter cites as the CEA's strengths the formal nature of its mandate, the lack of operational or procedural responsibilities that would detract from its analytic work, and the tradition of staffing the organization with secondees—largely from academia and the think tanks—who bring to their work a mix of practical experience and scholarly detachment.

Porter sees the CEA as continuing in its role so long as it eschews specific line responsibilities, bureaucratic infighting, expansion of its staff and assumption of coordinative responsibilities on behalf of incumbents. Whenever it loses sight of these caveats, the CEA runs the risk of compromising its greatest potential asset—namely, detached professionalism.

James Pfiffner turns our attention to the Office of Management and Budget. Some might take exception to Porter's favorable verdict on the CEA's ability to maintain its detached professionalism. However, virtually no one would challenge the assertion that OMB has lost virtually all semblance of neutral as opposed to responsive competence. And Pfiffner's analysis takes us a long way in pinpointing exactly why OMB has become so politically driven.

Most commentators cite Nixon's creation of (program) associate directors (PADs) as the decisive event in the politicization of OMB. By placing this layer of political appointees between career officials and the OMB director, Nixon preordained the marginalization of career officials' contribution within the presidential advisory system.

Pfiffner traces the process further back than 1970. He notes that both Kennedy and Johnson faulted the Bureau of the Budget, OMB's institutional predecessor, for lacking creativity and responsiveness. They turned things around so that BOB began to pursue the presidential agenda aggressively. In this respect, OMB became the victim of BOB's successful adaptation during the 1960s to Kennedy's and Johnson's styles. To this day, Republicans tend to view OMB's careerists as holdovers from the *ancien regime*. The OMB experience drives home two important lessons. Permanent officials must exercise discipline in their association with the goals of their political masters if they wish their institution to continue its role. Second, presidents must employ restraint in their attempts to win over career officials. That is, they cannot undermine these officials' claims to neutrality. Neither of these caveats seems to carry much weight with career officials or presidents these days.

William Plowden served for six years—from 1971 to 1977—as an undersecretary in Britain's Central Policy Review Staff (CPRS). Created in 1970 by Edward Heath, a Conservative prime minister, the CPRS usually consisted of some fifteen policy advisers. The staff included career civil servants, secondees from the private sector, and political appointees in roughly equal parts. As Plowden notes, Heath established the CPRS with a view to tapping, when required, countervailing advice to balance against whatever views the permanent Whitehall bureaucracy might serve up. Plowden's chapter provides an excellent overview not only of CPRS but the entire history of prime ministers' attempts to lodge—either in No. 10 Downing Street or the Cabinet Office—an independent source of advice.

Many reasons suggest themselves to explain why Mrs. Thatcher disbanded the CPRS in 1983. And Plowden maintains enough distance from CPRS to offer a solid diagnosis of what went wrong. At the end, however, Plowden touches on a very important point. Insofar as it worked, CPRS reaped the benefits of the legitimacy it had established in support of the head of government during a succession of administrations—Heath's, Harold Wilson's, and James Callaghan's—in which a reasonably strong sense of collective decision making prevailed.

Mrs. Thatcher, the other hand, chose to run a relatively non-collegial cabinet system. Thus, the CPRS—as an agency devoted to assisting the prime minister in cabinet consultation—lost its market. We should here recall Jones's observations about the elasticity of the prime minister's prerogatives. Plowden's analysis suggests an important qualification. Even if cabinet government does not collapse entirely under the pressure of a monocratic prime minister, some institutions upon which collective decision making has come to depend upon might not fare as well.

Stuart E. Eizenstat presents a very frank account of his experiences as assistant to the president for domestic affairs and policy during the Carter administration. He looks at the operation of the Council of Economic Advisers and the Office of Management and Budget in supplying the advisory and coordinative support that Carter required to function effectively as president. His many recommendations include clearly mandating an assistant to the president to coordinate the economic policy process, abolishing the practice whereby outgoing presidents present a full-blown budget which their successors immediately discard, taking the "M"—or management responsibilities—out of the OMB so that it can focus on the budget, and creating a permanent White House staff for more direct access to institutional memory for presidents.

Foreign and Defense Policy: No Easy Fixes

Many of the themes that emerge in part III resurface in part IV's consideration of systems for supporting presidents and prime ministers in the development of foreign and defense policy. Again, we find an area in which executive leaders and their advisers find it difficult to achieve a balance between political responsiveness and professional detachment. Kevin Mulcahy and Harold Kendrick examine the assistants to the president for national security from the first—Sidney Souers (who occupied a position then titled "executive secretary" of the National Security Council under the Truman administration)—to Colin Powell at the end of the Reagan administration.

Mulcahy and Kendrick categorize national security advisers (NSAs) according to the mix that they each achieved in policy-making and implementation roles. Thus, they term NSAs who rated low on both factors as *administrators,* those who made significant contributions to policy but did not engage in implementation as *counselors,* those who involved themselves only modestly in policy making but took implementation very seriously as *coordinators,* and those who vigorously pursued policy objectives and followed through to make sure that things actually happened as *agents*. By way of example, they classify Colin Powell as an administrator, Carter's NSA—Zbigniew Brzezinski—as a counselor, Reagan's third NSA—Robert McFarlane—as a coordinator, and Reagan's fourth NSA—John Poindexter—as an agent.

Mulcahy and Kendrick assert that administrators best fit the original concept of the NSA's role. The NSA was to serve the National Security Council as an executive-branch coordinative institution. As pressures built for the NSA to become the president's personal aide, the administrator function lost viability.

The authors note that NSAs will adopt styles that contrast with those of their immediate predecessors if the latter have performed ineffectively or behaved improperly. Thus, Brent Scowcroft (NSA under Gerald Ford) departed from his predecessor, Henry Kissinger (an agent), by adopting a more administrative style. In Mulcahy's and Kendrick's view, neither the *administrator* nor the *agent* approach recommends itself. That is, NSAs best fulfill the requirements of the modern presidency if they find a middle ground between aloofness from and immersion in pursuit of policy goals as well as implementation.

Lawrence Korb's chapter analyzes the styles of defense secretaries since the creation of a unified Department of Defense in 1949. He distinguishes the secretaries according to whether they manifested an active or passive approach to the department, and whether they sought to have a general impact on the entire administration or focused their efforts on the Pentagon.

Korb argues that presidents should appoint active defense secretaries who will challenge the military to justify their programs. He thus views Robert McNamara, secretary under Kennedy and Johnson, as an exemplary "active" secretary. At the other extreme, he characterizes Caspar Weinberger, secretary under Reagan, as an archetypical "passive" who became a seemingly uncritical advocate of Pentagon wish lists. Regarding Weinberger, his long tenure only makes sense if we recognize that the Reagan administration sought to throw a great deal of money into national security without getting bogged down in issues such as program effectiveness. Weinberger's desire to cater to Reagan's and the Pentagon's relentless claims upon resources made him virtually incapable of cautioning either about their excesses. Weinberger thus served neither the president, the military, nor the nation well.

In his chapter, Peter Hennessy provides a view of the national security advisory process in the United Kingdom. Congress patterned the U.S. National Security Council system after the British practice of using a standing cabinet committee to coordinate national security policy. Currently, the U.K. committee operates under the title Oversea and Defence. It does not own a statutory mandate. However, its membership includes the prime minister, all of the ministers responsible for departments that are immediately concerned with foreign and defense policies, and other cabinet officers—such as the secretary of the Home Office—whose departments' work significantly touches upon security and emergency issues. As with the U.S. National Security Council, Oversea and Defence also opens participation even further when the nature of an issue or the intensity of a minister's feelings about it appear to justify a more inclusive discussion.

Oversea and Defence operates with a fairly large secretariat located in the Cabinet Office. However, the officials in this staff come on secondment from other departments. Unlike the NSC staff, the secretariat includes no appointees from political or academic life. Thus, the secretariat rarely offers ministers advice that deviates very sharply from the types of stances that normally bubble up from Whitehall channels.

Hennessy characterizes this approach as a typically flawed British effort to entrust far too much to intelligent "force multipliers" who, notwithstanding their obvious abilities, lack experience in distilling disparate pieces of national security policy into a coherent whole. He argues that the secretariat should assume a higher profile and take on greater permanence in its career structure. This is an intriguing critique coming from the United Kingdom. American scholars have often viewed the Cabinet Office secretariat as superior to the NSC staff precisely because the former relies upon career civil servants and military officers exclusively. The NSC staff, on the other hand, includes a significant number of political appointees who—notwithstanding their academic credentials—bring little hands-on experience with government to their work.

The Limits and Perplexities of Personal Staff

Several issues come to the fore in any attempt to compare the personal staffs that support presidents and prime ministers. Even the settings of the staffs point up the immense differences between the four systems studied in this book. The U.S. president's personal staff occupies the West and East Wings of the White House and much of a huge office building next door. The most senior appointees crowd into cramped quarters in the West Wing so as to be as close as possible to the president.

The U.K. prime minister's staff crams itself into a medium-sized townhouse which the world knows as No. 10 Downing Street. To maintain the distinction between No. 10 and the Cabinet Office building, a coded security door guards the narrow passageway between the two. In Ottawa, the Prime Minister's Office (PMO) mostly occupies quarters on one side of the office building which it shares with the Privy Council Office (PCO)—Canada's equivalent to Britain's Cabinet Office. In Canberra, the Prime Minister's Office lodges itself in a bunkerlike suite in Australia's new Parliament House. Members of the Department of the Prime Minister and Cabinet (PM&C)—roughly the equivalent of Canada's PCO—work so far away that they must take chauffeur-driven cars to "the Hill" when briefing the prime minister or taking minutes at the meetings of cabinet or its committees.

These differences in physical placement and accommodation tip us to a number of more fundamental issues. To U.K., Canadian, and Australian observers, the number of political appointees working personally for American presidents has ballooned beyond all proportion. In the United States, great debates rage over whether the White House should run as a hierarchical organization with a strong chief of staff, a loose federation of White House barons, or some combination of both approaches. The issue of the organization—as opposed to size—of the prime ministers' staffs has attracted relatively little attention in the three Westminster systems. None has attained the complexity that would cause the prime ministers to multiply the layers of hierarchy in their immediate offices.

On the other hand, discussions about how many personal advisers prime ministers should have have absorbed a great deal of attention in Westminster systems among practitioners and scholars alike. We have already mentioned the concerns registered in some circles that prime ministers have presidentialized their systems when, like Mrs. Thatcher, they have paid less attention to the rubrics of cabinet consultation. Observers can become equally alarmed when it appears that prime ministers have built up their personal staffs excessively.

As well, the various systems have different norms about the distinction between the prime minister's staff and the cabinet secretariat. The security door between No. 10 and the Cabinet Office conveys the British view that the former serves the prime minister and the latter supports the entire cabinet. The Canadian arrangement whereby the PMO and PCO occupy the same building and are scarcely demarcated from each other hints at the degree to which the two tend to work collaboratively. The new spatial language in Australia indicates a new development: during the Hawke government, all cabinet members (not just the prime minister) have tended to rely upon their personal staffs much more than do their U.K. or Canadian opposite numbers. Thus, the PM&C joins the other two key Australian central agencies—Treasury and Finance—in learning how to operate once removed from its minister.

The four chapters in this section help immensely to assess the vagaries of this important area in the study of executive leadership. Joseph A. Pika begins with a look at the sense of disillusionment in the United States with the White House staff as a presidential resource. Citing Aaron Wildavsky, he asserts that the Brownlow Committee ushered in an age given to "organizational fixes" through which presidents tried to address the overwhelming responsibilities of their jobs by throwing more staff at intractable difficulties. During the Johnson and Nixon administrations, the diminishing returns of this approach began to hit home. Observers began to see damnation by staff—through their increasingly imperious behavior—as a major impediment to effective presidential leadership. Pika also notes that White House organization and staffing have remained relatively volatile—with presidents tending to overcompensate for the deficiencies of their predecessors by adding advisers and units and by shifting around boxes in the White House organizational chart.

Samuel Kernell's chapter focuses on the Reagan White House under Donald Regan, who served as chief of staff from 1985 to 1987. Kernell stresses the importance of placing studies of the White House within a historical perspective. He notes that presidents have struggled to maintain a degree of pluralism within the advisory system under the inevitable strains of an ever expanding organization.

Jimmy Carter's unhappy experience with the relatively loose spokes-in-a-wheel format that worked so well for Truman suggests that future presidents will be loath to try it again. Presidents just cannot afford to give all of their advisers equal access to the Oval Office. The size and complexity of the modern White House pretty much preordain that presidents choose either a modified spokes-in-a-wheel or a hierarchical format. The former worked well during Reagan's first term, in which James A. Baker, Edwin Meese, and Michael Deaver operated as hubs through which different sections of White House activity fed into the president.

In examining Donald Regan, Kernell brings us to the question of whether a strong, hierarchically oriented chief of staff can at least approximate the pluralism found in the modified spokes-in-the-wheel format. Kernell does not rule out the possibility. However, he underscores the degree to which the chief of staff must be politically astute and not just managerial. Regan proved to be a strong chief of staff who revealed a gross naivete about the political nature of White House business. Making the White House work involves an intricate system of bargaining relationships with networks of seasoned politicians. Within this context, the chief of staff's senior White House colleagues develop power bases and clienteles that give them considerable independent leverage. Not even the strongest and most secure chief of staff would wisely ignore or override such colleagues without an assessment of the political fallout.

We noted earlier that the Westminster systems are divided between prime ministers' staffs designated as personal offices and those meant to support the entire cabinet as well. Patrick Weller teaches in Australia, where the staff organization serving as the cabinet secretariat styles itself the Department of the Prime Minister and Cabinet. Understandably, thus, Weller does not press alarm buttons over suggestions that cabinet secretariats in Westminster systems owe a special responsibility to the prime minister. Many British practitioners and scholars, including George Jones, have, on the other hand, strenuously resisted any effort to characterize the U.K. Cabinet Office as a prime ministerial staff. Canadians would probably be unwilling to change the name of the PCO so as to incorporate "Prime Minister." However, they continue to turn a blind eye to the cohabitation of the PMO and PCO.

Meanwhile, new spatial language in Canberra, which assigns the Prime Minister's Office to the new Parliament House and keeps PM&C down in Barton—a precinct of functional departmental buildings beneath Parliament Hill, suggests that PM&C has become less "PM" and more "C." In all such developments and nuances, Weller sees a convergence whereby prime ministers— ever more the heads of government—tend to shape and mold their personal staffs and cabinet secretariats according to their stylistic preferences and the exigencies of the moment. This, Weller believes, does not suggest for an instant that they have become presidential. It does, however, indicate that prime ministers have reshaped the institutional resources and frameworks of cabinet government to make them more responsive to their own agendas and leadership.

Finally, Colin Seymour-Ure's chapter provides a timely comparative look at what has become a central theme in the study of executive leadership in the United States. As noted at the outset of this chapter, Samuel Kernell's *Going Public* (1986) asks whether presidents have resorted to direct appeals to the electorate over the heads of institutional forces in Washington to the point where effective governance begins to suffer. Seymour-Ure's chapter indicates that massaging public opinion through astute manipulation of the media has become a major element of prime ministerial leadership as well. Prime ministers in the United Kingdom, Canada, and Australia have employed similar strategies to concentrate news management in their personal offices. To the degree that they have succeeded in these approaches and, thereby, centralized and personalized their governments' media relations, prime ministers have heightened their leverage both over Parliament and over their cabinet colleagues.

Conclusion

The following chapters examine aspects of the progression of executive leaders—presidents and prime ministers—in Anglo-American systems from the age of government expansionism to the current minimalist era. In the study of either period, only a thorough consideration of context—the matrix of political and institutional environments—will allow us to begin to understand the folkways of executive leaders.

The contributors to this volume have all examined how presidents and prime ministers have attempted to work with and through their evolving executive establishments to rise to the leadership challenges they face. In an expansive age, these efforts tend to focus upon using organizational structures and resources, developing and honing individual management abilities and approaches, and designing and pursuing policy agendas. In the current era, marked by minimalism, the epicenter of executive leadership has shifted so that presidents and prime ministers focus at least as much attention to mending fences with political organizations outside of government and grappling with mercurial changes in policy demands and popular support.

We have, thus, seen the rise of special-interest and going-public politics. Interest groups drive the former, and the instant, sound-bite nature of public discourse brought on by the speed and pervasiveness of the electronic media has spurred the latter. Those who are optimistic about the potential role of the state and concerned about the clear deficiencies of the minimalist chief executive are tempted to judge current presidents and prime ministers harshly. However, as Wyszomirski has observed elsewhere, even the minimalist chief executive might embrace a style that, though catalytic rather than proactive, fits the art of the possible in a political era given to "organized anarchy."[29]

Many of the studies presented here also make clear that the institutional dimensions to executive leadership are hardly consistent or stable. The relationships between offices, agencies, departments, and chief executives vary greatly over time, often independently of the stylistic preferences of incumbent presidents and prime ministers. Thus, many of the chapters in this book will underscore the chameleonlike qualities of central executive institutions. In this respect, they capture the creative tension between predictability and changeability that permeates any truly adaptive organization.

Indeed, *tension* is manifested in myriad ways in all of the executive systems that this book covers. This should lead us to conclude that no system has discovered the philosophers' stone—a secret formula whereby the adoption of proven structures and practices might transform dysfunctional processes into efficient and responsive ones. Innovative executive leadership manages tensions creatively, it does not eliminate them. Our formulation of how presidents and prime ministers might reconcile the conflicting demands of partisan responsiveness and neutral competence serves as a case in point. It asserts that encompassing terms such as *policy competence* or *professional competence* convey the need for balance. Thus, neither the most party-political appointee nor the most technically competent career official adequately serves the political executive if s/he fails to achieve a creative mix between responsiveness to political exigencies and the rigorous assessment of the effectiveness of policies and programs.

We should add one final word about the legacy of the Brownlow Committee. Neither its "passion for anonymity" nor our current epoch's absorption with political marketing—which leads, of course, to the going-public syndrome of current executive leadership—adequately explains the intimate interrelationship between internal executive operations and external participatory, collaborative politics. Rather, as the following chapters make clear, contemporary executive leadership in the U.S. and Westminster systems fails to fit neatly into either the *personalized* or *institutionalized* category. Rather, each system achieves a unique and ever changing blend of personalized institutionalism.

Notes

1. For accounts of the effects of the Brownlow Committee report on development of the White House and the Executive Office of the President, see Larry Berman, *The Office of Management and Budget and the Presidency, 1921–1979* (Princeton, N.J.: Princeton University Press, 1979), pp. 10–15; John Hart, *The Presidential Branch* (New York: Pergamon, 1987), pp. 24–36; Emmette S. Redford and Marlan Blisset, *Organizing the Executive Branch: The Johnson Presidency* (Chicago: University of Chicago Press, 1981), pp. 4–6; Stephen Hess, *Organizing the Presidency,* 2d ed. (Washington, D.C.: Brookings, 1988), pp. 33–34.

2. James L. Sundquist, *Constitutional Reform and Effective Government* (Washington, D.C.: Brookings, 1986), pp. 78–79, and "Needed: A Political Theory for the New Era of Coalition Government in the United States," *Political Science Quarterly* 103 (Winter 1988–89), 613–35.

3. Richard E. Neustadt, *Presidential Power: The Politics of Leadership with Reflections on Johnson and Nixon* (New York: Wiley, 1976), pp. 11, 61.

4. Fred I. Greenstein, *The Hidden-Hand Presidency: Eisenhower as Leader* (New York: Basic Books, 1982), pp. 5, 40–42.

5. Samuel Kernell, *Going Public: New Strategies of Presidential Leadership* (Washington, D.C.: CQ Press, 1986), pp. 15, 23–24.

6. Kernell, pp. 137–38, 218.

7. George C. Edwards III, *At the Margins: Presidential Leadership of Congress* (New Haven, Conn.: Yale University Press, 1989), pp. 72, 109, 223.

8. Lou Cannon, *Reagan* (New York: Putnam), p. 45.

9. Roderick Kiewiet and Douglas Rivers, "The Economic Basis of Reagan's Appeal," in *The New Direction in American Politics*, ed. John E. Chubb and Paul E. Peterson (Washington, D.C.: Brookings, 1985), pp. 79–81.

10. James W. Ceasar, "The Reagan Presidency and American Public Opinion," in *The Reagan Legacy: Promise and Performance*, ed. Charles O. Jones (Chatham, N.J.: Chatham House, 1988), pp. 175, 206.

11. Barbara G. Farah and Ethel Klein, "Public Opinion Trends," in *The Election of 1988: Reports and Interpretations*, ed. Gerald M. Pomper (Chatham, N.J.: Chatham House, 1989), pp. 108–10.

12. Terry M. Moe, "The Politicized Presidency," in *The New Direction in American Politics*, ed. Chubb and Peterson.

13. Ibid., p. 258.

14. Richard F. Fenno, *The President's Cabinet: Analysis in the Period From Wilson to Eisenhower* (Cambridge, Mass.: Harvard University Press, 1959), pp. 5, 9; Stephen Hess, *Organizing the Presidency* (Washington, D.C.: Brookings, 1976), pp. 208, 212–16; Roger Porter, *Presidential Decision Making: The Economic Policy Board* (Cambridge: Cambridge University Press), pp. 15, 214–21; Lester M. Salamon, "The Presidency and Domestic Policy Formulation," in *The Illusion of Presidential Government*, ed. Hugh Heclo and Salamon (Boulder, Colo.: Westview, 1982), pp. 193, 199; Colin Campbell, S.J., *Managing the Presidency: Carter, Reagan, and the Search for Executive Harmony* (Pittsburgh, Pa.: University of Pittsburgh Press, 1986), pp. 25–57.

15. Moe, "The Politicized Presidency," pp. 239, 244–45.

16. Thomas E. Cronin, *The State of the Presidency* (Boston: Little, Brown, 1980), pp. 224–25, 248.

17. Bert A. Rockman, *The Leadership Question: The Presidency and the American System* (New York: Praeger, 1984), pp. 194–97; Campbell, *Managing the Presidency*, pp. 15–19.

18. Stephen Hess, *Organizing the Presidency*, 2d ed. (Washington, D.C.: Brookings, 1988), pp. 226, 231.

19. Richard Rose, *The Postmodern Presidency: The White House Meets the World* (Chatham, N.J.: Chatham House, 1988), p. 7.

20. Richard Rose and B. Guy Peters, *Can Government Go Bankrupt?* (New York: Free Press, 1978), pp. 33–34.

21. William F. Grover, *The President as Prisoner: A Structural Critique of the Carter and Reagan Years* (Albany: State University of New York Press, 1989).

22. V. O. Key, "A Theory of Critical Elections," *Journal of Politics* 17 (1955), 3–18; James L. Sudquist, *Dynamics of the Party System: Alignment and Realignment of Political Parties in the United States*, rev ed. (Washington, D.C.: Brookings, 1983). Early analysis of the rise of the Republicans under Reagnn tended to style it as a realignment. See, for instance, John E. Chubb and Paul E. Peterson, "Realignment and Institutionalization," in *The New Direction in American Politics*, ed. Chubb and Peterson, pp. 1–30; and Thomas E. Cavanagh and James L. Sundquist, "The New Two-Party System," in ibid., pp. 33–67. On the other hand, British scholars have tended to view Mrs. Thatcher's support as based more on dealignment, that is, the declining influence of traditional party and class loyalty on voting. See I. Crewe and B. Sarvik, *Decade of Dealignment* (Cambridge: Cambridge University Press, 1983).

23. Matthew Holden, "Imperialism in Bureaucracy," *American Political Science Review* 60 (1966), 943–51; Herbert Kaufman, "Administrative Decentralization and Political Power," *Public Administration Review* 29 (1969), 3–15; Joel D. Aberbach, Robert A. Putnam, and Bert A. Rockman, *Bureaucrats and Politicians in Western Democracies* (Cambridge, Mass: Harvard University Press, 1981).

24. Colin Campbell, S.J., and B. Guy Peters, "The Politics/Administration Dichotomy: Death or Merely Change?" *Governance* 1 (1988), 79–99; Colin Campbell, S.J., "The Political Roles of Senior Government Officials in Advanced Democracies," *British Journal of Political Science* 18 (1988), 243–72.

25. Patrick Weller, "Do Prime Ministers' Departments Really Create Problems?" *Public Administration* 61 (1983), 59–78; G. W. Jones, "Prime Ministers' Departments Really Create Problems: A Rejoinder to Patrick Weller," *Public Administration* 61 (1983), 79–84.

26. Kent Weaver and Bert A. Rockman, "Introduction: Assessing the Effects of Institutions," presented at a conference entitled *Political Institutions and Their Consequences*, Brookings Institution, Washington, D.C., February 2–3, 1990, p. 9.

27. Colin Campbell, "Cabinet Committees in Canada: Pressures and Dysfunctions Stemming From the Representational Imperative," in *Unlocking the Cabinet: Cabinet Structures in Comparative Perspective*, ed. Thomas T. Mackie and Brian W. Hogwood (London: Sage, 1985).

28. Thomas A. Hockin, ed., *The Apex of Power: The Prime Minister and Political Leadership in Canada*, 2d ed. (Scarborough, Ont.: Prentice-Hall, 1977).

29. Margaret J. Wyszomirski, "A Post-Modern Presidency?" *The Bureaucrat* 19 (Summer 1990), 58.

PART I

Executive Leadership:
Why the Sense of Malaise?

2

The Leadership Question:
Is There an Answer?

BERT A. ROCKMAN

If there is one thing that is clear about leadership, it is that there is no single conception of it. Indeed, like many other concepts of political analysis, it is a lumpy term. Yet it is central to political thinking and to the normative schemes we use to assess politics. Moreover, it also is pivotal even to our fundamental conceptions about human nature—about whether, for example, voluntarism and free will are the cornerstones of thinking about society and politics, or whether determinism and an organic social fabric are the foundations upon which to think about society and politics.[1]

Discussions such as these seem more appropriate to the halls of ivy than to the corridors of power. And yet, that is how ideas actually progress. Because ideas and politics are both powerful forces in the American environment, I want to work through in this chapter some ideas about an always vital topic (certainly one regarded as such within the Washington environs), that of presidential leadership. My hope is that these ideas will be applicable to appraising the present state of the presidency and its role as a political leadership institution.

I begin by talking broadly about the notion of leadership and the role of the presidency in providing it. Second, I discuss a set of factors conditioning presidential behavior, success, and leadership. Third, I note some ways in which we traditionally assess presidential performance and the problems associated therewith. Finally, I emphasize different tasks and styles of leadership and the difficulty of weaving together the diverse skills they require.

Leadership and the Role of the Presidency

Leadership and Outcomes

The most complicated issue concerning the exercise of leader-ship is identifying exactly what it is. How, in particular, can we dissociate its exercise from mere good or bad fortune? Machiavelli obviously struggled with this perplexing issue, and it is not clear that we have come very far since. During the 1988 election year, we witnessed the curious situation in which both the inside candi-date (Bush) and the outside candidate (Dukakis) each tried to represent himself as a successful leader by associating himself with good times—Bush as the representative of the Reagan "boom period" and Dukakis as the "Massachusetts miracle" man. To what extent are these outcomes the product of human engineer-ing or sheer luck? Can we ever know?

History often provides us with interesting paired comparisons. Think of such pairs as Buchanan and Lincoln, Hoover and Frank-lin Roosevelt, and Carter and Reagan. Almost always, we see the first in each pair as inept, unable to clarify direction, unable to inspire confidence or to lead. Equally, we tend to think of the second as able to do all the things the first could not. And yet, at least in the last two pairs—Hoover/FDR and Carter/Reagan—we know that FDR and Reagan mainly enlarged efforts and acceler-ated directions begun by Hoover and Carter. Hoover did bring government directly into play in trying to generate a recovery from the Depression, and Carter curtailed domestic spending, in-creased defense spending, and moved toward the deregulation of many areas of commerce. Moreover, in the case of Roosevelt, the objective conditions of the Depression did not greatly improve until the country mobilized its forces for war. And in the case of Reagan, the great economic recovery must be seen in the context of the great economic trough that occurred under his own, not Carter's, administration.

Is everything just a matter of timing? Or do policies matter? Is it better to be lucky than good? Or do only the good get lucky?

Although no precise answer can be given, Robert Putnam and several associates clear away some of the underbrush that clogs our ability to distinguish at least some differences that are the result of environment and those that might be the result of leadership.[2] In their study of the performance of Italian regional councils, they note the overwhelming power of a few basic fixed variables (such as socioeconomic development, political culture, and social stability) to predict nearly all of the raw performance of a region ($R^2 = .86$). The obvious analogy is that even with the most skilled diplomatic corps in the world, Gabon will not soon become a great power. However, what Putnam and his colleagues tried to do was to ask a different question: given what can be expected from any region's endowment, how much better or worse does it do? (In more technical language, how much above or below the regression line does a particular region perform, given our expectations of performance based on the prediction equation?)

Of course, this formulation hardly settles all matters of leadership. Nor is it easily applied to many situations. But even though it treats leadership as essentially a derivative, it points us in the right direction. More powerful givens determine basic outcomes. Within the range of outcomes that are determined, however, the quality of leadership can make a difference.

The Many Faces of Leadership

Obviously, leadership is deeply intertwined with and contingent upon situational factors, political culture (that is, prevailing value systems and norms), institutions, and the goals of leaders. This observation can be stated more concretely in the form of the following expectation: a collectivist system of leadership will tend to produce vastly different leadership styles than an individualistic or entrepreneurial system. A Japanese or Swedish prime minister, for example, is very different from an American president. For that matter, with some unanticipated exceptions such as Khrushchev and Gorbachev, a Soviet general secretary also is apt to be much more of an organization man and insider than a U.S. president.

Collectivist leadership styles emphasize insider politics. Such styles, therefore, tend to be low-key and focused on brokerage politics—or, in former Prime Minister Thatcher's inhospitable phrase, "consensus-mongering." Bold strokes and strong character lines are not the hallmarks of leadership in such systems. Indeed, leaders such as Nakasone in Japan and Palme in Sweden were sometimes regarded by local politicians as somehow "not Japanese" or "not Swedish" because they brought more attention

to themselves, were more personally directive, and were less attached to the prevailing consensus about styles of leadership than
was the norm.

The mode of policy change or political reform in such collectivist systems is mainly achieved through the syndication of risk—
making change appear to be the product of larger forces than
political decision making and by including more actors than simply the prevailing government.

By way of contrast, it is clear that any American presidential
candidate who offered to run on finding the "acceptable" view or
spreading the responsibility for leadership around would be quickly
derided as a wimp. Even more to the point, such a style of leadership does not easily flow from either the nature of American institutions or from the development of the modern presidency. Nor does
it flow from the manner in which presidents—and, more or less,
everybody else—get nominated and elected in the U.S. system of
electoral politics. The ingredients of collective decision making are
rarely present in the United States.

In systems such as Sweden and Japan, the prime minister is
most often a political orchestrator and manager, operating within
a fairly well-defined set of norms about how change may be
sought. Some individual leaders fit the prevailing forms more
clearly than others (Palme's and Nakasone's successors, for instance), but such forms are characteristically compatible with organizational style, brokerage, and the management of consensus.

This is not so in the United States, however, where entrepreneurial norms are more in demand and where outsider politics is more
prevalent in a political (and policy) game that itself is less clearly
structured and organized. American presidents, of course, also
differ in style, but entrepreneurship, direction, and advocacy are
the hallmarks of what we have come to think of as leadership
attributes appropriate to the American presidency. Staking out
space and expanding upon it is a norm for American presidents
because failing to act in such a manner, it is assumed, only encour-
ages their political and institutional competitors. Whether all these
assumptions are actually correct or not is less relevant than the
fact that they have tended to become the norm—a norm that over
the past generation and a half has derived from the coincidence of
institutional and (partisan) political division.

Norms are influenced, of course, by political conditions, political personality, and even learning. Unlike Ronald Reagan, President Bush's forte is not that of expressive symbolic politics. Because of his political circumstances and temperament, he appears more reluctant than his predecessor to go for the maximum short-term advantage. He also may have observed that except for one immensely important year, Reagan's strategy of pushing the maximum short-term advantage yielded little. By playing consensus, insider politics, however, George Bush has been criticized for lacking direction and theme.

While norms are at least moderately pliable, they nonetheless often differ across political systems. Such differences ultimately result from different attitudes about the proper equilibrium between decisive, clear-cut direction and nurturing interpersonal relations for attaining compromise.

Why Leadership Is Needed

Regardless of what we call it—whether leadership, steering, or statecraft—a leader must give direction and guidance. Governments, of course, often operate without giving any clear signals, and yet, in the short run at least, little is affected. Departments, through inertia, continue to follow a preexisting direction. The essential functions of government are maintained. The status quo, as Richard Rose once observed, is eminently doable because it is already being done.[3]

The stream of problems facing societies, however, is never constant. New problems emerge and old problems get dressed up in different garb. To generate *adaptations* to such problems (a term much preferred to *solutions*) requires selection from a repertoire of choices that also are rarely fixed. To have a chance of producing acceptable adaptations, leaders must send off signals that can be interpreted by followers and made persuasive. In the parlance of political science, leaders need to generate an agenda and offer some kind of philosophy that makes the agenda coherent. In other words, a leader needs a vision that others can understand and find persuasive.

The simpler this vision, the more likely it can be interpreted by others and the more clear-cut are the cues to be followed. In this regard, Aaron Wildavsky aptly noted one of the great secrets of Ronald Reagan's leadership: "Every official in Washington knows what Reagan wants—less. . . . Even when the president's ostensible aim is not achieved, his adherence to priorities achieves a sense of direction."[4] Wildavsky, thus, concluded: "Ronald Reagan has integrated public policy with political support so as to provide creative policy leadership."[5]

By contrast, Jimmy Carter had a more elaborate agenda, but one that emitted few consistent signals. If what Ronald Reagan wanted was less, no one could for certain tell what Carter wanted or precisely what he believed in.[6] These stark differences between Carter's elaborate agenda and Reagan's simple one, and the perceived differences in their success, no doubt result from factors far more complex than the personal shortcomings or skills of the two presidents. They testify at least as much to available opportunities (Reagan had an early opening that Carter lacked), and to the playing out and the marching in of policy ideas (Carter was responsible for managing a set of ideas then on the wane). Still, these variations in Carter's and Reagan's ability to send clear and consistent signals cannot be discounted. Reagan's message was understood; Carter's remained garbled.

Leaders who send strong signals may be furiously engaged (Mrs. Thatcher) or amiably detached (Mr. Reagan) from the details of their own program. One may dispute the wisdom of specific policy proposals and even their general direction, but there is little denying that if inertia needs to be arrested and if different adaptations are called for, these can be provided only by strong leadership cues and messages simply and economically understood.

At another level, however, there is the inevitable problem of wedding complexity and nuance of response to basic simplicity of design.[7] Bold strokes are often gross or blunt, but nuanced designs are often confusing. The policy leadership problem for any president is to give purpose without giving up on sophistication. The likelihood of combining sophistication with bold purpose is not necessarily great, but the likelihood of sophistication succeeding without purposeful design is virtually nil.

The President as Policy Retailer

In the American system, the presidency is the principal source from which leadership is expected. It is best, however, to view it as the retail outlet for *solutions* (more properly, *adaptations*) to the country's problems and even for defining what those problems are. We should not expect innovative thinking from the presidency; rather, it is a final filter, attentive to some subset of the rich flow of ideas about public policy that crosses the White House transom. The president's staff usually finds a way to work these ideas into proposals, speeches, or policy justifications.

The U.S. government is uniquely engaged with the society it governs. The actual situation is not as Jimmy Carter described it in his notorious "malaise" speech of 1979. Rather than being isolated from the vitality of the society, the government imbibes deeply from it, for two very strong reasons: (1) there is no encapsulating political party organization (so prevalent in Europe) that organizes all politics and frequently insulates politicians from the world of ideas, and (2) the civil service lacks the powerful role and status that might give it a monopoly over the fine grain of policy proposals. Related to this, of course, is the uniquely American "in and outer" system which brings new ideas into the government apparatus, although at the expense of continuity and, perhaps, sober judgment.

In short, there are many venues of leadership and innovation in American society—some governmental, but not always in Washington or at the federal level, and some nongovernmental. Not only are there many channels for leadership (one of the most potent American leaders of this century, Martin Luther King, never held government or party office), there are also many vendors of ideas both in government and outside. Permeability, in sum, is the hallmark of American government.

Within the federal government itself, idea leadership occurs in a variety of places, certainly not exclusively within the Oval Office. Members of Congress and, especially, their sizable staffs, are in the midst of the idea transmission belt—a far cry from the sleepier days when committee chairs had a stranglehold over agendas. Bureaucrats (both careerists and appointees), interest group staffs, public policy analysts in Washington think tanks and in universities, and big sectors of the White House staff are often linked to major policy debates, ideas, and analyses.

Wherever ideas actually start or wherever they are picked up, the president nonetheless commands center stage. If he is not the primary thinker, he is the final filter. *The president legitimizes ideas by signing off on them, packaging them, and attempting to sell them.* To do this successfully, he does not have to be a deep thinker. (One might perhaps exempt Thomas Jefferson and Woodrow Wilson—

and, on the outside, Herbert Hoover and Jimmy Carter—from this generalization.) What a president must be skilled at, however, is knowing which ideas to buy into, how to package them, and how to sell them. These attributes mark the two most influential of modern presidencies—those of Franklin Delano Roosevelt and of Ronald Reagan.

The Conditions for Presidential Leadership

Elsewhere, I have elaborated a scheme that sets forth the factors conditioning the opportunities for and exercise of presidential leadership.[8] This framework emphasizes four building blocks of analysis: (1) historical givens of the system, or *constants;* (2) *cycles* favorable or unfavorable to presidential opportunities; (3) secular *trends* in the system; and (4) *personal skills* and *styles.*

It is useful to think metaphorically of these factors as ripples in a pond (figure 1). When one throws a pebble into the water, the deepest indentation occurs at the point of impact. Yet the outermost ripples really define how far one can go, in other words, the real parameters of our capacity to disturb the water. The circle most distant from the point of direct impact may be most easily taken for granted. But these basic parameters set the outer limits of presidential direction. The immediate impact—the play of personalities—grips our attention and is often the talk of current politics. Yet, while personal factors such as skills and styles are by no means unimportant, they are less important than others in determining presidential success—which, admittedly, remains notoriously undefined.

Constants

At the outermost edge, then, are the basic endowments for leadership. These include obvious physical features such as the state's geography, wealth, population characteristics, and so forth. But politically, they also include factors such as the state's institutional arrangements (constitutional structure) and the political culture. Regarding the U.S. presidency, the peculiar system of separated institutions sharing authority has been juxtaposed to the seemingly more centrally driven, party-governed parliamentary systems.[9]

Recognizing that parliamentary systems actually function with considerable diversity and are not without their problems, it is fair

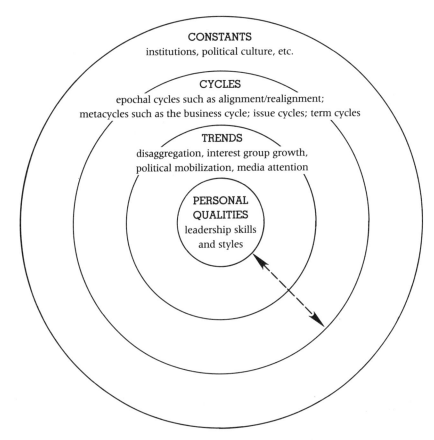

FIGURE 1. Conditions for Presidential Leadership

Note: Arrow between CYCLES and PERSONAL QUALITIES indicates the potential for interaction between opportunities and personal factors to effect outcomes.

to say that the American system of government is typically seen as an antileadership system that hobbles a president's ability to govern effectively. This is a matter of considerable debate, but the system does appear to inhibit presidents especially when they require legislation and lack strong congressional majorities or political support in the country. On other matters, however, where presidential initiative is decisive and creates *facts* around which others must act, such as military commitment, the American president has truly impressive latitude for action.[10]

Whether other factors in the political environment—such as the culture of localism, individualism, and popular participation, or

even such institutions as federalism—are more important than the
separation of powers system in determining the ability of presidents to lead cannot be established here. But, most broadly, the
conditions for presidential leadership are exactly as Richard Neustadt stated them over three decades ago: "The limits on command suggest the structure of our government. . . . The separate-
ness of institutions and the sharing of authority prescribe the
terms on which a President persuades."[11]

Cycles

Within the context of constant factors are cycles of varying
regularity and durability. One such cycle is that of political
alignment-dealignment-realignment. This topic holds much interest for political scientists and historians because periods of partisan
realignment have been associated with significant periods of policy change and innovation.[12] Realignment presumably injects
fresh gusts of political energy into the system and a period of party
government. Like spottings of the humpback whale, however,
observations of political realignment, at least in its classic expression, have been rare of late. Despite obvious evidence of electoral
change, the prospect of realignment seems only occasionally to
come into sight before again fading away.[13] More common is the
dissolution of party bonds. While realignment can give presidents
more opportunity to successfully push agendas because they enjoy
a time of party government, continuing dissolution of party forces
makes the problem of aggregating political support that much
greater for the president.

Cycles of shorter duration also can affect presidential prospects.
For example, the business cycle is given much attention in the
literature of political economy. Some analysts have focused on the
coincidence of elections and the political manipulation of economic benefits to increase potential voters' real income in the
short term.[14] How much of the business cycle can be politically
manipulated is an open question. Surely, however, the economy
influences the prospects of presidential candidates and incumbents. Herbert Hoover and Jimmy Carter both were caught in the
teeth of worldwide economic forces. In Carter's case, inflation and
unemployment rose together in a most unorthodox tandem. Neither Roosevelt nor Reagan created miracles; unemployment and
the use of industrial capacity remained at depression levels until

the onset of World War II, and Reagan's economic recovery merely meant emerging from the deep trough into which the economy had plunged earlier in his own administration. But it was Hoover who suffered the political effects of the Depression, not Roosevelt, and it was Carter who suffered for the stagflation of 1979–80, not Reagan, under whom unemployment rose to over 10 percent in 1982. As in baseball, it is better for a manager to inherit a team at the bottom than one at the top. One can only go up in the first instance and only down in the second.

Term cycles, or regularized patterns that occur within a given presidential term, are briefest. At the outset of their administrations, presidents know the least yet have the maximum opportunity to act if they are prepared to do so, both legislatively and in managing the executive branch.[15] Ironically, though, as Charles O. Jones points out, presidents who have maximally achieved early are likely to be on a downward spiral, especially through a second term when they must face up to the problems their achievements have caused.[16]

Trends

During the 1970s, many analysts pointed to trends that were making the exercise of political leadership, in general, and presidential leadership, in particular, more difficult.[17] The impact of the media, the decline of party strength, the expansion of the interest group universe, and the mobilization of more and more political forces in the society without equivalent means for aggregating them, all made the provision of direction seemingly less possible.

A trend is by nature hard to assess. Some eventually peter out, while others turn into cyclical phenomena. (Sometimes we just fail to interpret the symptoms correctly if we are dealing with a long cycle.) In any event, some of the political trends of the 1970s seem to have been deflected by the character of President Reagan's own leadership. To a considerable degree, the Reagan presidency was a period of high politics in which parties became increasingly important and in which congressional activity became more oriented to the floor.[18]

In the 1980s, however a different set of trendlike issues has emerged, mainly those dealing with the financial dependence of the United States on external sources of capital investment to carry the burden of American indebtedness. The issues of the 1970s seemed to reduce the scope of leadership discretion internally within the United States, but the issues of the 1980s and so far those of the 1990s emphasize limits on the discretionary scope of internal leadership imposed by external forces.[19]

Persona

The skills and styles of leadership that a president brings to (or develops within) the White House is the stuff of cocktail chitchat on the part of Washington political cognoscenti. It is usually great fun to delve into, and it is the basis of day-to-day casual discussion.

The personal attributes of the individual in the Oval Office actually are among the few real variables at work in the prevailing parallelogram of forces. If one, therefore, thinks of the framework presented here as focusing heavily on the interplay of capability factors, opportunities, and taking advantage of opportunities, then we can see especially the interactive nature of the second and fourth factors (cycles and persona) in the scheme (figure 1). For contemporary U.S. presidents, it is especially these two elements that tend to vary.

Presidential skills and styles will be discussed in more detail below. Now, however, I want to deal with an equally complicated matter, assessing presidential performance.

Assessing Presidential Performance

How can we measure presidential success? Presumably an effective leader is a successful one. Although there is no single way to grapple with the quality of presidential performance, there are rather a set of ways that together enable us to assess various kinds of performance.

Let us consider, then, some of the ways in which we might think about the meaning of presidential success.

Short-Run Political Success

Legislative Performance. When the phrase "presidential influence" is used by political scientists, that often means turning to the *Congressional Quarterly* (*CQ*) Index of Presidential Support. This is one of the most readily available and frequently used indicators of how the president is doing. This is not the place to discuss all of the potential pitfalls of this index, most of which *CQ* graciously notes in reporting it. Suffice it to say that a key problem (fortunately, there also are further clues in other *CQ* measures) is that presidential support rests merely upon presidential position taking. Thus, the index is unweighted.

Moreover, the index cannot tell us how much a president's score is likely to vary, given a particular distribution of seats. It is not normed, in other words. In recent decades, Republicans have faced Democratic Congresses—a condition likely to lower their scores, and Democrats have faced Democratic Congresses—which tends to work in their favor. Republican presidents would probably be most successful had they Republican Congresses to work with, since congressional Republicans tend to be more cohesive than Democrats. But that has happened fully only once since Eisenhower (1953–54), and with split control only three times (1981–86).

As table 1 illustrates, Democratic presidents are clearly more successful, as well they should be, in dealing with Congress than are Republican presidents. Republican presidents have an average legislative success rate of 65 percent, while Democratic presidents succeed at a rate of 81 percent. Since party division is increasingly the norm, we can conclude that presidents are having a more difficult time now in achieving success with Congress than in the past. Three of the past four years have produced the lowest success rates in the series. Moreover, in general, recent presidents have been doing less well with Congress than earlier ones (since Eisenhower), irrespective of party. Whether this is because Congress has been more resistant or presidents more unreasonable is not altogether clear. Notably, Ronald Reagan, whom I earlier described as one of the two most important modern presidents, ranks near the bottom in his averaged success rate with Congress.

A president can compile a pretty good legislative performance record by making few demands that are controversial or have deep impact. To a considerable extent, risk aversion helps explain Kennedy's performance during the three years of his presidency. His is by far the best legislative record, based on the support scores, of any president in the time series. Like a singles-hitter in baseball, Kennedy got on base frequently because he took short strokes. By contrast, Reagan has been the equivalent of a power hitter extraordinaire—some bases-clearing smashes offset by lots of whiffs.

TABLE 1. Average *Congressional Quarterly* Support Scores
from Eisenhower to Reagan

Administration	Years	Full Term Average Support Score (%)
Eisenhower (R)	1953–60	72.2
Kennedy/Johnson (D)	1961–68	83.4
Nixon/Ford (R)	1969–76	64.5
Carter (D)	1977–80	76.4
Reagan (R)	1981–83	61.8
Bush (R)	1989–90	54.7

Source: Congressional Quarterly 48, no. 51 (December 22, 1990), p. 4208. Table partially adapted from Charles O. Jones, "Ronald Reagan and the U.S. Congress: Visible-Hand Politics," in *The Reagan Legacy: Promise and Performance*, ed. Jones (Chatham, N.J.: Chatham House, 1988), p. 53.

Unweighted as it is, the so-called legislative record has to be viewed in two contexts: (1) What is a president's reputation on Capitol Hill? and (2) What forces outside of the president's direct control tend to account for the president's record, putting aside his own intentions to swing for home runs or percentage? The second question is by far the easier one because the explanation for most of the quantitative record of performance lies in partisan political forces, notably the distribution of congressional seats. The first question is a lot trickier because it also is intermingled with broader political considerations, such as public opinion. It is likely, but hard to prove definitively, that a president's reputation on the Hill counts for something—the willingness, for example, of members of Congress to accept even a modest risk on the president's behalf. However, the principal forces at work in accounting for actual performance are basically partisan and political rather than personal.[20]

Popular Approval. Another way to assess presidential performance is through the registered level of approval from the public. For about forty years, the Gallup survey has been asking the public a simple question regarding the performance of the incumbent: "Do you approve or disapprove of the way [the incumbent] is handling his job as president?" The frequency with which this question has been asked has accelerated over the years from once every few months during the Truman administration to every couple of weeks now.

Popularity is a valuable commodity (and unpopularity an albatross) for presidents, though the extent of their popularity is hardly the exclusive result of their own ministrations. Generally, when things go bad, presidents plummet in the polls. Such is the fate even of those with reputed "father" images (Eisenhower) or purported "Teflon" immunity (Reagan). To a lesser extent, when things go well, presidents also do better.

Although popular approval can help a president get what he wants, and disapproval hinders him, the relationships between popularity and achievement are rarely direct unless popularity itself is regarded as an achievement. Retaining popularity may itself be a relevant consideration if one views the role of the president as epitomizing a national consensus and avoiding deep division and controversy.[21] Richard Neustadt, of course, saw popularity as an instrument rather than an end, and was critical of Eisenhower's failure to invest it for policy purposes.[22] While Reagan's popularity mostly soared and sank with the economy, he did invest his currency heavily in his first-year legislative program. Yet ironically, Reagan became a president, unlike the Eisenhower of Greenstein's formulation, who was both popular *and* polarizing.

Popularity is obviously a measure of some form of political success (or luck), but precisely what it represents or can further account for is more complicated. To some extent, it can also be revalued retrospectively. For example, Richard Neustadt's image of Eisenhower at the end of his presidency fit the then prevailing and unflattering intellectual portrait of Eisenhower as a president with a bountiful crop of unharvested popularity who knew little about how to use it.[23] Over the years, however, as presidents got into increasing trouble and the political system itself seemed to become more unwieldy and less governable, the Eisenhower presidency looked better retrospectively. According to the revised intellectual perspective that was more skeptical of hyperactive presidents and activist government, Eisenhower was seen as a social peacemaker who steered the country away from division and controversy. A popular president ipso facto became a good—because more rare—thing.

The Management of Decisions

A president's success has to be measured through political indicators, in part, because the office is ultimately a political one.

Whatever his other accomplishments, a president's success or failure in the short run will be directly measured in ostensible political terms.

Yet there are other criteria—perhaps far more important ones—by which to evaluate presidents. Perhaps most important is the ability to manage decisions. In some respects, presidential campaigns create hyperbolic images around just exactly these issues—"Whose finger do you trust on the nuclear button?" The imagery conjures up visions of rashness and impulsiveness on the one hand, sobriety and judgment on the other.

Neustadt emphasizes the importance of what he calls "backward-mapping"—basically, tracing back the implications and consequences of decisions before they get made—as a key ingredient to successful decision making. Decisions are often only implied, rather than definitively made, in the White House. Consequently, decisions about how decision making should be managed (staffing and organization decisions) are often among the most important because such choices frequently determine how substantive policy decisions will get made and implemented. Presidential decision making, however, tends to be identified with those rare occasions for which the country actually needs a president—that is, crisis decisions.

Several examples come to mind. Carter's great attentiveness to detail and situational knowledge helped produce the Camp David accords. Reagan's lack thereof helped produce the Iran-contra fiasco. Eisenhower's military experience and judgment deterred an immediate U.S. military commitment in the face of the impending French colonial defeat at Dien Bien Phu. Kennedy's capacity to learn from his own earlier insufficiently skeptical behavior led to a more sober and calculating reaction (and decisional procedure) during the crisis over Soviet-installed missiles in Cuba.

To the extent that we can assess presidential candidates on the basis of personal attributes, we can get some hint of how they are likely to manage decisions as presidents. How curious are they about information? How skeptical are they in assessing solutions proposed by others? How aware are they of their stakes in the outcomes? And how aware are they of the stakes of others, including potential antagonists? Are they calm and collected, and yet persistent in finding out what they need to know? What in their experience would lead them to ask particular questions—or perhaps to ask none? How well can they think through the implications and consequences of what they or others propose? We cannot answer these questions exactly, but that does not diminish their critical importance.

Agenda Change

Presidents Roosevelt and Reagan, I have claimed, are the two most important of modern presidents despite Reagan's overall limited success in the legislative arena. The reason I offer this judgment is that each president has had considerable impact on his successor(s). The programs of the New Deal mostly remain today, leaving an institutional legacy and continuing popular constituencies for them, enlarged expenditure commitments, and a status of exemption from overt political change. In essence, Roosevelt's programs became institutionalized. Above all, they came to be accepted as part of the New Deal welfare state that Americans have shown little desire to pull apart despite more abstract attitudes denigrating "big government."

Although Ronald Reagan, like Roosevelt, did much to change the basic agenda of the federal government, his agenda did not displace the New Deal so much as it displaced or amended the less popular and more targeted programs of Lyndon Johnson's Great Society. The huge budget deficits run up by Reagan's tax cuts and, after the first year, the inability of his administration and Congress to agree on the quantity and distribution of expenditure reductions, meant that resolving the budget problem rose to the top of nearly everyone's list of policy priorities. Moreover, the deficit got linked to a massive international trade account deficit. Reagan's priorities effectively set an agenda that he favored; the question now is not what new program to begin but, rather, where cuts can be made. For the most part, that question continues to constrain policy initiatives in spite of (perhaps even because of) the budget agreement reached in the fall of 1990.

It remains to be seen just how constraining (or convenient!) the Reagan agenda will be for future presidents. Movement toward new social programs that cost money will require either offsets or earmarked revenues. Programs based on earmarked revenues, such as catastrophic health insurance, can prove to be catastrophic to the health of politicians. Program constituents will be reluctant to absorb costs that decrease the marginal benefit of the new service. While politicians find it more desirable to dip into general revenues, thus diffusing program costs, they will not be able to do so without offsetting these costs against present programs. Still, politicians interested in new spending programs are notoriously ingenious in finding ways to provide the means. So while program expansion or creation is currently down, it is by no means out.

Retrospective Judgment

History is the final judge, intones the conventional wisdom. History, of course, is written by flesh-and-blood historians who chip in their judgment as to who belongs in presidential halls of fame and infamy. Surveys of historians on this issue have become increasingly sophisticated, moving from mere unrationalized summary judgment to specified dimensions of evaluation.[24]

In general, the presidential rating game bears some resemblance to voting for the baseball hall of fame. For a certain period, placement is fairly fluid, and presidents (like baseball players) move up or down somewhat in the judgment of the cognoscenti. Estimations of Eisenhower, for example, moved up between the 1960s and 1980s, reflecting, no doubt, the troubled presidencies in between. Truman ascended fairly rapidly, and Kennedy now seems in danger of being thought less well of than earlier. Over longer stretches of time, however, reputations tend to get frozen. Whatever the real story, George Washington's reputation is firm and not likely to change.[25]

A recent analysis, however, of historians' polls indicates that their collective judgment can be equaled by a fairly simple prediction equation.[26] The results are reproduced below:

$$\text{GREATNESS} = 1.24 + 0.17 \text{ (years)} + 0.26 \text{ (war)} - 1.70 \text{ (scandal)} + 0.89 \text{ (assassination)} + 0.82 \text{ (hero)}$$

Put in the form of advice to future presidents to do well in the "greatness sweepstakes," one would have to say: (1) serve a long time; (2) have a war; (3) avoid scandal; (4) get assassinated (but only after serving a long time); and (5) be acclaimed before coming to office.

In sum, if history is to have the final word, the final word, it is fair to say, does not fully succeed in closing the leadership question.

Skills and Styles

There is no president for all seasons. The job plays to many and diverse audiences, thus requiring considerable virtuosity in two broad categories: policy and politics. In some ways, the two are likely to be related. A president good at small group and interpersonal (elite) politics at home might also be convincing and effective in give and take with leaders from other political systems. A president who is effective at political mobilization (outside politics) also might inspire confidence that his proposals are the country's solutions. But not everything fits together so well—and, indeed, there are likely to be many contradictory types of skills required for policy and politics, and even for different types of political needs.

Earlier in discussing the management of decisions, I referred to some of the key attributes important to making policy decisions—curiosity, empathy, the ability to comprehend consequences, and so on. The case of Jimmy Carter is evidence that impressive policy-thinking skills by themselves are not enough. Most often, Carter did better as a philosopher than as a king. The obverse is that those who do best as kings are often not overly skillful as philosophers.

There also is tension between two different types of political skills or styles—those of *insider politics* and *outsider politics*. Another way to understand this distinction is to think of a politics essentially structured by *cartels* and one structured by *markets*. Insider or cartel politics emphasizes mediation, consensus-mongering, and brokerage. Outsider or market politics stresses public presence, conflict, position-taking, symbolic or rhetorical engagement, and often a form of crude responsiveness to existing or anticipated group pressures.

Across political systems and across time, there have been changes in the balance of the insider/outsider mix. Organization is critical to insider politics; the capacity of a definable few to speak authoritatively for an organized many is its essence—at least within the context of democratic politics. Clearly, one way in which a Swedish or Japanese prime minister differs from a U.S. president is that the former are typically skilled in the arts of insider politics. That is the game through which Swedish and Japanese leaders are selected. Because American politics is less organizationally structured and more entrepreneurial, U.S. presidents are more likely to play an outsider game. From time to time, for example, presidents have threatened (or been urged) to circumvent their direct relationship with the Congress and "go to the people" so as to bring popular pressure on Congress.

As a general matter, it is probably true that outsider or market politics has been eroding insider or cartel politics, though at a different pace across different systems. That erosion also has been subject to short-term fluctuations. For approximately the last two decades, the tendency has shifted noticeably toward outsider politics. Consequently, in their political campaigns insider politicians (such as Mondale and Bush) strive to erase their insider images. To gain support from what he believed were key constituencies, Mondale was crudely responsive; to diminish the effects of his "aristocratic" origins, Bush was merely crude. Dukakis, in turn, sought to cast himself in the role of the outsider who could competently manage the inside political game.

Through the various enlargements of his classic, *Presidential Power*, Richard Neustadt traced the emergence of modern television politics as placing yet further demands on the search for potential presidents, by complicating even further the skills necessary to the arts of modern American politics. Insider politics does not play well on television, yet show-horse politics diminishes opportunities for productive cooperation. The politician who can play both games brilliantly is rare indeed. For even as Reagan showed extraordinary flair at the outside game, fundamental flaws in his inside game were notable.

Is There an Answer?

The American political system places large and often contradictory demands upon its presidents. The president is expected to take the lead without also holding the reins of government. The president is also expected to manage the federal executive branch with which he typically has no more than a nodding acquaintance. Above all, the president must be there to decide on those occasions when no one else can speak for him. A president needs to have knowledge and instinct. Above all, like any leader, a president has to have luck.

The leadership question turns out to be several different questions, and, as such, there is no single answer. Often, the answers run counter to one another because the elements of leadership simply are not additive. Different lessons, accordingly, are learned through the experiences of different presidents. Reagan's told us about the importance of an idea and organizing around it. That is the good news. The bad news is that it also told us about what happens when presidents fail to comprehend the limits that reality, and sometimes the law, impose upon their strongly held ideas.

Reputedly, Ronald Reagan, as presidential candidate, once said, "There are no complicated answers, only complicated questions." He was half right.

Notes

I am grateful to the late Marver Bernstein and Margaret Wyszomirski for their astute and helpful comments on an earlier draft of this chapter.

1. Donald D. Searing, "Models and Images of Man in Leadership Theory," *Journal of Politics* 31 (1969): 3–31.

2. Robert D. Putnam, Robert Leonardi, Raffaella Y. Nanetti, and Franco Pavoncello, "Explaining Institutional Success: The Case of Italian Regional Government," *American Political Science Review* 77 (1983): 55–74.

3. Richard Rose, *The Problem of Party Government* (New York: The Free Press, 1974).

4. Aaron Wildavsky, "President Reagan as a Political Strategist," in *The Reagan Legacy: Promise and Performance*, ed. C. O. Jones (Chatham, N.J.: Chatham House, 1988), p. 291.

5. Ibid., p. 290.

6. James Fallows, "The Passionless Presidency," *Atlantic* 243 (May 1979): 33–48.

7. Colin Campbell, *Managing the Presidency: The Search for Executive Harmony* (Pittsburgh, Pa.: University of Pittsburgh Press, 1986).

8. Bert A. Rockman, *The Leadership Question: The Presidency in the American System* (New York: Praeger, 1984); and Bert A. Rockman, "Constants, Cycles, Trends, and Persona in Presidential Governance: Carter's Troubles Reviewed," in *The American Presidency: A Policy Perspective from Readings and Documents*, ed. David C. Kozak and Kenneth N. Ciboski (Chicago: Nelson-Hall, 1985), pp. 449–74.

9. For example, see James MacGregor Burns *The Deadlock of Democracy: Four-Party Politics in America* (Englewood Cliffs, N.J.: Prentice-Hall, 1963); Lloyd N. Cutler, "To Form a Government," *Foreign Affairs* 59 (1980): 126–43; Samuel P. Huntington, "Political Modernization: America vs. Europe," *World Politics* 18 (1966): 378–414; and Don K. Price, "The Parliamentary and Presidential Systems," *Public Administration Review* 3 (1943): 317–34.

10. Bert A. Rockman, "The Modern Presidency and Theories of Accountability: Old Wine *and* Old Bottles," *Congress and the Presidency* 13 (1986): 135–56.

11. Richard E. Neustadt, *Presidential Power* (New York: John Wiley, 1960; rpt. 1980), pp. 26–27. The book was first published in 1960. It has been expanded again and published in 1990 by the Free Press.

12. David W. Brady, "Critical Elections, Congressional Parties and Clusters of Policy Changes," *British Journal of Political Science* 8 (1978): 79–99.

13. Paul Allen Beck, "Incomplete Realignment: The Reagan Legacy for Parties and Elections," in *The Reagan Legacy,* ed. Jones, pp. 145–71.

14. For example, see William D. Nordhaus, "The Political Business Cycle," *Review of Economic Studies* 42 (1975): 169–90; and Edward R. Tufte, *Political Control of the Economy* (Princeton, N.J.: Princeton University Press, 1978).

15. Paul C. Light, *The President's Agenda: Domestic Policy Choice From Kennedy to Carter* (Baltimore: Johns Hopkins University Press, 1982); James P. Pfiffner, *The Strategic Presidency: Hitting the Ground Running* (Chicago: Dorsey Press, 1988).

16. Charles O. Jones, "Ronald Reagan and the U.S. Congress: Visible-Hand Politics," in *The Reagan Legacy,* ed. Jones, pp. 30–59.

17. Anthony King, ed., *The New American Political System* (Washington, D.C.: American Enterprise Institute, 1978).

18. Steven S. Smith, *Call to Order: Floor Politics in the House and Senate* (Washington, D.C.: Brookings, 1989). Smith argues, "Both internal incentives and resources and external pressures have driven more important policy decisions to the floors of the House and Senate" (p. 11).

19. Richard Rose, *The Post-Modern President: The White House Meets the World* (Chatham, N.J.: Chatham House, 1988).

20. For example, see George C. Edwards III, *At the Margins: Presidential Leadership of Congress* (New Haven, Conn.: Yale University Press, 1989); and Jon R. Bond and Richard Fleisher, *The President in the Legislative Arena* (Chicago: University of Chicago Press, 1990).

21. Fred I. Greenstein, *The Hidden-Hand Presidency: Eisenhower as Leader* (New York: Basic Books, 1982).

22. Neustadt, *Presidential Power.*

23. Ibid.

24. Dean Keith Simonton, *Why Presidents Succeed: A Political Psychology of Leadership* (New Haven, Conn.: Yale University Press, 1987), pp. 166–228.

25. Barry Schwartz, *George Washington: The Making of an American Symbol* (New York: Free Press, 1987).

26. Simonton, *Why Presidents Succeed,* p. 201.

3

Executive Leadership in an Age of Overload and Retrenchment

B. GUY PETERS

The 1970s and 1980s have been an era of real or perceived fiscal difficulty for governments in most industrialized societies. Talk of cutting budgets, cutting public employment, and perhaps above all cutting taxes has dominated political life. These financial difficulties for the public sector have been in part a reflection of the uncertainty of future economic growth, following several decades of sustained and rapid economic growth.[1] Although economic growth in the mid- and late 1980s was more sustained and somewhat greater than in the decade immediately after the oil crisis of 1973, a nagging uncertainty remained in the minds of many policy makers. That practical uncertainty is accentuated by the absence of an accepted economic dogma to guide decision making after the collapse of Keynesianism.

The fiscal difficulties of government also are a function of a continuing commitment by governments to fund social programs begun in the 1950s and 1960s (or even the 1930s). Demographic changes, inflation, and political pressure to enhance benefits have made these entitlement programs more expensive. Increased program costs have been made even more uncontrollable by the indexation of benefits to meet increases in prices and/or wages.[2] The costs of these social programs have led some to question the advisability of their being continued. The desire to cut programs may actually be more deep-seated and ideological, but financial problems have provided a useful justification. In the language of the time, governments were "overloaded," with too much to do and inadequate resources to meet all their commitments.

Finally, after the initial financial shocks around the times of the oil crises, the apparent fiscal distress of governments has been generated as much by ideological changes and citizens' backlash against taxation as by real economic conditions. As noted above, economic growth has been more problematic in recent decades than in the late 1950s and 1960s, but growth continues to occur and for European countries appears likely to get stronger. The unpredictability that plagued the 1970s now appears to have been reduced, and growth is predictable if not always large. However, whether in California, Denmark, Wellington or wherever, groups have mobilized to lower or at least to stabilize taxes, and thereby have been able to wittingly or unwittingly place fiscal pressures on government.

The "era of retrenchment" has entailed more than just simple demands for government to spend less money or employ fewer people. In many countries it has been associated with a more sweeping indictment of government as usual and an attempt to impose an alternative ideological vision on government. While most political leaders of this era do not have *ideologies* in the sense of an integrated and coherent vision of state and society, they do have a set of beliefs about government. Further, they have had the capacity to communicate those ideas to their fellow citizens, and the tenacity to put their ideas into practice to an almost unprecedented degree.[3] This set of beliefs at the elite level has successfully permeated mass thinking about government in many countries: the notion of an "enterprise culture" in Britain is an obvious example. It appears that people no longer look first to government to solve social problems, but rather look to the private sector. The era of retrenchment and the leaders it has spawned have produced a major cultural change concerning government, and governing has come to mean coping with this cultural change as much as coping with its more tangible symptoms such as inadequate money and personnel. In the words of George Downs and Patrick Larkey, the public sector has now moved "from hubris to helplessness."[4]

Although retrenchment is usually discussed as a fiscal concept, it has numerous managerial and leadership ramifications as well. In the first place, some of the reasons behind the perceived need for budgetary retrenchment are managerial. Governments are usually discussed as "bureaucratic," bumbling, inefficient, and poorly managed (and those are the most polite terms used). Many critics of government see its fiscal problems arising as much from the inefficiency of its own internal management practices as from external fiscal pressures.[5] These critics then propose the private sector as the proper exemplar of good management for government to emulate.[6] Evidence of corruption—whether in defense procurement in the United States or the management of the Property Services Agency in Britain—only adds to the appearance of poor public sector management.[7] The terms "fraud, waste, and abuse" in the United States have come to encapsulate a general feeling that many of the financial problems of government can be laid at its own doorstep, and that something must be done to make government work better.

In addition to the managerial causes (again, real or perceived) of financial problems in government, there has been popular pressure on government to reduce taxes. However, citizens are not so willing to see reductions in government services. Numerous surveys have indicated just that; people want benefits but they do not want taxes.[8] Doing more with less is now a common demand placed on managers in the public sector, and those managers (and their nominal political superiors) have developed a number of mechanisms for coping with the difficult financial realities of government in the 1980s.[9] In some instances the responses are mere budgetary gimmicks;[10] some change little more than the style of presentation without any real impact on the level of public expenditure. Other responses fall under the general rubric of "cutback management"[11] and involve the micromanagement of organizations as they respond to declining resources and probably also declining personnel figures. Other responses involve large-scale changes in government organization and management. At one time or another, almost all governments of industrialized democracies have attempted all three types of reform, albeit with varying degrees of success.[12]

The new ideologues and their demands for management in turn require some rethinking of the role of political executives and the role of career civil servants. It may require even more careful rethinking for political leaders who follow the current crop of leaders into political office. The rules of the governing game have been changed, and in some cases changed very fundamentally. Those rules have been changed primarily to tilt the playing surface in the direction of the politicians' end of the field and to enhance their capacity to score goals. It may be that subsequent leaders can develop an even greater capacity to get things done with their own resources, or they may want to return to a managerial system with greater responsibility for the career service. If indeed times are tough it may pay to minimize responsibility for what happens and attempt to place the blame elsewhere. Whatever their desires, those future leaders will have to understand and react to the managerial and policy developments of the past decade.

This chapter will describe modern governments' reactions to their fiscal problems, as well as the problems produced by the image they have acquired in the minds of many citizens of poor management and general incompetence. Given the theme of the "executive establishment," the theme of this volume, we will focus on efforts to change aspects of that establishment. We will examine the reforms that have been undertaken to cope with overload, giving special attention to those reforms affecting executive leadership in both the political ranks and the civil service. Many of these reforms have involved rather minor tinkering with structures of government or with the processes for implementation.[13] However, it is in the relationships between political executives and their career civil servants that some of the most profound changes in public sector management have been occurring. Further, these relational changes appear to go a long way toward defining executive leadership in this age of retrenchment.

Attempting to Cope with Retrenchment

Governments have adopted a number of strategies to deal with their problems in the era of retrenchment. These coping strategies, ranging from very mundane tinkering to fundamental reorientations of the public sector, serve as a backdrop for subsequent attempts to address the crucial role of executive leadership. Few or none of these changes could have occurred without real executive leadership, but once undertaken, they will certainly alter the conditions under which future leadership will be exercised. Thus, we must attempt to understand what executive leadership will look like in a new style of government. Ironically, some of the reforms identified appear to reduce rather than enhance the leadership capacity of future political officeholders and would constrain any attempts they would make to place their own stamp on government.

Content of Reforms

One way to classify government attempts to cope with the need to retrench is to look at the content of those reforms. What problems in government were identified as needing "fixing" and provoked a particular intervention? While classification is difficult, we can think of these coping strategies in four categories: budgetary, structural, procedural, and relational.[14]

Budgetary Reforms. The simplest of these categories contains attempts to change the making of budgets, or the type of analysis or thinking that goes into their construction. As can be seen by reference to the second dimension of table 2, there are several styles through which this manipulation of the budgetary process has been tried.[15] Furthermore, to a greater or lesser extent, all the methods developed to cope with retrenchment appear to have had some successes, although usually less than promised by their advocates. These successes actually have been greater than most previous attempts at budgetary reform, that is, PPBS, RCB, and the like, in part because the goals of the recent reforms have been more modest. While many strategies for budgetary reform in the 1960s and early 1970s had something approaching comprehensive rationality as a goal, most contemporary budgetary reforms have had simpler intentions, such as reducing public expenditure.[16] Hence, strategies such as the Main Alternative for the Swedish budget[17] which is simply a 2 percent reduction of the previous appropriations, have very tidy and attainable goals. Even budgetary reforms with more analytic content, such as the reconsideration initiatives in the Netherlands,[18] have a fundamental goal of reducing public expenditures rather than more grandiose goals of achieving some Pigovian optimum of allocations among competing purposes. In the case of budgetary reform at least, the hubris may be gone but there is no sense of helplessness.

Structural Reforms. As the name implies, structural changes have involved transformations of the organizational framework that provides government services. These changes range from the simple jiggling and poking of the structure that is common in any era, faced with retrenchment or not,[19] to very fundamental changes in the institutional fabric that provides public services. It is by no means uncommon to think that if the organization of government

TABLE 2. Examples of Governmental Reform

Strategies	Reform Targets			
	Budget	Structures	Procedures	Relations
Load shedding	Privatization	Privatization	Deregulation	Corporate structure (New Zealand)
Snakes and ladders	Mandating subnational expenditures	*Projektgruppen* (Germany)	Regulatory review	Increased power for central agencies
Automaticity	Gramm-Rudman-Hollings Act (United States)	Personnel administration (Japan)	Sunset laws (United States)	—
Priority setting	Envelope budgeting (Canada)	—	MINIS (United Kingdom)	Politicization
Squeezing	Main Alternative (Sweden)	Grace Commission (United States)	Rayner scrutinies (United Kingdom)	—
Managerialism	Financial Management Initiative (United Kingdom)	SAFAD (Sweden)	—	Next Steps (United Kingdom)

Source: Author.

is correct, then those institutions will actually function smoothly. Unfortunately, however, despite its frequent use, structural reorganizations of government are really not very well understood either by those implementing them or students of government.[20] As a consequence, reorganizations frequently do not meet the goals— especially those of enhanced efficiency[21]—that have been set for them and often produce more disillusionment and disappointment than significant change.

Among the most fundamental structural changes tried has been shedding burdens through privatization and deregulation. Even when programs have been retained in government, there has been a tendency to hive them off into smaller, presumably more accountable and mission-oriented, organizations and to reduce the relative power and authority of the mainline departments. This has been seen, in among other examples, in the formation of *administrations de mission* in France and Belgium,[22] *Projektgruppen* in West Germany,[23] and in the proposed creation of mission-oriented agencies by the reform called "Next Steps" in the United Kingdom.[24] Also, there have been a number of efforts at decentralizing (or even centralizing) government to attempt to promote efficiency, accountability, and a host of other political values by involving other levels of government. It would appear that one common reaction to the perceived inability of existing government structures to deliver the goods in a manner that most people would desire is to attempt to alter the existing structures for delivering those services. This is hardly a new response to the problem, but it remains interesting the extent to which old reforms continue to become new problems.

Again, we should not be terribly sanguine about the capacity of structural reforms to produce any tangible improvements in the performance of the public sector. The reforms do have two advantages, however. The first is that they give the appearance of action in dealing with problems for which there may be no real solution, and political leaders may need that image created. Further, as with some of the budgetary "reforms," structural reforms may give the illusion that expenditures have been reduced when in fact they are only being made at another level of government, or by a quasi-public organization that does not show up in the budget.[25]

Procedural Reforms. Along with changing structures, governments have sought to alter the procedures by which they conduct their business and make their decisions. Again, unlike many of the nonbudgetary procedural remedies adopted during the 1960s and early 1970s, such as MBO, many of the procedural reforms emerging in the later 1970s and into the 1980s have been very little concerned with substantive rationality. Rather, they have been more concerned with the "simple" task of trying to improve productivity, or at a minimum making those who manage programs in government conceptualize their tasks in those terms.[26] Other reforms have been concerned with procedural rationality and providing the appearance that government does in fact perform its role properly.

Many of the components in the *procedures* category might be classified as structural reforms. Procedures rarely are introduced on their own but require an organization to develop and implement them. For example, were the Rayner scrutinies in Britain a procedural reform or were they a structural change, as for example the creation of the Efficiency Unit? We will be regarding these reforms as procedural because it was the change in procedure, or the addition of new procedures, that was designed to produce the result. Reorganization or the creation of a new organization was coincidental with the procedural change. Further, some procedural reforms may come very close to being budgetary in nature. The Financial Management Initiative in Britain, for example, had a good deal to do with spending money, although the primary purpose appeared to be altering how government did its business rather than focusing on the saving of candle ends through the formal budgetary process.

Similar to the budget and especially organizational reforms, however, some of the most important and effective procedural reforms have involved reducing the number of procedures. This is seen externally through deregulation and governments' decisions to impose fewer rules on the conduct of economic and social life in their countries. Internally, in government itself, this type of reform has manifested itself in several ways. One has been through Paperwork Reduction Acts and their equivalents. Another has been the abrogation of some procedures that may have protected civil servants, such as the Priestley system of pay research in the United Kingdom, or the principal of pay comparability between the public and private sectors in the United States. One meaning of "reform" has been simply to eliminate what were perceived as slow and costly procedures in favor of quick decisions by elected political leaders or their appointees.[27]

Relational Reforms. Finally, governments have sought to address their political demands for retrenchment through altering the relationships between the career civil service and temporary political executives. A dominant theme of most of the "ideological" governments in the 1970s and 1980s (especially those of the right) has been that policy making in those countries has been dominated by the career civil service. It has been argued that the poor management skills of the civil service, and their thinly disguised policy agendas, have been a fundamental cause of all that is wrong with government in Washington, Whitehall, or wherever. Further, the protection offered by civil service systems is argued to protect and disguise a cadre of organizational politicians who have their own views about policy and who have been successful in implementing those views.[28] With the popularity of this perception, the public bureaucracy has become a scapegoat for the very need for retrenchment, and political leaders have been effective in deflecting attention from their own managerial shortcomings onto the civil service.[29]

Given the above diagnosis of the illness of government, the remedies prescribed should not be surprising. In the 1980s, a number of attempts were made to interject more political control, and more political appointees, into the career service to the point where the politicization of the civil service has become a significant concern in a number of countries.[30] Even in countries such as the United Kingdom with a long tradition of an apolitical and largely respected and influential civil service, attempts have been made to impose greater political control and to involve outsiders.[31] In countries such as France and West Germany, where civil servants have been more identified with political parties, the importance of that identification appears to have intensified.[32] It now appears to be widely believed among elected political leaders that if they can only get more politically committed people into management and leadership positions in government, then the commonly identified problems of government will have been solved, or at least ameliorated.

Summary. Although the reform strategies and policies adopted by government are many and varied, they appear to fit into the four content categories outlined above. Each category is important and can help in ameliorating problems in governing, but none is a panacea. Decision makers appear to have very little guidance in their selection among these alternatives, so that fad or fashion appears as important as analysis and calculation. It does appear that the dominant fad in the late 1980s was to enhance the power of political leaders vis-à-vis their civil servants. This in turn has meant that governments have concentrated much of their attention on relational reforms as attempts to improve the capacity of *politicians* to exercise executive leadership.

Styles of Reform

In addition to dealing with the specific content of government problems, the reforms that have been adopted can also be classified according to the particular style of reform they attempt to impose. Although some styles appear closely tied to specific contents, such as automaticity with budgetary reforms, there is a rather wide distribution of almost all styles in the several content categories. Faced with the very daunting problem of attempting to change the manner in which government conducts its business, political (and administrative) leaders have cast their net wide and have tried a number of "solutions." What does appear general, however, is the denigration of "rationality" in favor of more political, ideological and nonanalytic responses to problems. These responses frequently involve the elimination of discretion, or shifting the location of decision making, or invoking the private sector as a solution rather than more systematic analysis and cogitation. This does not mean that all the tools taught in schools of public administration and policy around the country are being allowed to rust. Rather, the tools appear now to be used more overtly to justify preconceived notions rather than to "discover" new solutions and new information about the policy issues.

Load Shedding. One of the simplest strategies governments can adopt for dealing with the perceived need to retrench is to shed some of the burdens it has been carrying and allow the private sector to do more. We have already noted that this is infeasible for many large-expenditure entitlement programs, but it has proved to be very possible for a number of programs.[33] Even for the big-ticket items, however, some governments have undertaken serious evaluations of the possibilities of privatization. Further, international organizations such as the World Bank and the International Monetary Fund have been instrumental in carrying the gospel of privatization to many nonindustrialized countries, so that this has become a worldwide response to perceived governmental and economic failures.[34]

Load shedding need not just be privatization, however. Deregulation is another important form of load shedding that has been adopted in varying degrees in different countries. Not only has government eschewed the direct ownership of nationalized industries, but also it has sought to allow private industries greater autonomy in making their own decisions. This presumably both lessens the decision-making burden on government and permits greater economic progress through free-market solutions. It should be noted, however, that the two load-shedding strategies may not be possible simultaneously. Privatizing industries such as electricity that meet the usual criteria for regulation[35] may require those industries then be regulated. For example, very soon after British Telecom was privatized, the Office of Telecommunications was established in Whitehall to protect the public from a potential monopolist and to encourage competition.

Snakes and Ladders. Not all movement of power and decision making is between the public and private sectors. Another style is to redistribute the tasks of government among different actors within government as a response to its managerial ills, even if all the activities do remain government responsibilities. Some functions may be centralized and others decentralized, but if there is a problem, then shifting the level of government may be proposed as the answer. In other instances decision making may be shifted upward to politicians and away from the civil service. This is a simple solution that implies that policy problems can be corrected just by having someone else take responsibility for them.

Of course, all this shifting of responsibilities may only be a facade to hide the intractability of the problems; it may be simple an exercise in "blame avoidance."[36] Or it may be a means of one level of government trying to gain some apparent fiscal responsibility at the expense of others. This may be especially powerful for a goal of fiscal probity if the function can be forced onto a level of government that is not permitted to run a deficit, such as the states in the United States.[37] As with privatization as a solution, the same function performed elsewhere still costs somebody something, but the political appearance is often as important as the reality of the reform in having it adopted.

Interestingly, different governments when faced with somewhat similar demands for retrenchment, or at least improvement of governmental performance, have approached the problem of who does what somewhat differently. This to some degree may be a function of their respective starting points; highly centralized regimes could centralize further only with great difficulty. There may simply be a simple regression toward the mean as "solutions" are selected. This is not necessarily the case, however, as the United States, which began with a decentralized regime, became even more decentralized during the Reagan administration. Of the two types of response, decentralization has appeared to be the more popular choice. France, Spain, and Italy have undertaken major decentralization efforts in what had been centralized regimes.[38] Local government reforms in a number of European countries appear to have made giving more power to the localities a real possibility.[39] Only the United Kingdom has seen a major effort at centralization of control over local government,[40] albeit combined with a broad effort at load shedding to the private sector. Other countries have, however, centralized some functions in an attempt to enhance control.

Automaticity. As noted above, this strategy is especially closely associated with problems in the budget. It could be argued that it is hard for political organizations, or public organizations with close links to clients, to make difficult decisions about reducing public expenditure. Therefore, if those actors can agree on automatic mechanisms for imposing reductions, then some of the political onus will be removed from those decisions. American audiences will recognize the logic of the Gramm-Rudman-Hollings legislation in this statement, and similar mechanisms have been imposed in other political systems.[41] In some, like Japan, similar mechanisms have been applied to the civil service.[42] The fundamental idea here is to remove as much discretion as possible from those whose careers might be damaged by making decisions on cuts.

Automaticity has also been introduced as a means of preventing government from enhancing its revenues through inflation. With a progressive income tax, as incomes increase, taxpayers move into higher brackets and have to pay a larger proportion of their income in tax. If increases in income are due to inflation rather than real economic growth, individual taxpayers will retain a smaller real income. To correct for this, a number of governments have introduced automatic adjustments of bracket thresholds for inflation.[43] With this arrangement, if governments want more tax revenues, they have to go through the difficult political battle to change the law, rather than receiving a "fiscal dividend" of changes in price levels.

Priority Setting. One of the standard compliants about "big government" is that it has been allowed to grow without much rhyme or reason, and hence has grown in very incoherent, and therefore excessively costly, ways.[44] Thus, if clear policy priorities could be established, then the "burdens" of government could be reduced and better government produced for all. The need to set priorities is said to be especially great in budget matters, but also exists in a range of government activities.[45] Further, while some of the rational reforms of of the 1960s and 1970s also sought to impose priorities,[46] governments in the 1980s sought to determine those priorities by more political means.

Placing a greater emphasis on setting priorities in government will tend to drive decisions upward, away from the career civil service and toward the political executives. This is much the same idea as Campbell's "planning and priorities" style of executive behavior, and is to some extent similar to Dror's "central mind of government."[47] In moving decisions upward in the hierarchy, this style of governing will affect the relationships between civil servants and politicians. Thus, initiatives such as the Financial Management Initiative, and its sequel, Next Steps, in the United Kingdom have the impact of making civil servants the managers of frameworks established elsewhere and thereby of reducing their importance in governing.

Squeezing. If it is assumed that government budgets and staffs are almost by definition too large for the demands of the tasks that are to be performed, one important strategy to improve efficiency would be to squeeze the fat out of those budgets. While this may be done through the automatic methods discussed above, it can also be done more selectively. That selection may be done on the grounds of efficiency, for example, choosing targets regardless of their political popularity because they appear to have a great deal of available slack. Reviews of defense procurement (even prior to the bribery scandals of the 1980s) would be an example of this approach. A more common strategy would be to select as targets programs that are politically unpopular and then to scrutinize their budgets very carefully. Finally, often the most politically popular, even if logically undesirable, method of approaching this problem is across-the-board cuts, or "equal misery."

One way to produce the squeeze on government is to bring in people who have little or nothing to protect in the current programs and arrangements for administration. This is typified in the Grace Commission in the United States, with a very similar mechanism being employed in Canada in the form of the Nielsen Task Force.[48] Other countries that do not permit outsiders to come roaming through their governments cannot enjoy the benefits of these exercises,[49] but exercises such as the Rayner scrutinies in the United Kingdom serve much of the same purpose by using insiders.[50] This search-and-destroy tactic provides a great deal of ammunition for those who want to reduce the size of government, although it runs the risk of cutting the good with the bad. This is essentially true because, as we point out immediately below, the analogies between the public and private sectors may well be false.

Managerialism. Finally, there has been a major movement in government circles to attempt to make government itself more like private enterprise, and to make running government organizations more like private-sector management. This approach to governing sometimes parades under the banner of *managerialism,* as if there had been no managment in government before it was advocated. This approach tends to ignore all the warnings about the fundamental differences between government and business, and proceeds to attempt to transplant private-sector ideas to government.[51] As might be imagined, this approach has been championed especially by the political right, although it has not been without its more moderate and even liberal advocates. Managerialism has been characterized, however, by some scholars as almost hopelessly muddled and as a "reign of error."[52]

The managerial approach to improving government performance in the face of retrenchment has been widespread; it is very comforting to some to think that whatever is really wrong with government can be cured without addressing any fundamental value choices. The Reagan administration, through its general approach to government, characterized by projects such as the Grace Commission and "Reform 88," sought to make government function more like a business.[53] Similar themes have emerged in Canadian and Australian government.[54] Major efforts at understanding and improving government management are currently under way in the Scandinavian countries. Nowhere, however, has managerialism been a more visible and important strategy than it has been in Margaret Thatcher's Britain. Beginning with the MINIS information system,[55] going through the Financial Management Initiative,[56] and now pushing even further along the managerial trial with the Next Steps program,[57] Conservative governments since 1979 have been attempting to produce a basic change in the culture of the British civil service. The fundamental idea is that career civil servants should serve as managers, and policy ideas should be the province of the political executives. This thinking pervades several of the substantive areas of reform, but is especially evident in thinking about relational issues in governance. It is in many ways a restatement of the old "politics-administration" dichotomy whose obituary scholars wrote many years ago but which continues to live and breathe in the practical world of politics.

Summary

Governments have not been remiss in trying to cope with the problems presented by retrenchment politics. Rather, they have been extremely creative in producing reforms that address, if in no more than symbolic terms at times, the challenges they face. The classification and enumeration of reforms contained here only scratch the surface of the complexity of change. It does, however, serve as the background and prologue for an understanding of what these responses to the "crisis" of government now imply for the capacity of government executives, whether operating from a political or a career base, to supply real leadership for coping with the problems and crises that will inevitably arise. As is always the case for government, and other organizations, the last round of solutions becomes the source of the problems that the next wave of executives must confront.

Executive Leadership

Each type of reform mentioned above will impose some possible burdens, as well as provide some possible benefits, for subsequent executive leaders. We will discuss the implications of those reforms in discussing some of the general questions which the emphasis on retrenchment in government poses for executive leadership. As I have intimated, the climate for executive leadership may not now be as positive as that enjoyed by leaders who came to office just following the crises of the 1970s.

To Boldly Go

A general characteristic of executive leadership in government has been the ability to impose a vision on a government and make the operational components of that government respond to the vision. This may be done by force of personality, by good organization, or by mere persistence. In any case, effective leaders are usually thought to be those who produce a order-of-magnitude difference in what government does.

In the era of retrenchment, strong executive leadership has been associated with doing less rather than more. Political leaders such as Thatcher, Reagan, Mulroney, and to some extent many others, have made their marks on government by shedding responsibilities and making government smaller and less expensive.[58] This load shedding has now been done, and done rather effectively, in many countries. Although some ultraconservatives would certainly disagree, it appears that most programs that reasonably can be eliminated from the public sector have been so eliminated, and most reasonable cuts in the remaining programs have been made. The question now arises as to what comes next; what can subsequent executive leaders do to demonstrate their leadership and their vision of the good life for their countries?

The capacity for new executive leaders to appear to be doing something is especially constrained if we assume that many of the fiscal problems of government will persist—and, with increased interest payments on debts, some may be exacerbated. It will be made even more difficult if the negative conceptions of government that have been popular in many industrialized countries persist. The current stock of conservative political leaders have to some extent done the easy things, and have appeared effective thereby. Those that follow will face the difficult choice of being seen to do little or nothing, or be seen as violating what has become an apparent commitment of government to keep costs (and taxes) down. Either choice is unpalatable to most potential leaders.

The capacity to develop new policy initiatives is further inhibited by the crowding of the policy space that characterizes most industrialized countries.[59] Governments in most industrialized countries have a program, or more than one program, for most of the clientele groups and most of the identifiable problems in their societies; a dominant feature of overload may be the complexity and interconnectedness of programs in the public sector.[60] Policy making in this context becomes coping with coordination and integration of existing organizations and programs as much as pushing forward with new initiatives. It becomes "rationalizing politics" rather than "breakthrough politics."[61] As Heclo wrote in 1975:

The challenge confronting social policy is not a discontinuity but a cumulation of historical developments common to Europe and the United States. . . . Frontiers of policy development no longer stretch toward a horizon of unimpeded growth amid cheap resources but are now internal frontiers of integration, coordination, and trade-offs.[62]

This type of decision making is a particularly executive form of action, being focused on the structure of the executive branch of government and attempting to make that set of programs and institutions function better and with coordiantion. It also confronts the entrenched interests of clients and service providers. Certainly the legislative branch must be involved, because there are budgetary implications if nothing else, but it must function in a role secondary to that of executive officials.

Despite their central position in the process, dealing with coordinating existing policies presents some major challenges to executive leaders, especially those with a political base. This is very worthy activity, but it is difficult to make into exciting headlines for the nightly news. Therefore, the capacity of political leaders to *appear* to exercise policy leadership is diminished just when the need for such leadership is enhanced. The need is increased because moving into crowded policy spaces involves bumping up against existing programs with existing clienteles and workers.

Any intrusion into such an existing system is likely to produce more concern and resistancc than moving into relatively virgin territory.[63] The capacity of career civil servants to lead is perhaps even more constrained in these circumstances, given that most who are concerned with the issue area would be a member of one of the existing organizations, and would be expected to fight to defend that organization's turf rather than to cooperate in the name of sweet reason. This then puts political executives into a central postion, but one that is not very comfortable for them.

Still the Century of Corporatism?

The constraints on executive leadership are not just those arising within the executive branch of government, they also arise form the relationship between the public and private sectors in most industrialized countries. This is true on both the *input* and *output* sides of government, if we can use Eastonian language. First, on the input side, a dominant characteristic of politics in most industrialized societies during the 1960s and 1970s was some form of neocorporatism.[64] There was a linking of private sector interest groups to government, with a consequent loss of autonomy for both actors. This arrangement appeared to work well so long as there was growing affluence in these countries, with the quiescence of some groups toward certain decisions being repaid with their right to participate in all.

This agreed-upon system for sharing the fiscal dividend of growth enabled the corporatist countries to undergo large-scale economic and social change with a minimum of disruption. The system did not work so well on the downside, and many states have become virtual hostages to the participatory commitments they have made.[65] These commitments accumulated much as did states' commitments to provide social benefits and have severely limited the capacity of those countries to respond to a rapidly changing international marketplace and to make tough, redistributive decisions internally as required. If distributive politics works well in times of affluence, times of retrenchment appear to require politics that corporatism may not be able to supply.[66] Some political leaders in states with some tendencies toward corporatism have been able to grasp the nettle and break or modify the system, but for many there remains an apparent need for such decisive leadership.

The Loosening of Linkages

Some of the same loss of leadership capacity that resulted from linkages to the private sector on the input side also appears to occur on the output side. If we consider executive leadership in the age of retrenchment in terms of the literature on guidance and control in the public sector,[67] there is clearly some reduction in the steering capacity in most modern governments, when compared to governments of the 1950s and 1960s. This has been partly a function of popular attitudes, but has been in large part a consequence of the structural changes in the provision of public services described above, especially the tendency to use lower levels of government or nongovernmental organizations, to provide public services. Thus, even if the ostensible direction in a policy area is still determined by a central government organization, program implementation may not be, and that implementation may be crucial in defining the true nature of the policy.[68]

Further, old democratic values such as accountability may be threatened when a significant share of the portion of the real policy making in government is located outside organizations over which elective or appointive officials have direct control. The development of "third-party government" has produced some real benefits for government, but those benefits may have been purchased at some real cost as well.[69] Further, given the changes in popular attitudes, it may be difficult for future executives to return some of these functions to government administration, with the increased apparent cost that this would imply.

The tightness or looseness of the linkages in government need not, however, depend totally upon the use of third-party actors to implement public programs. Some political systems may be more closely linked within their own executive establishments than are others. For example, the decentralized and cross-pressured nature of the executive branch in the United States makes executive leadership a more difficult commodity to supply, even with the availability of more political executives to manage government.[70] This may be contrasted with the greater domination of the ministry structure in Britain which, combined with a rather tightly organized career civil service, puts government more directly in the command of the prime minister and the cabinet.

Other industrialized countries vary along this dimension as well, with factors such as the overall structure of the political system, the structure of ministries, the personnel system, and system of advice and analysis all influencing the relative degree of linkage within government. As I have argued before, a central point of departure for analysis of government is the ability of those at the top to manage it.[71] One can discern some substantial variations in effectiveness of executive leaders based on the closeness of the linkages within the political system. This closeness of linkage is certainly related to the political system's power to reduce its involvement in the economy and society, but also appears related to its ability to increase that involvement, as in the case of France under the Socialists.

Where Politicians Fear to Tread

Another barrier to executive leadership in the era of retrenchment is, to some degree, in apparent contradiction to the first: the problems that appear to face society are perhaps too massive or too inadequately understood to be solved by effective government intervention. Government is, at once, involved in everything, yet does not address some of society's fundamental structural problems. This is perhaps particularly evident in the United States where social dislocation, the widespread abuse of drugs, poor school performance, a rapidly aging population, an equally rapidly aging industrial structure, and a host of other major problems await some effective solution. At present, government does not appear to have answers to those problems and often seeks to run away from them. The aversion to these problems was most pronounced at the federal level in the Reagan administration, but to some degree is found in the states and cities where these problems are most dramatically manifested. This difficulty is not confined to the United States, however; most industrialized countries face similar problems.

The accumulation of large-scale problems for society poses at least two difficulties for executive leaders.[72] The first is directly related to the conventional, fiscal, interpretation of retrenchment: that is, any attempt to address most of these problems is likely to be very expensive. Previous attempts to address major public problems—whether they were social (the War on Poverty) or merely engineering (sending men to on the moon)—involved a commitment to spend, and to spend almost without limits. Such a deep-pockets strategy lost credibility in the 1980s with the real problems of public deficits and popular resistance to government taxation and expenditure.

The second problem is more political and perceptual, although linked with the cultural changes associated with retrenchment. This is that few politicians want to be associated with failures, and especially with expensive failures; avoiding blame may be preferable to the possibility of claiming credit.[73] The opportunities presented to politicians in this retrenchment period are primarily very risky, with a real possibility or even probability of failure. For most issues, government does not have a ready methodology for attacking the problem, any clear idea of the root "causes" of the problem, or even a very well-accepted definition of what the problem really is. In terms of Nelson's analogy of the "moon and the ghetto,"[74] the problems being faced are definitely moon-type problems for which there is no ready engineering solution. Governments may be able to address problems as experiments, but failure may produce human costs which would be unacceptable, as well as producing very fundamental questions about accountability.

Thus, if executive leadership is to be anchored in success, the possibilities of success are becoming more limited and so too are the possibilities of democratic political systems to encourage leaders with bold visions about the future who are willing to stake their careers and their futures on attacking wicked problems. Leaders may attempt to change the definition of success to include holding the line on those wicked problems and preventing them from getting worse. Even in an era that is skeptical of government, however, such minimalist visions of success are extremely unlikely to excite the public, or the political leaders themselves.

Conclusion: All Dressed Up and Nowhere to Go

The above analysis leads to a somewhat paradoxical, but even more a depressing, conclusion about the prospects for executive leadership in an age of retrenchment. This is especially the case if we conceive of leadership as making a significant addition to what might have been accomplished without the intervention of the leader. It appears on the one hand that executive leaders (meaning here primarily political leaders) have been blessed with a range of new leadership tools and possibilities. Some of the institutional politics of the 1980s has sought to reduce the role of the career civil service and to give political executives greater capacity. While most of the usual roadblocks to the power of political leaders remain, they are somewhat diminished. Further, when necessary, political leaders have developed novel mechanisms for circumventing or surmounting the barriers to policy change presented by the institutions they manage. Everything else being equal, political leaders should now have an enhanced capacity to put their ideas into action.

In fairness, there is a major caveat to the above generalization. Another reaction by political leaders to retrenchment has been to push so much of government out to "third-party" institutions, quasi-governmental organizations, other levels of government, and even regulated industries, that a good deal of control is lost, albeit at the gain of lower costs and less apparent responsibility. It appears that in many instances politicians have been quite willing to trade lower control and direction over policy for diminished responsibility if anything goes wrong. Even with that caveat, however, one consequence of the age of retrenchment is a new capacity for executive leaders to lead.

That having been said, there is a need to ask in what direction that executive leadership is to go. This dimension of leadership is less certain.[75] One might argue that there has been an exhaustion of political ideas, except for ideas about what tasks need *not* be done in government. While some of those ideas about minimizing government are creative and may require some leadership to bring to fruition, at a broader level there appears to be an absence of new policy directions in politics. That absence of direction appears inversely proportional to the number of times U.S. presidential candidates claim to offer a new direction to the voters.

The prevalence of the theme of new ideas and new policies in political campaigns does highlight some of the paradox mentioned above. Citizens apparently want government to do something positive for them, but they are very wary (and weary?) of the costs and the possible failures that this could involve. They are also skeptical about whether any new programs will benefit them, or only the politicians and special interests. How then can the political system

cope with these seemingly contradictory demands and expectations? A simple answer is to return to the theme of this volume
and to argue for greater leadership, but a leadership that shapes
ideas rather than merely reacts to them. As Lowi has argued for
years, policies shape politics and there may be a need for the
recognition of a new style of politics to cope with the new policy
demands.[76] It may be that Carter, rather than Reagan, is the wave
of the future. That is, this executive leadership may have to be
more technocratic (and bureaucratic) and less photogenic if it is to
be successful, in policy, rather than only political, terms.

Another response would be to enhance the capacity of the executive branch to provide direction to government. In the United
States at least, the Executive Office of the President has grown to
have the capacity (not always realized) to affect policy very directly. Political executives in other countries also appear to have
enhanced their capacity to influence policy, although that capacity
is often used for political, rather than policy, purposes. Likewise,
political executives could use their civil servants as allies in the
process of governing, rather than treating them as enemies, as has
been the case of a number of contemporary presidents and prime
ministers. These civil servants, and any political appointees, need
not be only implementers of policy; they also have vital roles to
play in generating policy ideas. In short, political executives need
not sit idly by while their programs are being opposed; they have
sufficient resources to make a good effort at doing what they want
while in office.

Another answer, somewhat more complex, might be that those
in government need to recapture a bit of the hubris of other times.
This would not mean relying on their rational methods to provide
solutions, but at least relying on their analytic methods to understand their actions. Any such analysis should focus as much on the
instruments of intervention as on a simple question of whether to
intervene or not. The same thing can be done in many ways, some
of which may provoke reactions against government and others
not. This has been well demonstrated for tax policies, and will
probably be true in other policy areas as well. If we return to
Gormley's ideas about institutional policy analysis, the need may
be for less coercive and more catalytic controls, and for very subtle
manipulations of instruments already in place. This may not be
the stuff of great political drama, but it may be the stuff of success-

ful executive leadership in an era of ongoing retrenchment and political skepticism. It may be that a little old-fashioned competence will solve more policy problems than all the political hype and photo opportunities.

Notes

1. Richard Rose and B. Guy Peters, *Can Government Go Bankrupt?* (New York: Basic Books, 1978).

2. R. Kent Weaver, *Automatic Government: The Politics of Indexation* (Washington, D.C.: Brookings, 1988).

3. Charles O. Jones, ed. *The Reagan Legacy* (Chatham, N.J.: Chatham House, 1988); Denis Kavanagh, *Thatcherism and British Politics: The End of Consensus?* Oxford: Oxford University Press, 1987.

4. George W. Downs and Patrick D. Larkey, *The Search for Government Efficiency: From Hubris to Helplessness* (New York: Random House, 1986), p. 183.

5. E. S. Savas, *Privatizing the Public Sector* (Chatham, N.J.: Chatham House, 1982); but see Charles T. Goodsell, *The Case for Bureaucracy,* 2d ed. (Chatham, N.J.: Chatham House, 1985).

6. Downs and Larkey, *The Search,* pp. 23–58.

7. A. Doig, *Corruption and Misconduct in Contemporary British Politics* (Harmondsworth: Penguin, 1984); Susan Rose-Ackerman, *Corruption: A Study in Political Economy* (New York: Academic Press, 1978).

8. David O. Sears and Jack Citrin, *Tax Revolt—Something for Nothing in California* (Berkeley and Los Angeles: University of California Press, 1982); Peter Taylor-Gooby, *Public Opinion, Ideology and State Welfare* (London: Routledge and Kegan Paul, 1985); Axel Hadenius, *A Crisis in the Welfare State* (Stockholm: Almgvist and Wiksell, 1985).

9. Yehezkel Dror, *Policymaking Under Adversity* (New Brunswick, N.J.: Transaction, 1985), pp. 51–72.

10. Daniel Tarschys, "Curbing Public Expenditure: Current Trends," *Journal of Public Policy* 5 (1985), 23–67.

11. Charles H. Levine, "Organization Decline and Cutback Management," *Public Administration Review* 38 (1978), 316–25; *Managing Fiscal Stress: The Crisis in the Public Sector* (Chatham, N.J.: Chatham House, 1980).

12. Patricia W. Ingraham and B. Guy Peters, "The Conundrum of Reform," *Review of Public Personnel Administration* 8 (1988), 3–16.

13. For a general critique see William T. Gormley, "Institutional Policy Analysis: A Critical Review," *Journal of Policy Analysis and Management* 6 (1987), 153–69.

14. See Ingraham and Peters, "The Conundrum."

15. Tarschys, "Curbing Public Expenditure"; Allen Schick, "Micro-budgetary Adaptations to Fiscal Stress in Industrialized Democracies," *Public Administration Review* 48 (1988), 523–33.

16. B. Guy Peters, *The Politics of Bureaucracy,* 3d ed. (New York: Longmans, 1989), chap. 7.

17. B. Ericksson, "Sweden's Budget System in a Changing World," *Public Budgeting and Finance* 3 (1983), 64–80.

18. Netherlands Scientific Council on Government Policy, *A Reappraisal of Welfare Policy* (The Hague: Netherlands Council, 1983).

19. B. Guy Peters and Brian W. Hogwood, "Births, Deaths and Metamorphoses in the U.S. Federal Bureaucracy 1933–1983," *American Review of Public Administration* 2 (1988), 119–34.

20. Arne Leemans, *Managing Change in Government* (The Hague: Nijhoff, 1976); Christopher Pollitt, *Manipulating the Machine* (London: George Allen and Unwin, 1984); Colin Campbell and B. Guy Peters, eds., *Organizing Governance, Governing Organizations* (Pittsburgh, Pa.: University of Pittsburgh Press, 1988).

21. Lester B. Salamon, "Reorganization—The Question of Goals," in *Federal Reorganization: What Have We Learned?*, ed. Peter Szanton (Chatham, N.J.: Chatham House, 1981).

22. Jacques Rigaud and Xavier Delcros, *Les Institutions Administratives Françaises* (Paris: Presses de la Fondation Nationale des Sciences Politiques, 1984).

23. Manfred Lepper, "Internal Structure of Public Offices," in *Public Administration in the Federal Republic of Germany*, ed. Klaus Konig, Hans Joachim van Oertzen, and Frido Wagener (Boston: Kluwer, 1983).

24. Kate Jenkins, Karen Caines, and Andrew Jackson, *Improving Management in Government: The Next Steps*. Ibbs Report (London: HMSO, 1988).

25. B. Guy Peters and Martin O. Heisler, "Thinking About Public Sector Growth," in *Why Governments Grow: Measuring Public Sector Size*, ed. Charles L. Taylor (Beverly Hills, Calif.: Sage, 1983); Christopher Hood and G. F. Schuppert, *Delivering Public Services in Western Europe* (London: Sage, 1988).

26. J. M. Lee, "Financial Management and the Career Service," *Public Administration* 62 (1984), 2.

27. See Jacques Fournier, *Le Travail Gouvernemental* (Paris: Dalloz, 1987).

28. Stuart Butler, Michael Sanera, and W. B. Weinrod, eds. *Mandate for Leadership II: Continuing the Conservative Revolution* (Washington, D.C.: Heritage Foundation, 1984); Sir John Hoskyns, "Whitehall and Westminster: An Outsider's View," *Parliamentary Affairs* 36 (1983), 137–47.

29. H. Brinton Milward and Hal G. Rainey, "Don't Blame the Bureaucracy," *Journal of Public Policy* 3 (1983), 149–68.

30. Francois Meyers, ed., *La Politisation de l'Administration* (Brussels: Institut International des Sciences Administratives, 1985).

31. F. F. Ridley, "Politics and the Selection of Higher Civil Servants in Britain," in *La Politisation*, ed. Meyers; Gavin Drewry and T. Butcher, *The Civil Service Today* (Oxford: Blackwell's).

32. Hans-Ulrich Derlien, "Reprecussions of Government Change on the Career Civil Service in West Germany: The Case of 1969 and 1982," *Governance* 1 (1988), 50–78; *Pouvoirs:* Special issue on "Des Fonctionnaires Politisés?" (1987).

33. Cento Veljanovski, *Selling the State: Privatisation in Britain* (London: Weidenfeld and Nicolson, 1987); E. S. Savas, *Privatization: The Key to Better Government* (Chatham, N.J.: Chatham House, 1987).

34. A. Premchand, *Government Budgeting and Expenditure Controls: Theory and Practice* (Washington, D.C.: International Monetary Fund, 1983), pp. 323ff.

35. Privatization may limit possibilities for deregulation. For example, privatizing firms like British Telecom has required the development of a capacity, that is, the Office of Telecommunications, to regulate the rates and operation of the new private firms.

36. R. Kent Weaver, "The Politics of Blame Avoidance," *Journal of Public Policy* 6 (1986), 371–98.

37. Richard P. Nathan and Fred C. Doolittle, *Reagan and the States* (Princeton, N.J.: Princeton University Press, 1987); David Beam, "New Federalism, Old Reali-

ties: The Reagan Administration and Intergovernmental Reform," in *The Reagan Presidency and the Governing of America*, ed. Lester Salamon and Michael Lund, Washington, DC: Urban Institute).

38. Michael Keating, "Does Regional Government Work? The Experiences of Italy, France and Spain," *Governance* 1 (1988), 184–209.

39. G. Gustafsson, "Local Government Reform in Sweden," in *Local Government Reform and Reorganization*, ed. Arthur B. Gunlicks (Port Washington, N.Y.: Kennikat, 1981).

40. George W. Jones, "The Crisis in Central-Local Government Relations in Britain," *Governance* 1 (1988), 162–83.

41. Schick, "Micro-budgetary Adaptations."

42. Michio Muramatsu, "Recent Administrative Developments in Japan," *Governance* 1 (1988), 468–78.

43. Richard Rose, "Maximizing Tax Revenue While Minimizing Political Costs," *Journal of Public Policy* 5 (1985), 289–320.

44. Bo Rothstein, *Den Socialdemokratiska Staten* (Lund: Studentlitterature, 1986).

45. See Peter C. Natchez and Irvin C. Bupp, "Policy and Priority in the Budgetary Process," *American Political Science Review* 67 (1973), 951–63.

46. Linda Challis et al., *Joint Approaches to Social Policy* (Cambridge: Cambridge University Press, 1988).

47. Colin Campbell, *Governments Under Stress: Political Executives and Key Bureaucrats in Washington, London, and Ottawa* (Toronto: University of Toronto Press, 1983), p. 24; Dror, *Policymaking Under Adversity.*

48. Vincent S. Wilson, "What Legacy? The Nielsen Task Force Program Review," in *How Ottawa Spends, 1988/89: The Conservative Heading into the Stretch*, ed. K. A. Graham (Ottawa: Carleton University Press, 1988).

49. I can say this with more reason than most, having served as an outside "expert" in the review of a state government in the United States.

50. Les Metcalfe and Sue Richards, "Raynerism and Efficiency in Government," in *Issues in Public Sector Accounting*, ed. A. Hopwood and C. Tompkins (Oxford: Philip Allan, 1984).

51. Graham T. Allison, "Public and Private Management: Are They Fundamentally Alike in All Unimportant Respects," in *Current Issues in Public Administration*, ed. Frederick S. Lane (New York: St. Martin's, 1986); Hal G. Rainey, Robert W. Backoff, and Charles H. Levine, "Comparing Public and Private Organizations," *Public Administration Review* 36 (1976), 223–44.

52. Les Metcalfe, "The Logic of Public Management," presented at the IPSA World Congress, Washington, D.C., 1988.

53. Chester A. Newland, "A Mid-Term Appraisal—The Reagan Presidency: Limited Government and Political Administration," *Public Administration Review* 43 (1983), 1–21.

54. Peter Aucoin, "Contraction, Managerialism and Decentralization in Canadian Government," *Governance* 1 (1988), 144–61; Peter Wilenski, "Administrative Reform—General Principles and the Australian Experience," *Public Administration* 64 (1986), 257–76; Anne Yeatman, "The Concept of Public Management and the Australian State in the 1980s," *Australian Journal of Public Administration* 46 (1987), 340–53.

55. Andrew Likierman, "Management Information for Ministers: The MINIS System in the Department of the Environment," *Public Administration* 60 (1982), 127–42.

56. J. M. Lee, "Financial Management"; Andrew Gray and William I. Jenkins,

"Accountable Management in British Central Government: Some Reflections on the Financial Management Initiative," *Financial Accountability and Management* 2 (1986), 171–85.

57. Jenkins, Caines, and Jackson, *Improving Management.*

58. The ability to shed responsibility is, as ever, especially valuable if the politician can shed responsibility for failures. Blame avoidance is as much, or more, valuable than credit claiming in the politics of most contemporary political systems. See R. Kent Weaver, "The Politics of Blame Avoidance."

59. Hugh Heclo, "The Frontiers of Social Policy," *Policy Sciences* 6 (1975), 403–21; Brian W. Hogwood and B. Guy Peters, *Policy Dynamics* (New York: St. Martin's, 1983).

60. Anthony King, "Overload: Problems of Governing in the 1970s," *Political Studies* 23 (1975), 284–96.

61. Lawrence D. Brown, *New Policies, New Politics: Government's Response to Government Growth* (Washington, D.C.: Brookings, 1983).

62. Heclo, "The Frontiers," p. 404.

63. Hogwood and Peters, *Policy Dynamics.*

64. Phillipe C. Schmitter and Gerhard Lehmbruch, eds., *Trends Toward Corporatist Intermediation* (Beverly Hills, Calif.: Sage, 1982).

65. A.J.G.M. Bekke, "Private Organizations and the State: Mutual Prisoners Blocking De-bureaucratization," in *Limits to Government: Dutch Experiences*, ed. I.T.M. Snellen (Amsterdam: Kobra, 1985).

66. Arthur F. P. Wassenberg, "Neo-corporatism and the Quest for Control," in *Patterns of Corporatist Policymaking*, ed. Gerhard Lehmbruch and Phillipe Schmitter (Beverly Hills, Calif.: Sage, 1982); Brigitta Nedelman and K. G. Meier, "Theories of Contemporary Corporatism: Static or Dynamic?" in ibid.

67. Franz-Xavier Kaufmann, Giandomenico Majone, and Vincent Ostrom, eds., *Guidance, Control and Evaluation in the Public Sector* (Berlin: DeGruyter, 1986).

68. Theo A. J. Toonen, "Implementation Research and Institutional Design," in *Policy Implementation in Federal and Unitary Systems*, ed. Kenneth Hanf and Theo A. J. Toonen (Boston: Martinus Nijhoff, 1985); Lawrence J. O'Toole, "Policy Recommendations for Multi-Actor Implementation: An Assessment of the Field," *Journal of Public Policy* 6 (1986), 181–210.

69. Lester B. Salamon, "Rethinking Public Management: Third-Party Government and the Changing Forms of Government Action," *Public Policy* 29 (1981), 255–75.

70. Harold Seidman and Robert Gilmour, *Politics, Position and Power*, 4th ed. (New York: Oxford University Press, 1986); Hugh Heclo, "The In and Outer System: A Critical Assessment," *Political Science Quarterly* 103 (1988), 37–56.

71. B. Guy Peters, "The Machinery of Government: Concepts and Issues," in *Organizing Governance*, ed. Campbell and Peters.

72. In this case we are using "large-scale" to describe problems very much as in Paul Schulman, *Large-Scale Policymaking* (New York: Elsevier, 1980). That is, a large-scale problem is one with relatively indivisible outcomes and that therefore must be addressed with comprehensive solutions. The NASA program to get a man to the moon is a classic example. It did no good to get the astronaut halfway, or even 99 percent of the way to the moon; it was all or nothing. This, in turn, required an undertaking by government of sufficient magnitude to ensure that this goal could be attained.

73. Weaver, "The Politics of Blame Avoidance."

74. Richard R. Nelson, *The Moon and the Ghetto* (New York: Norton, 1977).

75. This was the first dimension of leadership mentioned by Richard Rose, *The Problem of Party Government* (London: Macmillan, 1974).

76. Theodore J. Lowi, "Four Systems of Policy, Politics and Choice," *Public Administration Review* 32 (1972), 298–310.

4

The Discontinuous Institutional Presidency

MARGARET JANE WYSZOMIRSKI

Fifty years ago, the President's Committee on Administrative Management headed by Louis Brownlow implicitly noted a disjuncture in the executive establishment. After complaining about the "headless fourth branch" of government, the Brownlow Committee called for systematic functional centralization of the executive establishment and the provision of managerial and staff support to enable the chief executive efficiently and responsibly to provide "energy, direction, and administrative management."[1] In other words, the "help" that presidents came to acquire in what became known as the institutional presidency was intended to support the president's executive leadership and administrative management. Inspired by a desire to enhance presidential coordination and direction of the permanent executive establishment, the Brownlow Committee's call for expanded staff resources gave birth to an equally anomalous entity, the discontinuous institutional presidency.

Prior to the establishment of the Executive Office of the President (EOP) in 1933, a president's executive assistance consisted primarily of appointive political executives, particularly the heads of the cabinet departments. During the early years of his presidency, FDR augmented this group through the inclusion of a proliferation of New Deal agency appointees as well as by a small personal staff consisting of a few presidential assistants, an informal "brains trust" and "kitchen cabinet," and a contingent of detailees from various departments and agencies.

Since 1939, a greatly expanded and diversified Executive Office of the President has become the preeminent component of a president's advisory and staff support, even as political appointees heading the executive departments and agencies have come to occupy a less assured centrality in presidential councils. Indeed, it has become common to characterize the executive establishment as consisting of two branches: the presidential branch[2] (often called the institutional presidency) and the executive branch, which apparently encompasses not only the former "headless fourth branch" of independent regulatory agencies but includes executive departments and agencies as well.

Whereas the long historical roots of the executive branch predate even the constitution (for example, in a postal service), the presidential branch is of more recent vintage. From one perspective, the establishment of the EOP marked the institutionalization of the presidency,[3] implying that the presidential branch sprang, rather like the Athena of legend, fully developed at birth. Conversely, from another perspective, the creation of an EOP in 1939 can be viewed as a first step in the evolution of an institution with distinctly chameleonlike properties. Or to maintain the classical metaphor, the institutional presidency would appear to be an oxymoron akin to the river described by the Greek philosopher Heraclitus—a thing that retains its integrity amid continuous change.

What Is Presidential Institutionalization?

Although the term *presidential institutionalization* has become commonplace, its usage is seldom precise or consistent. Indeed, the presidential literature exhibits at least four uses of the term.

Perhaps most frequently, institutionalization is used narrowly to refer to the establishment and growth of the Executive Office of the Presidency. This rather static definition fails to accommodate the more dynamic process orientation characteristics of comparative and sociological literature on institutionalization. Under this narrow definition, institutionalization occurred in response to the Brownlow Committee's recommendation to provide the president with staff assistance and was embodied in the creation of the EOP in 1939. Subsequently, the growth and diversification that has occurred during the last fifty years appears to be simply an elaboration of the original phenomenon. A variation of this approach focuses upon the "generic staff distinction"[4] posed in the Brownlow report between personal and institutional staff. The presumption is that with the establishment of institutional staff (notably,

the Bureau of the Budget), the presidency became institutionalized. Within this approach, some observers have argued that the
politicization of personal and institutional units has resulted in a
process of deinstitutionalization. Alternatively, as institutional
staff has become politicized and personalized, other scholars have
concluded that the original generic difference has become increasingly indistinct and indistinguishable, and therefore of decreasing
analytical utility.

A second usage conceives of institutionalization as a style of
management that is highly routinized and bureaucratized. Hence,
institutionalization involves the development and use of collegial
consultation devices, established decision-making procedures, and
hierarchical administrative routines. From this perspective, while
FDR's competitive and experimental management style may have
been conducive to the invention of the modern presidency, it was
left to later presidents to consolidate, routinize, and elaborate his
legacy into the institutional presidency.

The third definition casts institutionalization as an ongoing process and, variously, focuses on what prompts the process to engage
or on the comparison of how different support structures develop.
In either case, a central concern is to explain the growth and complexity of the EOP. For those analysts who regard institutionalization as internally induced,[5] a closed-system approach is adopted.
As a consequence, the explanatory emphasis focuses, paradoxically, either on bureaucratization[6] or on personalization (in the
sense of organizational responsiveness to individual presidential
management and leadership styles).[7] Other analysts who consider
the process to be essentially externally induced, employ an open-
system approach, emphasizing organizational adaptation as a response to changes in the environment. This approach underlies
discussions of the development of staff functions such as legislative
liaison or personnel management as responses to changes in congressional operations or in the role of political parties. The two
perspectives can even be combined into an internal-external approach. For example, Terry M. Moe argues that the logic of institutional development lies in "the extent to which existing structures
making up the institutional presidency are congruent with the incentives and resources of the president."[8]

Finally, a sociologically based definition focuses on institutionalization as a behavioral phenomenon whereby informal or innova-

tive behavior becomes organized, regularized, and legitimated as a norm. It therefore emphasizes roles, values, normative expectations, and the behavior of organizational actors so as to discern predictable patterns.[9]

Although each of these conceptions has its merits, a most promising approach combines the third and fourth conceptualizations, thereby stressing the explanation and analysis of the process of institutional development. Few analysts have attempted the ambitious task of following through the entire process from identifying stimuli that begin the process, through various developmental steps including assessing indicators of institutional change, and finally to evaluating the impact and value of the results of the process. Nor have scholars subjected all components or aspects of the institutional presidency to comparable attention. Rather, researchers tend to concentrate on phases of the process,[10] or produce case histories of particular EOP agencies and functions,[11] or are concerned with the evolution of a particular norm or value within the institutional presidency.[12]

What Becomes Institutionalized?

A comprehensive examination of the institutionalized presidency would constitute a major undertaking, since it would require a layered and interactive analysis of both the various subunits as well as their various effects upon the development of the whole. Furthermore, analysis would need to account for changes both within and among subunits as well as change in response to different external forces and internal preferences and priorities. Additionally, a fully developed analytical framework would need to integrate the patterns and effects of prior institutional change into an understanding of how expectations and behavior of presidents, of presidential subunits, and of other political institutions have constituted an ever shifting backdrop to the changing state of the institutional presidency. Thus, we have only begun to come to grips with the task of analyzing the institutional presidency.

As a start, we have begun to assemble an understanding of some of the parts at certain times. As these accumulate, like the pieces of a jigsaw puzzle, a clearer picture of the whole starts to emerge. Thus, if researchers have not been concerned with the totality of the institutionalized presidency, what has been studied? Or, to put it another way, *what* has been institutionalized?

There is no one answer to that question. Instead, many answers—each a part of the total institution—have been the subjects of investigation. Although I cannot give a full catalogue of these studies here, at least subjects of study can be identified. These range from what might be considered a causal factor that sets off a sequence of organizational responses to specific routinized procedures or products.

Some scholars have argued that what I have referred to as a "causal factor" involves the initiation, routinization, and legitimation of presidential roles, such as economic policy maker or administrative manager or political communicator. These roles impose responsibilities and create public expectations for the president. To meet these responsibilities and expectations, the president requires assistance and support resources. Hence a second category of institutionalized phenomenon is supportive organizational structures and personnel that emerge in response to newly developed presidential roles. These agencies, offices, and/or positions may become institutionalized, particularly if their roles persist despite changes of presidents and party. If the role does not persist, it is unlikely that the support structures will continue (unless turned to a different but nonetheless useful purpose).

A third possible answer to the question of what becomes institutionalized is relational roles or patterns of presidential staff or of staff agencies. The original Brownlow distinction between *personal* and *institutional* staff was hinting at relational role patterns. Another way to conceive of these is to construct ideal types of relationships that might exist between presidents and their supportive resources. At least four such types of subunits or personnel patterns can be advanced: *agents* of the president, *advisers* to the president, *advocates* with the president, or *administrators* for the president. Each of these relational patterns can be characterized by functions, authority, constraints, and expectations. Certain subunits or functions might exhibit only one legitimate relational pattern, while others may develop a repertoire of relational patterns playing different parts in response to varying circumstances or presidential preferences.

A fourth answer would suggest that routines, practices, or procedures—whether for decision making, conducting press conferences, personnel screening, or program planning—can become institutionalized. Last, a product answer indicates that certain outputs, such as an annual economic report, the annual budget, or an annual State of the Union message can become institutionalized.

Assessing Institutionalization

The preceding sections have examined the definition of institutionalization and the elements that can become institutionalized. The next logical question might be, "How can one determine when and to what extent something is institutionalized?" Identifying the indicators of institutionalization has been problematic for many studies of organizations. The problem is acute when dealing with a discontinuous institution such as the U.S. presidency. Indeed, most studies of institutionalization can presume at least the superficial continuity, routinization, and rationalization of the organization under analysis. In contrast, students of the presidency must presume discontinuity, redefinition, and personalization of the object of their scrutiny. Because of the paradoxical character of the institutional presidency, much of the analytical framework developed for the study of other political and social institutions cannot simply be applied to the presidency but rather must be adapted if it is to be useful.

The classic works of Samuel Huntington and Nelson Polsby constitute a common reference point for discussing the institutionalization of political organizations.[13] With regard to the study of the presidency, however, both theorists have been found wanting. Huntington's work is frequently considered vague, inherently contradictory, and difficult to operationalize.[14] Conversely, Polsby has developed and applied a set of analytical criteria designed for the study of the legislative, not the executive, institution. Therefore, his method can only provide analogous suggestions for assessing the presidency. Despite these shortcomings, elements of both approaches can be used for a combined nominal and empirical assessment of the presidency.

In his general theoretical framework, Huntington proposed four major nominal elements of institutionalization:

- Adaptability
- Complexity
- Autonomy
- Coherence

Variously, it has been argued that adaptability may be incompatible with coherence, or that autonomy may impede adaptability, and so on. Leaving aside the merits of such arguments regarding other kinds of institutions, one can argue that the case of a discontinuous institution (such as the presidency) not only highlights such apparent contradictions but, indeed, requires their accommodation in a conceptual approach.

Therefore, Huntington's elements of institutionalization might be transformed into four sets of paired attributes, as follows:

- Adaptability—Continuity
- Complexity—Coordination
- Autonomy—Linkage
- Coherence—Personalization

Each of these pairs represents a dynamic tension in which both attributes are not only present but must be balanced within the institutional presidency. Although there is no one equilibrium point for each set of attributes, a pronounced disequilibrium is likely to result in organizational behavior that is detrimental to the institution and/or politically damaging to the president (and perhaps the political system at large). In other words, failure to maintain a balance between each set of attributes may produce deinstitutionalization in the presidency (or of component parts of it). If such deinstitutionalization is not resolved by a new dynamic equilibrium, specific presidential agencies, assistants, or even presidents will lose legitimacy. Ultimately, such delegitimation can undermine presidential roles and responsibilities, perhaps even the presidency itself.

Both Huntington and Polsby provide suggestions regarding possible indicators of these paired nominal characteristics. *Adaptability* has been called an "acquired organizational characteristic" that reflects responsiveness to environmental challenge and implies age.[15] Organizational age and persistence, however, presume at least a degree of *continuity*. Indeed, adaptation is not only a process of responding to external conditions and demands imposed upon the organization, but also of modifying existing organizational attributes and procedures. As James Pfiffner observes about the relation of the permanent government to changing presidencies, "There can be no change unless there is a certain amount of stability in institutions and personnel."[16] Thus, adaptation occurs in relation to some established status quo.

Organizational age—whether chronological or generational age, counted by presidential or partisan successions—is an implicit measure of adaptability and an explicit measure of continuity. For example, the Council of Economic Advisers (CEA) and the National Security Council (NSC) are two senior subunits of the institutional presidency. Established in 1946 and 1947, respectively, both agencies have weathered eight presidential successions and five changes of party. In contrast, other EOP subunits are approximately half this age: the Office of Special Representative for Trade Negotiations (est. 1963) is twenty-eight, has served seven presidents and has undergone three party changes, while the Office of Administration (est. 1978) is thirteen, served three presidents, and has seen only one change of party. Typically, other EOP agencies have had rather short life spans. For example, the Office of Economic Opportunity (1964–75) lasted only eleven years, under two presidents, before becoming a casualty of partisan change. Similarly, the Cost of Living Council (1971–73) lasted only two years, served one president under one party, while the Council on Wage and Price Stability (1974–81) reached the age of seven, served three presidents before being abolished by a fourth, and survived one party transition, only to become the victim of a second.

Alternatively, the extent of an organization's institutionalization may be assessed in functional or purposive terms. The presidency and its component parts were created to perform certain tasks. Their raisons d'être may be exhibited formally or informally, or may be redefined over time. For example, the Bureau of the Budget (BOB) was created to draft the executive budget and to offer "impartial advice" to the president on "the proper business functioning of government."[17] While retaining its budget preparation function, BOB gradually acquired other tasks, including program review and planning, legislative clearance, and administrative coordination. Upon its reorganization as the Office of Management and Budget (OMB) in 1970, the agency acquired public advocacy and policy implementation responsibilites. Finally, under President Reagan, OMB became the primary architect of the administration's general economic policies as well as a virtual line agency to oversee deregulation.

An equally interesting and successful, though less studied, adaptation occurred in the emergency management and planning agency. An EOP agency charged with emergency management coordination and planning existed for over thirty years, between 1940 and 1972. Although this agency experienced many name changes and reorganizations, its functional responsibilities were handed down from one incarnation to the next, sometimes with additions and other times with exemptions. The line stretches from the Office of Emergency Management (1940–43), the Office of War Mobilization (and Reconversion), the National Security Resources Board, the Office of Defense Mobilization (1950–58), the Office of Civilian and Defense Mobilization (1958–61), to the Office of Emergency Planning Preparedness (1961–72). Established to help coordinate war planning just before World War II, then concerned with the cold war, the Korean War, and eventually the Vietnam War, the agency finally outlived its usefulness in an era of détente following the end of the draft. Under its various identities, the agency grew to a ripe age, served six presidents, survived three party changes, and undertook emergency planning for four major wars. In other words, the emergency planning agency proved very adaptable and yet maintained its continuity in the face of considerable external change. Thus, organizational age and functional character are two indicators of an organization's adaptability/continuity.

With regard to the American presidency, institutional adaptability is a prerequisite for its continuation. Electorally induced and periodic change repeatedly subjects the institutional presidency to variations in leadership and management style, in political support and opposition coalitions, and in policy demands and preferences. Indeed, this conjunction of adaptability and continuity was noted by the Brownlow Committee when it stated,

As an instrument for carrying out the judgment and will of the people of a nation, the American Executive occupies an enviable position among the executives of the states of the world, combining as it does, the elements of popular control and the means for virgorous action and leadership—uniting stability and flexibility.[18]

Alternatively, given the systemic imperatives for effective presidential performance, no incoming president has the luxury of creating an institutional presidency from whole cloth. Rather, each president inherits a legacy of roles, including substantive and procedural expectations, that must be addressed, albeit within a flexible range of personal, political, and administrative styles.

For instance, during the past thirty years, presidents have found it necessary and expedient to have their White House staffs assist in the performance of recurring functions, including congressional liaison, communications, and personal recruitment and selection. For a president to ignore any of these duties spells political as well as administrative disaster. In part, the institutional presidency must perform these functions because other modern presidents have done so. Also, such tasks are necessary to the functioning of the larger governmental and political systems. For example, a White House congressional liaison function began to be formalized during the Eisenhower presidency. This occurred, in part, because the president was relatively new to both governance and partisan politics and hence needed (and wanted) assistance in meeting expectations regarding his performance as Chief Legislator. Additionally, once the opposition Democratic party regained majority control of Congress, interbranch communication and cooperation could not follow party patterns but, instead, required continual bipartisan cultivation. Thus, in adapting to internal, presidential needs as well as to external political circumstances, the response of the Eisenhower organization created a functional legacy that has been maintained and elaborated upon in subsequent presidencies.

Indicators of the *complexity/coordination* dimension are perhaps the most obvious and classically defined. Common indicators of complexity are organizational size and diversity. The larger the organization—whether in terms of manpower, financial resources, or number of assigned functions or tasks—the more complex it is likely to appear. Size, however, it not the key factor; complexity typically reflects a combination of size and diversity. Diversity may be exhibited in the variety of tasks or functions performed; the different types of personnel employed (that is, career, appointive, or personal staff); or the various types of skill they possess (that is, substantive expertise, political experience, or managerial/administrative ability). If an institution is to cope with such complexity effectively, it customarily develops routinized and rationalized internal organizational structures and practices. In a word, complexity gives rise to bureaucratization.

Indicators of bureaucratization have been identified by organizational theorists since at least the time of Max Weber. These include the development of rationalized structures such as the specialized division of labor involving the multiplication of organizational subunits and the recruitment of specialized, credentialed personnel. It is also characterized by hierarchy as well as by the differentiation and interdependence of functionally separate subunits. Bureaucratization is also likely to involve the regularization of expectations concerning overall and subunit roles (such as advisor, administrator, advocate, or agent)[19] and activities (the preparation of annual reports or budgets, or program planning procedures). Hence, it should be noted that in this assessment scheme, institutionalization is not regarded as synonymous with bureaucratization; rather, bureaucratization is a factor contributing to institutionalization as well as a mechanism for managing complexity while achieving coordination.

The necessity to manage great and changeable complexity amid the discontinuity of successive presidencies has led to functional specialization among White House staff subunits while it has encouraged versatility among staff members. Specialization in political tasks such as congressional liaison, public liaison, or intergovernmental relations cannot be kept hermetically distinct from policy expertise in economic, national security, or domestic affairs nor from administrative functions such as communications, scheduling, or secretariat support. One way of coordinating and integrating these specialized components of the presidential leadership mosaic is through staff personnel who have multiple competencies even as they are responsible for specialized tasks. One such combination finds expert policy in-and-outers who have also had prior administrative experience or often political experience as campaign issues advisers (a pattern often found in senior national security, domestic, and economic policy assistants). Bert Rockman points to the emergence of Image IV types, or a new breed of political executives who "straddle the world of politics and that of expertise and technical competence"[20] as evidence that dual functions (political-managerial and techno-analytic coordinating functions) exist at the top of the executive establishment and require multiple-competency staff. Reagan's budget director David Stockman is an example of such a multiple-competency staffer. Similarly, Colin Campbell points to the growing presence of what he calls amphibians[21] (individuals who combine policy expertise with political ties) and that Hugh Heclo has called political careerists.[22] Such personnel bring a coordinative sensitivity to political considerations even as they provide substantive policy expertise or an awareness of administrative capacity, or any combination of the three.

A second specialized coordinative practice that has developed in the institutional presidency to manage complexity is duplication and overlap of purpose. If strict specialization and division of labor were followed in the executive establishment, democratic chief executives might easily become doctrinaire, insulated from multiple sources of advice and information, and indeed a captive of their own (and their staff's) perspectives and preferences. Instead, various analysts, including George, Plowden, and Kernell, have argued for the utility and necessity of multiple-advocacy, pluralistic, or countervailing advice systems.[23] In other words, in the institutional presidency, complexity cannot be managed simply through specialization and bureaucratization but instead requires coordinated specialization and a integrative bureaucratization.

The third set of organizational attributes are *autonomy* and *linkage*. Institutional *autonomy* concerns the extent to which an organization differentiates itself from its environment as well as from other organizations in that environment. Polsby refers to these indicators as boundaries, including specific factors such as the particularization of personnel and its concomitant limited interchangeability both between subunits of an organization and between an organization and others in its environment. With regard to the institutional presidency, particularization may be assessed concerning personnel (1) among the various EOP subunits; (2) between ostensibly institutional EOP personnel and personal staff in the White House Office; (3) between EOP personnel and other appointive executive personnel; and (4) between EOP personnel and personnel in other political organizations such as Congress, political parties, campaign organizations, the judiciary, and interest groups.

Other measures of boundaries concern the rationalization of selection and promotion criteria and the internal development and selection of leaders. In other words, recruitment characteristics are likely to involve relevant training or experience, often attested to by the requirement of certain basic credentials (such as an advanced economics degree for members of the CEA). Furthermore, promotion and advancement are likely to be based on prior service, particularly in a lower-level, apprenticeship capacity. For example, between 1939 and 1989, seven of the twenty-one BOB/OMB directors had previously served as deputy director. Similarly, most chairmen of the CEA have seen prior service as council members.[24]

Given the discontinuous character of the institutional presidency, such apprenticeships may not immediately precede appointment to leadership positions. Rather, a "leapfrog" pattern is likely wherein individuals who have served an apprenticeship return to be promoted in subsequent administrations of the same party but under a different president. Such discontinuous apprentice-to-director patterns characterized the careers of Richard Allen and Martin Anderson, whose earlier service in the Nixon NSC and Domestic Council, respectively, prepared them for a return as the heads of these agencies in the Reagan administration. Similarly, Max Freidersdorf and E. Pendleton James saw prior service in the Nixon-Ford White House staffs, concerned with congressional liaison and personnel management, respectively, before coming back to head these units for the Reagan administration. Indeed, this pattern of partisan leapfrog apprenticeship might be regarded as a form of institutional memory particularly appropriate for a discontinuous institution.

In the modern institutional presidency, personnel and leadership boundaries with campaign organizations are permeable. Indeed, the temporary campaign organization—if successful—has come to serve as a socializing force as well as a testing ground for prospective presidential personnel. Such campaign apprenticeships may be particularly relevant and transferable to tasks that involve outreach functions to the public, such as press relations and communications, public opinion polling, and constituency group liaison. Conversely, campaign service provides political experience that is functionally distinct from that of governance. The oft-made complaint that presidents (and their staffs) have become increasingly competent at electoral and campaign politics but have proven less adept at the politics of governance suggests that campaign organization skills are only partially appropriate for a presidential governance organization. This is not because competence, loyalty, and esprit are lacking in the campaign organization but that these qualities have been proven with regard to functions, tasks, expectations, and circumstances that are different from those facing a president.

These differences are, perhaps, most notable in the difference between a cultivated capacity for linkage as opposed to outreach. Unlike a candidate, a president operates within a system of interdependent institutions. To paraphrase Richard Neustadt, the American system of government is not merely premised upon separate institutions (autonomy) but upon shared powers (linkage). Presidential campaign organizations have displayed little need or desire to develop linkages with other political institutions. Indeed, the trend in recent decades has been to diminish historic linkages with political parties, congressional candidates, or career bureaucrats. Although scholars such as Paul Light and Charles Jones have argued that a president's capacity for legislative leadership is enhanced by a coattail effect in congressional elections,[25] presidential candidates seldom seriously try to cultivate this congruence. For example, each party in Congress has developed its own separate campaign support structures (such as the Democratic Congressional Campaign Committee and the National Republican Senatorial Committee). Furthermore, individual congressional candidates have been more likely to seek to avoid a negative coattail effect (that is, to dissociate themselves from an unpopular presidential candidate heading the national ticket) than to make common cause with their own party's presidential candidate.

Similarly, and even more pronounced, is the indifference of presidents to forging links with the permanent bureaucracy. Presidents, especially since their assertion of a managerial presidency, seem to regard the permanent executive establishment either unrealistically, expecting to dominate it, or antagonistically, expecting it to obstruct a president's ideological or policy agenda.[26] Hence, it can be argued that a productive equilibrium between autonomy and linkage has seldom been maintained during the last twenty years. This apparent imbalance can, in turn, be seen as contributing to problems in effective governance that have confronted recent presidents.

Finally, the fourth pair of organizational attributes involve *coher-*

ence and *personalization. Coherence* derives from those aspects that cultivate organizational unity and a distinctive esprit and style; these enhance the organization's ability to accomplish its purposes. Coherence also gives the institution, its functions, procedures, and structures, inherent and affective value. These aspects include the use of universal rather than particular decision-making criteria and of automatic rather than discretionary methods for conducting internal business. The establishment and adherence to rules and precedents, the use of merit criteria (rather than personal favoritism), and the evolution of informal operational and behavioral norms are specific examples. Paradoxically, in the institutional presidency, the kinds of "objective" affective value and identification usually requisite for organizational coherence seem to be suspect and therefore insufficiently integrative unless balanced with a personalized "subjective" loyalty and identification with the incumbent president. Similar tendencies can be discerned in the executive establishments of parliamentary systems where the combined phenomenon is referred to as presidentialization.

The tension between this pair of nominal attributes is central to both systemic and presidential expectations concerning the legitimate and successful functioning of the institutional presidency. Indeed, reconciling coherence with personalization may be seen as having prompted operational redefinitions of key canons of administrative behavior.

For example, while many presidential reorganization efforts (including the recommendations of the Brownlow Commission) were designed to increase executive efficiency and economy,[27] those norms have taken on a distinctive meaning within the presidential context. Efficiency in the institutional presidency is not simply, as the Brownlow Committee declared, a matter of responsible, up-to-date, and well-managed government machinery for carrying out the will of the nation. It is also a qualitative measure of the social good attained from the management of given resources.[28] From the president's perspective, efficiency not only includes this meaning but has also, perhaps predominantly, acquired the connotations of effectiveness and timeliness. This sense of efficiency is manifest in the concern of presidential staff and assistants to meet "fire-fighting" and "crisis-management" demands. In this sense, efficiency in the institutional presidency can be conceived of as prompt and effective assistance with the "must-do" demands made upon presidents by the press of events, schedules, etcetera.

Similarly, economy in the presidency is not merely a matter of cutting financial costs and of saving money, but also a calculation of political resources, costs, and potential benefits to maximize the return on a president's investment. Again, as the Brownlow Committee put it, the quest for economy "rests not alone on the idea of savings . . . but upon better service to society," including not only "the provision of adequate managerial machinery" but also "the cutting of costs, of improving the service, and of raising the standards of performance."[29] Thus, in each instance, a classic administrative norm has taken on a different shade of meaning when viewed through the personalized lens of the presidency.

Similarly, many commentators on the managerial presidency have noted the apparent decline of neutral competence as a norm. The alternative, as labeled by critics, is generally referred to as *politicization*, although a less judgmental term may be *responsive competence*. Indeed, the norm of neutral competence has become increasingly questionable both with regard to neutrality and with regard to competence.

On *neutrality:* the history of the permanent U.S. civil service suggests that the concept of neutrality emerged from a confluence of two developments, neither of which supported presidential management. On the one hand, "The strong bias against politics, especially . . . machine politics"[30] evinced by good government reformers at the turn of the twentieth century gave rise to the normative distinction between politics and administration.[31] In the process, the policy-making prerogatives of the president were recognized but divorced from his ministerial capacity to implement policy. Second, the recurrent interbranch battle over control of federal patronage that had raged throughout the nineteenth century resulted finally in a pyrrhic presidential victory. Even as presidents asserted their power to fire executive appointees, Congress moved to limit their hiring jurisdiction through the creation of a permanent civil service (1883) and the designation of qualified immunity from dismissal for other appointments, such as regulatory commissioners (1887). Thus, from a presidential perspective, neutrality has long carried the connotation of insulation from the necessity to be fully responsive to the chief executive.

While this is an oversimplification, it illustrates that the assessment of political neutrality is likely to lie in the eye of the be-holder. Indeed, virtually all modern presidents have come to office with the expectation that the permanent bureaucracy—ostensibly the "neutral" civil service—will be unenthusiastic, if not outright opposed, to the new president's program and philosophy. Indeed, FDR, who inherited a bureaucracy that had been built up and staffed during decades of predominantly Republican control of government, sought to bypass, augment, and reform the perma-nent government whenever possible. To varying degrees, similar sentiments were strongly voiced by Eisenhower, Kennedy, Nixon, and Reagan. Even presidents who have succeeded members of their own party (such as Truman, Johnson, and Bush) seem to have considered personnel attuned to their predecessor to be some-what suspect.

Finally, regardless of partisan cast, recent presidents have often regarded the so-called neutral civil service as anything but neutral with regard to its own bureaucratic self-interest and, conse-quently, have disparaged it as obstructionist and opinionated. The tendency to run against the Washington establishment and against big government was obvious in both the Carter and Reagan cam-paigns. Thus, in a variety of ways, neutrality has seldom been regarded by modern presidents as a legitimate administrative norm.[32]

Another question concerns the political feasibility of neutral competence. Neutral competence may be possible and acceptable to presidents regarding the performance of functions or tasks that are essentially nondiscretionary, noninterpretive, and administra-tive. Relatively few such tasks are performed within the institu-tional presidency; as a fundamentally political institution,[33] issues of power, influence, authority, opinion, and judgment are inher-ent to its nature. Indeed, the original Brownlow Committee asser-tion of a distinction between institutional and personal staff (which implied a distinction between neutrality and politiciza-tion) may have enshrined a public administration principle (the administration-versus-politics dichotomy) that was even at that time being criticized and questioned. Subsequently, as the focus has shifted from viewing politics, policy, and administration as separable to regarding these as intertwined aspects of governance, very few executive functions are carried out in an atmosphere of neutrality.

In a related vein, neutral competence was rooted in the quest for nonpartisan administration of the government's decisions with the implicit expectation that one party would lead both elected branches and thus give a common direction to the bureaucratic establishment. In the current era of divided government, executive personnel have difficulty in maintaining a neutrality that is institutionally rather than party-oriented. That is, when one party commands the White House and the opposition controls Congress, executive personnel face a dilemma in which partisan neutrality may easily be mistaken for unresponsiveness to either (or both) elective institutions. Hence, from the Oval Office, responsiveness—whether premised on partisan, political, or personal bases—may seem distinctly preferable to neutrality.

Idealistic expectations of neutral competence have been undercut from the *competence* side as well. As the institutional presidency began to acquire substantive advisory functions, it was soon recognized that if expert assistants were to influence their chief client— the president—their own normative values, judgments, and objectives had to be in general accord with those of the president. This is certainly a lesson learned by the CEA and by the National Security Assistant and his staff. It is also a maxim repeatedly demonstrated by its breach—that is, the loss of influence, the "freezing out" of uncongenial advice and interpretation or its transformation into the role of devil's advocate. The recommendation that presidents construct "multiple advocacy" advisory systems implies not only the existence of different competent opinions, but also different expert perceptions of facts and issues.

Indeed, one can argue that the pool of experts and expertise that presidents can draw from has itself become increasingly politicized during the past two decades. This phenomenon has attracted more comment with regard to foreign affairs than domestic or economic policy. In the foreign policy realm, the breakup of the postwar establishment consensus gave rise to alternative clusters of professional policy elites, each of which represents different assumptions and philosophies. Similarly, a baseline economic consensus was revealed as weakened, if not repudiated by the disagreement between supply-siders and Keynesian demand-siders. Although in domestic affairs the splits are more complex and highly segmented according to specific issue, the different assumptions and expectations that generally characterize liberal and conservative analysts are rife. Indeed, the ongoing debate about and awareness of the politics of numbers and the unreliability and interpretability of "facts" highlights the pervasive weakening of the idea of objective or neutral competence.[34] Hence, presidents can scarcely be faulted for preferring responsive competence when the available pool of expertise is itself not neutral but notably politicized. They can however be criticized—and are likely to find it self-defeating—when they eschew competence for the sake of responsiveness.[35]

The foregoing discussion of the norms of economy, efficiency, and neutral competence and how they have been redefined in practice in the institutional presidency reveals a form of institutional adaptation. Other norms might also be analyzed, especially the meaning of loyalty or trustworthiness. The significant point is that in each case the norm that helps to give coherence to the institution has acquired a particular meaning within the presidential context that attempts to bring the organization's interests into congruence with those of the president of the moment. In other words, norms of the institutional presidency seem to display the paradoxical character of having institutionalized personalization.

Evaluating and Interpreting the Results of Institutionalization

Ostensibly, the purpose of analytical efforts to define, explain, measure, and understand the institutionalization of the presidency is similar to that of institutionalization—namely, to enhance effective and responsible presidential leadership and performance. What observations can be deduced from this analysis?

First, has institutionalization, to the extent that it has occurred, helped to support presidential leadership and performance? While this question has no single answer, various frames for answers can be suggested. On what basis can one assess whether institutionalization is good or bad? Clearly, institutionalization need not result in rigidity or inflexibility. Indeed, institutionalization in the presidency must incorporate a considerable degree of flexibility to accommodate the personalism inherent in the unitary office of the presidency. If the normative criteria for evaluating institutionalization are unclear, can one, instead, identify less preferable alternatives, such as politicization or deinstitutionalization? In other words, can it be established what would be "bad" and therefore be avoided in the development and functioning of the institutional presidency?

Such a back-handed approach presents other evaluative questions. What makes politicization an objectionable characteristic? After all, the presidency is preeminently a political institution. To deny the presidency the legitimacy of acting in a political fashion is to confront one of the paradoxes of the modern presidency.[36] Indeed, the quest for an effective managerial presidency presiding over enlarged executive and presidential branches may have raised public expectations unrealistically. It may simply be impossible for the president to meet such expectations. Even if it could be accomplished, such as through some administrative presidency strategy, might not that "success" be viewed as illegitimate, either as means or as ends?[37]

Conversely, if some form of deinstitutionalization is occurring, is this necessarily bad for presidents or for effective and responsible governance? There is some evidence that certain boundary elements between the executive and presidential branches have become more permeable. It has become more common to consider personnel at the highest levels of each branch—senior White House staff and cabinet secretaries and deputy secretaries—to be transferable. White House Chief of Staff James Baker moved over to head the Treasury Department, while Treasury Secretary Regan moved to the White House Office. Similarly, other White House assistants such as John Herrington or Elizabeth Dole have also moved to the cabinet. When such a socialization process was used at a lower level in the Nixon administration, it was considered something of the equivalent of planting presidential loyalists as infiltrators in executive agencies and departments. In the Reagan administration, it seems to have enjoyed more acceptability, even applause as a strategy in demonstrating effective presidential leadership and dispelling the notion of a impotent presidency.

One observer's lament about deinstitutionalization might be another's hopeful sign that the presidential branch is continuing to develop, perhaps attempting to reintegrate the presidential and executive branches into an enlarged institution for effective presidential leadership and political governance. A discontinuous institution may appear to be a contradiction in terms, but to paraphrase

Sherlock Holmes, when all likely explanations have proven inadequate, than the improbable must be considered.

Notes

1. *Administration Management in the Government of the United States: Report of the President's Committee on Administrative Management* (Washington, D.C.: GPO, 1937; rpt. Chicago: Public Administration Service, 1947), p. 2 (hereafter referred to as *The Brownlow Committee Report*).

2. John Hart, *The Presidential Branch* (New York: Pergamon Press, 1987).

3. This is sometimes referred to as the narrow definition of the institutionalized presidency. See comments in Lester G. Seligman and Cary R. Covington, "The Comparative Institutionalization of Presidential Roles," presented at the annual meeting of the American Political Science Association, Washington, D.C., 1979, pp. 1–2; and Cary R. Covington, Joseph Pika, and Lester Seligman, "Institutionalization of the Presidency," presented at the annual meeting of the American Political Science Association, Chicago, 1983), p. 1.

4. This discussion of the various definitions of institutionalization draws upon the excellent work of Covington, Pika, and Seligman, "Institutionalization of the Presidency," p. 9.

5. Covington, Pika, and Seligman raise the distinction between an internally and an externally induced process in ibid., pp. 10–11.

6. An example of the concern with organizational responses to essentially internal stimuli—in the sense of routinized presidential roles—can be found in Dorothy Buckton James, *The Contemporary Presidency* (Indianapolis: Bobbs-Merrill, 1974). Another variation on this theme might be found in the interpretation that an organizational response of the modern presidency has prompted its pluralization (that is, a delegation of presidential responsibilities to staff officials in specialized offices). Lester Seligman raises this interpretation in "The Presidency and Political Change," *Annals* 466 (March 1983), 182.

7. Although not presented as a study of institutionalization, the set of administration case studies that Richard Tanner Johnson presents in *Managing the White House* (New York: Harper & Row, 1974) provides information about the various organizational adjustments to differing presidential management styles from FDR through Nixon.

8. Terry M. Moe, "The Politicized Presidency," in *The New Direction in American Politics*, ed. John E. Chubb and Paul E. Peterson (Washington, D.C.: Brookings, 1985), pp. 235–71.

9. Examples of this sociological approach include S. N. Eisenstadt, *Essays in Comparative Institutions* (New York: John Wiley, 1965); and Charles Loomis, "Social Change and Social Systems," in *Sociological Theory, Values and Sociocultural Change*, ed. Edward A. Tiryakian (New York: Free Press, 1963).

10. An excellent general discussion of the stages of the process by which a presidential role becomes institutionalized is presented in Covington, Pika, and Seligman, "Institutionalization of the Presidency," pp. 22–34. On the institutionalization of an advisory role for the vice-president and the attendant development of adequate organizational and staff resources, see Paul C. Light, *Vice Presidential Power* (Baltimore: Johns Hopkins University Press, 1984).

11. Various studies on individual EOP agencies include: Lester G. Seligman, "Presidential Leadership: The Inner Circle and Institutionalization," *Journal of*

Politics 18 (1956), 410–26, which focuses on the Council of Economic Advisers; Cary R. Covington, "The Council on Environmental Quality: A Prodigal Presidential Agency," presented at the 1983 meeting of the Midwest Political Science Association; Anna Kasten Nelson, "National Security I: Inventing a Process (1945–1960)," in *The Illusion of Presidential Government*, ed. Hugh Heclo and Lester M. Salamon (Boulder, Colo.: Westview Press, 1981), pp. 229–62: and I. M. Destler, "National Security II: The Rise of the Assistant (1961–1981)," pp. 263–85 in ibid., pp. 263–85; and Margaret Jane Wyszomirski, "A Domestic Policy Office: Presidential Agency in Search of a Role," *Policy Studies Journal* 12 (1984), 705–18. Perhaps the most studied presidential agency has been the Bureau of the Budget/Office of Management and Budget. Among the best known of these studies are Allan Schick, "The Budget Bureau That Was: Thoughts on the Rise, Decline, and Future of a Presidential Agency," *Law and Contemporary Problems* 35 (1970), 519–39; Hugh Heclo, "OMB and the Presidency," *Public Interest* 38 (Winter 1975), 80–98; and Larry Berman, *The Office of Management and Budget and the Presidency* (Princeton, N.J.: Princeton University Press, 1979).

Space does not permit a full bibliography of studies of specific institutional presidency function. Two early and classic studies are Richard E. Neustadt, "Presidency and Legislation: The Growth of Central Clearance," *American Political Science Review* 48 (1954), 641–71; and Elmer E. Cornwell, "The Presidential Press Conference: A Study in Institutionalization," *Midwest Journal of Political Science* 4 (1960), 370–89. For a more recent study of the position and function of White House chief of staff, see Samuel Kernell, *Chief of Staff* (Berkeley and Los Angeles: University of California Press, 1986).

12. Terry Moe discusses the development of politicization and centralization in "The Politicized Presidency." As part of a general agency history, Edward S. Flash, Jr., discusses what later comes to be called "responsive competence" as it developed at the Council of Economic Advisers. Flash calls this "objectivity within subjectivity." See his *Economic Advice and Presidential Leadership* (New York: Columbia University Press, 1965). Margaret Jane Wyszomirski discusses the interrelationship of competence and politicization as it evolved in four EOP agencies—BOB/OMB, the CEA, the NSC, and the domestic policy agency—in "The De-Institutionalization of Presidential Staff Agencies," *Public Administration Review* 42 (1982), 448–58. In *The Presidential Branch* John Hart gives considerable attention not only to the breakdown in the distinction between institutional and personal staff but also to the development and congressional practice of a "peculiar comity toward the presidential branch."

13. Samuel P. Huntington, "Political Development and Political Decay," *World Politics* 17 (1965), 386–430; Nelson W. Polsby, "The Institutionalization of the U.S. House of Representatives," *American Political Science Review* 62 (1968), 144–68.

14. For example, see Robert S. Gilmour, "The Institutionalized Presidency: A Conceptual Clarification," in *The Presidency in Contemporary Context*, ed. Norman C. Thomas (New York: Dodd, Mead, 1975), p. 150. Also see Mark Kesselman, "Overinstitutionalization and Political Constraint," *Comparative Politics* 3 (1973), 21–44.

15. Huntington, "Political Development and Political Decay," p. 394.

16. James Pfiffner, *The Strategic Presidency* (Chicago: Dorsey Press, 1988), p. x.

17. This was the understanding of the first budget director, Charles G. Dawes. Quoted by Percival Flack Brundage, *The Bureau of the Budget* (New York: Praeger Publishers, 1970), p. 16.

18. *Brownlow Committee Report*, p. 1.

19. For the development of these relational roles from a basis in the law of representation, see Margaret Jane Wyszomirski, "The Roles of a Presidential Office for Domestic Policy: Three Models and Four Cases," in *The President and Public Policy*, ed. George Edwards, Steven Shull, and Norman C. Thomas. For a analysis of different role-playing experiences in the foreign policy arena, see Cecil V. Crabb and Kevin V. Mulcahy, *Presidents and Foreign Policymaking: From FDR to Reagan* (Baton Rouge: Louisiana State University Press, 1986).

20. Joel D. Aberbach and Bert A. Rockman, "Image IV Revisited: Executive and Political Roles," *Governance* 1 (1988), 6.

21. Colin Campbell, S.J., *Managing the Presidency: Carter, Reagan and the Search for Executive Harmony* (Pittsburgh, Pa.: University of Pittsburgh Press, 1986).

22. Hugh Heclo, "In Search of a Role: American Higher Civil Service," in *Bureaucrats in Policymaking: A Comparative Overview*, ed. Ezra N. Suleiman (New York: Holmes and Meier, 1984), pp. 18–20.

23. Alexander L. George, *Presidential Decisionmaking in Foreign Affairs* (Boulder, Colo.: Westview Press, 1980).

24. For more details on these personnel characteristics, see Wyszomirski, "The De-Institutionalization of Presidential Staff Agencies."

25. Paul Light, *The President's Agenda* (Baltimore: Johns Hopkins University Press, 1982); Charles O. Jones, "Presidents and Agendas: Who Defines What for Whom?" in *The Managerial Presidency*, ed. James Pfiffner (Chicago: Dorsey Press, 1990).

26. James P. Pfiffner, "Political Appointees and Career Executives: The Democracy-Bureaucracy Nexus in the Third Century," *Public Administration Review* 47 (1987), 57–65. For advice on how to manage the bureaucracy, see Michael Senera, "Implementing the Mandate," *Mandate for Leadership II: Continuing the Conservative Revolution* (Washington, D.C.: Heritage Foundation, 1984), pp. 457–560.

27. Lester M. Salamon calls the (re)organizational goals of economy and efficiency "potent political symbols" even though progress toward these goals is difficult to assess and may not prove to be as desirable as generally presumed. Nonetheless, economy and efficiency have been "the primary goal of reorganization in every reorganization statute" at least since 1947. See *Federal Reorganization: What Have We Learned?* ed. Peter Szanton (Chatham, N.J.: Chatham House, 1981), pp. 64–68.

28. Peri Arnold comments on the particular form efficiency has taken on for twentieth-century presidents. See *Making the Managerial Presidency* (Princeton, N.J.: Princeton University Press, 1986), p. 20.

29. *Brownlow Committee Report*, p. 45.

30. Colin Campbell and B. Guy Peters, "The Politics/ Administration Dichotomy: Death or Merely Change?" *Governance* 1 (1988), 80.

31. Hugh Heclo points out that the politics-policy-administration distinction is "actually a normative political doctrine" not a rule of "social science theory." See "The In-and-Outer System: A Critical Assessment," *Political Science Quarterly* 103 (1988), 40.

32. Terry Moe makes this argument with regard to the composite of neutral competence in "The Politicized Presidency," p. 239.

33. Charles Walcott and Karen M. Hult focus on the political nature of the institutional presidency in "Institutionalizing the Presidency: The Structural Development of the White House Staff," presented at the annual meeting of the American Political Science Association, Chicago, 1987).

34. See, for example, the recent book by William Alonzo and Paul Starr, eds.,

The Politics of Numbers (New York: Russell Sage, 1987). A notable milestone on this path toward the mutability of "facts" was revealed in the infamous *Atlantic Monthly* interview with OMB Director David Stockman in which he admitted that budget numbers were fictitious and "cooked" to present interpretations and "facts" that fit the administrations political needs and policy preferences.

35. For a discussion of problems of declining competence and tenure in political executives, see Patricia W. Ingraham, "Building Bridges or Burning Them? The President, the Apparatus and the Bureaucracy," *Public Administration Review* 47 (1987), 425–35.

36. Thomas Cronin, *The State of the Presidency,* 2d ed. (Boston: Little, Brown, 1980) identifies a number of paradoxes that make the job of the modern president particularly difficult.

37. For an example, Richard Nathan's analysis of President Nixon's administration strategy argues that its procedural illegitimacy were abuses of executive powers. Conversely, Richard Schlesinger's analysis in *The Imperial Presidency* infers an illegitimacy of presidential policy ends concerning the Vietnam War. See Richard P. Nathan, *The Plot that Failed: Nixon and the Administrative Presidency* (New York: Wiley, 1975); and Arthur Schlesinger, Jr., *The Imperial Presidency* (Boston: Houghton, Mifflin, 1973).

PART II

Cabinet Government: A Clean Bill of Health?

5

Presidentialization
in a Parliamentary System?

GEORGE W. JONES

Two well argued-over themes converge in the assertion that Westminster parliamentary systems have been transformed into presidential or quasi-presidential systems. They are that prime ministers dominate cabinets, and that parliaments have declined. The
essence of a presidential system is that decision-taking power is
exercised by one person, the president, independently of another
executive body, the cabinet, and of the legislature, parliament.
The cabinet is an entourage of advisers to the president, not a
body that acts as the collective executive in which the head, just
as much as the other members, is bound by the doctrine of
collective responsibility. He has his own administrative resources
in the form of a team of staff—a department—loyal only to him.
The president has a direct relationship to the people who elected
him, and his continuation in office does not depend on his always maintaining the support of the legislature, nor must he
ensure that all his governing acts are acceptable to the legislature.
In presidential systems, presidents may have to engage in some
bargaining with their cabinets and legislatures to get their way,
but in parliamentary systems, cabinets and parliaments are much
more significant constitutional constraints on the head of the
executive.[1]

In Britain in 1988 the two propositions that provide the main
foundations of the case that the system of government has become
presidential—that prime ministers dominate cabinets and that parliaments have declined—seem plausible, as an interventionist
prime minister, who had led her party to its third election victory
in a row, seemed to hold sway over not only a compliant cabinet
but also a House of Commons in which her party had an overall

majority of one hundred and her opponents were in disarray. She had given her name to the prevailing doctrine in policy making, Thatcherism, and there was no coherent and convincing alternative on offer.[2]

The decline of Parliament has been deplored for years. The cause is depicted as the growth of government which has enhanced the executive, putting power into the hands of civil servants who are not fully accountable to ministers or to Parliament. Government tasks have been allocated to a complex of boards beyond the reach of close parliamentary scrutiny, and Parliament itself by delegated legislation has granted the executive extensive discretion to act through regulations. The growth of party is said to have made Parliament a puppet of the executive, since the government can always rely on the votes of its supporters to sustain it in office and back its legislation. Parliament's procedures are regarded as outdated and cumbersome, failing to fit it to be an effective counterweight to the executive. Policy making is depicted as taking place in the processes of intergovernmental bargaining or in discussions between executive bodies and pressure groups, both of which are free from parliamentary control.

The claim that the prime minister overshadows cabinet is not recent.[3] From time to time it has surfaced about Lloyd George, Neville Chamberlain, Winston Churchill, Anthony Eden, Harold Macmillan, and Harold Wilson; and it has been asserted against John Gorton in Australia, Pierre Trudeau in Canada, and Robert Muldoon in New Zealand.[4] However, although such prime ministers may have exercised great influence in cabinet over some—indeed, very many—issues, they set no patterns to be followed nor institutionalized prime ministerial power for their immediate successors. The latter usually adopted a different style, more consensual and conciliatory, often deliberately to distance themselves from their predecessors. Commentators who proclaim that there has been a shift to prime ministerial predominance neglect the constraints on the holder of that office, both structural and—more important—political.

The perennial attractiveness of the thesis of prime ministerial power lies in its simplicity. Richard Crossman, before he became a minister, was greatly impressed with the thesis when he found it expounded by John Mackintosh.[5] So enamored was he that although his diaries of his time in office failed to find consistent confirmation, he nevertheless employed Mackintosh to draft his Godkin lectures which propounded the myth.[6] It also fits in with the needs of the media to personalize politics and government and to treat public affairs as a branch of the entertainment industry. It also saves them effort, since by concentrating on the activities of one person they are spared the expense of deploying extra staff and technology to keep others under review. A belief in prime ministerial power appeals to iconoclasts who revel in debunking traditional views, however true; and it appears the modern line for the fashionable who follow American trends. If they have presidents, so should Britain; and if they have a stronger legislative assembly, again so should Britain.

Academics now rarely see government in such simple terms. The widest survey of prime ministers in Westminster systems, *First Among Equals* (1985) by Patrick Weller, takes account of key constraints on prime ministers in the United Kingdom, Australia, Canada, and New Zealand.[7] Weller also concludes, "In none of the cases can it be argued that parliamentary government no longer exists or that the Westminster system has been destroyed."[8] It shows a considerable resilience. Philip Norton in his inaugural lecture also judges that the decline of Parliament is a premature verdict. Often such "decline" is simply deviation from the golden age of the middle years of the nineteenth century, or from some ideal that never existed, or from the congressional model. Increasingly, the British Parliament, both Commons and Lords, has in recent years forced governments to think again and modify their proposals;[9] procedural reforms have strengthened Parliament's capacity to scrutinize the executive; and M.P.s have become more active in representing their constituents. Polls of public opinion show no evidence of growing widespread public dissatisfaction with Parliament.[10]

The topics of prime ministerial power and the decline of Parliament are the commonplaces of the media and undergraduate essays. Recently, however, new ammunition has been found to sustain the case that Britain under Mrs. Thatcher became presidential. It would be interesting to assess whether similar trends have appeared elsewhere and have been interpreted likewise. Four aspects are emphasized.

First, as Peter Hennessy has noted, Mrs. Thatcher reduced the number of cabinet and cabinet committee meetings and relied on more informal ad hoc meetings of a few ministers and their advisers with herself and her advisers, where she could introduce her views into the policy-making process more effectively.[11]

Second, she made a direct appeal to the public through the media, whose manipulation on her behalf was centralized in the hands of her chief press secretary, Bernard Ingham.

Third, she politicized the civil service by intervening in top appointments to inject her favorites.

Fourth, she built up her own personal staff in the Policy Unit which, with the Private Office, served to ensure that her voice was heard at the early stages of policy making, challenging departmental views with the prime minster's perspective.[12]

Prime Ministers and Parliament

Before commenting on these current observations of British trends, I will examine the traditional relationship between the prime minister and Parliament.[13] Little research has been carried out on the involvement of prime ministers in parliamentary proceedings. Most explorations have been into relationships between prime ministers and cabinets, and between cabinets and parliaments. Even Patrick Weller's chapter on prime ministers and parliaments contains only a small amount on the contributions of prime ministers to parliaments. He observes that Parliament looms large for the prime minister, since one's performances in it can make or unmake a reputation. "Parliamentary performance may be one of the first indications that a prime minister is slipping."[14] A prime minister's political standing depends on how well he or she performs in Parliament.

For prime ministers, the most challenging time they face on a regular basis is question time, which in Britain is a twice-weekly session of fifteen minutes on Tuesdays and Thursdays while the Commons is sitting.[15] Prime ministers are very apprehensive about their answers and spend much time rehearsing with their closest advisers. One private secretary spends almost all his time handling the preparation of the prime minister's replies. The jousts between the prime minister and the leader of the opposition are well reported and often broadcast on radio. Weller observes that in Australia, Canada, and New Zealand, question time is not so formalized and that less attention is paid to the prime minister, although prime ministers attend question time every day and may have questions directed at them without notice on any occasion.[16]

The questions to and answers given by British prime ministers can range over all activities of the government, and usually relate to issues regarded as the most politically significant of the day. Although the initial question asked, which is on the order paper, may seem bland and innocuous, often referring to visits or speeches by the prime minister (since mention of a substantive topic would cause the question to be transferred to the minister responsible), supplementaries carry the sting and cover almost everything done, or not done, by the government. Because of this potentially comprehensive scope, prime ministers have to interest themselves in the work of all departments. Thus M.P.s themselves have encouraged prime ministerial intervention in departmental affairs by asking such all-encompassing questions.

The second mode of prime ministerial involvement in parliamentary proceedings is through making statements to the House of Commons. This type of intervention has declined over the years and has changed in nature. It once covered statements about forthcoming business of the House. That role has been unloaded onto the Leader of the House since the two offices (of prime minister and Leader of the House) were formally separated in 1942. It covers statements about ceremonial occasions, like royal births and marriages, and tributes to the eminent deceased, and about important and controversial topics and policies.

Two significant changes have occurred in the subject matter of statements since 1970, between Edward Heath and Margaret Thatcher. Excluding statements of a protocol and ceremonial kind, the majority of Heath's statements (76 percent) were on domestic affairs, mainly economic, industrial, and social issues, and on Northern Ireland. Of his foreign affairs statements, most were about meetings of the EEC Council. With Wilson, too, between 1974 and 1976 most statements (58 percent) were on domestic affairs; but with Callaghan from 1976 to 1979 most were on foreign affairs (58 percent), and the majority were again about the EEC Council. With Mrs. Thatcher, between 1979 and November 1988, foreign affairs statements amounted to 83 percent of all her statements, and once again the EEC (later EC) Council provided the majority; meetings of Commonwealth heads and other multilateral summits made up the bulk of the others. Of the 17 percent of her statements on domestic affairs, most dealt with national security. Only one related to economic, industrial, and social issues: in June 1985 on football hooliganism. The inference might be drawn from this evidence that Mrs. Thatcher is more concerned with foreign affairs and less with domestic, leaving the latter more with her responsible ministers.

The third mode of prime ministerial intervention is making brief interjections in debates, apparently spontaneously and in response to the speaker at the time. These interventions have also declined. Indeed Mrs. Thatcher made none at all in the sessions of 1985–86, 1986–87, and 1987–88. She was not an active participant in the cut and thrust of parliamentary debate.

The fourth mode of intervention is making major set-piece speeches, prepared in advance, either on specific matters or as wider ranging reviews. These events have declined, especially under Mrs. Thatcher, and she shifted the balance of topics. With Heath, Wilson, and Callaghan, most (excluding the Debate on the Address) were on domestic issues: economic, industrial and social affairs. For Heath, 83 percent, and for Wilson, 90 percent, while Callaghan made no foreign affairs speeches at all. With Mrs. Thatcher, between 1979 and 1988 52 percent were on domestic and 48 percent on foreign affairs, and just under a half of the latter were about the Falklands Islands. Again the evidence shows that Mrs. Thatcher was more involved in foreign than domestic issues, which she left to the ministers responsible for such domestic matters.

This shift in the subjects of prime ministerial involvement in Parliament can lead to two different interpretations. On the one hand, it can support the presidentialization thesis, since a concentration on foreign affairs may enhance the image of the single leader of the nation amid world statesmen, uniting the people to her as the national champion, whereas taking a lead in domestic matters may be more divisive. On the other hand, by not taking a lead in Parliament on domestic issues, she is leaving such matters more to her ministers, thus strengthening their roles. Or perhaps she is becoming more presidential in foreign affairs and less so in domestic, but prime ministers in the past have frequently participated more in foreign than in domestic matters. Table 3 presents data about Mrs. Thatcher's interventions in Parliament in the session of 1987–88. Table 4 presents data about Mrs. Thatcher's interventions in the Commons for the whole period since she became prime minister in

TABLE 3. Margaret Thatcher's Interventions in Parliament, 1987–88

Types of Intervention	No. of Days (Total = 224)	% of Total
Answering questions	78	34.8
Making statements	7	3.1
Making minor interventions in debates	0	0.0
Making speeches	3	1.3
Total interventions	84	37.5

TABLE 4. Margaret Thatcher's Interventions in the House of Commons, 1979–88

Types of Intervention	No. of Days (Total = 1,588)	% of Total
Answering questions	566	35.6
Making statements	65	4.1
Making minor interventions in debates	16	1.0
Making speeches	35	2.2
Total interventions	622	39.2

1979 to the end of the session 1987–88 in November 1988. Table 5 shows the pattern of interventions by Mrs. Thatcher in Parliaments to indicate trends during her terms of office.

These tables indicate that Mrs. Thatcher in the session of 1988 kept very much to her previous pattern, not making minor interventions in debates, rarely delivering a major speech, making few statements, and concentrating her performances in the House on answering questions. These appearances on Tuesdays and Thursdays from 3:15 to 3:30 P.M. were the main occasions when she involved herself personally and directly in the officially recorded proceedings of the Commons. These characteristics accentuated during her time as prime minister. Compared with her earlier terms, by 1988 she was making fewer speeches, statements and minor interventions, answered questions less often, and generally was less involved in Parliament. She could not be called an enthusiastic parliamentarian, seeming to prefer an executive role, as head of the government, rather than to sit in the chamber and participate in its activities. Her increasing aloofness from Parliament could be taken as evidence of presidentialization.

TABLE 5. Margaret Thatcher's Interventions in Parliament, 1979–88
(percent of days)

Types of Intervention	Sessions		
	1–4 1979–83 (694 Days)	5–8 1983–87 (670 Days)	9– 1987–88[a] (224 Days)
Answering questions	36.5	35.1	34.8
Making statements	4.8	3.7	3.1
Making minor interventions in debates	1.4	0.9	0.0
Making speeches	3.2	0.9	0.0
Total interventions	41.1	37.6	37.5

a. First session only.

Mrs. Thatcher's interventions in the Commons, at the rate of just below 40 percent of the days in a session, put her very much at the bottom end of the list of prime ministers since 1868. She has intervened fewer times than any prime minister since Lloyd George, equaling Macmillan's rate. Table 6 presents data on the total number of days prime ministers have intervened in the Commons since Disraeli in 1868.

Table 6 shows that Mrs. Thatcher, of prime ministers since the mid-1950s, is the most distant from proceedings in Parliament, except for Harold Macmillan. Since the time of Churchill, the rate of interventions has tended to cluster between 39 percent to 45 percent, with Thatcher's record at the bottom. More generally, the table shows that Thatcher was far removed from great parliamentary performers, like Balfour, Gladstone, Asquith, and Baldwin, whose rates ranged from 66 to 76 percent. The prime minister who intervened most in Parliament was Chamberlain, with a rate of 77 percent, the result largely of his having to answer in the Commons not only for domestic but also for foreign affairs. He virtually directed foreign policy, since his foreign secretary was in the Lords and his opponents sought to question him closely. The prime minister most detached from Parliament was Lloyd George, with a rate of only 25 percent, well below that of any other prime minister. He, like Mrs. Thatcher, much preferred to be an executive director of government than to participate in the Commons. He fell from office because he lacked a strong parliamentary following, to some extent a consequence of his personal neglect of Parlia-

TABLE 6. Prime Ministers' Interventions in Parliament since 1868

Prime Minister	Total Days	Days Intervening	% of Total
1. Chamberlain	478	368	77
2. Balfour	420	319	76
3. Gladstone	1,655	1,234	75
4. Asquith	1,292	883	68
5. Baldwin	964	641	66
6. Campbell-Bannerman	334	210	63
7. Disraeli	438	267	61
8. MacDonald	1,063	578	54
9. Attlee	1,025	517	50
10. Law	81	40	49
11. Wilson	1,306	590	45
12. Eden	269	121	45
13. Callaghan	518	226	44
14. Churchill	1,225	545	44
15. Heath	611	264	43
16. Home	155	66	43
17. Thatcher	1,588	622	39
18. Macmillan	1,089	420	39
19. Lloyd George	889	224	25

ment. The most presidential of British prime ministers was the least active in Parliament, and suffered because of it: perhaps M.P.s had not seen enough of him. Mrs. Thatcher and Harold Macmillan were both accused of presidential proclivities, and they after Lloyd George were the least involved in the Commons. However, Chamberlain was also seen as a presidential figure and yet had the highest intervention rate of all. Perhaps he suffered because M.P.s saw too much of him. He fell in the end because he could not command the confidence of his colleagues in the House, that is, because of the policy catastrophes with which he was associated.

If Lloyd George and Chamberlain are treated as special cases, then the table shows that there has been a decline in the involvement of prime ministers in parliamentary proceedings from the late nineteenth century. Roughly from the 1860s to the 1920s and 1930s, the participation rate was in the 60–76 percent range; with MacDonald it fell and stayed until the 1950s around 50 percent. From Churchill's government in 1951–55, it fell further to the fortieth percentile, where it has remained. Some might want to use these figures as an index to show that as executive power increased, legislative power declined, but it does not necessarily follow from a decline in prime ministerial involvement in Parliament that there has been a decline in legislative power relative to the executive.

Tables 7–10 analyze the changing patterns of interventions since 1868. Mrs. Thatcher is the prime minister with the lowest rating ever for intervening in the course of debates: not for her the cutting interjection during a heated debate (see table 9). To complete the coverage of prime ministers since 1868, table 11 presents data about the intervention rates of prime ministers in the House of Lords.

A number of general points emerge from these tables. Appearance at question time is the main mode of involvement for prime ministers in the Commons. Since the regular twice-weekly grilling was instituted in Macmillan's period, in 1961, prime ministers have tended to limit their interventions to these occasions, constituting between 33 and 43 percent of days in a session. Mrs. Thatcher was at the bottom end of this group, along with Macmillan. This intervention rate is well below that of prime ministers like Chamberlain, Balfour, Asquith, and Baldwin. They also indicate that Gladstone, although a high scorer on speech making and making interventions in debates, was not as assiduous in answering questions.

In making statements, Mrs. Thatcher is revealed as a midway prime minister, although somewhat out of line with her predecessors in the 1970s who had much higher scores: Callaghan had double her rate. But the figures are small in total and reveal that statements are not a major mode of involvement.

Nor is making minor interventions in debates, with Mrs. Thatcher posting the lowest number since 1868—1 percent of total days. Since the nineteenth century, there has been a considerable decline in the rate at which prime ministers have made such interjections, the most obvious fall coming with Lloyd George. Mrs. Thatcher stood out. She clearly did not relish the unrehearsed remark. Her preference was for the stage-managed performance for which she was well prepared, like question time.

But Thatcher was also not inclined to make major set-piece speeches in the Commons. Again, she was the worst-rated prime minister since 1868. She reduced this type of speech making below that of her immediate predecessors, Callaghan, Wilson, Heath, and Home. Compared with the behavior of nineteenth-century prime

TABLE 7. Prime Ministers' Days Answering Questions in Parliament since 1868

Prime Minister	Total Days	Days Answering Questions	% of Total
1. Chamberlain	478	358	75
2. Balfour	420	270	64
3. Asquith	1,292	819	63
4. Baldwin	964	601	62
5. Gladstone	1,655	981	59
6. Campbell-Bannerman	334	187	56
7. MacDonald	1,063	542	51
8. Attlee	1,025	517	50
9. Law	81	35	43
10. Wilson	1,306	554	42
11. Disraeli	438	165	38
12. Home	155	57	38
13. Churchill	1,225	455	37
14. Heath	611	221	36
15. Callaghan	518	187	36
16. Thatcher	1,588	566	36
17. Macmillan	1,089	363	33
18. Eden	269	77	29
19. Lloyd George	889	138	16

TABLE 8. Prime Ministers' Days Making Statements in Parliament since 1868

Prime Minister	Total Days	Days Making Statements	% of Total
1. Eden	269	31	12
2. Wilson	1,306	140	11
3. Callaghan	518	44	8
4. Attlee	1,025	85	8
5. Home	155	13	8
6. Macmillan	1,089	88	8
7. Churchull	1,225	84	7
8. Heath	611	38	6
9. Gladstone	1,655	76	5
10. Thatcher	1,588	65	4
11. Balfour	420	11	3
12. Asquith	1,292	27	2
13. Disraeli	438	10	2
14. Lloyd George	889	16	2
15. Chamberlain	478	5	1
16. Baldwin	964	10	1
17. Campbell-Bannerman	334	2	1
18. MacDonald	1,063	6	1
19. Law	81	0	0

TABLE 9. Prime Ministers' Days Making Minor Intervention
in Debates in Parliament since 1868

Prime Minister	Total Days	Days Intervening in Debates	% of Total
1. Gladstone	1,655	911	55
2. Balfour	420	179	43
3. Disraeli	438	163	37
4. Asquith	1,292	358	28
5. Campbell-Bannerman	334	83	25
6. Chamberlain	478	100	21
7. Law	81	16	20
8. Baldwin	964	142	15
9. MacDonald	1,063	124	12
10. Heath	611	74	12
11. Eden	269	31	12
12. Lloyd George	889	111	12
13. Home	155	17	11
14. Churchill	1,225	138	11
15. Wilson	1,306	101	8
16. Attlee	1,025	76	7
17. Macmillan	1,089	62	6
18. Callaghan	518	15	3
19. Thatcher	1,588	16	1

TABLE 10. Prime Ministers' Days Making Major Speeches in Parliament since 1868

Prime Minister	Total Days	Days Making Major Speeches	% of Total
1. Gladstone	1,655	234	14
2. Balfour	420	54	13
3. Chamberlain	478	41	9
4. Disraeli	438	33	8
5. Lloyd George	889	73	8
6. Eden	269	18	7
7. Asquith	1,292	95	7
8. Law	81	5	6
9. Baldwin	964	46	5
10. Churchill	1,225	62	5
11. Callaghan	518	19	4
12. Macmillan	1,089	42	4
13. Heath	611	22	4
14. Wilson	1,306	52	4
15. Home	155	6	4
16. Attlee	1,025	37	4
17. MacDonald	1,063	46	4
18. Campbell-Bannerman	334	12	4
19. Thatcher	1,588	35	2

TABLE 11. Interventions in the House of Lords by
Prime Ministers Salisbury, Beaconsfield, and Rosebery

Prime Minister	Total Days	Days Intervening	% of Total
Answering questions			
Salisbury	1,238	184	15
Beaconsfield	325	37	11
Rosebery	130	13	1
Making minor interventions in debates			
Salisbury	1,238	336	27
Rosebery	130	24	18
Beaconsfield	325	41	13
Making major speeches			
Beaconsfield	325	15	5
Salisbury	1,238	46	4
Rosebery	130	4	3
Total interventions			
Salisbury	1,238	490	39
Rosebery	130	42	32
Beaconsfield	325	82	25

ministers, there has been a significant reduction in the delivery of major speeches by prime ministers in the Commons.

To be comprehensive, I include tables for prime-ministerial involvement in the Lords. There is no table for the number of days a prime minister made statements, since these occasions were so infrequent; they have been merged into those for minor interventions, thus inflating the latter category a little. The tables show that prime ministers have not intervened as much in the proceedings of the House of Lords as in the Commons. It was not such a demanding institution for prime ministers. Overall, it was only as demanding on a prime minister as is the Commons today under Mrs. Thatcher.

The data about prime ministerial involvement in Parliament might at first glance seem to sustain the argument that prime ministers have become more presidential and that Parliament has declined as the shaper of their behavior. Indeed, there has been an appreciable reduction during the twentieth century, and significantly under Mrs. Thatcher, in the use of Parliament as the forum in which the prime minister operates and gives an account of his or her leadership of the government, and the prime minister's participation in Parliament is focused on the narrow activity of answering questions twice a week for a quarter of an hour in a rowdy adversarial clash distinguished more by its heated confrontations than by its contribution to enlightenment.

However, other changes should be taken into account. The reduction of prime-ministerial involvement is matched by an increase in the involvement of ministers. As government and departmental responsibilities have grown, ministers are doing more and have to account for more before Parliament. The prime minister's cabinet colleagues perform more in Parliament and have more opportunities to enhance their reputations through a display of parliamentary expertise. They are able to win support from their backbenchers and build up their own followings, which enable them more securely to resist the prime minister's policy preferences, and even to appear to challenge the prime minister's leadership. An important function of Parliament is to assess ministers, to make and unmake their political reputations. If the prime minister is less active in parliamentary proceedings, they are more prominent. The extensive legislative program of Mrs. Thatcher's government provided ministers with many opportunities to shine in Parliament, and the establishment in 1979 of fourteen select committees to scrutinize the work of government departments further increased the occasions on which ministers are engaged formally in parliamentary proceedings.[17] Through successful performances they can acquire political support and become significant counterweights to the prime minister inside the executive, in cabinet, and in cabinet committees. Bad performances, however, can erode their support and even lead to their fall from office, as Leon Brittan discovered in 1986.

The standing of the government does not depend on the prime minister alone. Its general competence rests on ministers in charge of departments and on their performances in Parliament. The impression they create as a team will go a long way to determining whether the government will be reelected next time. Their activities have a bearing on the reputation of the government more than in a presidential system.

The data presented above do not capture the full range of interactions between prime minister and Parliament. They cover only what is formally recorded in Hansard and omit involvement in party meetings in the House, conversations with M.P.s in the prime minister's room in the Commons, informal talks in the corridors and lobbies, or over meals or drinks, or simply sitting in the chamber listening to proceedings. It is impossible to quantify this activity without access to the prime minister's diary, which will never be able to give a full account. Lord Donoughue has analyzed the diary arrangements of Wilson and Callaghan from 1974 to 1979 and counted 200 meetings with individual M.P.s and 130 meetings of the Parliamentary Labour party, in addition to 400 question times and 50 major Commons speeches and statements.[18] Mrs. Thatcher was well aware that one reason she ousted Edward Heath as Conservative leader was his neglect of his party colleagues in the Commons. A "peasants' revolt" of Conservative back-benchers brought Mrs. Thatcher to power, and she was sensitive to the need to woo them. Her parliamentary private secretary during her first administration, 1979 to 1983, Ian Gow, was assiduous in his cultivation of back-benchers on behalf of the prime minister. He kept her in touch with her supporters. She made sure she was about the House available to meet M.P.s in a more accessible way than ever Heath was. She invited M.P.s to No. 10 Downing Street for discussions, and restored honors for political services, which included back-benchers whose loyalty was recognized by knighthoods. In her later administrations, her parliamentary private secretaries did not show such a deft touch as Gow, and she was not as accessible in the Commons as earlier—which played a part in losing her some support,[19] and could be taken as evidence of her growing aloofness from the Commons.

Since the government's very existence depends on retaining the confidence of the Commons, the prime minister has to be concerned to keep it content, especially her back-benchers. Those ministers with responsibility for managing Parliament, the chief whip, and the leaders of the Commons and the Lords, were particularly close to the prime minister, advising her and cabinet about appropriate tactics to ensure high morale among their back-benchers and to prevent their sullen acquiescence or outright mutiny. They do not always succeed. Since the late 1960s and especially since Heath, back-benchers have shown an increasing propensity to rebel against governments—which, together with the large majorities enjoyed by Mrs. Thatcher, made management of the party in the Commons more difficult.[20]

Party, which is often portrayed as debilitating the power of Parliament by giving the executive an instrument with which to enforce discipline on the legislature, is a means of enhancing the influence of Parliament. It constrains the prime minister, since she had to conform to party policy and the manifesto and cannot deviate too much without provoking outcry from her back-benchers. They acquire their potency from being elected as party candidates. Similarly, interest groups have strengthened Parliament, making use of select committees to feed in their views on policy and administration. They provide M.P.s with a constant supply of information and argument, which is deployed in Parliament against the prime minister and government.[21] Parties and pressure groups are not weakening Parliament ̖and sustaining presidential government but reinforcing parliamentary government, that is, government which has to be carried out in Parliament, account to it, and is held responsible to it.

Parliament looms large in the deliberations of the executive, exercising its influence largely through the law of anticipated reactions but also through more overt expressions. Parliament is no back number for the prime minister. Mrs. Thatcher could not treat it with contempt or be aloof from it. It was the source of her authority and a constraint on her power. She had reached executive power through a career in the Commons, in which she had held a number of important opposition posts. Long service in the Commons socializes a prime minister into respect for the values of the parliamentary process, which is reinforced by the prime minister still being an M.P. with all the duties of an M.P. to carry out, including voting for the party, often in the early hours of the morning.[22] The prime minister is no president: she was deeply embedded in the legislature.

Refuting Conventional Wisdom

It would be informative to compare interactions between prime ministers and parliaments across countries with Westminster-based systems. Such investigations would reveal whether the structural and political characteristics of the Westminster model form obstacles to the emergence of presidential or quasi-presidential systems, as suggested by analysis of British experience. Similarly, cross-national inquiry could assess whether some further recent developments observed in Britain have appeared elsewhere and have so enhanced the power of the prime minister that the nature of the governmental system can be said to have been transformed into a presidential or quasi-presidential model.

There is alleged to have occurred a devaluation of cabinet by greater reliance on cabinet committees and, more important, on ad hoc meetings of ministers and officials, together with the prime minister and her advisers, in which policy is determined, leaving cabinet either not involved or a body that merely notes decisions taken earlier in the smaller group.[23] However, cabinet committees are not new; neither are meetings of the prime minister with a few other ministers or even a single minister. Both types of occasion were common in the nineteenth century. Cabinet committees, serviced by the Cabinet Office, can be distinguished from ad hoc informal meetings by function. The former are part more of the decision-*taking* process, the latter part more of the decision-*making* process. In the former, decisions may be taken, while in the latter discussions occur preparatory to later decision by a minister, by cabinet committee or by cabinet itself. Mrs. Thatcher made more use of such meetings of both types because she found them sensible and efficient ways of conducting business that in fact made cabinet as a whole operate more effectively.

The composition of cabinet committees, and meetings where decisions are taken, is crucial in ensuring they do not detract from the cabinet itself. Invariably they consist of two types of minister: those with a departmental interest in the subject under consideration—the functional ministers most directly concerned, who would take the lead in full cabinet and be listened to with the most deference by their colleagues—and other ministers not so closely involved but with weight in cabinet, "who will be important when it comes to selling it in Cabinet."[24] Thus such gatherings are, in Gordon Walker's words, "partial cabinets," composed of those who would carry the cabinet if it had itself decided on the matter.[25] They are in effect mini-cabinets in which all members are virtually represented and operate as if they were full cabinet, but with the proviso that the minister most directly concerned with the topic under consideration, and the chairman, have the right to take the issue to full cabinet if they are unhappy with the sense of the committee. These cabinet committees anticipate the likely reactions of their colleagues in full cabinet, whose views they know well from close working acquaintance over many years in party and Parliament, and from

current Whitehall networks of information. Thus such committees do not damage cabinet government; they enhance it.

Similarly with the ad hoc and more informal meetings, of nar-
rower composition and not so likely to take decisions: here much
preliminary work can be cleared away, early soundings take place
and ground prepared—sifting out matters on which agreement
can be reached and highlighting issues in dispute between ministers on which further work is needed. They enable ministers, including the prime minister, to be better informed about topics on
the government's agenda: indeed they strengthen ministers' collective involvement in policy making by enabling them to participate
at an early stage in the process, perhaps previously left to civil
servants. Mrs. Thatcher's use of such meetings, far from presidentializing the system, increased the contribution of her ministerial
colleagues, both individually and collectively.

Mrs. Thatcher's approach to cabinet government can be seen as
making cabinet more effective, especially its main task of resolving
disputes unable to be settled earlier. Without prior sieving, cabinet
might have become clogged. Instead it was able to concentrate on
divisive issues. Thus, cabinet has been able to survive as the central decision-taking institution of British government despite the
vast increase in governmental activity. Mrs. Thatcher streamlined
government without losing its essential collective nature.

This streamlining was welcome to her ministerial colleagues,
since it not only saved time but also helped keep cabinet together.
Two types of issue can be handled in cabinet committees and
ministerial meetings: those not contentious which can be easily
dealt with and those very divisive. Ministers may be pleased not to
have to experience grueling arguments over such sensitive matters
in full cabinet, such as over defense issues for Labour or public
expenditure for all governments. Ministers may be happy to leave
their resolution to the ministers most involved, together with others, to look after wider aspects, which includes the prime minister.
She had the function of acting as guardian of collective government. Her assertiveness was not necessarily to promote her personal policy predilections: it might be to advance the collective
view of cabinet. In committees and ministerial meetings, she assured members of cabinet not present that cabinet as a whole was
not forgotten. Thus cabinet committees and ministerial meetings
are not necessarily evidence of presidential government, but can

bear witness to the continued vitality of collective cabinet government;[26] and since ministers are also parliamentarians, overwhelmingly from the House of Commons, they bear witness to the continued vigor of parliamentary government.

The second recent development said to be making Britain more presidential is the prime minister's increasingly direct appeal to the public and the centralization of her relationships with the media through her chief press adviser. Colin Seymour-Ure is currently engaged on comparative research into prime ministers' relationships with the media, and until his findings are published judgments must be tentative.

For a long time, prime ministers in Britain have shown a keen interest in how the media depict them and their governments. In the nineteenth and early twentieth centuries, prime ministers personally maintained close contact with editors and reporters, and sought to ensure that a favorable line was presented, even distributing honours as a reward for helpfulness. Until 1931 one of the prime minister's secretarial staff usually kept the press informed day-to-day about the prime minister's views. In 1931 the first press adviser to the prime minister was appointed, and since then No. 10 Downing Street has housed a press or public relations adviser, sometimes a former journalist, sometimes a member of the government information service, and sometimes a civil servant from a line position. His role has been to project the prime minister through the media and advise him or her on how to gain good reports. The staff of the adviser have grown, and from time to time attempts have been made to bring the information officers and press departments of ministers under closer supervision from No. 10 Downing Street.

Mrs. Thatcher's chief press adviser, Bernard Ingham, was an ebullient and assertive character devoted to pushing the prime minister's case. He came to No. 10 Downing Street in the spring of 1980, and was the longest serving official there after the prime minister. When he spoke to the media, he was taken to be acting on her behalf. He attempted to unify the government information service under his leadership and to exert control over the activities of departmental press offices. They were increasingly staffed by officials who had served for a time in his office. However, his influence should not be exaggerated. Ministers and their departmental officials were eager to preserve their autonomy and, although efforts were made to coordinate the timing of departmental statements, they did not accept subservience to Ingham. They kept open their own lines to the media and ensured that their case was purveyed, even to counter that of the prime minister. Reports in the press and broadcasting do not rely only on prime-ministerial guidance or a steer from Ingham. Veteran *Times* reporter Geoffrey Smith has stated that his judgments are much influenced by his talks with ministers, and that his assessment of the government comes from the impression ministers create as a team.[27]

British prime ministers indulge in nothing like the presidential press conference. Mrs. Thatcher gave occasional interviews on television and radio, often on popular programs and not just serious broadcasts about public affairs; she gave occasional interviews to the press, often again popular journals; and she exploited travels around the country to provide "photo opportunities" for media coverage. She also made during the course of a year a number of major speeches, or lectures, at formal gatherings of her party or of national institutions, and she made some prepared speeches at events abroad. Her main channels of communication to the public remained Parliament, especially question time, when she came under constant attack, and regular daily briefings by her press staff. Other ministers, too, use the same means. The way they perform in Parliament and their briefings to the media have an important effect on the standing of the government. The media do not simply focus on the prime minister. Their reporting shaped the reputations of her colleagues, building up some as counterweights to the prime minister. She was not able to dominate news management, as a president can.

The third development said to contribute to presidentializing the system was the politicization of the civil service by Mrs. Thatcher through appointments to its top ranks. The prime minister since the 1920s has had to give approval to the leading civil service positions, the most important of which are permanent secretaries, the official heads of the departments. She was reputed to ask of names put before her: "Is he one of us?" More than earlier prime ministers, she took an interest in these appointments, and not just of those at the very top, and because of her longevity as prime minister she was responsible for the appointment of most leading civil servants, including now all the permanent secretaries. Some of them were not thought to be the favorite candidates of the official hierarchy and had often served in her private secretariat at Downing Street or had come to her attention at meetings she attended.

However, a recent study by the Royal Institute of Public Administration, *Top Jobs in Whitehall,* concluded that there was no evidence that appointments were made on party-political grounds.[28] The prime minister was seeking to change the culture of the civil service and was doing so partly through appointing to leading positions officials oriented to action, constructive problem solvers, who will energetically find ways to achieve the political objectives of the government. Mrs. Thatcher did not favor the traditional style of urbane skepticism that focused on pointing out difficulties and pitfalls that lay ahead.

Her approach was in fact likely to lead to a reduction of political, including prime-ministerial, control over the civil service. Her goal was to make the civil service operate in a more businesslike manner.[29] She supported through the "Rayner" efficiency scrutinies, the Financial Management Initiative and, most recently, "The Next Steps" proposals of Sir Robin Ibbs, a series of changes in civil service operations and processes.[30] They involve decentralizing to line managers responsibility for achieving set objectives within specified budgets, and payment increasingly by results measured in relation to objectives. Already the culture of the civil service has much changed since 1979. The emphasis is on cost-cutting, setting clearer goals, and devising performance indicators, particularly output tests. Civil servants are increasingly regarded less as policy advisers and administrators than as managers. The implication of this change is that ministers will set strategic policy guidance and leave civil servants to manage. Whether that development will occur is not yet clear, but it would mean a considerable reduction in detailed ministerial intervention in departmental activities. Thus the end result will not be to reinforce a presidential system. Further fragmentation into policy communities and networks looks the most likely outcome of the process, enhancing the influence of the bureaucracy and those interest groups with whom bureaucrats come into close contact during the course of their work.

The fourth development said to be sustaining a presidential, or quasi-presidential system, is the building up of the prime minister's own staff at No. 10 Downing Street, both in her Policy Unit and through individual special advisers, coupled with the abolition in 1983 of the Central Policy Review Staff which acted as a "think tank" for cabinet as a whole.[31] Through these personal advisers she was said to be able to penetrate the policy-making process earlier and deeper than had previous prime ministers, ensuring that her views had more impact. However, her team of advisers was small-scale, fluctuating in composition, comparatively young and inexperienced when set alongside the staff available in departments to serve ministers, and not matching in expertise and weight departmental resources. They may have raised questions about departmental proposals, but were unlikely to prevail to promote a whim of the prime minister. She had not at her personal disposal the staff available to help presidents, or even prime ministers in other Westminster systems. Pressure for the establishment of a Prime Minister's Department was defeated largely on the grounds that it would stimulate antagonism from ministers and their departments and would signify a change in the British Constitution from cabinet to prime-ministerial government. That Britain still has no Prime Minister's Department is symbolic that it is not a presidential system.[32]

The role played by Thatcher's personal advisers may in fact strengthen collective government. The danger to policy making in Britain arising from the expansion of government, along with the retention of a medieval governmental structure and set of key values, is departmentalism. The collective is menaced by pressures of fragmentation. The prime minister, as chairman of the cabinet, is the guardian of collective government, with responsibility to keep the ministers together. He asserts himself to maintain collegial government, using his staff to ensure that ministers and their departments do not pursue a maverick course. His staff help him keep up with his ministers, so that he is briefed to participate in meetings with them. Otherwise they would roll over both him and cabinet. Whether the analytical capacity of the center of British government is adequate, and where it should be located, are frequently discussed in Britain.[33] Given that his ministers have much more analytical resources than are available to him, and comparing the balance between the two now and in the early years of the century, the British prime minister is weakly endowed. He is no president in his staff resources.

Concluding Observations

Since the mid-nineteenth century, the chamber of the House of Commons has declined as a forum in which the prime minister operates and gives an account of the government. Mrs. Thatcher took that trend a significant stage further than her predecessors. Her participation in parliamentary proceedings was concentrated on twice-weekly appearances at question time. She did not relish the cut and thrust of making speeches and debating. However, prime ministers are involved with Parliament in other ways than those formally recorded in Hansard, and she did not behave in a cavalier way toward the institution on which the very existence of her government depended. Parliament looms large in the work of the executive and cannot be ignored. The reputation of the government—above all, the impression of its competence or incompetence—is shaped by performances in Parliament of not only the prime minister but, more important, ministers. Parliament provides political support for ministers, her colleagues in cabinet, who act as a constraint on any potentially presidential inclinations she may have harbored.

Mrs. Thatcher was the most assertive prime minister in policy making since Lloyd George. She led from the front, constantly scrutinizing departmental activities and advancing her views. She did not always get her way. Her cabinet was apparently more an obstacle to her proposals than it ever was to the imperious Edward Heath. In any case, her interventions can be seen as keeping her colleagues to the collective line of party and government strategy. She brought to government a particular style, not a change in structure. Cabinet was streamlined but without losing its capacity to determine those issues that could not be settled earlier and to set the guidelines within which ministers had to work. The civil service was not transformed into her personal fiefdom and is likely to become more detached from political control. She did not create a Prime Minister's Department, but continued to rely on a small and frequently changing group of advisers who did not match the administrative and advisory resources of her ministers. She was not the sole channel of communication to the public about government. Despite paying great attention to the presentation of government information, seeking to control it more from

Downing Street, she never managed to monopolize the public relations of government.

The office of prime minister is like a piece of elastic: it can be stretched to accommodate an active, interventionist prime minister, like Mrs. Thatcher, but it can also contract to contain a more passive prime minister. Mrs. Thatcher was a prodigious worker and covered far more than most prime ministers. As with earlier ones, she paid particular attention to foreign affairs and any other issues that reached the top of the daily political agenda. But that did not make her a president or quasi-president. She did not operate outside the confines of cabinet and parliamentary government. She was constrained by their constitutional structures and political pressures. Like all prime ministers, she had to engineer consensus out of a fissiparous group of colleagues with their own power bases in Parliament and the party. She was only as strong as they allowed her to be. Her style was not to seek the lowest common denominator of agreement between them, but the highest to accord with her judgment of party policy. As long as her style brought success to her party, it was accepted, but when times changed and she appeared a liability, she was dropped and another leader with a different style emerged. The elastic was reshaped to fit a new prime minister.

The last word can be left to the British people's electoral judgment. "When the Harris exit poll asked voters [in the 1987 general election] for the ONE most important reason 'which decided their vote' only 6 percent mentioned a party leader."[34] Butler and Kavanagh explain, "Voting behaviour is more often influenced by the individual's calculation about what is best for his or her family.'[35] Elections are determined more by "the social structure, prosperity and the mood created by the events of the previous years" than by the prime minister.[36] By the tests outlined at the start of this chapter, Mrs. Thatcher was no president.

Notes

I wish to thank my colleagues Desmond King and Brendan O'Leary for their comments on a first draft of this chapter.

1. A recent analysis of differences between presidential and parliamentary systems appears in Fred W. Riggs, "The Survival of Presidentialism in America: Paraconstitutional Practices," *International Political Science Review* 9 (1988), 247–78.

2. For a wide-ranging analysis, see K. Minogue and M. Biddiss, eds., *Thatcherism: Personality and Politics* (London: Macmillan, 1987); R. Skidelsky, ed., *Thatcherism* (London: Chatto and Windus, 1988).

3. See A. King, ed., *The British Prime Minister*, 2d ed. (London: Macmillan, 1985), esp. chaps. 7–9.

4. See, for example, C. A. Hughes, *Mr. Prime Minister* (Melbourne: Oxford University Press, 1976); T. A. Hockin, ed., *Apex of Power*, 2d ed. (Scarborough: Prentice-Hall of Canada, 1977); H. Gold, ed., *New Zealand Politics in Perspective* (Auckland: Longman Paul, 1985); R. Mulgan, *Democracy and Power in New Zealand* (Auckland: Oxford University Press, 1984).

5. J. Morgan, ed., *The Backbench Diaries of Richard Crossman* (London: Hamish Hamilton and Jonathan Cape, 1981), p. 1028.

6. The Godkin Lectures are in R. Crossman, *Inside View* (London: Jonathan Cape, 1972). Mackintosh's role in their drafting is shown in R. Crossman, *The Diaries of a Cabinet Minister*, vol. 3: *Secretary of State for Social Services, 1968–70* (London: Hamish Hamilton and Jonathan Cape, 1977). The first two volumes of his diaries (1975 and 1976) cover his time as minister of housing, 1964–66 and as Lord President of the Council and Leader of the House of Commons, 1966–68. Critical comments on Crossman's views are in G. W. Jones, "Crossman and Cabinet Government," *Contemporary Record* 1 (1987), 25–26; and G. Jordan, "Central Co-ordination, Crossman and the Inner Cabinet," *Political Quarterly* 49 (1978), 171–80.

7. P. Weller, *First Among Equals* (Sydney: Allen and Unwin, 1985). See also for comparison with presidential systems, R. Rose and E. N. Suleiman, eds., *Presidents and Prime Ministers* (Washington, D.C.: American Enterprise Institute for Public Policy Research, 1980).

8. Weller, *First Among Equals*, p. 209.

9. Even to the extent of defeating a government bill at Second Reading. See P. Regan, "The 1986 Shops Bill," *Parliamentary Affairs* 41 (1988), 218–35.

10. P. Norton, *Parliament in Perspective* (Hull: Hull University Press, 1987). Also see M. Ryle and P. G. Richards, *The Commons Under Scrutiny* (London: Routledge, 1988). On the House of Lords, see D. Shell, *The House of Lords* (Deddington: Philip Allan, 1988); and A. Adonis, "The House of Lords in the 1980s," *Parliamentary Affairs* 41 (1988), 380–401.

11. P. Hennessy, *Cabinet* (Oxford: Blackwell, 1986).

12. Recent expositions of the prime-ministerial power thesis are in M. Burch, "The British Cabinet: A Residual Executive"; and M. Doherty, "Prime Ministerial Power and Ministerial Responsibility," *Parliamentary Affairs* 41 (1988), 34–67. See also R. Holme, *The People's Kingdom* (London: The Bodley Head, 1987); and G. Jones, "Mrs. Thatcher and the Power of the Prime Minister," *Contemporary Record* 3 (1990), 2–6.

13. The following section updates my earlier article, "The Prime Minister and Parliament," *British Politics Group Newsletter* 47 (Winter 1987), 17–22. I must thank the Staff Research Fund of the London School of Economics and Political Science for providing financial assistance over the years for a number of research assistants who delved for data in Hansard, and June Burnham for compiling many of the later tables.

14. Weller, *First Among Equals*, p. 179.

15. G. W. Jones, "The Prime Minister and Parliamentary Questions," *Parliamentary Affairs* 26 (1973), 260–73.

16. Weller, *First Among Equals*, p. 171.

17. See G. Drewry, ed., *The New Select Committees* (Oxford: Oxford University Press, 1985); and I. Marsh, *Policy Making in a Three Party System* (London: Methuen, 1986). An elaboration of the data presented here can be found in P. Dunleavy, G. W. Jones, and B. O'Leary, "Prime Ministers and the Commons: Patterns of Behaviour, 1868 to 1987," *Public Administration* 68 (1990), 123–40.

18. Bernard Donoughue, "The Prime Minister's Day," *Contemporary Record* 2 (1988), 16–19.

19. Mrs. Thatcher's impact on politics and government is well covered in the symposium "The Thatcher Years," *Contemporary Record* 1 (1987), which also contains a good bibliography (p. 31).

20. Philip Norton has illuminated the phenomenon of back-bench dissidence in a series of studies. See his *Dissension in the House of Commons 1945–74* (London: Macmillan, 1974); *Conservative Dissidents* (London: Temple Smith, 1978); *Dissension in the House of Commons 1974–79* (Oxford: Oxford University Press, 1980); and his edited volume, *Parliament in the 1980s* (Oxford: Blackwell, 1985), esp. chap. 2.

21. See Drewry, ed., *New Select Committees;* and I. Marsh, *Policy Making in a Three Party System.*

22. Mrs. Thatcher's record of voting in the Commons while prime minister has not been assessed. However, in the MM Political Services analysis of M.P.s' voting between June 1987 and July 1988, Mrs. Thatcher was eighth from the bottom, having voted in only 19.7 percent of divisions (*The Observer,* August 14, 1988, and *The Times,* August 15, 1988).

23. The following section draws on G. W. Jones, "Cabinet Government and Mrs. Thatcher," *Contemporary Record* 1 (1987), 8–12.

24. P. Hennessy, "The Prime Minister, the Cabinet and the Thatcher Personality," in *Thatcherism,* ed. Minogue and Biddiss, p. 63.

25. P. Gordon Walker, *The Cabinet* (London: Fontana/Collins, 1972), pp. 87–91.

26. Cabinet committees are examined in comparative perspective in T. T. Mackie and B. W. Hogwood, eds., *Unlocking the Cabinet* (London: Sage, 1985).

27. G. Smith, "The Prime Minister and the Press," in *Presidents, Prime Ministers and the Press,* ed. K. W. Thompson (Lanham: University Press of America, 1986).

28. Royal Institute of Public Administration Working Group, *Top Jobs in Whitehall* (London: RIPA, 1987). Also P. Hennessy, "Mrs. Thatcher's Poodle? The Civil Service Since 1979," *Contemporary Record* 2 (1988), 2–4.

29. Assessments of changes in the civil service appear in L. Metcalfe and S. Richards, *Improving Public Management* (London: Sage, 1987); A. Harrison and J. Gretton, eds., *Reshaping Central Government* (Oxford: Policy Journals, 1987); and G. K. Fry, "The Thatcher Government, the Financial Management Initiative, and the 'New Civil Service,' " *Public Administration* 66 (1988), 1–20.

30. The Efficiency Unit, *Improving Management in Government: The Next Steps* (London: HMSO, 1988). See also *Civil Service Management Reform: The Next Steps,* the government reply to the eighth report of the Treasury and Civil Service Committee, sess. 1987–88, HC 494-1, Cm. 524 (London: HMSO, 1988).

31. See T. Blackstone and W. Plowden, *Inside the Think Tank* (London: Heinemann, 1988).

32. The advisory networks of the British prime minister are examined in G. W. Jones, "The Prime Minister's Aides," in A. King (ed.), *op.cit.,* and in G. W. Jones, "The United Kingdom", in *Advising the Rulers,* ed. W. Plowden (Oxford: Blackwell, 1987). The latter volume covers advisory systems in a number of countries. See also J. Walter, *The Ministers' Minders* (Melbourne: Oxford University Press, 1986).

33. See the exchange between P. Weller and G. W. Jones in *Public Administration* 61 (1983), 59–84; and K. Berrill, "Strength at the Centre—The Case for a Prime Minister's Department," in *The British Prime Minister,* ed. King, pp. 242–57.

34. D. Butler and D. Kavanagh, *The British General Election of 1987* (London: Macmillan, 1988), p. 249.

35. Ibid., p. 273.

36. Ibid., pp. 263–64.

6

Cabinet Government in Canada: Corporate Management of a Confederal Executive

PETER AUCOIN

Under the Canadian system of parliamentary government there is a separate executive, the prime minister and members of the cabinet, which is also part of the legislative branch of government, Parliament, and at the same time "responsible" to the elected chamber of this branch, the House of Commons. As an executive that is responsible to the elected House of Commons, it must function as a corporate body: it is formed and maintained by the confidence of the Commons. Although Parliament does establish ministerial authority over departments and agencies, both the prerogative powers of the prime minister and statutory authority vested in the prime minister make the organization of the executive, in effect, a matter of prime ministerial discretion. Further, the actual management of cabinet is entirely subject to prime ministerial dictate, subject only to the political dynamics within the governing party in the House of Commons. This applies to the decision-making structures and processes of the cabinet, the assignment of responsibilities to members of the cabinet, the use of partisan political staff to advise the prime minister and cabinet, and the design of public service "central agencies" to serve the cabinet as a corporate executive.

The consequence of this constitutional design is that prime ministers have some considerable autonomy to shape the executive system to suit their individual philosophies of leadership, management styles, and political objectives.[1] At the same time, however, there are political realities which they must consider if they are to be effective in the design and management of their executive system. The purpose of this chapter is to outline the most important of these realities and to describe how cabinet government in Canada in recent decades has been affected by them. The most important of these realities are the following: the need for the cabinet to be "the effective representative body at the centre of government,"[2] especially with respect to the representation of regional interests in national policy; the extensive role of the federal government in the direct delivery of public services and enforcement of regulatory laws, including the provision of joint programs with provincial governments; and the tradition of a "neutral" public service reaching to the highest echelons of the federal bureaucracy.

The Cabinet as a Representative Body

The fact that the federal cabinet must be, and must be seen to be, a "representative body" derives essentially from the design of the Canadian political system. This design sought to combine the efficiency of parliamentary government, with the strong role assigned to the cabinet as a separate but responsible executive, with a federal distribution of powers between two levels of jurisdiction: federal and provincial. The Canadian design of "responsible government" meant that the second chamber of Parliament, the appointed Senate, although based on the principle of representation by "regions," could not function as a federalist check on either the House of Commons, as a legislative body based on representation by "population," or the Cabinet as formed from and maintained by it.[3] If regional interests in national policy were to be accommodated at all effectively, they had to be adequately represented in cabinet. This was acknowledged in the construction of the first cabinet following confederation in 1867, and has been a feature of cabinet composition ever since.

The role of ministers as regional representatives within the cabinet has been largely informal in character.[4] The assumption is that the regional distribution of cabinet positions should secure attention to the regional dimensions of public policies as they are considered by cabinet as a corporate body. The formal assignments of ministers is to head departments of government; their regional responsibilities have been added to individual portfolio responsibilities. Although Canadian cabinets have always been relatively large because of the need to secure regional representation, and to

do so as to give greater representation to some regions, this requirement meant, for many decades, that the preferred mode of operation for decision making was the full cabinet. As the business of
cabinet increased with growth of government in this century, cabinet had to meet with increasing frequency.

Beginning in the 1960s with the election of the Liberal Pearson
government (1963–68), however, cabinet turned to the device of
cabinet committees to handle the increasing volume of business
that required cabinet attention.[5] With this change, issues generally
went to standing cabinet committees before they went to cabinet
for final decision. Before he left office, Pearson introduced a Priorities and Planning Committee, a quasi-inner cabinet. Upon assuming office from Pearson, Trudeau further reorganized the cabinet
committee system so that cabinet committees could make what, in
effect, were cabinet decisions. The short-lived Clark government
(1979–80) took this system even further, with a full-fledged inner
cabinet and a system of cabinet committees to which policy and
expenditure decision-making powers were delegated.

Over almost two decades, the regional representative character
of the cabinet was clearly at odds with the increasingly formalized
design of the corporate executive. The increased size of the cabinets during this period, with Pearson at 25–26, Trudeau at 27–33,
and Clark at 30, meant that full cabinet became less and less
effective as a decision-making body; indeed, the Clark government did not even use full cabinet for decision making.[6] Cabinet
committees obviously helped the executive to deal with its increasing volume of business, but they restricted the capacity of the
cabinet to ensure that regional interests were adequately represented in the several decision-making parts of such a system. For
some time following the introduction of this system by the Pearson government, this was implicitly acknowledged by the policy
of the government not to make public the composition of these
committees.[7] It also was acknowledged by the policy whereby any
minister could attend meetings of committees, except for the Priorities and Planning Committee/Inner Cabinet, of which they were
not a member.

Trudeau's first cabinet, after his overwhelming electoral victory
in 1968, acknowledged the convention of regional representation
in cabinet composition. But four factors served to play down the
importance of regional representation in cabinet decision making.

First, Trudeau wished to take a much more aggressive position in federal-provincial relations; in his view the Pearson government had been to inclined to compromise national interests in order to promote "cooperative federalism," especially as this related to the status of Quebec. Ministers of Trudeau's government, in contrast, were to adopt a "national," rather than a regional, perspective.[8] To this end, the subject matter of federal-provincial relations became even more a corporate concern of the federal cabinet. The prime minister took the lead role in this, and the prime minister's public service department/cabinet secretariat, the Privy Council Office, strengthened its capacity in this regard. By the mid-1970s, a separate central agency was created for this function—the Federal-Provincial Relations Office. Second, Trudeau was much enamored of the "scientific" approach to politics; in his view public opinion polls conducted by professionals were a more sophisticated way to gauge public opinion, across the nation, than a reliance on regional ministers and their partisan political networks of amateur party politicians.[9] Third, Trudeau was interested in direct relations between the prime minister and the party, and even citizens; "participatory democracy" was one of his principal themes. This meant by-passing intermediaries, such as local members of Parliament and regional ministers. The creation of "regional desks" in his Prime Minister's Office, to monitor and assess political developments and public opinion in the regions, was perhaps the most concrete expression of this approach.[10] Fourth, Trudeau's paradigm of "rational management" placed greater emphasis on the intellectual merits of policy initiatives than on the degree to which policy proposals accommodated regional, that is "parochial," interests. Under this approach, regional ministers might still perform the required function of political patronage; for the more critical functions of the state, they were an anachronism. At best, they could help to refashion local and provincial party associations to become agents for a new style of politics, as was attempted by Trudeauites within the federal wing of the Quebec Liberal party, for example.

Within the tenure of the Trudeau government from 1968 to 1979, compromises had to be made between the above approach and the demands of the party, often led by regional ministers. Following the government's near defeat in 1972, when it emerged as a minority government, that is, without a parliamentary majority, the system of regional desks in the Prime Minister's Office was disbanded, and greater attention was paid to the roles of regional ministers as well as to the party's legislative caucus. The attainment of a parliamentary majority in 1974, however, saw a partial resumption of the original approach.

A number of factors contributed to the defeat of the Trudeau government in 1979. Among them were the criticisms directed at the government for the degree to which the government was regarded as as out of touch with political realities as a consequence of its technocratic approach to governance. The short-lived Conservative minority government of Joe Clark stumbled badly, however. It structured its executive system in a manner which exceeded the formalization of even the Trudeau regime. Its inner cabinet, for example, had weak representation from Quebec, and no representatives from three provinces, notwithstanding the fact that the full Cabinet did not meet for decision-making purposes. It also miscalculated badly on the trade-offs between important regional interests, particularly in regards to energy policy.[11]

The return of Trudeau's Liberal party to power, less than a year later, eventually witnessed a more explicit recognition of the role of regional ministers in cabinet decision making. Its initial economic strategy was predicated on the development of major energy, and energy-related, megaprojects, which fortuitously were considered feasible in all regions of the country. When a number of factors forced the government to scrap this strategy, an attempt was made, through a major reorganization, to bring regional development concerns to the forefront of economic development policy.[12] The major sectoral committee of cabinet, namely, the Cabinet Committee for Economic Development, was given this new mandate, and thus was renamed the Cabinet Committee for Economic and Regional Development. Its membership included all important regional ministers. It was served by a central agency, the Ministry of State for Economic and Regional Development, which became the first central agency with senior officials located in each province. Although the experience varied from province to province, these officials became an important staff support to many regional ministers; indeed, in some cases, they became, in effect, the public service deputy to their regional minister, marking the first such explicit deployment of senior bureaucratic support for ministers in their capacities as regional ministers. For the first time as well, regional ministers were officially recognized in formal cabinet decision making, as they were given an explicit role in the development and design of federal programs and contributions under federal regional economic development agreements with individual provincial governments, and in the allocation of expenditures under special employment programs and special capital expenditure projects.[13]

By the end of Trudeau's second term in office, the role of regional ministers had assumed an importance that had not been evident for many decades. In many respects, the patronage and policy roles of ministers had been linked in ways that made patronage more blatant on the one hand, and program expenditures decisions more regionally focused on the other. By 1984, the cabinet was more a confederation of regional ministers than the collegial decision-making body of Trudeau's rational management paradigm.

The Conservative government of Brian Mulroney, elected in 1984, assumed office with a commitment to what was called "national reconciliation." This was taken to mean, among other things, an accommodation of regional interests in the formulation of national policies. The first appointments to the Mulroney cabinet reflected this consideration: for instance, eleven of forty members were from the west, and seven of the fifteen on the Priorities and Planning Committee were from this region. Recognition of the need for brokerage politics, a traditional approach to cabinet goverance in Canada, also required a departure from the design and management of the executive system that had developed over the past two decades. Two elements of this departure need to be emphasized here.

The first departure involved the establishment of major portfolios designed as organizations based on "place."[14] To this end, the government has created, to date, three portfolios with explicit and exclusive responsibilities for specific regions. These portfolios are responsible for the Atlantic Canada Opportunities Agency (ACOA), the Western Economic Diversification Office (WEDO), and the Northern Ontario Development Corporation (FEDNOR). There are variations in the roles to be performed by these organizations, for their mandates are region-specific, given the particular needs and opportunities of each region. But, in each case, the logic of the design of these portfolios is to coordinate the policies and programs of line portfolios and departments as they relate to economic development in each of these regions, and to act as an advocate of the region in the policy development process of the federal government.

In these crucial respects, these agencies build upon the Trudeau experiment with the decentralized apparatus of the Ministry of State for Economic and Regional Development (MSERD), which, as noted, brought significant professional staff support to regional ministers for the first time. In fact, that particular dimension was so successful that when the short-lived Turner Liberal government (1984) eliminated MSERD as a central agency, its decentralized offices survived and were transferred to a line department, but as a separate set of offices thereof. ACOA and WEDO were built upon the base of these offices in each of the four Atlantic and Western Canadian provinces, respectively. Although under a single minister in each case, they also provide staff support to other ministers in each region. As the minister responsible for ACOA put it:

What you get . . . now is an agency that acts almost as a department to these Atlantic Ministers *in their role as Atlantic Ministers*. . . . The law gives to that agency an advocacy role, and so the Ministers have resources, staff, and the ability to do research in order to come to the [cabinet] table with information.[15]

The second departure from the practice of the past two decades has been a diminution in the role of cabinet committees as integral parts of a formalized decision-making system. This will be discussed in greater detail later. Here, I simply note that the Mulroney government devolved greater authority to individual ministers for the management of their portfolios as well as for the discharge of their regional responsibilities.

These most recent changes reflect an effort to design the executive system so as to provide for a better fit between the informal dynamics of cabinet politics, on the one hand, and the need for greater formality to ensure that there is a measure of corporate management within the cabinet system, on the other. Cabinets prior to the 1960s did this, albeit at some cost to efficiency, especially after the Second World War, by deploying the full cabinet as the principal and formal decision-making forum. Beginning in the 1960s, the development of the cabinet committee system, with its central agency apparatus, sought greater efficiency, but at the price of a considerable mismatch between the formal structure and the informal organization of political power.

Portfolio Differentiation and Integration

From a comparative perspective, the Canadian executive system is well known for the size of its cabinet, its highly institutionalized structure, and its extensive use of central agencies to support corporate decision making and management.[16] In part, of course, the size of the Canadian cabinet derives from its character as a regionally representative body. Other factors have been at play as well. Among the most important of these are those which derive from the character of the federal system.

The scope and involvement of the federal government are extensive for essentially two reasons. First, the jurisdiction of the federal government has meant that it has a wide range of responsibilities to undertake directly: it does not merely establish policies and programs which are implemented, in whole or part, by provincial (or local) governments, as is the case in some federal systems. Second, the competitive nature of Canadian federalism has led successive federal governments to emphasize the need for direct federal government involvement in program management, even in areas of provincial jurisdiction, where the principal constitutional basis on which it acts is its spending power. Although the federal government has negotiated joint programs with provincial governments, collectively and individually, where provincial delivery of programs has been the norm, a federal presence has been maintained in order to highlight its "visibility."[17]

As a result, the federal executive system reveals considerable organizational differentiation in portfolio and departmental design. There are approximately twenty "line" portfolios/departments, as well as three "common services" portfolios/departments (Revenue, Public Works, and Supply and Services). The line portfolios, with only two or three exceptions, are large and complex organizations with major policy and operational responsibilities. Although many of these have been rearranged over the past twenty-five years, at least twelve were in existence before the major expansion of the federal government that occurred in the 1960s in expenditures and public service staff. This fact cannot be overemphasized: considerable portfolio differentiation clearly existed prior to the advent of what Campbell aptly describes as the "Canadian fascination with coordinative machinery."[18]

When one adds to this complement of portfolios those with corporate responsibilities—that is, for the Prime minister, for finance, external affairs, and justice, at the least—it is obvious why Canada has had a good-sized cabinet for many decades. In addition to the increase in the number of line portfolios, two other developments have increased the size of the cabinet further. The first has been the creation of new corporate portfolios, such as a separate portfolio to head the Treasury Board and its secretariat as the cabinet committee and central agency responsible for the general management of the government, including the preparation of the expenditure budget, the establishment of the ministerial position of deputy prime minister, and the institution of "ministers of state for designated purposes"—portfolios that have been established, with horizontal policy responsibilities but without line authority, to develop integrated policies to be implemented by way of the programs of operational departments.[19] The second development has been the institution of "minister of state to assist" portfolios.[20] These ministers are full members of the cabinet as a corporate body, but their responsibilities are assigned by prime ministerial prerogative and do not possess statutory authority. Rather, as "junior ministers," these ministers assist senior ministers in the discharge of one of their responsibilities.

The development of "the minister of state to assist" portfolios obviously could only take place following the introduction of a formalized and differentiated cabinet system. The original impetus in this direction was the result of the report and recommendations of the Royal Commission on Government Organization (1960–62), which pointed to major deficiencies in government organization for the "wholly collective concerns" of the cabinet. The "needs for central direction," it claimed, were "in varying states of underdevelopment," except for "the preparation of the budget."[21] Cabinet, it was argued, had to function less as a "confederacy" of line department ministers, concerned primarily with their own specific mandates, and more as an integrated team that would address the corporate dimensions of government policy and administration.[22]

The minority context of the first Pearson government (1963–

68), wherein a priority had to be given to coordination, provided the necessary political incentive to proceed with organizational reforms. These reforms included the development of a greater policy advisory capacity at the center, in both the Prime Minister's Office and the Privy Council Office, the creation of a separate portfolio to chair the Treasury Board—the president of the Treasury Board—along with an expansion of the board's secretariat, and the introduction of a "planning, programming, and budgeting system."[23] In addition, the Pearson government introduced major reforms to the executive system by way of its use of cabinet committees. In part, this was simply to cope with the volume of cabinet business. In part, it was to provide a mechanism, other than the full cabinet, to integrate what was now recognized as a highly differentiated set of portfolios.

These several, but related, developments were carried even further by the Trudeau government, which assumed office in 1968. In addition to an expansion to the number of line portfolios, the Privy Council Office and Treasury Board Secretariat were expanded considerably, as Trudeau relied heavily on the "superbureaucrats" in his central staff agencies to bring a corporate, and coordinating, perspective to the cabinet's decision-making process.[24] The full blossoming of the cabinet committee system, with its Priorities and Planning Committee as a quasi-inner cabinet, provided ample opportunities for increased coordination and collegial decision making. The need for the same was also increased by the introduction of more than one new line portfolio with a mixture of line and horizontal responsibilities, the latter of which mandated these ministers to secure policy integration across a range of other government departments and agencies. In addition, there were created the first two "ministers of state for designated purposes," for science and technology and for urban affairs, respectively.

Over the 1970s, this increasingly "matrix" structure of the executive system was elaborated upon in essentially three ways. First, there was a further differentiation of the central agency apparatus serving the corporate executive. Second, the Trudeau government, and the short-lived Clark government, reorganized the Cabinet committee system, and the decision-making process, into what was called the Policy and Expenditure Management System (PEMS).[25] This involved the integration of policy making and expenditure decision making, so that those cabinet committees that were responsible for major "sectors" of government policy and expenditure programs—namely, economic development, social development, foreign and defense policy, and government operations—were given sectoral budgets ("envelopes," as they were labeled) to allocate to existing, and any new, departmental programs in each sector. The Priorities and Planning Committee/Inner Cabinet determined the size of each sector's budgetary envelope (and had its own envelopes for the "public debt" and "fiscal arrangements"). To assist the three major sectoral committees—Economic Development, Social Development, and Foreign and Defence Policy—three new central agencies were created. These new central agencies were to advise the committees in developing sectoral plans, to coordinate policy development by the departments in their sector, and to assess program and expenditure proposals for their policy and expenditure implications. Third, throughout this period there was a further elaboration in the use of "functional," or "horizontal," cabinet committees, including the Treasury Board, the Legislation and House Planning Committee, the Federal-Provincial Relations Committee, and the Communications Committee. These committees added further elements to the matrix character of decision making, as many ministerial policy proposals were required to make their way through these committees, as well as through the relevant sectoral cabinet committees.

By 1984, when John Turner took over as Liberal party leader and prime minister, it was clear that this complex matrix system had not achieved its desired result. As noted, it frustrated the representation of regional interests in the executive system, but it could not eliminate this crucial political function of ministers: powerful regional ministers pursued their regional responsibilities largely through informal means, thereby undermining the formal process. The same phenomenon occurred with powerful line ministers. In many cases, of course, these powerful line ministers were also powerful regional ministers. As a consequence, trade-offs and compromises had to be made, usually outside the context of formal decision making, at the cost of an obvious lack of discipline in the expenditure decision-making system.[26]

Turner recognized all this when he assumed office. He eliminated the three new central agencies which served the three sectoral committees, as noted above. He further consolidated the cabinet committee system, although not its basic structure, and

initiated a process whereby the collective decision-making requirements of the cabinet would be reduced. He also reduced the
size of the cabinet, from thirty-seven to twenty-nine members.
The system he inherited, he said, was "too elaborate, too complex, too slow, and too expensive," and had "diffused and eroded
and blurred" the responsibilities of individual ministers.[27]

The Mulroney government did not reverse the organizational
changes made by Turner, although his cabinet was increased to
forty. Over the first four years, however, a number of significant
changes were effected.[28] PEMS, dubbed a "pretty expensive management system" by one senior official, has been all but abandoned in practice.[29] With this, the sectoral cabinet committees
have been reduced in significance, especially regarding expenditure decision making. The government has also delegated further
authority to line department ministers to act on their own.

The position of deputy prime minister has assumed a role that
has transformed this portfolio into that of a "general manager" of
the cabinet. This has been accomplished by way of an Operations
Committee, chaired by the deputy prime minister and consisting
of a small number of key corporate and regional ministers. This
committee manages the work plan of the cabinet, especially with
respect to major issues, coordinates interministerial assignments,
and, most important, serves as the focal point for the budgetary
trade-offs to be made among major policy and program initiatives.
In all of these ways, it constitutes a major departure from the
Policy and Expenditure Management System. It also represents a
greate centralization of power than was meant to be, or was,
present under PEMS.

The result of all the above is that there has emerged an "inner
circle" of ministers which revolves around the prime minister, on
the one hand, and a working group headed by the deputy prime
minister, on the other. This means that, in a number of important
respects, the cabinet structure has a built-in informal dynamic. As a
multifaceted pattern of relationships between ministers, including
the prime minister, this inner circle does not lack organizational
coherence. At the same time, however, the flexible character of this
arrangement gives the prime minister room to maneuver; he is able
to broker competing interests in an ad hoc manner. The centralization inherent in this approach to the coordination of the highly
differentiated portfolio system has replaced the more collegial ap-

proach to coordination that had characterized the structure put in place in the mid-1960s.

The Neutral Public Service

When Brian Mulroney assumed office in 1984, it was widely assumed that there would be a major change in the role and character of the federal bureaucracy.[30] In sometimes explicit and sometimes implicit ways, Mulroney and key members of his party's leadership had indicated that a Conservative regime would assert the role of ministers and diminish the role of bureaucrats in policy development and decision making, enhance the role of political staff, and politicize staffing at the senior levels of the bureaucracy. In each regard, significant departures from the Canadian tradition were expected.

The tradition of a neutral public service, coupled with a powerful role for the federal bureaucracy, was based upon a number of factors. First, public service staffing, by 1984, had been subject to the merit principle, as implemented by an independent public service commission, for well over half a century.[31] The application of this principle applied to the staffing of all positions below the level of deputy minister, the administrative heads of departments who continued to be appointed by the prime minister. In the spirit of this merit principle, moreover, prime ministerial appointments at this level were expected to be made from within the public service or, at the least, to reflect the nonpartisan character of the public service.

A second factor in the development of what Canadian scholars have regarded as a first-class federal public service was the ability of the service, beginning in the 1920s, to attract, at senior levels, exceptionally able professionals.[32] Two factors were critical to this development. On the one hand, the bureaucracy was dominated by a group of mandarins who functioned with a remarkable esprit de corps. This was reinforced by the respect of their political masters, and by the role in policy development which this respect afforded them. On the other hand, this development was facilitated by the long period of one-party dominance. The Liberal party held office from 1921 to 1957, interrupted only twice: for three months in 1926, and five years in the next decade (1930–35). Throughout this period, one prime minister, Mackenzie King, a former bureaucrat, headed three governments for a total of twenty-two years (1921–26; 1926–30; and 1935–48). A symbiosis between the public service and the Liberal party was the result; indeed, the idea of a "neutral" public service serving the "government party" came to be taken as the natural state of affairs.[33]

The consequences of this state of affairs through this period, extending to 1957, were twofold. On the one hand, ministers did not need political staff; the Liberal party machinery was sufficient for political advice, if ministers needed it. On the other hand, bureaucrats provided policy advice. They did so for ministers individually through departmental bureaucracies; for ministers collectively through interdepartmental committees; and, especially, by participating in meetings with ministers—ad hoc meetings, or cabinet committee meetings. More important, the principal mode of policy coordination was provided by the interactions of the mandarinate. This meant that deputies, and their subordinate officials, were to reconcile any departmental differences in pursuit of a coherent government policy. The norm was that interdepartmental relations were to be "informed by a common concern to identify the collective national interest": they were not to be forums, as they later became, in the 1960s, as one former official put it, "where departments negotiated with each other and jockeyed for position."[34]

This symbiosis was so well developed by the 1950s under King's Liberal successor, Louis St. Laurent, that for the 1957 election campaign, "The Liberal programme, such as it was, was that of the government. Not fashioned to suit the exigencies of the 1957 election, it had, in the main, evolved gradually as the consequences of the continuous interaction of the cabinet and the leading experts in the civil service."[35] The defeat of the "government party" in 1957 ushered in the Conservative party under John Diefenbaker, whose government, understandably, was deeply suspicious of the bureaucracy. Diefenbaker, however, refused to politicize the staffing of the service, even at the deputy level, including the position of secretary to cabinet (in effect, the prime minister's public service deputy). He also refused to bring in a cadre of political advisors; indeed, he ignored his one policy advisor in the Prime Minister's Office. Rather, he turned to the use of Royal Commissions to obtain an independent examination of a number of critical policy and organizational issues.

The return of the Liberal party to power, in 1963, under Lester Pearson, himself a former senior bureaucrat, did not result in a complete return to the style of the "government party." It did not do so in two important respects. First, Pearson appointed to the Prime Minister's Office a senior policy advisor, Tom Kent, who was intended to, and did, have an enormous influence over the implementation of Liberal party policy, which he had greatly influenced in the first instance.[36] For the first time, the PMO possessed a policy role, albeit consisting of a one-person policy staff. The breadth and depth of Kent's mastery of public policy issues, however, enabled him to exercise an influence unprecedented for a nonelected official. Second, there began the increased differentiation of the bureaucratic central agencies serving the cabinet. This was reflected in the increased differentiation of the Privy Council Office itself, in order to serve the new cabinet committee system, and the separation of the Treasury Board Secretariat from the Department of Finance, so that the former could assume its new corporate role as the principal advisor on the development of expenditure budget priorities.

These changes were not undertaken as a result of any general antipathy toward the bureaucracy, as was shown during the Diefenbaker regime, but rather constituted a recognition that the development of the bureaucracy over the preceding three decades had become increasingly departmentalized. Furthermore, the government had become too large for deputy ministers, acting as a collectivity, to provide for the required interdepartmental coordination. A greater capacity for policy direction and coordination from the center was now demanded. Under Pearson, this was provided by a blend of political and bureaucratic central agents.

Under Trudeau, this approach was also adopted, at least initially. The expansion of the central apparatus, however, was based as much on Trudeau's desire to insert a system of checks and balances into the system as on a desire for coordination. The result was threefold. First, the decision-making and management systems became increasingly subject to overlapping authorities and responsibilities. Second, the Prime Minister's Office became increasingly unable to perform policy advisory functions; at best, it could focus only on a few strategic priorities of the prime minister. This was the case in part because Trudeau did not expand its policy staff significantly, but rather relied increasingly on the expanded Privy Council Office to coordinate the policy agenda of the government. Third, the government again allowed bureaucrats to engage extensively in the policy deliberations of the cabinet, especially in cabinet committee forums.

The return to greater bureaucratic participation in the policy process was reminiscent of the golden days of the King–St. Laurent mandinarate: with two critical differences. On the one hand, deputies of the line departments were no longer the expert and experienced heads of specialized departments. Rather, they were bureaucratic generalists, skilled primarily in the processes of the system, who were rotated around the system with increasing frequency. Second, the key players were the "superbureaucrats" in the highly differentiated central agency apparatus. Although the prime minister's personal stamp on the character of his regime was clearly evident in the staffing of key positions at the senior bureaucratic levels, the "partisan" character of the bureaucracy was essentially in the mold of a technocracy. This technocratic orientation accounted, in large measure, for the perpetuation of the norm of a neutral bureaucracy.

Both the Clark and Turner interludes were too short to produce substantial change in the position of the public service, although each government took steps indicating that it recognized the need to do so. Clark, for example, fired Trudeau's secretary to the cabinet, because he refused to leave on his own: he claimed he was a neutral public servant. He was replaced, nevertheless, by a public servant, and not by an outsider. Turner, as noted, began to dismantle the central agency apparatus, and, equally important, eliminated the procedure whereby central agency officials "assessed" the policy proposals of ministers.

The Mulroney government has asserted the primacy of ministers over policy making. It has been able to do so, primarily because it came to power with an agenda which encompassed the major sectors of federal policy. The policy role of the bureaucracy has been reduced, as a consequence, simply because the government requires less advice on those matters where the government has had a clear idea of what it has wanted to do. The government has also found little obstructionism from the bureaucracy; indeed, the economic policy orientation of the new government was welcomed in many quarters, particularly in the Department of Finance.

The Mulroney government did take steps to enhance the role of its political staff—what one former official has called "the political arm of government."[37] The Prime Minister's Office was enlarged, and the number of policy advisors was increased. The principal political advisors to individual ministers were elevated in their status and salary, as "chiefs of staff." Their appointments were coordinated under the direction of the PMO. All of this was done to ensure that the political dimensions of coordination were emphasized over the technical dimensions: the political trade-offs inherent in the interdependence of policies were to be given a higher priority than had been the case under Trudeau.

These efforts were not entirely successful. This was partly because of the inadequacies of the persons appointed, who, with precious few exceptions, lacked the requisite governmental experience, in Ottawa or elsewhere. Following a disastrous first two years, changes were made. First, there was the secondment of a seasoned federal diplomat from the Department of External Affairs to the PMO, to become chief of staff to the prime minister. This was a new position in the PMO, given that the incumbent principal secretary was not dismissed. This chief of staff was given responsibility for handling the prime minister's affairs as leader of the government, including relations with the various bureaucratic central agencies in the administration of cabinet business. Second, the role of the deputy prime minister, as "general manager," was enhanced with the creation of the Operations Committee, as previously noted.

The combination of these two changes has made for better integration of politics and policy responsibilities at the center, but without a return to the technocracy of the previous regime. This has meant that deputies of line departments are now more fully involved, once again, in policy development. Equally important, this new approach has enabled the government to better accommodate the interests of regional ministers within the regular structures and processes of the executive system. This has become particularly critical, given the introduction of the new region-specific portfolios created for Western Canada, Atlantic Canada, and Northern Ontario. What has become clear is that ministers are as much, if not more, concerned with the need to sensitize the bureaucracy to the regional politics of governance as they are with the need to overcome any bureaucratic resistance to the governing party's ideological orientation.

Finally, it should be noted that the Mulroney government has not taken steps to politicize appointments to the bureaucracy. Less than a handful of senior bureaucrats have been pushed out, although a number of them have left on their own. Moreover, less than a handful of deputy minister positions have been filled by appointments from outside the service, and in each case they were policy professionals who made it clear that they intended to function as public servants, and have done so. The norm of appointments from within has thus been maintained. At the same time, Mulroney has used the practice of rotating deputies, which began under Trudeau, so that, by 1988, no deputies were in the same position they occupied in 1984.

Conclusion

There have been essentially three major approaches in the structure of the executive system. The first is constructed around strong ministers and line departments. This requires a significant measure of ministerial autonomy and a clear demarcation between the mandates of the line departments. Coordination, when required, is effected by an elite group of regional ministers, who also occupy the most senior portfolios, supported by their deputy ministers. The latter are responsible for ensuring that only the most politically sensitive matters requiring ministerial coordination come to the cabinet table. For intractable problems, especially involving conflicts among regional interests, the prime minister must act as a broker. This "ministerialist"[38] or "departmentalized"[39] approach characterized the King and St. Laurent regimes. The Diefenbaker government varied from this approach only in its mistrust of the bureaucracy. The Turner government gave some indication that such an approach would be adopted if it had survived the 1984 election.

The second approach is constructed around a cabinet committee system in which collegial or collective decision making, supported by corporate portfolios and central agencies, is the norm. Ministerial autonomy is limited by the perceived need to reconcile the policy interdependencies among the mandates of departments. This requires that ministers participate in a number of sectoral committees where these interdependencies can be coordinated. In addition, the executive also requires a number of corporate portfolios and functional committees to manage those policy functions which cut across the several sectors of line operations. Finally, the committee system itself must be orchestrated at the center, under the direction of the prime minister, and the corporate portfolios must have separate staff—hence the crucial roles, and yet differentiation, of the central agency apparatus. This approach characterized the Pearson and Trudeau regimes. The former, however, had a better balance of the political and bureaucratic elements at the center.

The third approach is a more hierarchically structured cabinet and central agency system. Under this approach, an inner group of ministers functions as the effective executive decision-making body of the cabinet. It determines the policy and expenditure priorities and work plan of the entire executive. Coordination is effected by way of a top-down process of decision making. The central executive agencies, however differentiated they may be, are also subject to the stratification inherent in this approach. This approach has characterized the Clark and Mulroney regimes. The former was more "bureaucratized" in terms of its formal Inner Cabinet, the Policy and Expenditure Management System which it established, and the elaborate central agency apparatus which PEMS required. The latter has been more "politicized" in terms of its use of an informal inner circle of ministers to effect the hierarchical principle, to assert ministerial primacy over the professional bureaucracy, and to provide for the representation and brokering of regional interests.

Notes

1. Peter Aucoin, "Organizational Change in the Machinery of Canadian Government: From Rational Management to Brokerage Politics," *Canadian Journal of Political Science* 19 (1986), 3–17.

2. Colin Campbell, "Cabinet Committees in Canada: Pressures and Dysfunctions Stemming from the Representational Imperative," in *Unlocking the Cabinet: Cabinet Structures in Comparative Perspective,* ed. T. T. Mackie and B. W. Hogwood (London: Sage, 1985), p. 61.

3. Peter Aucoin, "Regionalism, Party and National Government," in *Party Government and Regional Representation in Canada,* ed. Aucoin (Toronto: University of Toronto Press, 1985), pp. 137–60.

4. Herman Bakvis, *Regional Ministers: Power and Influence in the Canadian Cabinet* (Toronto: University of Toronto Press, 1991).

5. I. D. Clark, "Recent Changes in the Cabinet Decision-Making System in Ottawa," *Canadian Public Administration* 28 (1985), 185–201.

6. R. D. French, *How Ottawa Decides* (Toronto: James Lorimer, 1980), pp. 133–46.

7. Colin Campbell and George Szablowski, *The Superbureaucrats: Structure and Behaviour in Central Agencies* (Toronto: Macmillan, 1979).

8. D. E. Smith, "Party Government, Representation and National Integration in Canada," in *Party Government and Regional Representation in Canada*, ed. Peter Aucoin (Toronto: University of Toronto Press, 1968), pp. 1–68.

9. F. Schindler and C. M. Lanphier, "Social Science Research and Participatory Democracy in Canada," *Canadian Public Administration* 12 (1969), 481–98.

10. D. Smith, "President and Parliament: The Transformation of Parliamentary Government in Canada," in *The Canadian Political Process*, ed. O. M. Kruhlak et al. (Toronto: Holt, Rinehart, and Winston, 1970), pp. 367–82.

11. Jeffrey Simpson, *The Discipline of Power* (Toronto: Personal Library, 1980).

12. Peter Aucoin and Herman Bakvis, "Regional Responsiveness and Government Organization: The Case of Regional Economic Development Policy in Canada," in *Regional Responsiveness and the National Administrative State*, ed. Aucoin (Toronto: University of Toronto Press, 1985), pp. 51–118.

13. Bakvis, *Regional Ministers*.

14. Peter Aucoin, "Organization by Place, Regional Development and National Policy: The Case of the Atlantic Canada Opportunities Agency," presented at the annual meeting of the Canadian Political Science Association, 1988.

15. Canada, House of Commons, *Minutes of Proceedings and Evidence of the Legislative Committee on Bill C-103*, 10 March 1988, 5:92, emphasis added.

16. Colin Campbell, *Governments Under Stress: Political Executives and Key Bureaucrats in Washington, London and Ottawa* (Toronto: University of Toronto Press, 1983).

17. D. J. Savoie, *Regional Economic Development* (Toronto: University of Toronto Press, 1985).

18. Campbell, *Governments Under Stress*, pp. 77–99.

19. Peter Aucoin and Richard French, *Knowledge, Power and Public Policy* (Ottawa: Information Canada, 1974).

20. J. A. Chenier, "Ministers of State to Assist: Weighing the Costs and Benefits," *Canadian Public Administration* 28 (1985), 397–412.

21. Canada, *Report of the Royal Commission on Government Organization* (Ottawa: Queen's Printer, 1962), p. 53.

22. Canada, Privy Council Office, "Responsibility in the Constitution," Prepared for the Royal Commission on Financial Management and Accountability (Ottawa: Privy Council Office, 1977), p. 31.

23. G. Bruce Doern, "The Budgetary Process and the Policy Role of the Federal Bureaucracy," in *The Structures of Policy Making in Canada*, ed. Doern and Peter Aucoin (Toronto: Macmillan, 1971), pp. 79–112.

24. Campbell and Szablowski, *The Superbureaucrats*.

25. Richard Van Loon, "The Policy and Expenditure Management System in the Federal Government: The First Three Years," *Canadian Public Administration* 26 (1983), pp. 255–85.

26. Colin Campbell, "Review Article: The Political Roles of Senior Government Officials in Advanced Democracies," *British Journal of Political Science* 18 (1988), 243–72; Richard Van Loon, "Planning in the Eighties," in R. D. French, *How Ottawa Decides*, rev. ed. (Toronto: James Lorimer, 1984).

27. Canada, Office of the Prime Minister, *Release*, 17 September, 1984, p. 1.

28. Colin Campbell, "Mulroney's Broker Politics: The Ultimate in Politicized

Incompetence?" and Peter Aucoin, "The Mulroney Government, 1984–1988: Priorities, Positional Policy and Power," in *Canada Under Mulroney: An End-of-Term Report*, ed. Andrew B. Gollner and Daniel Salee (Montreal: Vehicule Press, 1988), pp. 309–34, 335–56.

29. Aucoin, "The Mulroney Government, 1984–1988," p. 346.

30. David Zussman, "Walking the Tightrope: The Mulroney Government and the Public Service," in *How Ottawa Spends, 1986–87: Tracking the Tories*, ed. M. J. Prince (Toronto: Methuen, 1986), pp. 250–82.

31. Kenneth Kernaghan and David Siegel, *Public Administration in Canada* (Toronto: Methuen, 1987), pp. 465–69.

32. J. L. Granatstein, *The Ottawa Men: The Civil Service Mandarins, 1935–57* (Toronto: Oxford University Press, 1982).

33. R. Whitaker, *The Government Party: Organizing and Financing the Liberal Party of Canada, 1930–1958* (Toronto: University of Toronto Press, 1977).

34. T. W. Plumptre, *Beyond the Bottom Line: Management in Government* (Halifax: Institute for Research on Public Policy, 1988), p. 72.

35. John Meisel, *The Canadian General Election of 1957* (Toronto: University of Toronto Press, 1962), p. 37.

36. G. Bruce Doern, "The Development of Policy Organizations in the Executive Arena," in *The Structures of Policy Making in Canada*, ed. Doern and Peter Aucoin (Toronto: Macmillan, 1971), pp. 49–50.

37. Gordon Osbaldeston, "The Public Servant and Politics," *Policy Options* 8 (1987), 3.

38. Whitaker, *The Government Party*.

39. J. Stephan Dupre, "Reflections on the Workability of Executive Federalism," in *Intergovernmental Relations*, ed. Richard Simeon (Toronto: University of Toronto Press, 1985), pp. 1–32.

7

A View from the Cabinet in Canada

THOMAS HOCKIN

An American might well wonder, "What in the world could I possibly learn about my own system of government by studying Canada's?" The answer to this question has been given by Samuel Beer, who has argued that one's own governmental system, especially those parts most "common and familiar," become better illuminated through contrast or comparison with the government of another country. Beyond doubt, an examination of how policy advice is funneled to the political executive in Canada, keeping one eye on how the same function is performed in the United States, draws attention to some marked differences between the two systems. Those differences are deeply rooted in Canadian and American constitutions and political cultures.

The merits of the comparative approach do not, however, justify forcing one country into another's frame of reference. The exercise of executive power differs greatly between Canada and the United States, and we should not be led astray by some superficial similarities between their respective institutions.

First, the U.S. presidency is an institution built around an individual officeholder. The entire apparatus of the executive branch, both in the departments and agencies and in the White House, is tasked with advising the president and carrying out the president's decisions. In contrast, the Canadian prime minister has traditionally been regarded as primus inter pares, and, although his role and powers have expanded enormously during the twentieth century, the structure and character of the exercise of executive power are still, in an important sense, collegial. By law, authority and responsibility are vested, individually and collectively, in ministers. The governor-in-council, which is, in fact, the cabinet, is constitutionally the executive, not the prime minister alone. This is a crucial point distinguishing the Canadian system of government from that of the United States. Though the prime minister wields the paramount influence in shaping the government's decisions, his cabinet colleagues are not there just to advise him but also to participate actively in making those decisions and to join their leader in taking responsibility for them before Parliament. Canadian ministers are governed by conventions of cabinet secrecy and collective responsibility, and when they leave the cabinet room, they must all publicly uphold the same point of view. The prime minister also appoints them.

U.S. presidents not infrequently come into office professing the intention to hold frequent cabinet meetings, but their number dwindles as the term progresses. A Canadian prime minister, on the other hand, may alter the structure of cabinet committees, but must pay continuing and consistent attention to the cabinet.

The prime minister must also pay attention to the parliamentary party which he leads, but on which he also greatly depends for his political strength and for assistance in shaping his political judgments. At the apex of power, advice-giving is melded with the continual pulls and pressures that characterize the deliberations of elected politicians. Admittedly, there are, standing at one remove from the government, advisory bodies such as the Economic Council of Canada and, within the government, a variety of mechanisms for advising the prime minister and cabinet ministers. The central roles are, however, played by cabinet and caucus.

The Cabinet

The Canadian cabinet, though superficially similar in appearance to that in the United States, is the major instrument of decision making in government. Policy is formulated for consideration by cabinet, policy is coordinated through cabinet and its committees, policy is decided by cabinet, and policy is articulated and enacted only with cabinet approval. To keep this mechanism in working order, cabinet has at its disposal a supporting secretariat called the Privy Council Office.

As of July 1991, the Canadian cabinet is made up of thirty-eight members. Most of its work is carried out in committees and each minister may sit on several committees, most of which meet weekly or biweekly. The most important "policy" committees are those concerned with economic policy, cultural affairs, the environment, federal-provincial relations, trade, social policy, foreign policy, and defense. Their work is funneled up to the Priorities and Planning Committee, which is, in effect, the "executive committee of cabinet" and on which twenty-one senior ministers sit.

The prime minister's chief involvement in this process comes by way of his chairmanship both of the cabinet and of the Priorities and Planning Committee[1] and through his broader responsibility for determining the structure and operations of the cabinet system. One of the prime minister's basic functions is to provide the setting within which collective decision making can take place. This is what enables mininsters to concert their diverse views into a single position before Parliament and the public.

The effectiveness of the Canadian cabinet hinges not only on the leadership of the prime minister but also on the representative character of its membership. In the first place, each member normally carries departmental responsibilities and must reflect those responsibilities in deliberations with his or her colleagues. For example, the minister of finance must necessarily strive for fiscal responsibility, the secretary of state for external affairs must insist that due regard to be paid to Canada's international commitments, the minister of agriculture must press the interests of the Canadian farmer, and so on.

In addition to their departmental responsibilities, most members of the cabinet have political responsibilities, as representatives of different regions of the country. When issues arise respecting a particular region, the minister representing that area will be expected to get involved in those issues regardless of the department under whose purview they come. The minister's job is to keep in touch with his or her region and to communicate its interests to the prime minister and other cabinet colleagues. Outside advisers are not, generally speaking, called on to perform this role.

The principle of regional representation enhances the importance of the cabinet as an institution. While the prime minister may well have political advisers from the party organization and from his own office, the cabinet always enjoys the first claim on his attention. The prime minister is likely to give great weight to the views of cabinet colleagues not only because they share the convictions and experience of working in the same political party, but also because the prime minister depends on them to be effective representatives of regions and of other interest groups, and to keep the government's lines of communication open to those regions and groups.

The Parliamentary Caucus

Nowhere does the prime minister hear more forthright presentation of different views than at the weekly meetings of the parliamentary caucus which are held on Wednesday mornings. These meetings are closed to the press and the rule of caucus secrecy prevails. The exchange of views is frank and often critical. These views are bound to carry weight with the prime minister and with ministers because they are expressed by parliamentary colleagues who are in close touch with the attitudes and opinions held in their respective constituencies.

Attendance at the regular weekly caucus meetings is virtually obligatory for ministers. I cannot recall Prime Minister Mulroney himself having missed more than a handful of such meetings each year since the election of the government in 1984. (At the beginning of the Persian Gulf War, he met caucus three times in a single week.) The agenda of caucus includes reports from the M.P.s who are the regional and provincial chairmen (no minister can play this role), as well as discussions of items high on the current political agenda. What are the deeply felt concerns being voiced in the various regions of the country? What complaints are being heard about government action or inaction? What should be brought to the government's attention that it might not otherwise hear as quickly or as clearly from its professional advisers in Ottawa? The paramount significance of this airing of issues comes from the fact that it is done in front of the prime minister and, of course, almost all ministers. The present prime minister regularly makes a response at the end of the meeting of the Conservative caucus. Not infrequently, he makes commitments on the basis of what he has heard.

This forum is perhaps the private member of Parliament's best opportunity to press his or her advice upon the party leadership. By undertaking a thoroughgoing reform of Parliament, the present government has opened up other avenues for that advice as well. Parliamentary committees now have staff, research help, and, not infrequently, substantial budgets. Before becoming a minister, for example, I chaired the Special Joint Committee of the Senate and the House of Commons on Canada's International Relations which undertook a good deal of research and travel, plugging into the best intellectual views as well as those of ordinary Canadians in order to be able to advise the government on Canadian foreign policy. Almost all the committee's recommendations were accepted by the government.

Parliamentary committees are now in a position to be tough on ministers. This might not appear novel to Americans, but in the context of the Canadian parliamentary system it is striking to see private members differing vehemently with a minister of the same party. Indeed, it is not going too far to say that one of the major innovations of the Mulroney government has been to elevate the status of the private member of Parliament, to make this individual a significant source of policy ideas and interest group representation.

The Prime Minister's Office (PMO)

Just as the White House bureaucracy has expanded greatly in the postwar period, the Prime Minister's Office has grown in response to the increasing size and complexity of modern government and to the need for political direction. The PMO still numbers just over a hundred, which is quite a bit larger than is the case in the United Kingdom or Australia, but a tiny fraction of the size of the Executive Office of the President of the United States. Of these individuals, only a handful are engaged in substantive advisory roles. In addition to advice on political strategy and tactics, the responsibilities of the PMO include the prime minister's agenda and press relations, speech writing, correspondence, travel and Order-in-Council appointments.

The way in which each prime minister organizes his support reflects, of course, his personal style. The major innovation undertaken by the Mulroney government is to give the deputy prime minister responsibility for chairing the "operations committee" of cabinet and managing the government's week-by-week agenda.[2]

The PMO is inevitably drawn into political troubleshooting and only occasionally acts as a mechanism for providing comprehensive policy advice. The office does not try to mirror the main departments or agencies of the government. Nor has Canada followed the United Kingdom's example of developing a policy unit attached to Downing Street. I have observed, however, that the PMO does offer a route for novel ideas (ideas that might not be very enthusiastically taken up within the professional public service) to be brought to the attention of policy makers.

The overriding importance of the representative principle is seen in the constraints that bind the PMO. It cannot monopolize channels of advice to the prime minister because the principle of representation makes the cabinet central in the decision-making process and bolsters the role of the caucus in policy deliberations.

The Privy Council Office (PCO)

In contrast to the United States, Canada separates political support from public service support to the prime minister and ministers. The role of the Privy Council Office is both advisory (facilitating the flow of advice upward) and implementational (ensuring the flow of decisions downward).

The PCO has about a hundred professional staff, middle-level and above, mostly occupied in preparing advice for the cabinet secretary to present to the prime minister. The PCO's job is to advise the prime minister on the structure and functioning of the government apparatus, to manage the process of making appointments to senior positions in the public service, to provide advice and support in setting and managing government priorities, to provide support for cabinet meetings and cabinet committees, and to assist the prime minister with his particular responsibilities in the area of national security.

The PCO is divided into secretariats, each reflecting loosely one of the sectoral divisions of government. It is important to note, however, that the PCO is *not* a miniature replica of the goverment. If it is doing its job properly, it is serving the prime minister and the cabinet, not duplicating what is going on in the departments. The PCO supports, but should not impinge upon, the role of the cabinet and ministers when it comes to giving advice.

The Public Service

Finally, of course, policy advice comes from the departments and agencies that together compose the massive machinery of government and house the greatest quantity of expertise. We are all familiar with the differences in the management of professional bureaucracies in the Canadian and U.S. systems. The United States undertakes a wholesale change of administration with each new president, whereas a change in government in Canada brings a switch of only a relatively small number of people, political advisers to ministers. The career public service remains in place. Deputy ministers, who are the senior advisers of ministers, are chosen by the prime minister, but they usually come from the ranks of the public service and they do not automatically leave office with a change in government. One of the current deputy ministers has served as such for fifteen years, in five different departments for eight different ministers.

It would be inaccurate, however, to think of the prime minister as receiving two separate streams of advice, one from political advisers and the other from career officials. To my surprise, I have found that there is generally a synthesis of political and officials' views at many levels of government. A good deal of policy does, indeed, "bubble up" from the public service, but, in my experience, it has been formulated to accord with an agenda determined by the political leadership.

For example, when the Mulroney government took over in 1984, the public service was ready to meet it with a set of plans and policies that accorded with, and fleshed out, the platform on which the government had been elected. Presumably, it was ready with different plans and policies had either of the opposition parties been successful in the election. In that respect, the public service is, of course, politically sensitive, but it also guarantees continuity and consistency in policy that is not totally political in emphasis.

Canadian and American Systems Compared

We must always be mindful that a political leader should not be dependent on a single source of advice, but should rather be able to test the opinions of senior advisers against a number of differing points of view. Otherwise, he or she could be oblivious to important facts that ought to enter into the calculation of policy outcomes, and would probably not even be equipped to ask the right questions when confronted by the recommendations of close advisers.

When it comes to applying this principle, the Canadian and
United States systems of government stand in striking contrast.
Americans have built up a large apparatus in the Executive Office
of the President with sensors and receptors of advice and ex-
tradepartmental mechanisms, such as the Council of Economic
Advisers. Any inclination that Canadians might have had to go as
far in the same direction has been reined in by the principles of
ministerial responsibility and of cabinet collegiality and solidarity,
by the importance that Canadians place on regional and interest-
group representation, and by the newly enhanced role of elected
members of Parliament. Whereas U.S. presidents have gone outside the formal institutions of government to supplement the advice received from these quarters, Canadian prime ministers and
their cabinet colleagues have not done so to nearly the same extent. How this difference of approach may be reflected in the
decisions that the respective governments take would be a fitting
subject for academic inquiry.

Notes

1. The prime minister also chairs the Cabinet Committee on Security and
Intelligence and may, from time to time, create or chair other committees.
2. As a result of the changes in the cabinet made on April 21, 1991, the leader of
the government in the House of Commons now chairs the Operations Committee.

PART III

Advice to Presidents and Prime Ministers on Domestic and Economic Policy

8

The Council of Economic Advisers

ROGER B. PORTER

The Council of Economic Advisers (CEA) was created by congressional initiative in the Employment Act of 1946. Two years later, Rexford Guy Tugwell, one of the New Deal's most prominent enthusiasts and an experienced Washington observer, concluded that the CEA did not "possess very great survival value" and that it was "vulnerable to its natural enemies and possesses no strength of its own." He viewed it as an "experiment" that would finally be "liquidated."[1]

The "experiment" survived. Of the forty-five entities lodged at one time or another in the Executive Office of the President, the CEA is one of only eleven that remain.[2] Given the nature of its roles and the resources at its disposal, it has shown remarkable resilience and staying power.

In many respects, the Council of Economic Advisers is unique. It has no close parallel among the institutions at the center in governments outside the United States. In other governments, to the extent that they undertake the functions the CEA performs, they are lodged, for the most part, within major departments or ministries. Likewise, there are few analogous entities within the U.S. government. Measured by the nature of its formal mandate, its lack of operational or procedural responsibilities, and the basis for the selection of its staff, there is no entity like the CEA in the foreign policy or domestic policy arenas. This chapter will examine the CEA's origins and what its founders thought they were creating, trace briefly its historical evolution, describe its structure and personnel, examine its roles, and evaluate why it has survived and the contributions it makes.

Origins

The events of the 1930s and 1940s and the administration of Franklin D. Roosevelt transformed the presidency. With the modern presidency came the idea of the chief executive as the element in the U.S. political system responsible for formulating initiatives. It was accompanied by deepened expectations for presidential action in formulating a federal response to problems.

The nation's experience throughout the 1930s with prolonged economic hard times dramatically altered the notion of the government's responsibility for shaping economic outcomes. The growth of federal programs to cushion the effects of economic downturns, to facilitate economic adjustments, and to promote and encourage economic activity all combined to create the perception of a new presidential responsibility. In Clinton Rossiter's words, the president is the "Manager of Prosperity."[3]

Finally, there was the recognition that the modern president, in fulfilling these expectations, needed help in the form of staff. The creation of the Executive Office of the President in 1939, based on the recommendations of the Brownlow Committee, provided a formal structure for placing a wide variety of staffs at the center to support the president.

In 1945, the approaching transition from a wartime to a peacetime economy occasioned much discussion about the federal government's objectives and responsibilities. Fear that a rapid demobilization of the armed forces would produce a return to the high unemployment levels experienced during the 1930s dominated the drive for what became the Employment Act of 1946, enacted in February of that year.

The act not only outlined goals with respect to employment, production, and purchasing power, but also called on the president to transmit to the Congress each year a report on the economic health of the nation and a program for carrying out the policy objectives of the act. Initially little thought was given to the mechanics for producing such a report. The new president, Harry Truman, who had assumed office on April 12, 1945, following Roosevelt's death, supported full-employment legislation.

My objective was to carry out, during the reconversion period, the economic bill of rights which had been formulated by President Roosevelt.

By full employment I meant the opportunity to get a good peacetime job for every worker who was ready, able, and willing to take one. Making jobs, or making people work, was in no sense a part of the full-employment program. I did feel, however, that it was the responsibility of the government to inspire private enterprise with confidence by giving assurances that all the facts about full employment and opportunity would be gathered periodically for the use of all; assurance of stability and consistency in public policy, so that enterprise could plan better by knowing what the government intended to do; assurance that every governmental policy and program would be pointed to promote maximum production and employment in private enterprise; and assurance that priority would be given to doing those things first which stimulated normal employment most.[4]

But Truman did not propose creating any new entity to assist him in carrying out his responsibilities under the act. As the legislation evolved in Congress, several alternatives were considered. One idea was to have the principal economic advice to the president come through a cabinet committee, as provided for in the Employment Stabilization Act of 1931. Also considered was the creation of an economic commission serving both the president and the Congress and consisting of presidential appointees, members of Congress, and representatives of the public. Establishing an independent agency responsible to the Congress rather than the president was suggested, as was placing responsibility in "a quasi-public body similar to the Federal Reserve Board."[5]

In the first drafts of the legislation, the Bureau of the Budget was given responsibility for preparing a National Employment and Production Budget. By the time the legislation was formally introduced, responsibility for preparing the national budget was vested "in the Executive Office of the President under the general direction and supervision of the President, and in consultation with the members of the Cabinet and other heads of departments and establishments."[6]

There was considerable discussion and differences of opinion over whether a new entity should be created to assist the president. Some wanted to establish an "Office of the Director of the National Budget," with its director appointed by the president and subject to congressional confirmation. But Senate sponsors felt the "wisest course" would be "to allow the President to work out this problem in consultation with his Cabinet."[7]

Several factors influenced congressional deliberations on the matter. Among them were the concepts of accountability and visibility. As one advocate of creating a new entity argued, "Planning of this economic program is extremely complicated and cannot possibly be done by the President himself. It should be done by an identifiable group, responsible to the Congress and the people, as well as to the President, and not by an anonymous group of economic planners."[8]

Creation of a Council of Economic Advisers was first proposed by the House Committee on Executive Expenditures as a staff of professional economists in the Executive Office of the President.[9] Its chief proponent, Representative Will Whittington (D-Miss.), pushed for creating

a permanent agency devoted to one thing and one thing alone, and that is to the implementing of the legislation that we pass to prevent unemployment, and that is to the studying of trends, with a staff at their command to . . . give to the President of the United States the best available expert advice of the leading economists, the leading thinkers, the soundest planners of the country, that will enable them to make sound recommendations to the Executive and then to Congress.[10]

The administration was not enamored with the idea of a new, independent, permanent entity. Responding to a request for his comments on an early draft of the House bill, Treasury Secretary Fred Vinson argued:

The members of the Council, while appointed by the President, require Senate confirmation. Their terms of office are fixed at five years, with one member's term expiring each year. This technique is altogether too rigid to succeed. It fails to give the President that degree of flexibility and adaptibility which will be necessary if we are to constantly improve our reporting and forecasting techniques and allow for speed modification if these prove essential. Moreover, you confront a newly elected President, bearing a direct mandate from the electorate, with the virtual necessity of having the National Budget or Economic Report prepared by a body of men not elected by the people and not appointed by him. I am confident that this certainly was not the intention of your subcommittee, but unfortunately it seems to be the case.[11]

Vinson proposed creating a cabinet committee, chaired by the treasury secretary, to perform the functions of the proposed economic council. Elsewhere within the administration, the staff of the Office of War Mobilization and Reconversion outlined plans for "a permanent coordinating and planning staff along the lines of the O.W.M.R. in a reorganized Executive Office of the President."[12]

The concept of a separation of powers helped guide the final product of the legislative deliberations, which included both a new entity to advise the president (the CEA) and a new joint committee on the economic report to perform a similar function for the Congress. The legislation envisioned the council as a collegial body with three members equal with respect to compensation and in authority to hire and direct staff. One was to be designated chairman by the president and another vice-chairman, but the notion of a collegial body dominated. The preference for a collegial structure seems to have been driven both by a desire to encourage the achievement of a balanced view and by the ideal of professional integrity.

Congress also viewed the CEA as "a presidential communications center both within the government and between the government and the private economy."[13] It was expected that the CEA would coordinate with other federal departments and agencies in preparing economic reviews each six months and that its annual report would be reviewed and discussed on an interagency basis. Moreover, it was envisioned that the council would actively participate in the administration's deliberations on economic policy issues.[14]

The congressional architects of the CEA thus determined to do more than merely enshrine the goals of maximum employment, production, and purchasing power as objectives of the federal government. They established within the president's office a three-person council composed of individuals who, as a result of their "training, experience, and attainments" were "exceptionally qualified to analyze and interpret economic developments, to appraise programs and activities of the Government . . . and to formulate and recommend national economic policy."[15]

Edwin Nourse, the CEA's first chairman, and Bertram Gross, a key congressional staffer during the drafting of the Employment Act, observed soon after the CEA was created, "Both the Council and the Joint Committee have to learn how best they can serve and be used by the President and by Congress. They face manifold problems of fitting themselves into a complex governmental structure. Each must look forward to a long period of growth and maturing."[16]

Beginnings

President Truman appointed the three members of the council five months after signing the Employment Act. In his initial appointments he seems to have sought to balance scholarly attainments, governmental experience, and ties to major outside groups. Edwin G. Nourse, age sixty-three, the chairman, was a noted agricultural economist with a Ph.D. in economics from the University of Chicago. At the time of his appointment, he was vice-president of the Brookings Institution. Leon H. Keyserling, the vice-chairman, was twenty-five years younger than Nourse. He had not completed his graduate studies in economics but had opted for a career in government with the coming of Franklin Roosevelt's administration, serving as a legislative assistant to Senator Robert Wagner and in a variety of positions with the U.S. Housing Authority and the National Housing Agency. John D. Clark, a year younger than Nourse, held a Ph.D. in economics from Johns Hopkins, had been a successful oil industry executive, and then had pursued an academic career as dean of the University of Nebraska School of Business.

During its first year of operation, the council struggled to attract a high-quality staff as the nation adjusted to peace and university enrollments swelled. (Many universities were reluctant to grant leave to their best faculty at this time.) The professional staff were selected on the basis of their general competence in economics and their capacity to grapple with public policy problems. Most came from other positions within the federal government or had prior government service.[17]

Some substantive staff committees were formed to address issues that cut across individual subject areas, but for the most part the CEA's internal organization followed a "somewhat rambling and highly flexible administrative pattern."[18] President Truman initiated the practice of having the council appear each quarter at a cabinet meeting to present for discussion a survey of economic developments and problems.

What dominated the early days of the CEA, however, was the combination of its collegial structure and the range of views represented by its members. Relations among the three original members of the council were uneasy at best. A norm of public agreement was established, but developing this agreement was, as two staff members later wrote, "a tortuous process."[19] Deadlines were difficult to meet, and ultimately the effort to produce unanimous statements yielded to a pattern of issuing separate statements by individual members on various issues. Some issues were avoided, and the entire process was characterized by cautiousness. Within a matter of months, it was apparent to some observers that a more hierarchical structure was needed if the council was to serve the president adequately.[20]

Some congressional sponsors of the legislation publicly expressed concern about what they considered the "aloofness" of the council in its relationship with Congress in general and the Joint Committee on the Economic Report in particular.[21]

While tensions within the council were partly caused by specific policies, they focused on the role the council was to play and the way it would conduct its affairs.

Edwin Nourse, the chairman, adopted a distinctly scholarly approach. His vision of the council was that it should exhibit "the highest qualities of technical competence, mature wisdom, practical realism, and intellectual objectivity that can be found in the country." Leon Keyserling, whose formative experiences were in the rough-and-tumble of the New Deal, sought a much more politically active role for the council. He envisioned a council that was more visible, more publicly engaged, and more of an advocate both inside and outside the administration.

Nourse held the view that the council should confine itself to dispensing objective, detached advice. Engaging in advocacy once administration policy had been determined could only endanger its primary mission, which was apart from the struggles of the political process. He explained his interpretation of the council's mandate:

The first function of the Council will be to piece together a complete and consistent picture of the economic state of the nation. . . .

The second function . . . is to interpret all available literal facts into the soundest possible diagnosis as to the state of the nation's economic health and the causes which explain any evidence of current ill health which threaten to produce unhealthy conditions in the future. . . .

The Council of Economic Advisers is . . . a scientific agency. . . . There is no occasion for the Council to become involved in the advocacy of particular measures or in the rival beliefs and struggles of the different economic and political interest groups.[22]

Nourse steadfastly held to a purist view of the role of the CEA as a dispassionate dispenser of advice. The issue that occasioned the most public display of differences was whether CEA members should give congressional testimony. Nourse felt that council members would face congressional efforts to drive a wedge between the president and his advisers, would of necessity be cast in the role of advocates of the president's policies, and thus would undermine the notion of the professional integrity of the council's advice. Truman sought to resolve the dispute within his council by indicating that members were permitted to testify if they wished but were not required to do so.

By the fall of 1949 continuing tensions within the council led to Nourse's resignation on November 1. Leon Keyserling served as acting chairman for over six months before President Truman designated him its chairman on May 10, 1950. The ascendancy of Keyserling produced a more visible and activist council that sought "objectivity within subjectivity." Truman, who seems never to have been very enamored of the idea of the CEA in the first place, was not impressed and appears to have made little use of the Council.[23]

Congressional support also waned, and the CEA's modest appropriation was reduced twice. With limited presidential or congressional enthusiasm for the experiment, the first Hoover Commission recommended abolishing the council and replacing it with an Office of the Economic Adviser.[24]

By the end of the Truman administration, there was serious question as to whether the CEA would be continued. Congressional cuts in the agency's budget were coupled with permission to spend all the funds during the first nine months of the fiscal year. By March 1, 1953, less than six weeks after Dwight Eisenhower took office, the CEA's appropriation was depleted and most of the staff, many of whom had been with the CEA since its creation, dispersed. Eisenhower requested a three-month supplemental to continue funding for the remainder of the fiscal year, but congressional action provided funds only for a single economic adviser.[25]

Eisenhower, on the advice of Gabriel Hauge, his administrative assistant for domestic and economic affairs, invited Arthur Burns to serve as his economic adviser and to make recommendations on the fate of the council. Burns recalls, "Eisenhower was by no means certain that he wanted a CEA. In fact, he was inclined not to continue it. . . . He suggested that he would prefer to have me alone as his economic adviser, but that he also wanted my best thoughts on the subject."[26]

Burns consulted widely on Capitol Hill and across the administration before recommending to Eisenhower that a reorganized CEA be continued. Reorganization Plan No. 9 of 1953, which Eisenhower approved and submitted to the Congress, reconstituted the council establishing the chairman as preeminent.[27] Responsibility for employing staff, specialists, and consultants was transferred from the council to the chairman, as was the formal function of reporting to the president on the council's views and activities.[28]

Personnel and Relations with Other Government Officials

The Council

The reconstituted three-member council with the chairman preeminent has remained unchanged for three and a half decades. While the Employment Act simply states that each member is to be a person with "training, experience, and attainments," the pattern has been to appoint academically trained economists.[29] Most of them have held appointments at prestigious universities or research institutes.

Fourteen individuals have served as chairman, an average tenure of three years. Thirty-seven individuals have served as one of the two members not designated as chairman with an average tenure of just over two and a quarter years. Drawing the bulk of its professional staff also from academia has meant that the CEA has little institutional memory. What institutional memory exists has often been provided by the chairmen, who have tended to combine professional reputation and government experience. Nine of the fourteen chairmen had previously held senior government positions before being made chairman. Leon Keyserling, Raymond Saulnier, Gardner Ackley, Arthur Okun, Paul McCracken, and Herbert Stein had all served as council members before becoming chairman. Charles Schultze and Murray Weidenbaum had previously served as council staff members and had held significant posts elsewhere in the executive branch: as director of the Bureau of the Budget and assistant secretary of the treasury for economic policy, respectively. Beryl Sprinkel had served as under secretary of the treasury for monetary affairs.[30]

Newly elected presidents, more often than not, have appointed as the CEA chairman an individual whom they have not known well before their election.[31] Once in office, when the chairmanship has become vacant, their tendency has been to designate one of the existing members or an individual serving elsewhere in the executive branch.[32] Professional reputation and stature have weighed more heavily than political connections or personal relationships in the appointment of CEA chairmen. This pattern has served to enhance the CEA's professional reputation while representing a challenge for CEA chairmen seeking to establish themselves within the administration's economic policy community.

Most members are selected on the recommendation of the chairman with a relatively routine clearance by the White House personnel office. Paul McCracken described his experience in the appointment of the first Nixon council:

As we walked to the door to go down to the press conference [announcing McCracken's nomination], he [Nixon] said, "Now, let's see, there have to be two other members of the Council. Do you have any ideas about this?" I said at that time, "Well, the first person I would like to talk to about this would be Herb Stein." As I recall, he said, "I don't think I know him personally, but I know who he is." He had no problem with either Herb or Houthakker. . . . These names had to be cleared, but the selection was mine.[33]

Other presidents have similarly granted wide leeway to the chairman in the selection of the other two members. This has helped prevent a repetition of the experience of the first Truman council. As McCracken explains:

This is not just to make sure that life is nice, but because these people do have to work as a team. . . . Any chairman who's worth his salt is not going to try to throw his weight around or treat the other two people as second-class citizens. On the other hand, you don't want a debating seminar taking votes two to one in favor of a tax cut.[34]

In almost all councils, there is a good deal of collaboration and joint work on issues. Generally, one of the members is known as the "macro" member and takes the lead in the forecasting exercises and on fiscal and monetary policy issues. The other member generally focuses much of his time and attention on a broad array of microeconomic and regulatory issues. Despite this typical division of labor, in most councils the chairman and the members spend a good deal of time working closely with one another.

The Staff

What is most remarkable about the CEA staff over the last forty-two years is its constant size. Despite assertions that the staffs serving the president have grown ever larger in the post–World War II period, the size of the CEA staff was slightly smaller in 1988 than when founded in 1946.[35] By Washington standards, it is extremely modest, rarely exceeding eighteen to twenty professional economists, including the members for a total staff of between thirty-five and forty, including secretaries and the statistical unit.

The Eisenhower administration brought a shift in the composition of the staff. Thereafter, less reliance was placed on previous government experience and more professional staff came directly from the groves of academe. A Ph.D. in economics for the senior staff was only the first threshold that needed to be cleared.

The major criterion used in selecting staff is clear evidence of professional competence. The recruitment process begins in late winter and early spring and is conducted entirely within the confines of the council. No clearance through the White House personnel office is required. Prospective staff are not asked about their political affiliations. As one former chairman put it:

The work of the CEA is carried on in an atmosphere of professionalism and, in large measure, nonpartisanship. As is customary with a change in administration, I inherited the staff recruited by my Democratic predecessor. Except for career statisticians and secretaries, the staff traditionally consists of non-career appointees, most of whom are on leave from their respective universities and research institutes. I found each one of them a loyal and dedicated professional economist. In fact, I asked several of them to stay on beyond their initial appointments.[36]

The senior economists are typically assistant or associate professors. Occasionally, full professors are selected. Most are between thirty and forty-five years of age, with the majority in their mid-thirties. Typically, the junior staff economists have all the work completed for their doctorate degree except the thesis. They are taking a year off to find out for sure what they are interested in, perhaps to pick up some ideas for a thesis topic, and to get some hands-on experience at policy making at a young age.

Staff turnover at the CEA is typically very high. Most staffers stay for only a year; some remain for two years. One reason for this high rate of turnover is that it is difficult to attract many of the finest academic economists for longer than a year. As one former staffer commented, "If you want to attract the people you really want to get, you have got to live with having them for one year."[37]

Most councils in recent years have had senior staff with expertise in macroeconomics, money, and finance; international macroeconomics and trade; public finance and taxation; energy, transportation, environmental protection, and regulation; agriculture; labor; and health, education, and welfare.

Both the size of the staff and the nature of its work contribute to the informality of the council's internal working relationships. There are few communications problems at the council. As one former staffer put it, "People are close and they are bonded by a certain view of the world. We have lunch together every day and talk. We're quite close. Staff meetings don't perform the general function they do in other organizations, which is to make sure people just don't go off on their separate ways. That was no problem when I worked there."[38]

The Executive Branch Economic Policy Community

In the late Eisenhower years an informal relationship between the chairman of the CEA, the secretary of the treasury, and the Budget Bureau director emerged for discussions with the president, or among themselves, on major economic policy issues. Sometimes they would be joined by the chairman of the Board of Governors of the Federal Reserve System. This relationship became more regular during the Kennedy and Johnson administrations and acquired the name of the Troika, or Quadriad when the Federal Reserve was included.[39]

For macroeconomic forecasting purposes, the remnants of the Troika arrangements remain intact. But for the broad range of economic policy issues, the Troika is now usually supplanted with some formal or informal grouping—it varies from one administration to another and often within administrations as personnel change—that is somewhat larger.

An important trend that has made the economic policy development processes within the executive branch potentially more porous is the growth of policy planning and analysis units in executive departments and agencies. Many of these are heavily laden with economists. A parallel development has been the increased interrelationships between the domestic and international economies; on many issues, it is impossible to consider the two separately.

These trends have resulted in more departments and agencies pressing to get involved in deliberations within the administration on economic policy issues. This mean both a larger and a smaller role for the CEA staff.

To understand this paradox, reflect on the view of the world and the responsibilities of White House staffers who organize the economic advice given to the president. They want the best information and analysis available. They often face extremely short deadlines. They must do a good deal of sifting and sorting, determining what is going to the president and what is not. They need quick evaluations of proposals popping up inside and outside the administration. They prefer to keep administration members happy, other things equal, by dispensing due process—making sure that people feel involved and included.

In one respect this means a smaller, less exclusive role for the CEA staff. Their monopoly or near monopoly on economic advice is gone and will never return. One senior economic official who returned to government in the late 1970s after more than a decade, described the change that had occurred:

In the 1960s there were a lot of people who would have liked to get into the game but just did not have the staff. They were unsupported and when you weren't supported, you couldn't carry the issue. Nobody had a group of economists to evaluate all these issues for them. CEA had a monopoly on it along with a few people at the Treasury. What has changed today is that every agency has an economic policy and planning group and it is not easy to tear their arguments apart. CEA cannot blow people out of the water with the depth of its analysis like it could in the 1960s. Few people understood what the term "multipler" meant in the 1960s much less were able to argue with CEA's arguments about a tax policy to stimulate the economy. When CEA said that the effect of a specific tax action on investment was such-and-such there wasn't any other agency doing its own empirical work to argue with it. But now, Treasury may say, "No, it's Y." And Labor, "It's Z."[40]

On the other hand, the greater concentration of decision making at the center, the larger the number of interagency issues requiring resolution, the greater the need for the kind of help and expertise that the CEA is well positioned to provide. Throughout these changes, the CEA has retained its essential characteristics—small, professional, nonpartisan, noncareer, and advisory.

Roles and Functions

The CEA was created to provide advice. Throughout its history the council has consistently avoided expanding its mission by taking on line responsibilities, such as managing wage and price controls, reviewing inflation impact statements, evaluating proposed regulations, or supervising federal statistical agencies. Perhaps even more significantly, the CEA has resisted procedural responsibilities such as coordinating the development of economic policy within the executive branch. To be sure, there have been some forays into this arena—such as chairing the Advisory Board on Economic Growth and Stability (ABEGS) during the Eisenhower administration. But virtually all of the formal and informal efforts to systematically coordinate economic policy advice to the president, foreign and domestic, have been managed by White House or Department of the Treasury staff.[41] By confining itself to advice, the council has focused its efforts in three major endeavors.

Macroeconomic Forecasting

Since its inception, the president and administration economic policy officials have relied heavily on the CEA for macroeconomic assessments and for the economic assumptions used in key administration documents. The formal development of the economic assumptions used in the budget has generally come through a three-tiered process involving the Troika agencies—CEA, the Treasury, and the Office of Management and Budget.[42] The lead in forecasting has generally been taken by the CEA, and in some administrations the CEA has essentially assumed sole responsibility.[43] The tremendous impact of economic assumptions on both the revenue and spending aggregates in the budget have often made this exercise a highly charged and fiercely contested event. Typically, the CEA has pushed for a set of assumptions that are within the band of most well regarded private forecasts.

Advocate for Efficiency

One of the central contributions of the CEA flows from its independence of any constituency other than the economics profession. It possesses a view different from any other institutional actor. In this respect, Charles Schultze has argued, the council serves as an advocate for efficiency. "The CEA ought to be there literally as a professional, pushing efficiency as opposed to the politically wise decision."[44] As an advocate for efficiency, the CEA tends to represent the views of the economics profession. Schultze observes,

On most, although not all microeconomic issues that typically are the bread and butter of daily White House decisions, the economics profession does have a relatively wide consensus. Under both Republican and Democratic Presidents, the CEA tends to take roughly similar stances on such issues; . . . the reason for this is that most microeconomic issues are seen as long term structural problems and there is wide professional agreement that in the long run, and under most circumstances, markets and the price system do a better job of allocating resources than other alternatives. The Democrats will have to lean against colleagues who see externalities lurking in every corner and the Republicans against colleagues who don't recognize any. But in general they all carry on the same fights against secretaries of Labor and Commerce on trade matters, against secretaries of Agriculture on farm subsidies, and often against administrators of EPA and OSHA on excessively command-and-control approaches to environmental and safety matters.[45]

As Schultze emphasizes, "There are precious few advocates of efficiency itself."

Franklyn Raines, who served in senior positions on both the Domestic Policy Staff and at the Office of Management and Budget during the Carter administration, described the role of the CEA staff as reality testing. CEA staff members often serve in internal policy discussion as "expert witnesses." They are looked to, not for their political acumen but as a reservoir of expertise, some of it general in nature, some of it very technical.[46] The CEA members and senior staff often spend a good deal of time with White House and OMB staff discussing, debating, weighing, and challenging various proposals and alternatives.

Economics Educator

In addition to its crucial forecasting role and its advocacy for efficiency on a wide range of day-to-day issues that flow through the presidential policy development process, the CEA also serves as an educator. Its principal student is the president. There are no formal classes or mandatory subjects, but there are innumerable opportunities to explain and articulate economic principles, to relate from the vantage point of economics why something has happened or is likely to happen. Senior administration officials are similarly often eager for explanations and ready to be educated.

The CEA provides the president with a brief memorandum informing him the night before of the following day's statistical releases and explaining for him what is behind the numbers and what may be some of their implications. Most CEA chairmen have also established a pattern of regular briefings with the president, either one-on-one or involving a small group of the administration's senior economic officials, to review economic developments outside of the context of making a decision on a specific issue.

The Annual Report

The council's principal public product is its annual report. The report consists of chapters discussing economic trends and macroeconomic policy in general, followed by more specialized chapters on particular topics. The topical chapters generally concern issues of current interest and are selected by the council members in an iterative process from a lengthy original list. These chapters often cover topics that have not been treated in a number of years and that will be relevant to policy decisions to be made in the near future.

In an effort to enhance relationships with department and agency heads, Beryl Sprinkel established the practice of visiting each cabinet member about the annual report early in the process, once the chapter topics had been determined and the basic themes were emerging. He explained:

I go around with one of the members and a senior staff person and talk to each cabinet member that I think has either a direct or an important indirect interest in that year's report. I tell them what we're going to do and why we are going to do it. I solicit their advice, their ideas, find out who the contact person should be, and we discuss it in great detail.

The secretary of state is interested in all of the chapters because he happens to be an economist and he's had broad experience. The secretary of the treasury has a broad interest and so we will go through all of the chapters with him.

Later we send them text and solicit their comments. This has avoided all kinds of potential problems. They don't get any surprises. They know what's coming. They've agreed to what is coming. They have been a part of the process.[47]

While the economic report is an administration document, its drafting is dominated by the CEA. After the initial drafting is done by the council, it is sent to departments and agencies for comments; they are asked to respond within a relatively short time. Its most important audience, according to some council members and staff, are officials within the administration.

Murray Weidenbaum has observed that the annual report provides an opportunity to delicately "raise new issues and to move policy along." He gives the following example: "It was widely known in Washington that I had advocated making sizeable reductions in the rapidly expanding military budget. This was a subject area in which I had done research for over two decades. The 1982 Economic Report was, I believe, the first one that raised serious questions about the economic feasibility of the defense program of the Administration then in office."[48]

Public Spokesman

The Truman CEA was riven over the issue of how public a profile the council should take. The particular issue over public testimony by the CEA chairman has now been settled decisively in favor of giving testimony. In doing so, he is viewed as an administration spokesman in the same sense that other presidential appointees are.

The choices made by the CEA chairman and members about the frequency of their public appearances and the nature of their public remarks can influence not only public discussion and debate on economic issues, but also their relationships with other economic officials within the administration and with the president.

Weidenbaum argues that the norm for the CEA members and chairman is to keep a low public profile: "The public role of the Council of Economic Advisers is normally the proverbial tip of the iceberg. Usually, the CEA chairman is expected to develop public understanding of and thereby enhance the popular support for the President's economic program. Yet some of the most successful chairmen kept the lowest profiles, avoiding speechifying and press conferences."[49]

This brief review by no means exhausts the role and activities undertaken by the CEA in the over four decades of its existence. What is striking is how much of what the CEA does that makes a difference depends on the skills, the credibility, and the persistence of those who fill its positions.

Conclusions

The Council of Economic Advisers, created by congressional initiative and enjoying at first only limited executive-branch enthusiasm for the "experiment," has survived for over forty years amid a remarkable turnover of offices and councils in the Executive Office of the President. It has little institutional memory to offer new administrations and no identifiable constituency base other than the economics profession. What accounts for its longevity? How substantial is its contribution?

The CEA has survived in part by having a clearly defined mission and by not allowing its reach to exceed its grasp. It fulfills an important role that is not duplicated elsewhere, and it does not attempt to do more than it is capable of doing. It has succeeded in part by not accepting added responsibilities that are inconsistent with its principal capabilities. It has *not* assumed line-operating responsibilities, even though such opportunities have arisen and many have urged it to accept them. It has *not* become a bureaucratic threat to any of the other major players in the economic policy community. It has *not* expanded its staff, nor retreated into long-term studies or detailed reports.

It has been filled with competent, energetic, and able economists able to turn around high-quality, understandable analysis quickly. This skill is at a premium in the environment in which it operates. Rather than retiring into an ivory tower, the CEA has spent the overwhelming bulk of its time on day-to-day economic decisions that require presidential attention.

Likewise, it has not sought or accepted responsibility for managing processes, for coordinating the stream of economic advice to the president. There is nothing to suggest that professional economists have a comparative advantage as process managers or policy coordinators. Other Executive Office entities that have accepted responsibility for both coordinating policy and providing policy advice or advocacy have shown how difficult it is to marry these twin roles. Much of the prestige that the CEA enjoys flows in part from the fact that it is not confused about its role.

In an important sense, the greatest responsibility of the Council of Economic Advisers is to exhibit a particular type of professionalism and a particular type of detachment. Such detachment is possible only because it does not have either operating or coordinating responsibilities. Charles Schultze puts it well:

The President should expect most of his advisers, in providing him with advice, to balance substantive concerns about a particular issue with a consideration of political opportunity costs.

The CEA, on the other hand, while not quite unique in government is different. The CEA Chairman sits at the Cabinet-level policymaking committees, and has (or should have) frequent direct access to the President. But its whole "raison d'être" is to provide advice *as economic professionals* to the President. It is the nearest equivalent to the Joint Chiefs of Staff. The CEA's advice has less political weight but its Chairman has more routine access to the President. In theory the President's Science Advisor has an analogous position, but with far smaller scope and usually with less access and power. Given its professional role, the Chairman or members of the CEA, unlike the economist turned Secretary of the Treasury or Secretary of Commerce, should not ordinarily be expected to weigh their substantive economic findings against political considerations large and small and arrive at a balanced judgment in giving their economic advice to the President. Their principal task ought to be the application of professional economic reasoning to the task at hand, very importantly including the limitations and uncertainties of existing knowledge about the connections between policy action and economic consequences.[50]

The CEA is clearly part of an administration. It is detached but not dispassionate. Those who serve at the CEA are as interested as other officials in the success of the president and his policies. What the CEA can provide is a type of professional advice that presidents need even when for good reasons they do not heed it.

The CEA has kept itself renewed with a steady infusion of new talent. Some have suggested that greater institutional memory is what is needed in the Executive Office of the President and that the CEA should rely less on itinerant academics for its professional staff. The CEA has opted instead to maintain its links with the academic world.

The United States has long been one of the most dynamic countries with respect to the quantity and quality of its research institutions and research universities. A great challenge is to ensure that the ideas generated by scholars and academics are efficiently transmitted to policy makers. James Sundquist has suggested the creation of a sequence or series of links between academic researchers, academic intermediaries, research brokers, and policy makers. Crucial in this sequence is the link between academic intermediaries and research brokers. The latter are individuals within the government who are familiar with the best work being done in university and research institutions and who have the capacity to translate that work so as to make it accessible to policy makers. In this sense, the kind of academics that comprise the CEA and its staff represent a reservoir of expertise that helps connect the worlds of scholarship and government. In this respect the CEA is unique among U.S. government institutions. There is no parallel body in the foreign policy and domestic policy arenas.

Given that it has only advice to offer—no line authority or responsibilities, no process that it controls—the CEA is incredibly dependent on its relationships with the president and with those around him. It depends on its credibility and the quality of its analysis.

The CEA is an educator, taking the world of economics and economic analysis and making it accessible to those responsible for making policy decisions. Presidents normally have not known their CEA chairmen well before they were selected. But this has not prevented them from often developing extremely close working relationships with them.

The CEA has had its ups and downs—its times of influence and periods when its advice was ignored or perhaps only rarely even sought. Yet it has succeeded in providing enough good analysis and offering enough good advice that it is unlikely any administration in the foreseeable future would seek to abolish it. It has carved out this niche by keeping its mission limited and its resources focused. It has flourished when its members, and particularly its chairman, have had a close working relationship with the president and with those around him.

History suggests that the greatest danger the CEA faces is not that it will be viewed as an apologist for the president and his policies, but that it will so distance itself from the administration of which it is a part that it will be seen as of little use to its principal client. Professional integrity is important to maintain. So is loyalty to the boss.

Notes

1. R. G. Tugwell, "The Utility of the Future in the Present," *Public Aministration Review* 8 (Winter 1948), 57–59.
2. Of the eleven existing entities within the Executive Office of the President,

only the White House Office and the Office of Management and Budget (formerly the Bureau of the Budget) have greater longevity than the CEA.

3. Clinton Rossiter, *The American Presidency* (New York: New American Library, 1960), pp. 34–36. See also William E. Leuchtenburg, "Franklin D. Roosevelt: The First Modern President," in *Leadership in the Modern Presidency,* ed. Fred I. Greenstein (Cambridge, Mass.: Harvard University Press, 1988), pp. 7–40.

4. Harry S. Truman, *Year of Decisions* (Garden City, N.Y.: Doubleday, 1955), p. 491.

5. Edwin G. Nourse and Bertram M. Gross, "The Role of the Council of Economic Advisers," *American Political Science Review* 42 (April 1948), 287–88.

6. S. 380, 79th Cong., 1st sess., sec. 4(2) (January 22, 1945), cited in Stephen A. Bailey, *Congress Makes a Law* (New York: Columbia University Press, 1950), pp. 167–68.

7. U.S. Senate, "Assuring Full Employment in a Free Competitive Economy," *Report from the Committee on Banking and Currency,* S. Rpt. 583, 79th Cong., 1st sess., September 22, 1945, p. 36, cited in Bailey, *Congress Makes a Law,* p. 168.

8. U.S. Senate, "Assuring Full Employment in a Free Competitive Economy," *Minority Views from the Committee on Banking and Currency,* S. Rpt. 583, p. 2, 79th Cong., 1st sess., September 24, 1945, p. 2, cited in Bailey, *Congress Makes a Law,* p. 168.

9. Nourse and Gross, "The Role of the Council of Economic Advisers," p. 285.

10. Bailey, *Congress Makes a Law,* p. 169.

11. Ibid., p. 170.

12. Ibid., pp. 169–70.

13. Bertam M. Gross and John P. Lewis, "The President's Economic Staff During the Truman Administration," *American Political Science Review* 48 (March 1954), 121. Sec. 4(e) (1) of the act provides that the council "may constitute such advisory committees and may consult with such representatives of industry, agriculture, labor, consumers, State and local governments, and other groups as it deems advisable."

14. As one of the architects of the legislation later reflected: "It was precisely the Council's developing status as a key part of the formal machinery for formulating current programs that most clearly distinguished it, as a planning instrument, from the National Resources Planning Board" (Gross and Lewis, "The President's Economic Staff," pp. 122–23). For an assessment of the role played by the National Resources Planning Board, see John D. Millett, *The Process and Organization of Government Planning* (New York, 1947).

15. Employment Act of 1946, Sec. 4(a).

16. Nourse and Gross, "The Role of the Council of Economic Advisers," p. 286.

17. David Naveh, "The Political Role of Academic Advisers: The Case of the U.S. President's Council of Economic Advisers, 1946–1976," *Presidential Studies Quarterly* 11 (Fall 1981), 496.

18. Gross and Lewis, "The President's Economic Staff," p. 128. One of the characteristics of the Truman CEA was its network of advisory committees. A business advisory committee, an agriculture advisory committee, a consumer advisory committee, and advisory committees for the American Federation of Labor, the Congress of Industrial Organizations, and the Railway Labor Executives Association held meetings roughly each quarter. The sessions were informal and off-the-record and centered around current problems, recent reports, and assessments of the economy. There is little evidence that much in the way of substantive contributions to the formation of policy came from these sessions. The sessions

did, however, represent an interest and willingness on the part of the Council to consult with representatives of a variety of outside groups. See Nourse and Gross, "The Role of the Council of Economic Advisers," p. 292; Gross and Lewis, "The President's Economic Staff," p. 123.

19. Gross and Lewis, "The President's Economic Staff," p. 126.

20. Millett, *Process*, pp. 167–68.

21. See Ralph E. Flanders, "Administering the Employment Act—the First Year," *Public Administration Review* 7 (1947), 221–27.

22. Edwin G. Nourse, *Economics in the Public Service* (New York: Harcourt Brace, 1953), p. 107.

23. The CEA rates only passing mention in one of Harry Truman's two-volume memoirs (Harry S. Truman, *Year of Decisions* [Garden City, N.Y.: Doubleday, 1955], pp. 493–94). The relatively modest role of the council during its early years is reflected in the sparse references to its activities found in the major works on the Truman years. See Merle Miller, *Plain Speaking: An Oral Biography of Harry S. Truman* (Berkeley, Calif.: Berkeley Publishing Corporation, 1973); Barton J. Bernstein and Allen J. Matusow, eds., *The Truman Administration: A Documentary History* (New York: Harper and Row, 1966); Bert Cochran, *Harry Truman and the Crisis Presidency* (New York: Funk and Wagnalls, 1973), pp. 193, 216; Cabell Phillips, *The Truman Presidency: The History of a Triumphant Succession* (London: Macmillan, 1966); Margaret Truman, *Harry S. Truman* (New York: William Morrow and Co., 1973), pp. 308, 449, 451; Robert J. Donovan, *Conflict and Crisis: The Presidency of Harry S. Truman, 1945–1948* (New York: W.W. Norton, 1977), pp. 170, 339–41.

24. Commission on Organization of the Executive Branch, *General Management of the Executive Branch* (Washington, D.C.: GPO, 1949), pp. 16–17.

25. See Margaret Jane Wyszomirski, "The De-Institutionalization of Presidential Staff Agencies," *Public Administration Review* 42 (September/October 1982), 450; Edward S. Flash, Jr., *Economic Advice and Presidential Leadership* (New York: Columbia University Press, 1965).

26. Erwin C. Hargrove and Samuel A. Morley, eds., *The President and the Council of Economic Advisers* (Boulder, Colo.: Westview Press, 1984), p. 95.

27. Reorganization Plan No. 9 of 1953 (67 Stat. 644). See also "Special Message to the Congress Trasmitting Reorganization Plan 9 of 1953 Concerning the Council of Economic Advisers," June 1, 1953, *Public Papers of the Presidents: Dwight D. Eisenhower, 1953* (Washington, D.C.: GPO, 1960), pp. 355–59. The chairman of the Council of Economic Advisers is an Executive Level II official. The other two members of the council are Executive Level IV officials.

28. The position of vice-chairman of the council was abolished.

29. All forty-five individuals who have served as members of the council have had graduate training in economics. All but four have held Ph.D.s in economics at the time of their appointment. Thirty-nine of the forty-five had held professorships at a wide variety of universities.

30. Edwin Nourse was the first chairman and Arthur Burns the first Republican appointee. Only Walter Heller, Alan Greenspan, Martin Feldstein, and Beryl Sprinkel were appointed chairmen without previous council service after it had become an established entity.

31. See Hargrove and Morley, *The President and the Council*, pp. 95, 319–20, 413.

32. Of CEA chairmen appointed in the midst of a presidential term, Keyserling, Saulnier, Ackley, Okun, and Stein were serving as CEA members and Sprinkel as

undersecretary of the treasury for monetary affairs. The exceptions to this pattern have been Alan Greenspan (first approached about the position by the Nixon White House but formally appointed by Gerald Ford) and Martin Feldstein.

33. Paul W. McCracken, interview in Hargrove and Morley, *The President and the Council,* p. 320.

34. Ibid.

35. In Agusut 1988, the CEA staff totaled thirty-seven people, including three members, eleven senior staff economists, and six junior staff economists.

36. Murray L. Weidenbaum, "The Role of the Council of Economic Advisers: Theory and Reality," presented at the annual meeting of the Southern Economic Association, Dallas, November 25, 1985, p. 7.

37. Interview with Kathleen Utgoff, March 23, 1988.

38. Ibid.

39. See Hargrove and Morley, *The President and the Council,* p. 190.

40. Quoted in Roger B. Porter, "Organizing Economic Advice to the President: A Modest Proposal," *American Economic Review* 72 (1982), 357.

41. See Roger B. Porter, "Economic Advice to the President: From Eisenhower to Reagan," *Political Science Quarterly* 98 (Fall 1983), 403–26.

42. An excellent description is found in Arthur M. Okun, "The Formulation of National Economic Policy," *Perspectives in Defense Management* 2 (December 1968), 9–12.

43. The latter was true during the Carter administration. Interview with Charles L. Schultze, July 26, 1988.

44. Ibid.

45. Charles L. Schultze, "Some Excerpts from a Political Handbook for Economic Policy Advisors," May 23, 1988, manuscript in possession of the author.

46. Interview with Franklyn Raines, June 29, 1988.

47. Interview with Beryl W. Sprinkel, April 13, 1988.

48. Weidenbaum, "The Role of the Council of Economic Advisers," p. 7.

49. Ibid., pp. 2–3.

50. Schultze, "Some Excerpts," pp. 6–7.

9

OMB: Professionalism, Politicization, and the Presidency

JAMES P. PFIFFNER

Though the Bureau of the Budget was created by the Budget and Accounting Act of 1921, BOB really came into its own as a general staff arm of the presidency when it was transferred from the Treasury Department to the newly created Executive Office of the President in 1939. The move was made in response to the Brownlow Committee's judgment that "the president needs help," and in accordance with its operating assumption that "Strong Executive Leadership is essential to democratic government today."[1]

Under the leadership of Harold Smith, appointed in 1939, the Budget Bureau grew in size, stature, and power. "Smith saw himself as the prospective "chief" of a general-utility "institutional" staff, mainly a career group, quite distinct from personal aides, but tackling in depth, at another level, a range of concerns as wide as theirs."[2] In 1939 the Budget Bureau had forty-five employees; by 1945 it had about 600, roughly its present size.

The Bureau of the Budget, renamed the Office of Management and Budget in 1970, has grown to be the cornerstone of the Executive Office of the President. It is the EOP's most institutionalized component, but in recent years critics have charged that it has become too politically responsive to the president.

This chapter will examine the development of BOB/OMB with respect to professionalism, including its budget-making power, central legislative clearance, and its management role. Next examined will be *politicization,* a term that has been used by critics of the development to denote an increasing number of political appointees and the responsiveness of the agency to the personal political interests of the president rather than to institutional interests of the presidency. Finally, OMB's development will be fit into the broader contours of the presidency in the past five decades.

Professionalism

From the beginning, BOB's role has been to offer nonpartisan service to the president in the pursuit of economy and efficiency. According to its first director, Charles Dawes (who turned down an offer to be secretary of the treasury in order to be budget director):

The Budget Bureau has no control of policy and is concerned simply with economy and efficiency in the routine business of government. The Bureau of the Budget is simply a business organization whose activities are devoted constantly to the consideration of how money appropriated by Congress can be made to go as far as possible toward the accomplishment of the objects of legislation.[3]

The term *professionalism* includes expertise, continuity, and responsiveness to the president. One of Dawes's "principles" was: "The Budget bureau must be impartial, impersonal and nonpolitical."[4]

The Budget Bureau's workhorses have been the budget examiners, the people with the green eyeshades, the bean counters, who scrutinize carefully all agency expenditures. They know where the bodies are buried, which skeletons are in which closets, and where the soft spots are in each agency's budget. The bureau's role of responsiveness to the president was expressed by a career staffer in the 1980s:

We always talk in this institution first about accountability to the president. We work for him. We are all fed with stories about the beginning of this institution when the first director asserted that if the president said you have to shovel garbage on the front steps of the White House you do it; . . . what we're trying to do is give the president the best information possible . . . to keep the president out of trouble. We are supposed to be a career service which provides . . . a continuity of government.[5]

Traditionally, BOB had also played an important role in transitions from one president to another. Career staffers used to follow campaign promises and analyze the cost implications and present the analyses to the winning candidate after the election. There is an old OMB story that if Martians invaded the earth, everybody would leave Washington except the OMB career staff who would stay to prepare for an orderly transition.[6]

OMB staffers' self-image has remained remarkably consistent over the years. Nevertheless, there has been a constant stream of criticism that OMB has been too responsive to individual presidents and their personal political agendas and in the process has become less able to fulfil its traditional role of service to the institutional presidency.

Budget Making

The main source of the Budget Bureau's power has always been its control over the budget of the executive branch. With respect to agencies, it has had virtual final say over funds, with very occasional appeals to the president. With respect to Congress, the president's budget has, since 1921, set the agenda and framework for consideration of budgetary matters. Until the Congressional Budget Office was created in 1974, BOB had a monopoly on the technical information necessary to make informed budgetary decisions. But the way BOB has exercised its power over the budget has changed over the decades.

In the past, OMB's power was based on the budget examiners' intimate familiarity with their agencies and their program expertise. This knowledge was born of many years of examining agency budgets; the examiners brought the perspective of the presidency to agency budgets, and presidential priorities rather than agency wishes prevailed. The traditional formulation of the executive budget was an iterative, bottom-up process conducted within an annual budget cycle: OMB general policy guidance in the spring, agency requests in the summer, final OMB mark and any appeals in the fall. The combination of guidance from the top and details from below has always existed, but the balance has shifted over the years.

The bottom-up process predominated from 1921 to the 1960s, when the emphasis began to shift to a top-down perspective. The 1960s were marked by a Keynesian perspective on fiscal policy, and economic expertise was highly valued in OMB. Initially, the macro approach of the 1960s was accompanied by economic growth; then, in the 1970s, the need to fight inflation spurred the continuation of OMB's concern with aggregate spending. The careful scrutiny of agency budgets continued to play an important role, given the need to reduce federal spending.

In the 1980s the imperatives of deficit reduction and formula budgeting profoundly reinforced top-down budgeting. The focus on fiscal policy, and budget aggregates, overwhelmed OMB's traditional concentration on agencies and programs. The Reagan administration came to power determined to make massive cuts in the domestic budget. The main concern was not to prune programs carefully, but to cut budget aggregates and eliminate domestic programs whenever possible. Budget Director David Stockman focused on the aggregate effect of all spending decisions and was not interested in programs except in trying to cut them. OMB staffers strained to be responsive to Stockman, and OMB was reoriented. Budget examiners began to focus on their own aggregates and to emphasize budget cutting (which came naturally) at the expense of program analysis (which they also had traditionally done).

In order to achieve the type of budget cuts he wanted, Stockman had to negotiate constantly with Congress. He needed "real time" answers to his "what if" questions about changed economic assumptions or program levels. The Central Budget Management System was developed to give the director the on-line information necessary for his negotiations. This included the ability to track the status of legislation on the Hill in each committee and in the congressional process. It also included "scorekeeping" ability, that is, to tell what the effect of each successive change in a spending bill would mean to the totals.

This sophisticated capacity was developed in OMB under Stockman's leadership and gave the director the information he needed to conduct his negotiations on the Hill. The Stockman era accelerated the change in the budgetary process from an annual exercise with defined stages to a state of virtually continuous budgeting in which economic projections, assumptions, and program estimates changed constantly. As a result of the budget stalemate between President Reagan and the Congress, appropriation bills were often not passed before the beginning of the fiscal year, and it was necessary to use continuing resolutions to fund the government, sometimes for a full fiscal year.

David Mathiasen, assistant director for budget review in the Reagan administration, describes OMB's institutional reaction to budget developments in the 1980s:

The recession-induced deficits or the changes in budget priorities proposed by the administration would have been enough to alter the institutional focus of OMB. Together they made it inevitable. The tradition of focusing on many small and large individual pieces was supplemented by top-down, across-the-board budgeting; by negotiated budget agreements in some years; and by intense concern with legislative outcomes. . . . Formula budgeting finally became enacted in the two versions (1985 and 1987) of Gramm-Rudman-Hollings. To carry them out, highly complex, across-the-board formulas needed to be analyzed and calculated in ways that literally had no programmatic content and for which normal policy analysis was irrelevant.[7]

The emphasis on bill tracking and scorekeeping and the development of the Central Budget Management System drew staff resources from OMB's traditional functions of building the executive budget from the bottom up. With the emphasis on aggregates, the importance of detailed program knowledge declined, since examiners were more concerned with saving dollars than with program effectiveness.

OMB has also become much more involved with getting the president's budget through Congress. The trend began before Stockman, with OMB Director James McIntyre adding four staffers to the congressional liaison section of OMB. But the trend was drastically accelerated with the priorities of David Stockman. Career OMB staffers were expected to play a much more active role in negotiations on the Hill than before. In the past, much of the advocacy for legislation was done by departments and agencies who were affected by the legislation, but since 1981 OMB has taken the lead and the legislative liaison staff has taken on more responsibility and importance.[8]

The norms for career staff have changed to meet the new role expectations of active engagement in lobbying Congress. When BOB officials went to the Hill to testify in the past, career staffers generally provided facts and data, but were careful not to advocate policies or negotiate with congressional staffers.[9] In the Stockman era, both of these norms have shifted to support a more active role for career OMB staffers in advancing the president's budget.[10]

The thrust of these developments has been to shift the focus of OMB's efforts from the development of the executive budget to the shepherding of the president's budget through the congressional budgetary process. Career staff expertise and efforts have shifted from detailed knowledge of agencies and programs to focus on the aggregate, while legislative tracking has overshadowed the traditional OMB budget analysis role.[11]

Central Legislative Clearance

One of the Budget Bureau's most important sources of power has been its power of central legislative clearance. The power was established in 1921 in Budget Circular 49, which stated that all agency proposals for legislation, "the effect of which would be to create a charge upon the public treasury or commit the government to obligations which would later require appropriations," must be submitted to the Budget Bureau before legislative action was sought.[12] After some initial resistance from executive-branch agencies and selective enforcement, it became an important tool for economy under President Coolidge, who used it actively to limit spending.

Central clearance was used primarily to save money through the 1930s. But in 1934 President Roosevelt decided to use the clearance mechanism for legislative matters of substantive policy as well as for fiscal savings. The decision was formalized in Budget Circular 336 in 1935, and the clearance was conducted through the National Emergency Council. In 1937 Budget Circular 344 provided that substantive legislative proposals, even without fiscal implications, would be routed to the Budget Bureau for clearance. In 1938 Director Bell allocated a full-time staff to coordinate legislation.

The central legislative clearance function became firmly established in the 1940s under Harold Smith, when the Legislative Reference Division was created and the process was routinized. During this period the division was staffed by career civil servants, and legislative clearance as well as the enrolled bill process were carried out by career staffers through the Truman and Eisenhower administrations. During that time, the directors of the Legislative Reference Division (LRD), Roger Jones (1949–57) and Philip (Sam) Hughes (1958–65) made most final determinations as to whether legislative proposals were in accord with the president's program. They had regular contact with White House staff members to ensure that their policy decisions accurately reflected the president's preferences.

In the 1960s Presidents Kennedy and Johnson took a much more active approach to policy initiation and each felt that the career agencies were not as creative as they would like. With the emphasis on new presidential initiatives the White House became more involved in legislative clearance, and a "two-track" system developed whereby legislation that involved issues of special interest to the White House was taken out of the routine system.[13] This development was reinforced by the new head of legislative reference, Wilfred H. Rommel, who distinguished carefully between routine and policy decisions and felt that the latter were clearly the province of political officials.[14]

This trend was reinforced with the creation of OMB in 1970 and the creation of program associate directors in OMB. Legislative reference decisions of a nonroutine nature were shifted to the PADs, who were in closer touch with White House preferences. These developments signified "a gradual erosion in the scope and influence of the clearance process over time. The LRD, no longer the haven for generalists led by a career executive aggressively pursuing the presumed institutional interests of the Presidency, is now comfortable with a less visible, less controversial staff role."[15]

Centralizing decisions about legislative clearance contributed to blurring the distinction between the merits of legislation and the president's personal political stake. The trend was intensified by the expansion of domestic policy-making function in the White House. The Legislative Reference Division still handles a large volume of matters, but its policy role and power has declined significantly since the days of Jones and Hughes.

Management

The Budget Bureau's claim to play a major role in federal management lies in section 209 of the Budget and Accounting Act of 1921, but its interest in management issues, aside from a narrow focus on economy and efficiency, did not come to the fore until the late 1930s. It began with the concern of the Brownlow Committee for the administrative role of the president in the constitutional system and the necessity of consolidating administratively the plethora of programs spawned by the New Deal.

BOB's prominent role in managing the federal government began with the creation of the EOP in 1939, shortly after which FDR appointed Harold Smith to be its director. Smith created the Division of Administrative Management (AM) and appointed Donald C. Stone to lead it. The AM division had about seventy-five people in 1942 and over one hundred by the end of the war. Smith built the Budget Bureau into a general staff arm for the presidency, and the Administrative management Division was the core of BOB. The duties of the division included government-wide organizational and procedural matters, setting up and improving management systems within individual agencies, initiating new programs, revamping old ones, and putting out administrative fires.[16] "Through its reputation and prestige, it was able to recruit top-grade personnel. Furthermore, it became a major source of managerial know-how and information as well as a bastion of qualified personnel available for detail or transfer to other parts of the bureau and to other federal agencies, not excluding the White House itself."[17]

A number of factors accounted for the success and dominance within BOB of the Division of Administrative Management during this unique period in the Budget Bureau's history.[18] The institutional capacity in number of personnel, but more important the high quality of personnel, allowed the division to act effectively. The division was led by Donald Stone, with the full support of Director Smith. Smith had President Roosevelt's confidence and a mandate to play a major role in managing the federal government. He headed the bureau from 1939 to 1946 while the economy was in a stage of expansion after the Great Depression, and mobilizing for World War II required an emphasis on positive managerial skills rather than economy and efficiency.

BOB had a virtual monopoly on management expertise in the federal government at this time. But most important, the president felt that good management was essential to his political and governmental leadership, and he assigned high priority to the Budget Bureau. Another reason for BOB prominence during this period was that the White House staff was so small that if the president wanted staff resources for his priorities he had to rely on BOB.

After Smith's tenure, James Webb, a strong advocate of the AM division, took over and injected new energy into the agency.[19] During Frederick Lawton's term as director of BOB, however, the AM division began to decline in influence and management became a less important function of the Budget Bureau. Lawton's reorganization of BOB in 1952 merged its management functions with other parts of the agency, and its staff was significantly reduced. But these were merely symptoms of the major cause of the decline of administrative management: presidential priorities were changing. Though President Eisenhower had a sophisticated appreciation of organization and management and used them very effectively in organizing his White House and cabinet, he did not value giving BOB a broad role in managing the federal government. He felt that management of departments and agencies fell within the proper sphere of his cabinet officers to whom he delegated the responsibility. But more important, Eisenhower was very concerned with saving money and bringing the budget into balance, and his use of BOB reflected this priority. Eisenhower valued the role of BOB in the federal government, but gave top priority to budget-cutting, not management.

The thrust of the Kennedy and Johnson administrations was initiating programs to solve the great problems in American society. Neither thought the Budget Bureau had the creative energy needed to develop New Frontier or Great Society initiatives.

Richard Nixon believed that the organization and machinery of government made a difference. In implementing the Ash Council's recommendation to reorganize BOB into the Office of Management and Budget (which was almost named the Office of Executive Management), he decided that management should become a major concern of the Bureau. But Nixon's approach to management stemmed from his antibureaucratic strategy and his distrust of the civil service. He wanted to bring the agencies of the executive branch under tighter White House control. His vision of management became one of presidential control of the government, particularly during his second term.

On the surface, the intention of Reorganization Plan No. 2 of 1970 was to separate policy from administration. "The Domestic Council will be primarily concerned with *what* we do; the Office of Management and Budget will be primarily concerned with *how* we do it, and *how well* we do it." Frederick Mosher points out the irony that what in fact happened after the reorganization was that the distinction between the roles of policy making in the White House and administration in OMB were further blurred. John Ehrlichman, the head of the Domestic Council, increasingly called upon career members of the OMB staff to work on special projects, and George Shultz, director of OMB, took an office in the West Wing. He was primarily an advisor to the president rather than a manager of OMB.[20]

President Carter came to office with an avowed interest in management and promised that reorganizing the government would be one of his primary objectives. The management staff of OMB was beefed up and headed by a newly created Executive Associate Director for Reorganization and Management, Harrison Wellford. While the Carter reorganization effort had a number of successes, most notably the Civil Service Reform Act of 1978, the whole effect did not result in a major reorientation of the federal government, nor did the management side of OMB resume the prominence and power of its glory days in the 1940s.

The Reagan administration undertook a number of management initiatives, including the President's Management Improvement Program—Reform '88, the President's Council on Integrity and Efficiency, the President's Council on Management Improvement, the Cabinet Council on Management and Administration, and the President's Private Sector Survey on Cost Control (the Grace Commission). These efforts made progress on a number of important issues, including credit control, cash management, and financial control; but they did not add up to a broad and coherent approach to managing the government. The Reagan approach was criticized by Comptroller General Bowsher for overemphasizing central control of the executive branch by the central management agencies rather than focusing upon management issues in departments and agencies.[21] It was also criticized by the National Academy of Public Administration for emphasizing central control rather than decentralization and support for program managers in departments and agencies.[22]

One of the major objectives of the Reagan administration was to limit federal regulation of business. The actions of OMB in this area have been significant and amount to a major increase in presidential control over the executive branch. Through Executive Orders 12,291 and 12, 498, OMB can review all potential executive branch regulations (except for those of independent regulatory agencies) to assure that they are in accord with the president's priorities, and it can prevent many of them from being formally proposed or implemented.[23] While these initiatives are certainly concerned with management, it is management with a very narrow focus of control.

In summary, there has been only one period in the history of BOB, the ten years under Harold Smith and James Webb, in which the management function has been highly valued and powerful.[24] On the other hand, management in the sense of tight centralized control over the executive branch has, along with budget control, been highly valued by most presidents. The Budget Bureau has consistently been the president's primary arm in the search for control. Ronald Moe makes a crucial distinction:

If management is principally conceived of as "control," then most observers agree that OMB appears to be managing many agencies and programs reasonably well through its regulatory review processes. However, if management is principally conceived of as providing the organizational planning, human and material resources, and leadership to assist agencies and managers to accomplish their statutory mission, then critics assert that OMB is falling short.[25]

Politicization

The Budget Bureau has always been put to political uses in the broad sense of the term. It was used to achieve economy and efficiency in the 1920s and to consolidate the New Deal and coordinate the war effort in the 1940s. It was used to implement the Reagan budget objectives in the 1980s. It has always been responsive to presidential priorities which is its raison d'être. But critics of recent developments have argued that OMB has become increasingly politicized in recent decades and that this has been detrimental to OMB as an institution and to its role as a presidential staff agency. They have focused on the development of OMB in three major areas: the blurring of the distinction between an institutional staff and a personal staff, the increasing number of political appointees, and the use of OMB leadership for political advocacy.

From Institutional to Personal Staff

Richard Neustadt argues that Franklin Roosevelt made an important distinction between his personal staff and the institutional staff of the presidency. His White House staff represented him personally and interacted with him on a day-to-day basis.

The things he personally did not do from week to week, the troubleshooting and intelligence he did not need first-hand, were to be staffed outside the White House. The aides he did not have to see from day to day were to be housed in other offices than his. This is the origin of the distinction which developed in his time between "personal" and "institutional" staff. The Executive Office was conceived to be the place for "institutional" staff; the place, in other words, for everybody else.[26]

What Roosevelt wanted from the Budget Bureau as the institutional staff of the presidency was as follows:

First, he wanted cool, detached appraisals of the financial, managerial, *and* program rationality in departmental budget plans and legislative programs. *Second,* he wanted comparable appraisals of the bright ideas originating in his own mind, or the minds of his political and personal associates. *Third,* he wanted the White House backstopped by preliminary and subsidiary staff-work of the sort his own aides could not undertake without forfeiting their availability and flexibility as a small group of generalists on his immediate business.[27]

James H. Rowe, Jr., one of Roosevelt's personal White House aides, explained that his job "was to look after the President," and the Budget Bureau's job was to protect the interests of the presidency.[28]

Though contemporary critics cite the 1940s and 1950s as a period of professionalism at BOB, it was Director James Webb (1946–49) who first began moving the agency closer to the White House. According to Larry Berman, Webb "believed that the fundamental difference between himself and Harold Smith was his predecessor's protectiveness of the Bureau, whereas Webb thought that the Bureau was strong enough to stand on its own feet and swim in perilous waters."[29] So Webb proceeded to get the bureau more involved with congressional relations and program development.

Despite this increased involvement with presidential concerns, by the 1960s the bureau was criticized for not being flexible enough to take the positive role in program development that Presidents Kennedy and Johnson wanted. According to Allen Schick, "The Bureau's failure to orient itself to the service of the President was due largely to its institutional status. As it became the institutionalized presidency, the Bureau became separated from the President."[30] Ironically, this period is what later critics were to point to, along with the management era in the 1940s, as the "golden days" of the Budget Bureau. William Carey, an assistant director of BOB, describes the lack of responsiveness to presidential desires: "Lyndon Johnson spent the better part of a year badgering the Budget Director to assign 'five of the best men you have' to drag advance information out of the agencies about impending decisions and actions . . . but the Budget Bureau never came anywhere near satisfying him because its own radar system was not tuned finely enough."[31]

This concern for responsiveness to presidential concerns and thus a concern for the power of the bureau was also expressed by the career staff of BOB. In a 1959 self-evaluation there was strong support for recommending that political appointees be placed in lower-level line positions.[32]

In 1967 an internal study by the "steering group" advanced similar arguments that the bureau was not politically relevant enough and thus not of maximum use as a general staff agency to the president. The steering group's report identified the elements of a presidential staff agency, including defending administration positions, providing managerial intelligence, and early warning about potential problems.[33] It concluded that in order to best fulfill its primary mission of serving the president, BOB had to change its traditional style and to subordinate all functions that were not essential to responding to presidential priorities.

A staff paper for the study concluded, "The Bureau is almost completely without people who have political sensitivity and who read the signals."[34] By the end of the Johnson administration, the "problem" was solved, and LBJ used the bureau for all sorts of special projects. According to Berman, this was the end of the bureau's function as an institutional staff arm of the presidency. After this it became difficult to distinguish institutional from personal staff support. There is an irony here: the politicization that has recently been decried by OMB staffers and alumni was, in part, initiated by career professionals in trying to make the Budget Bureau more responsive to the president.

The problem of lack of responsiveness was attacked structurally in 1970 by President Nixon's reorganization of BOB into OMB, with politically appointed Program Associate Directors and use of the OMB director as a personal adviser to the president. When OMB was created, Nixon replaced Robert Mayo as director with George Shultz, who took an office in the West Wing to be more available to the president. Stockman's tenure as director was to exhibit even more the director's role as political advisor to the president rather than as leader of an institutional staff of the presidency.

Political Appointees: The Rise of the PADs

Another aspect of the "politicizing" of OMB is the increase in the number and role of political appointees. From its beginning in 1921, the director has been a presidential appointee, and with the change of the presidency to another party each director and most deputy directors have also changed. Almost all directors until President Carter had prior federal experience, and most deputies were drawn from the career ranks.[35] All others in the bureau were career civil servants, and even in the Eisenhower administration which appointed four or five assistant directors, most of these appointees were career civil servants.

The major change toward political direction came with the Nixon reorganization when the positions of Program Associate Directors (PADs) were created to place political appointees directly in charge of the examining divisions. The Carter administration created the positions of Executive Associate Director, of which there were two, one for budget and one for reorganization and management. By the 1980s there were about twelve line political positions among thirty to forty total noncareer positions.

The purpose of these political appointees was to make the bureau more directly responsive to presidential political priorities. But their creation has been criticized for undermining the professionalism of the bureau. "Critics charge that the Pads are too political, possess too little program knowledge, remain in OMB too short a time to obtain that program knowledge, do not trust careerists, and, by handling the political interface which the Director used to handle, have eroded the independence of division chiefs and the decision-role of the Director."[36] A career OMB official put it this way: "The PADs, for the most part, are people who come and leave within a year and a half or two years. The good ones get an institutional feel for things; most of them don't. Therefore, they tend to see issues on a case-by-case basis, almost a personal basis. They are impatient with the history of an issue, the lessons that have been learned and so on."[37]

One of the problems with the political orientation and responsiveness of the PADs is that the professional and analytical perspective of career OMB staffers may not be available for presidential consideration. The argument is not that career perspectives should prevail; policy decisions are legitimately the domain of the president and his agents, the political appointees. The point is that the president will be able to make a more fully informed decision if he has institutional as well as political input.

The question then arises: at what point is political, as opposed to institutional, input most appropriate and useful? It used to be that the career staff of BOB would present their best analysis of the interests of the presidency. Then White House staffers would insert their political judgment, and the president would decide the appropriate balance. With the PADs, the political spin of what is best for *this* president is put on issues *before* they are brought up for higher-level decision.[38] According to Elmer Staats, President Truman would say: "Give me your best professional analysis, I'll make the political judgement."[39]

These criticisms of the increasing number of political appointees are not shared by all OMB alumni. Dale McOmber, former assistant director for budget review, argues that the changing role of OMB in the 1980s requires a greater political sensitivity at lower levels than in the 1950s and 1960s, and that the increased number of political appointees is thus appropriate. James T. McIntyre, President Carter's OMB director, argues that more, rather than fewer, political appointees at OMB would be preferable.[40]

Public Advocacy and Visibility

The third element of politicization is the extent to which OMB has become a public advocate for the president's political priorities and the director has played a visible partisan role. The 1970s saw the beginning of a more public role for OMB directors, partly because of the importance of their roles as presidential advisers and partly because of the controversial policies they were implementing. According to Hugh Heclo, "There has been a fundamental shift in OMB's role from wholesaling advice to the Presidency and towards retailing policy to outsiders. The Bureau of the Budget had carefully shunned public visibility and served as an administration spokesman only infrequently and in specialized areas."[41] Bert Lance played a highly visible role during the transition and early months of the Carter administration not because of his budgetary expertise, but because of his close relationship with the president.[42] But the extreme case of the public visibility of an OMB director was David Stockman during President Reagan's first term.

Stockman was a highly visible advocate for the Reagan agenda even before his designation as OMB director; after his appointment, he became the lead administration official directing Reagan policy priorities for the first year of the administration.[43] In addition to Stockman's visibility, his style of leadership of OMB was a major departure from all previous directors. Despite his nontraditional approach to the office his qualifications were impeccable. Senator Pete V. Domenici, the ranking Republican on the Budget Committee, said: "Stockman was a bamboozler and a conniver, but in terms of knowledge he was totally and absolutely the epitome, the essence of a budget director."[44]

In Hugh Heclo's analysis, Stockman treated OMB as an organizational tool to accomplish his short-run objectives at the expense of the longer-term interests of OMB as a presidential staff agency.[45] In the words of one OMB staffer: "He bangs on you for information on the day that he needs it. He doesn't think about how to strengthen the agency's general ability to provide what is wanted. He gets what he wants when he wants it and wherever he can. He doesn't say to himself, 'I'd better get an organization and process in motion to be able to supply what is needed.' "[46]

One of the effects of OMB's politicization has been its loss of credibility with Congress. Sam Hughes, who was in charge of Legislative Reference from 1958 to 1965, says that since 1970 OMB's credibility as a source of neutral competence has been undermined and that it is viewed as more of a political tool than the source of neutral expertise it used to be.[47]

This lack of credibility has come in part from the controversial nature of the policies of the presidents for which it has worked. During the Nixon administration, OMB defended and implemented Nixon's impoundment policies that withheld funds provided in law from programs that the president wanted to eliminate or scale back. In a series of more than seventy court cases culminating in a Supreme Court decision, the Nixon administration was rebuffed in its impoundment of funds.[48]

OMB's credibility was also undermined by the consistently optimistic economic assumptions with which it defended the past several presidents' budgets. The projections were optimistic and predicted the elimination of the deficit by the end of the president's term. The projections were invariably proved wrong by economic events. OMB's credibility was challenged by the Congressional Budget Office, a nonpartisan agency created by the 1974 Budget Act. CBO's less optimistic economic projections consistently turned out to be more accurate than OMB's.[49] The optimistic projections and "rosy scenario" of the supply-side theory of fiscal policy that dominated OMB in the early months of the Reagan administration did severe damage to OMB's economic credibility.[50]

Another element of politicization, according to OMB's critics, has been the downgrading of career staff. This slighting of the expertise, professionalism, and experience of the career staff has been a continuing problem at least since the White House staff began to take a more active role in policy development in 1960. Harold Seidman, a senior BOB official for twenty-five years, said of the Johnson White House: "They didn't use the Budget Bureau as an institution. They used individual Budget Bureau staff as legmen to do pick and shovel work. This was not using the Budget Bureau."[51]

The *Budget of the United States*, the budget proposal sent to Congress by the president each year, has always been a defense of the president's budgetary agenda, but it used to be also a relatively objective statement of the best professional judgment about the state of the economy and the federal government's budgetary situation. In recent years, however, it has become a more blatant advocacy document. In Allen Schick's judgment, the "Major Accomplishments" section of the 1981 Carter budget "was the first time that the president's budget office incorporated a campaign tract into its budget documents."[52] Bruce Johnson, however, traces the beginning of this trend to President Ford's budget director, James T. Lynn. According to Johnson, this practice was carried to new heights in the Reagan administration. "The agency began using a new document that attempted to 'sell' rather than just describe the budget. The 'advocacy papers' contained in this document had a more argumentative tone and plainly contrasted with the explanatory language of the traditional budget documents."[53]

Under Budget Director James Miller, OMB became more actively engaged in selling the president's budget priorities to the public. This took the form of writing speeches and preparing op-ed pieces for placement in newspapers. These were written by both political and career OMB staffers. In addition, career staffers under Miller prepared a set of more than fifty documents that were intended to illustrate the "wasteful" nature of congressional spending. These "pork pieces" were written not in support of any particular presidential policy initiative, but rather merely to criticize Congress.[54]

It is tempting for career OMB staffers to move beyond professional analysis and toward advocacy of policy positions, but this is dangerous because their credibility as objective analysts can easily be undermined both at the institutional and the individual level. In the words of one OMB career official, "The organization is becoming more vulnerable the more it gets associated with particular public positions. By doing things for this and not that group, selling this and not that deal, we become more politically identified with one administration."[55]

OMB and the Presidency

OMB has not been the only presidential institution to undergo these developments; they are part of a broader historical trend over the past several decades to increase centralized control of the executive branch in the White House. OMB is only one part of that trend.

According to Terry Moe, the trends of centralization and politicization have been caused by the incongruence between voters' high expectations of presidents and the inability of presidents to fulfill these expectations because of the fragmentation of power in the U.S. system. "The expectations surrounding presidential performance far outstrip the institutional capacity of presidents to perform; . . . politicization and centralization have grown over time not because of who presidents are or what they stand for, but because of the nature of our institutions and the role and location of presidents within them. The basic causes are systemic."[56]

As a result, presidents tend to be less concerned with governance than with popularity and control of the government. The permanent institutions of government are seen as obstacles to their success, and career civil servants are treated as enemies to be vanquished rather than as allies in an enterprise. Presidents often feel that their personal political success cannot be entrusted to civil servants or even to their own political appointees in the departments and agencies. This has led to efforts to centralize power in the White House, including the formulation of domestic policy and national security policy.

This centralizing trend has led to an increased number of political appointees throughout the executive branch and the domination of the selection of all political appointments in the White House in unprecedented ways.[57] The development of OMB fits into this general pattern of increasing presidential control of the government and centralization of power in the White House, and we should not expect major reversals of the situation in the near future.

The major political and budgetary reality of the 1990s will be the necessity to deal with the huge national debt accumulated during the 1980s. For OMB, this will ensure the continued domination of aggregates at the expense of fine tuning or good management of programs. Focusing on aggregates will ensure the continuation of top-down control of the budget from OMB. Thus OMB's management function will continue to take a back seat unless a new president feels that he has a stake in the long-run management of government programs and agencies. On the other hand, presidents may discover that good management is as essential in a steady-state or cutback mode as it is when the government is expanding.

With the focus on aggregates, the congressional budget process will continue to be of primary concern to presidents, and OMB's new capacity to follow closely the ins and outs of congressional budgeting will continue to be valued.

Presidents will find OMB's new ability to control the regulatory decisions of executive branch agencies to be a useful tool of control, and they will be unlikely to abandon the new powers developed in the Carter and Reagan years and fought through the courts. An administration, however, without the ideological orientation of the Reagan administration may use the power in a more selective manner.

Presidents will hesitate to give up the newly created political positions of the past two decades, but they might be convinced that competence and continuity will be of greater use to them than merely having their own people in positions. In the words of Aberbach and Rockman:

Politicization and centralization are appropriate presidential responses in efforts to define the terms of the relationship—to a degree. Beyond that unspecifiable point, however, strategies for achieving presidential responsiveness turn into tactics for exclusive presidential rule. Efforts to achieve that level of aggrandizement are ruinous for governance in the American system; that is, they are collectively irrational. They also are ultimately ruinous for presidents whose political well-being probably is essential for effective governance and are thus likely to be individually irrational as well.[58]

The Office of Management and Budget, with its traditions of professionalism and service to the presidency has continued to adapt to the needs of the president. Despite the misgivings of some of the career staff and its alumni, it has had no choice. As Heclo argues, "Lacking any outside clientele in Congress or interest groups, OMB can resist only through inactivity; its choice is to be of use to the President of the day or to atrophy. OMB preferred to be of use."[59]

In 1985 an associate director of OMB was asked whether the career staffers could be counted on to support fully Reagan administration priorities. PAD Constance Horner replied:

The decisions my career staff and I make are surprisingly consensual. To exaggerate, but not by much, they would kill for the president. Any president. They are often accused of being rigid and lacking in political sensitivity. But they consider themselves the technical keepers of the president's policy. . . . In so far as [OMB] has a bias, I'd say that the examiners live for efficiency and abhor sloppiness; . . . even if the political types were quite different, the examiners would be applying their same set of basic standards.[60]

This sounds strikingly similar to the traditional role the Budget Bureau has played over the years. OMB's role may be changing, but Charles Dawes would recognize it.

Notes

For comments on an earlier version of this essay, the author would like to thank the following people: Samuel Cohn, Alan Dean, Stuart Eizenstat, James Fesler, Dwight Ink, Herbert Jasper, Dale McOmber, Richard Nathan, Roger Porter, Edward Preston, Charles Schultze, Donald Stone, Margaret Wyszomirski.

1. The President's Committee on Administrative Management, *Report with Special Studies* (Washington, D.C.: GPO, 1937), p. 6.
2. Richard Neustadt, "Roosevelt's Approach to the Budget Bureau," Attachment B to his memo, "Staffing the President Elect," October 30, 1960, p. 3.
3. C. W. Dawes, *The First Year of the Budget of the United States* (New York: Harper and Brothers, 1923), p. 178.
4. Dawes, in U.S. Bureau of the Budget, *Report of the Director of the Bureau of the*

Budget to the President of the United States (December 5, 1921), pp. xxi–xxii, quoted in Frederick C. Mosher, *A Tale of Two Agencies* (Baton Rouge: Louisiana University Press, 1984), p. 40.

5. Quoted by Colin Campbell, *Managing the Presidency: Carter, Reagan, and the Search for Executive Harmony* (Pittsburgh, Pa.: University of Pittsburgh Press, 1986), p. 165. There is an irony in how the relative constitutional places of the executive and legislative branches have changed in organization mythology. The "garbage" reference is to Charles Dawes's statement in his book on the first year of BOB: "We have nothing to do with policy. Much as we love the President, if Congress in its omnipotence over appropriations and in accordance with its authority over policy, passed a law that garbage should be put on the White House steps, it would be our regrettable duty, as a bureau, in an impartial, nonpolitical, and nonpartisan way to advise the Executive and Congress as to how the largest amount of garbage could be spread in the most expeditious and economical manner" (*The First Year of the Budget of the United States*, p. 178.

6. Interview with Dale McOmber, Washington, D.C., July 21, 1983. McOmber was deputy director for budget review from 1973 to 1981.

7. David Mathiasen, "The Evolution of the Office of Management and Budget Under President Reagan," *Public Budgeting and Finance* 8 (Autumn 1988), 10.

8. See David G. Mathiasen, "Recent Developments in the Composition and the Formulation of the United States Federal Budget," *Public Budgeting and Finance* 3 (Autumn 1983), 103.

9. Interview with Samuel Cohn, July 28, 1983.

10. See Shelley Lynn Tompkin, "Office of Management and Budget—Congressional Relations During the Reagan Administration," presented at the annual convention of the American Political Science Association, New Orleans, 1985.

11. See Bruce Johnson, "The Changing Role of the OMB Budget Examiners in the Reagan Era," presented at the national conference of the Association for Public Policy Analysis and Management, October 30, 1987, p. 21.

12. Quoted in Richard E. Neustadt, "Presidency and Legislation: The Growth of Central Clearance," *American Political Science Review* 48 (1954), 644.

13. See Stephen Wayne, *The Legislative Presidency* (New York: Harper and Row, 1978), pp. 80–82.

14. See Joel Havemann, "OMB's Legislative Role is Growing More Powerful and More Political," *National Journal*, October 27, 1973, p. 1596.

15. Ronald C. Moe, "Central Legislative Clearance," in Senate Governmental Affairs Committee Print, *OMB: Evolving Roles and Future Issues* (Washington, D.C.: GPO, February 1986), p. 182.

16. Memorandum from Donald Stone to the author, October 26, 1988.

17. Mosher, *A Tale of Two Agencies*, p. 104.

18. An authoritative analysis of the reasons for the rise and decline of the Administrative Management function in BOB is contained in Donald C. Stone, "Lessons to be Derived from BOB/OMB Experience," preliminary draft, December 3, 1980. Valuable advice on how OMB can play a positive role in government management is also contained in a letter from Stone to Dwight Ink, then assistant director for executive management of OMB, dated October 30, 1970. These manuscripts were provided by their authors, whose generosity is gratefully acknowledged.

19. Memorandum from Donald Stone to the author, October 26, 1988.

20. Mosher, *A Tale of Two Agencies*, p. 133.

21. Charles A. Bowsher, "Building Effective Public Management," *The Bureaucrat* 13, no. 4 (Winter, 1984–85), 26–29.

22. NAPA, *Revitalizing Federal Management: Managers and Their Overburdened Systems* (Washington, D.C.: NAPA, 1983). For a summary of criticisms, see Peter M. Benda and Charles H. Levine, *The Reagan Legacy* (Chatham, N.J.: Chatham House Publishers, 1988), 129–31.

23. For analyses of OMB's new regulatory powers see: William F. West and Joseph Cooper, "The Rise of Administrative Clearance," in *The Presidency and Public Policy Making,* ed. George Edwards, Steven Shull, and Norman Thomas (Pittsburgh, Pa.: University of Pittsburgh Press, 1985); Cooper and West, "Presidential Power and Republican Government," manuscript; National Academy of Public Administration, "Presidential Management of Rulemaking in Regulatory Agencies," NAPA Panel Report (January 1987); Morton Rosenberg, "Regulatory Management at OMB," in Senate Governmental Affairs Committee Hearings, *OMB: Evolving Roles and Future Issues* (Washington, D.C.: GPO, February 1986), pp. 185–234; Peter M. Benda and Charles H. Levine, "Reagan and the Bureaucracy: The Bequest, the Promise, and the Legacy," in *The Reagan Legacy* (Chatham, N.J.: Chatham House, 1988).

24. There was a brief resurgence of management from 1969 to 1972 that included the Federal Assistance Review program and the proposed reorganization of the executive branch, but White House interest declined with the opening to China and the coming of the 1972 elections. Interview with Dwight Ink and Alan Dean on November 3, 1988.

25. Ronald C. Moe, "Assessment of Organizational Policy and Planning Function in OMB," printed in Senate Governmental Affairs Committee Print, *OMB: Evolving Roles and Future Issues,* p. 147.

26. Richard Neustadt, "Roosevelt's Approach to Staffing the White House," attachment A to the memo: "Staffing the President Elect," October 30, 1960.

27. Richard Neustadt, "Roosevelt's Approach to the Budget Bureau," attachment B to "Staffing the President Elect," October 30, 1960.

28. Quoted in Harold Seidman, *Politics, Position, and Power* (New York: Oxford University Press, 1988), p. 74.

29. Larry Berman, *The Office of Management and Budget and the Presidency: 1921–1979* (Princeton, N.J.: Princeton University Press, 1979), pp. 41–42.

30. Allen Schick, "The Budget Bureau that was: Thoughts on the Rise, Decline, and Future of a Presidential Agency," *Law and Contemporary Problems* 35 (1970), 532.

31. William Carey, "Presidential Staffing in the Sixties and Seventies," *Public Administration Review* 29 (1969) p. 453.

32. See Hugh Heclo, "OMB and the Presidency," p. 87.

33. Berman, *The OMB and the Presidency,* p. 91.

34. Quoted in ibid., p. 120.

35. See Mosher, *A Tale of Two Agencies,* p. 130.

36. Berman, *The OMB and the Presidency,* p. 118.

37. Quoted in Stephen Wayne, *The Legislative Presidency,* p. 100.

38. Statement of Herbert Jasper at the Presidency Project Panel meeting of the National Academy of Public Administration, May 17, 1988.

39. Statement at the Panel meeting of the Presidency Project of the National Academy of Public Administration, May 17, 1988. Elmer Staats was the chair of the panel.

40. Interview with James T. McIntyre, May 9, 1986.

41. Hugh Heclo, "OMB and the Presidency—The Problem of 'Neutral Competence,' " *The Public Interest* 38 (Winter 1975), 89.

42. Interview with Bert Lance, Calhoun, Georgia, June 21, 1983.

43. For an analysis of Stockman's role in 1981, see James P. Pfiffner, "The Reagan Budget Juggernaut," in *The President and Economic Policy,* ed. Pfiffner (Philadelphia: ISHI Press, 1986).

44. Judith Havemann, "The Man Who Isn't David Stockman," *Washington Post National Weekly Edition,* September 8, 1986, p. 6.

45. Hugh Heclo, "Executive Budget Making," in *Federal Budget Policy in the 1980s,* ed. Gregory B. Mills and John L. Palmer (Washington, D.C.: Urban Institute, 1984), p. 286.

46. Quoted in Hugh Heclo, "Executive Budget Making," p. 280.

47. Statement at a the panel meeting of the Presidency Project of the National Academy of Public Administration, May 17, 1988.

48. For an analysis of the political, institutional, and legal aspects of the impoundment issue, see James P. Pfiffner, *The President, the Budget, and Congress: Impoundment and the 1974 Budget Act* (Boulder, Colo.: Westview Press, 1979).

49. See Robert D. Behn, "The Receding Mirage of the Balanced Budget," *Public Interest* 67 (Spring 1982), 118–30; also Rudolph G. Penner, "Forecasting Budget Totals: Why Can't We Get it Right?" in *The Federal Budget: Economics and Politics,* ed. Michael J. Boskin and Aaron Wildavsky (San Francisco: Institute for Contemporary Studies, 1982).

50. See William Greider, "The Education of David Stockman," *The Atlantic,* December 1981; Hugh Heclo and Rudolph Penner, "Fiscal and Political Strategy in the Reagan Administration," in *The Reagan Presidency,* ed. Fred I. Greenstein (Baltimore: Johns Hopkins University Press, 1983). See also John Gist, "The Reagan Budget: A Significant Departure from the Past," *PS* 14 (Fall 1981), 745.

51. Quoted in Berman, *The Office of Management and Budget and the Presidency,* p. 80.

52. Allen Schick, "The Problem of Presidential Budgeting," in *The Illusion of Presidential Government,* ed. Hugh Heclo and Lester M. Salamon (Boulder, Colo.: Westview Press, 1981), p. 105.

53. Bruce Johnson, "OMB's New Role," *Journal of Policy Analysis and Management* 3 (1983–84), 507.

54. Bruce Johnson, "The Changing Role of the OMB Budget Examiners in the Reagan Era," presented at the Ninth Annual Research Conference of the Association for Public Policy Analysis and Management, October 30, 1987, p. 26.

55. Quoted in Hugh Heclo, "OMB and the Presidency," p. 90.

56. Terry Moe, "The Politicized Presidency," in *The New Direction in American Politics,* ed. John E. Chubb and Paul E. Peterson (Washington: Brookings, 1985), p. 269.

57. See James P. Pfiffner, *The Strategic Presidency: Hitting the Ground Running* (Chicago: Dorsey Press, 1988), ch. 4; *Leadership in Jeopardy,* National Academy of Public Administration, 1985. See also the report of the National Commission on the Public Service (the Volcker Commission), and its task force report, "Politics and Performance: Strengthening the Executive Leadership System," 1989.

58. Joel Aberbach and Bert Rockman, "Mandates or Mandarins?: Control and Discretion in the Modern Administrative State," *Public Administration Review* 48 (March/April 1988), 609.

59. Hugh Heclo, "OMB and the Presidency," p. 88.

60. Quoted by Suzanne Garment, "Budget Process Is Just Fine, Thank You," *The Wall Street Journal,* February 2, 1984.

10

Providing Countervailing Analysis and Advice in a Career-Dominated Bureaucratic System: The British Experience, 1916–1988

WILLIAM PLOWDEN

Analysis and advice for whom, and countervailing what? Basically, *for* elected decision makers heading governments (frequently, "ministers"); and *countervailing* any other form of advice reaching them from within the government organization: that is to say, from any of a number of sectional interests—individual departments and agencies, finance ministries, their own colleagues, and, especially, the bureaucracy as a whole.

The last of these, the entire bureaucracy, is the interest most often seen as requiring countervailing influence. Elected heads may perceive a need for countervailing analysis and advice for several reasons: the competence of the bureaucracy; bureaucrats' mind-set, the value system or organizational culture; the nature of decision making within the bureaucracy. The combination of these three factors in particular may lead to failure to explore—let alone to present—all available policy options, failure to take account of politicians' priorities or sensitivities, or failure to follow their instructions. Where the executive machine is dominated, at all levels, by lifetime career bureaucrats, politicians may well feel that the bureaucrats' competence is skewed, that their values take too much account both of the status quo, of established policies, and of their own long-term professional interests. Conversely, where those bureaucrats have only recently been working for an administration of a different political complexion, politicians may feel that they are unduly conditioned by a different set of political priorities. Political leaders who approach the decision-making process as outsiders may well feel that it is too slow, too ponderous, and too intolerant of radical thinking.

Heads of government may face, or feel that they face, peculiar problems in their capacities as both governmental and political leaders. They may feel that the pursuit of the government's overall objectives is hampered by sectional interests within, or allied with, separate government departments. This sectionalism may be reinforced by the personal ambitions of the head of government's colleagues (and sometimes rivals) in charge of departments.

The solutions attempted to these perceived problems, in different systems of government, include the following: (1) excluding career bureaucrats from key posts in the bureaucratic hierarchy, that is, mainly at the top, and substituting for them people implicitly or explicitly sharing the politicians' own views; (2) allowing politicians to manipulate at least the senior ranks of the bureaucracy to ensure the presence there of people in whom they feel relatively greater confidence; (3) giving politicians personal support in the form of supporting teams of their own choice (drawn from within or without the bureaucracy).

In Britain, to an extent rare among industrialized democracies (and indeed even rarer elsewhere), virtually no use at all has been made of the first two stratagems. Only intermittently has the third been used. Anticipating the account that follows, I will make three general points about the British experience. First—recalling that the modern merit-based civil service dates only from the last quarter of the nineteenth century—the professional civil service has thoroughly consolidated its near monopoly of advice to ministers within fifty years of the introduction of the merit system. Second, there have been only modest attempts to furnish ministers with alternative sources of advice that might be considered "theirs," compared with arrangements in the United States, Canada, Australia, France, Germany, and other advanced countries. Third, there has been little cumulative evolution in the arrangements attempted over the last seventy years. Discontinuity has been the theme; ground captured by one administration has been surrendered by its successor not so much without a fight as without thought; politicians—divided as they are among different parties—have failed to build up any kind of institutional memory on these questions.

As a consequence, in British government positions in the advisory hierarchy right up to the top are still held by career bureaucrats who have managed over the years to defend and maintain the principle that the appointment of partisan or sympathetic outsiders, and even intervention by politicians in the internal processes of appointing insiders, would be a significant breach of constitutional convention. Even under the Thatcher administration since 1979, although much more emphasis has been placed on appointing to senior positions people of a certain type, virtually all appointments made have been from within the ranks of career officials.[1]

This chapter outlines the use made of the third stratagem during the twentieth century. Support teams to provide countervailing advice for politicians are not a new idea; as will be seen below, the first experiment in this line in Britain was made over seventy years ago. But the practice has been extraordinarily slow to take root and is far from established even today. It is widely felt—by adherents as well as by opponents—that its basic principles still need defending. The systems and processes involved remain ad hoc and personal, in marked distinction to the entrenched and deeply institutionalized procedures of the administrative machine, dominated by the career bureaucracy, whose advice these teams have been intended to countervail.

Lloyd George, the Cabinet Secretariat, and the Garden Suburb

The first systematic attempt in modern times to insert countervailing advice into decision making was made by one of Britain's two outstanding wartime prime ministers, David Lloyd George. Lloyd George ousted his Liberal party colleague, H. H. Asquith, as prime minister in 1916 at a time of widespread doubt about the competence and drive of the country's government in managing the war against Germany. Both the office of prime minister, and the cabinet which the prime minister chairs, date in their modern form from that moment. The war cabinet secretariat then established, under Col. Maurice Hankey, contained all the essential elements of the modern cabinet secretariat. But it was then, and to a large extent it remained, what its name implies: a *secretariat* concerned mainly with processing decisions rather than with their content or their implementation, and a secretariat for the cabinet, with no formal acknowledgment that, within the cabinet, the prime minister might have some special claims and requirements.

The modernity of Lloyd George was reflected in his simultaneous establishment of the prototype of a prime minister's office. The cabinet secretariat, then as for many years afterward, concentrated on the relatively mechanical work of organizing meetings, preparing the papers for them, recording the outcome and, as part of this, ensuring that chairmen (the prime minister, in the case of the cabinet) were properly briefed. The prime minister's official civil service secretariat handled his day-to-day relations with the rest of Whitehall. By contrast, the "garden suburb," housed in temporary huts in the garden of No. 10 (hence the name), was very much concerned with policy. Under the leadership of an Oxford don, Professor W. G. S. Adams, the new body was in effect the earliest of a number of attempts to strengthen the prime minister's hold over central government.

The "garden suburb" was an early response to a problem summarized over half a century later by a former secretary of the British cabinet:

Of course, in theory, advice to the Prime Minister is given by departmental ministers, but that tends to bring the prime minister in very late, and I am afraid that events over the past 20 years or so have shown that prime ministers want some staff whom they feel are their own . . . and to whom they can look to watch their interests and to bring to their notice options that have perhaps been buried away and ought to be examined.[2]

During its brief life between December 1916 and 1918, the "garden suburb" processed information for Lloyd George, before and after meetings of the War Cabinet; it commented on departmental and ministerial proposals coming forward to cabinet or to No. 10 Downing Street, and acted as "progress-chaser" after decisions had been taken. Like many similar staffs, its members also helped in resolving difficulties and interdepartmental disputes, thus relieving the prime minister and the cabinet of all but a formal responsibility for the outcome.[3]

But with the end of the war and the return of normal times, Lloyd George's innovations in the machinery of government were treated, like changes in other aspects of national life, as having been exceptional responses to an exceptional situation. Nor did they fit the approach to policy making of a different set of politicians. They were decried by his opponents. From mid-1918, as the war drew to a close, the "garden suburb" melted away, its members drifting one by one into other careers. When the Conservatives under Bonar Law replaced Lloyd George's government in October 1922, the temporary huts in the garden of No. 10 were demolished. (Hostility to the centralizing style of Lloyd George was so great that the cabinet secretariat itself was denounced as unconstitutional; during the 1922 election campaign the leader of the opposition actually promised to abolish it.) Though the cabinet secretariat survived, in the years between the wars the prime minister's office evolved slowly into a unit staffed entirely by civil servants.

Twenty years passed. In the years between the world wars, the advice received by British ministers from within government was dominated—indeed, virtually monopolized—by career officials. When there was criticism of the personal arrangements made by the last prime minister of peacetime and first prime minister of World War II, Neville Chamberlain, this was because he was felt to be placing undue reliance on a single career official, Sir Horace Wilson.

The Prime Minister's Statistical Section

With the outbreak of war in 1939, as in 1916, exceptional times produced an exceptional man. He, like Lloyd George before him, had a taste for exceptional arrangements. When Chamberlain appointed Winston Churchill to be first lord of the admiralty in 1939, Churchill, determined to take "positive action," saw this as depending on constant access to the facts and figures about the navy and the naval war. In his first month of office he was arguing the case for a "central body which should grip together all Admiralty statistics, and present them to me in a form increasingly simplified and graphic."[4] Shortly afterward he appointed his old friend and adviser, Professor Frederick Lindemann, who had already been acting as his personal scientific advisor, to be the head of a new statistical section also reporting to Churchill personally. Half a dozen young academics were recruited. This team was to work for Churchill throughout the war.

The job of "S Branch" was not only to pull together the statistics; it was also to conduct what Churchill described as "special enquiries," analyzing papers submitted to cabinet (of which Churchill was a member) from other departments, and commenting on

wider matters discussed by cabinet. It was, in fact, providing countervailing advice. As one of its members later recalled, "Churchill
felt that he wanted an independent mind to digest and criticise
[other cabinet ministers'] papers. It was not enough, amid the
heavy pressure of his duties at the Admiralty, to have cursory
knowledge of matters outside his province; he wanted to have a
deeply critical knowledge."[5]

When, less than a year later, Churchill became prime minister
and moved to No. 10 Downing Street, he took Lindemann and S
Branch with him. Lindemann became Lord Cherwell in 1941, and
a minister himself in 1942, and the staff advised and briefed him
as well as Churchill. Staff members also took part in other Whitehall activities, such as interdepartmental committees. But their
main task continued to be supplying the information that Cherwell then passed on to the prime mininster, their principal client.

The work and the general approach of the section were well
described in an article written by one of its members shortly after
the end of the war.

The total establishment was in the neighbourhood of twenty. On the
average there were perhaps half a dozen economists; one scientific officer, one established civil servant (with economic training) to help keep
the amateurs on the rails, some half a dozen [human] computers; two or
three typists and clerks; and last, but not least, a number of what were
called "chartists"—about four were fully employed in the early period
when there was much drawing of new charts and diagrams.

The staff had contacts with nearly every Ministry, most of all with the
service and supply departments. They dealt with departmental officers at
all levels, and Lord Cherwell had much conversation and correspondence
with the various Ministers. Work was informal and intimate, and Lord
Cherwell spent much of his time in discussion with his staff.

The main method of communication with the Prime Minister, apart
from tables and charts submitted regularly, was through minutes from
Lord Cherwell supplemented by his frequent discussions with the Prime
Minister.

Some of the minutes were comments on official papers circulated to
the Cabinet or Cabinet committees; some commented on minutes sent by
other Ministers to the Prime Ministers; many were written in response to
requests by the Prime Minister for information and an opinion on specific
topics; many raised matters which Lord Cherwell, on his own initiative,
wished to bring to the Prime Minister's attention.

A minute from Lord Cherwell recommending action might occasionally form the basis of a directive by the Prime Minister, after consultation
with the Ministers concerned. More often the Prime Minister would
address an inquiry to the appropriate departmental Minister or Ministers,

or ask a Minister without departmental responsibility to conduct an inquiry and report. The Ministerial reply would normally be passed to Lord Cherwell for comment. When a new line of policy was settled the Prime Minister would sometimes ask for periodic progress reports which would in turn be examined by the Section.[6]

Just as had happened with Lloyd George, Churchill and his methods were to be regarded as exceptional responses to exceptional circumstances. Churchill's government lost office even before the end of the war. Churchill went, and with him Lord Cherwell and S Branch. Exactly as before, for the following twenty years advice to ministers was, at least in principle, monopolized by the career bureaucracy.

The Chief Planning Officer

One partial exception, in practice, was provided by the creation by Clement Attlee's postwar Labour government of a new position of chief planning officer (CPO). The task of this senior official was, formally, to coordinate the conversion of the British economy from a wartime to a peacetime footing and to plan economic policy for the longer term. This was, indeed, to remain the central focus of the chief planning officer and his staff. As things turned out, however, the CPO did become in some contexts a semi-institutionalized source of countervailing advice. The first and only holder of the post was Sir Edwin Plowden, a former businessman who had had a successful wartime career as one of the many outsiders brought into government as temporary civil servants.

The countervailing role of the staff followed naturally from Plowden's own view of its role. As he wrote later, "My wartime experience in Whitehall convinced me that the staff . . . should see its job as quite distinct from that of departments, who were there to carry out policies in areas for which they were responsible, while our task was to advise and to co-ordinate."[7]

This mode of operation was reinforced by Plowden's own position as a very senior official who, almost uniquely, was employed on a short-term (albeit renewable) contract. In his words, "I never undertook to stay for more than a year, and I had a job to which I could return whenever I chose. This allowed me much greater independence than would have been the case had I been an established civil servant. Indeed from time to time established civil servants would ask me to lobby Ministers on their behalf because of the greater influence and flexibility the unique nature of my position offered."[8]

Even if he sometimes acted as an amplifying conduit for the view of the career bureaucracy, Plowden inevitably from time to time put in his own views, in his own way. He later recalled the comment made by one of the chancellors of the exchequer for whom he worked, the Conservative R. A. Butler. Butler, discussing Plowden's style of work in the Treasury, said, "The difference between you and all others, Edwin, was that you used to burst into my room and say 'Rab, you must do this' or 'Rab, you must do that.' The others used to knock on the door and say, 'Chancellor, if I may respectfully suggest. . . . ' "[9]

It is worth noting that, even if his value to ministers was as a source of advice countervailing that of the line career bureaucracy, Plowden shared with the latter their ability to serve administrations of more than one party. Although appointed by the *dirigiste* Labour government of 1945–51, he worked equally effectively for the very different Conservative government of Winston Churchill that followed.

Plowden was based in the Treasury and, although formally the government's economic adviser, was in practice largely acting as a personal adviser to the chancellor of the exchequer. But ministers other than the chancellor had no such sources of advice. During the 1960s the only partial exception to this were prime ministers, of both parties; they had individual confidants who sat in No. 10 Downing Street, with titles such as prime minister's personal secretary. But these were indeed personal arrangements, virtually appointments at court, of a kind that would have been familiar in the eighteenth century. With Harold Macmillan was John Wyndham, later Lord Egremont; with Harold Wilson between 1964 and 1970 was Marcia Williams, later Baroness Falkender. But the artless descriptions of these informal arrangements in the protagonists' memoirs makes it clear that since the days of the "garden suburb" or S Branch, there had been no progress at all.

Countervailing Advice for the Cabinet: The CPRS

While Mrs. Williams was advising Harold Wilson, the foundations for something much more systematic were being laid by the leader of the Conservative opposition, Edward Heath. In the spring of 1968 he set up a small working group chaired by a former senior civil servant, Baroness Sharp, to advise him on various aspects of the machinery of government and, in particular, on the scope for providing a future Conservative prime minister with advice to countervail that reaching him from individual departments. A major objective of this would be to help develop a "government" view rather than to hope that something plausibly resembling it would emerge from the sum and multiple of departmental views, clashing in cabinet. As Lady Sharp later recalled:

In the particular sphere in which I worked—local government, housing, new towns, land use, planning, etc.—the machinery [of government] did not work well. There was a great deal of overlapping between departments and a great deal of friction. I remember bitter arguments between myself and the Board of Trade (responsible for the distribution of industry) about the siting of new towns; and again of course with the Ministry of Agriculture. Sometimes these disputes were taken to the Cabinet for settlement which took up a lot of their time and did not necessarily produce the right result.

There was also a lot of chopping and changing in the distribution of responsibilities between Departments. . . . But there seemed to be no way of settling the Departmental pattern in the interests of good government. It was nobody's business.[10]

Lady Sharp added that as she watched overburdened ministers plowing through their official papers, she wondered if they ought to have more help in considering subjects outside their own departments' fields but on which they might be expected to make sensible comments in cabinet or cabinet committees.

Lady Sharp's account continued:

"One day . . . Mr. Macmillan, then Prime Minister (whom I had known well at the Ministry of Housing and Local Government) asked me to lunch. . . . One thing he said was "It's a strange thing that I have now got the biggest job I have ever had and less help in doing it than I have ever known." And that clicked with my growing notion that there was a gap in the machinery of government at the centre. Should there be a Prime Minister's Department? Or a staff to serve the Prime Minister and Cabinet Ministers?"[11]

Discussions between Lady Sharp and Mr. Heath led to his asking her to lead a small group of advisers—all former civil servants—to help him in thinking about the machinery of government. One of the topics on which the group advised was the issue of whether or not to create a "Prime Minister's Department." The group commented on the cabinet's preoccupation with short-term problems. It noted also the weak position of the prime minister himself, who, despite his central role "has normally had no agency on which to call for objective advice or for help in evaluating his colleagues' ex parte statements, other than the tiny personal staff located at No. 10."

The report's solution to these problems was to create a new Office of the Prime Minister and Cabinet, with the basic tasks of "co-ordination, planning, research and study, management and organization services at governmental levels." Its responsibilities were to include the cabinet secretariat, civil service personnel management and management services and, most important, the planning of priorities—"the crucial task of enabling the Government to identify its main objectives, to relate individual decisions to their wider context and, in doing so, to co-ordinate its own activities." This task would be performed by a small central staff, alongside the cabinet secretariat and headed by a "chief planning officer" equivalent in rank to the cabinet secretary. It was to be supported by a permanent research unit. Its advice would

enable the Government, once its major purposes had been established, to ensure that the means by which these were implemented were compatible with each other; and whether existing activities were compatible with them . . . ; and to determine whether apparently unrelated proposals coming forward from departments were consistent with them, in both the short and long-term.[12]

Edward Heath discussed this report with its authors, but kept his own counsel about his reaction to its recommendations, including that for an Office of Prime Minister and Cabinet.

While the group was at work, Heath had in fact some rather similar advice—which was shown to the group—from another source. Lord Plowden and Lord Roberthall, formerly chief planner and chief economic advisor, respectively, sent Mr. Heath a short memorandum noting the long felt need by prime ministers and nondepartmental ministers for "impartial advice on matters with a high context of expertise which come to Cabinet from Departmental Ministers." Cabinet Office briefing was of little help, being at most "the quintessence of civil service impartiality—'On the one hand . . . on the other. . . . ' " What the prime minister and his nondepartmental colleagues needed was a "relatively small staff of able people who can examine proposals from Departments . . .

from the point of view of the whole national interest in the short and especially in the long-term. . . . Such a body could also bring out the real issues at the root of a conflict of advice, which can usually be resolved into different views about the aims of policy or differrent estimates of probability." This staff would work to a senior minister, possibly the prime minister himself; especially since it would be "bitterly opposed by existing Whitehall departments," the prime minister would need to make clear his own backing for it and to ensure that the cabinet was agreed on the need for it.[13]

The eventual upshot, in which the advice of Lady Sharp's group and that of Lord Plowden and Lord Roberthall was combined with the thinking of several senior civil servants, was the creation after the Conservative victory of 1970 of the so-called Central Policy Review Staff (CPRS). The tasks outlined for the CPRS, in the government statement of its purposes, included helping ministers to "take better policy decisions by assisting them to work out the implications of their basic strategy in terms of policies in specific areas, to establish the relative priorities to be given to the different sectors of their programme as a whole, to identify those areas of policy in which new choices can be exercised and to ensure that the underlying implications of alternative courses of action are fully analysed and considered."[14] In other words, it was to try to ensure that departmental bureaucracies and their ministers did not hinder the achievement of the government's objectives by ignoring them, by stampeding the cabinet into decisions without a sense of their context, or by failing to make clear, when putting proposals to cabinet, what the real consequences of accepting those proposals might be.

The body, whose countervailing advice was intended (among other aims) to prevent the career bureaucracy from distorting the achievements of an elected government, was novel in composition, in activities, and in style. Uniquely in modern British government, its members were chosen wholly at the discretion of its director. Never more than twenty in all, about half of them were career civil servants seconded from departments, the rest recruited from outside (business, management consultancy, the universities). Except in the early (Conservative) years, CPRS members were not chosen for their partisan sympathy with the government in power. Nor, even, was the director. The average length of service in the CPRS was two years. Its four directors included a polymath research scientist (the flamboyant Lord Rothschild), an academic economist, a businessman, and a merchant banker.

The case for the CPRS, at the time it was set up and later, was expressed largely in terms of its contribution to "strategic" and "synoptic" thinking on the part of the cabinet collectively. Its attempts to do this, especially by helping the cabinet to think through and to assess events and policy options in the widest possible context, remained important throughout its life. But in practice, almost as important (if less explicit) in the CPRS's own view of itself, was its role in providing an antidote, or at least an alternative, to the advice reaching ministers through departmental channels dominated by career civil servants. Edward Heath, creator of the CPRS, said later that in his view its role included "to examine interdepartmental issues which came to the cabinet *including the exposure of fallacies in departmental papers*"; James Callaghan, who made much use of the CPRS during his premiership in 1976–79 saw its tasks as including *"to inject a new angle in agreed interdepartmental papers."*[15]

Though they did not say it in as many words, both former prime ministers might have added that this task was probably perceived as most valuable not by cabinets but by prime ministers, trying with their small official staffs to interpret and to evaluate the advice reaching them through the career hierarchy and through their cabinet colleagues. A similar view was expressed by the CPRS member (a career official on secondment) who summarized the role of the CPRS as "to sabotage the over-smooth working of the bureaucratic machine."[16]

The CPRS did its job in three main ways. First, especially in the early years, it organized and provided the papers for wide ranging "strategic" meetings of the cabinet. The aim of these was to enable ministers to discuss, confirm, develop, or revise the major themes of their current program, undistracted—as at conventional cabinet meetings—by specific events and by departments' immediate responses to them. These meetings were not intended to lead to decisions; they were meant to provide, or at least to strengthen, the policy framework within which specific decisions could later be taken.

Second, the CPRS conducted quite detailed, long-term studies into particular issues that might be thought to have strategic significance: energy policy, the computer industry, the motor car industry (and the scale and nature of government support in both cases), the role and effectiveness of the foreign service. These reports, some of which were published, were intended to tackle such issues from a perspective wholly within the executive machine but not unduly influenced by any special interest (of the kind which might occasionally "capture" particular departments and the career officials who staffed them).

Third, the CPRS saw itself as having a continuing open-ended responsibility for monitoring, as far as it could, developments both in the world at large and in government policies, and for intervening when it thought fit with advice to ministers. The technique developed by the CPRS was directly addressed to the problem that had been pointed out by Lord Plowden and Lord Roberthall: that for almost every issue raised in cabinet or cabinet commmmittee, one or more ministers advised by their relatively expert departments would circulate a paper arguing their own special case in whatever terms seemed likely to be persuasive. Meanwhile, the chairman would have a broadly neutral (and sometimes not very expert) brief provided by the cabinet secretariat and the rest of the group might be lucky enough to have some departmental interest and thus some departmental briefing—or might not, in which case they would simply have to do as best they could on the basis of their native wit, or remain silent. The result was that ministerial discussions always risked being dominated by special interests, with no certainty at all that the national or even the collective government case would be argued, let alone prevail.

The CPRS dealt with this problem by producing what it called "collective briefs." These were, literally, papers that aimed to look at an issue from a collective point of view and were circulated collectively—that is, to all the ministers involved, and not to the chairman alone. A hypothetical but familiar type of case might thus see a paper prepared by a "spending" department describing a situation and arguing for more resources to deal with it, and a counterpaper from the Treasury claiming that public spending was already far in excess of the budget and that consequently nothing could be done that cost money—and a third paper from the CPRS trying to set both the issue and these two responses to it in the context of the government's current strategy and of likely future contingencies. Collective briefs frequently also posed what the

CPRS saw as key questions that needed answering before a rational decision could be taken. Whatever that decision might be, a collective brief could be said to have achieved its objective if it at least prevented ministers from steamrollering colleagues through their own unexamined assertions.

As the above illustration shows, the CPRS at different times found itself sometimes supporting, sometimes opposing the various Whitehall departments. Its relationship with the Treasury was especially variable, and especially significant. The CPRS was often at one with the Treasury in questioning the justification for spending departments' bids for funds; it also often sided with departments in insisting that a government had objectives—social, industrial, military—that might sometimes have higher priority than the Treasury's objective of holding public spending down to a preordained level.

In all these activities, the CPRS was conscious of its formal position as adviser to the cabinet collectively; it had not been intended to be a prime minister's department. Its "strategy" papers, and virtually all its big reports and collective briefs, were circulated to all ministers in the cabinet (and thus to their departments, consequently lessening the CPRS's countervailing force against those departments and their continuing policies). But an important minority of CPRS output was destined for the prime minister of the day alone; some of what it produced often went unseen, its existence unknown, by anyone outside the prime minister's personal secretariat.

This privileged access ensured CPRS advice a direct route to the top. On the other hand, since such advice went unseen by other cabinet members, and by the civil service, it was all too easy for them to believe (or profess to believe) that the CPRS was doing nothing useful. There was often a choice between deploying advice in a semipublic forum around the cabinet table, earning credit for it but risking that it would be neutralized, and advising the prime minister privately in the hope that the prime minister, at least, would value and remember this service.

The Prime Minister's Policy Unit

The lifetime of the CPRS coincided with the reintroduction of one institution already tried (and mentioned above) and the introduction of another—both still in the mainstream of established practice in attempting to provide countervailing advice by inserting outsiders into the interstices of the policy-making hierarchy, rather than by intervening in the structure of that hierarchy itself. The first of these was the recreation, in 1974, of a body that David Lloyd George or Winston Churchill would certainly have recognized, even if its title were new: a Prime Minister's Policy Unit. Harold Wilson, unexpectedly winning an unexpected general election for Labour in early 1974, had spent little time (unlike Heath, in the 1960s) in thinking ahead about refinements to the machinery of government. It seems to have been largely as a last-minute afterthought that he set up, after his victory, a small unit in No. 10 Downing Street headed by a former academic and Labour supporter, Bernard Donoughue. Donoughue was given a free hand in staffing his unit, which he led until Labour's defeat in summer 1979; its members, totaling about seven or eight, were drawn mainly from academic life, though they also included people from business and the trade unions. All were Labour supporters.

The unit's function has been described as "forward policy analysis, medium and long term, on domestic and overseas policy. They could act on their own initiative. . . . They also acted in response to a Prime Minister's request. . . . The Policy Unit gave the Prime Minister a view that was different from that of the official machine and from that coming to him from separate departments. They commented on and probed the advice coming in from these sources."[17]

James Callaghan inherited Donoughue and his unit and made no changes in the role of either. Margaret Thatcher, replacing Callaghan, established a very similar unit of her own. Initially led by a businessman, the Thatcher policy unit was later headed by a journalist, a banker (now a member of Parliament), and an academic. The latter resigned with Mrs. Thatcher in November 1990. Mr. Major replaced him with an economic journalist (married to a middle-ranking government minister).

Like its predecessor, the Thatcher/Major unit was small—never more than eight or nine professionals. Many of its members were seconded from the private sector. A large proportion of its members were active members of the ruling Conservative party. Initially (unlike the Wilson/Callaghan unit) it included a few serving civil servants, on secondment. A former member of the Thatcher unit saw it as having seven main functions: (1) as think tank, developing and presenting new ideas to the prime minister; (2) as adviser, commenting on the work and on the advice of departments; (3) as progress-chaser, following up the implementation of policy decisions; (4) as drawing to the prime minister's attention issues that might otherwise be handled within individual departments; (5) as an additional channel of communication between the prime minister and departments; (6) as a source of informed, "non-Whitehall," comment on the sometimes "strangely generalized" advice reaching the prime minister from the bureaucracy; and (7) as suggestion box, receiving and transmitting to the prime minister suggestions originating elsewhere.[18]

The Wilson and Callaghan units, and the Thatcher unit for its first four years coexisted with the continuing CPRS. In 1974 it was widely thought that Wilson's establishment of his own unit would change the role of the CPRS and possibly even cause its demise. That this did not happen was probably due to the rather different roles played by the two organizations, during a period when collective decision making, through the cabinet, was very much a reality. The official line was that the Policy Unit was concerned with the short term, the CPRS with the medium and longer term. There was little force in this distinction. More important in practice was the fact that where the CPRS worked for ministers collectively, from time to time taking on specific tasks for the prime minister, the Policy Unit worked exclusively—and privately—for the prime minister. Its advice—as continued to be the case under Thatcher— was seen by nobody except its recipient; CPRS papers were normally circulated widely to ministers and consequently were seen, and briefed on (or against), by civil servants. In addition, the small size of the Policy Unit limited its ability to do large pieces of work or to produce long reports.

Both under Labour and under Thatcher, the CPRS and the Policy Unit were on good terms and, on occasion, worked closely together. Both shared a common interest in keeping abreast of thinking and planning in departments and in ensuring that sectional interests did not hijack government policy; both saw themselves as having a clearer view of ministerial priorities and sensitivities than did departmental (that is, career) civil servants, and as being more likely to work enthusiastically to reflect these in practice. They shared a common disdain for those departments, and the officials in them—whom they regarded as unduly subservient to outside interests or unduly wedded to a particular view of the world—and a common suspicion that ministers in charge of such departments might "go native" and themselves come to reflect exactly the same influences. To this extent they saw themselves as actually, or potentially, a source of countervailing advice for the head of government—the difference being that between 1971 and 1979 (under Heath, Wilson, and Callaghan) government was led in a more genuinely collective style than under the relatively autocratic Thatcher.

However, the CPRS and the Policy Unit coexisted during only the first Thatcher administration. Immediately after Thatcher's second election victory, in 1983, the CPRS was abolished. The reasons given for this in an official statement at the time were that its original role of providing "policy analysis and collective advice to Ministers" was now being adequately performed by departmental policy planning units, the cabinet secretariat, the prime minister's policy unit and ministers' special advisers. A member of the Policy Unit subsequently argued that there were, in fact, "four crucial reasons": (1) the CPRS's propensity to respond to problems with large-scale, long-term strategic reviews rather than immediate advice on tactical options set in a strategic framework; (2) the strong chance that its advice, circulated to ministers collectively, would be leaked by one of them; (3) the risk that CPRS comments on departments' policy proposals could themselves become the focus of discussion and could thus undermine departments' sense of responsibility for their own policy areas; and (4) the inevitably transitory nature of any institution at the center of government.[19] Two of these points were confirmed by Mrs. Thatcher in a discussion with me. "All those leaks!" was the first reason she gave for establishing the CPRS. The second was the poor quality of its reports—"Guffy stuff, like Ph.D. theses. We could do that kind of thing ourselves."[20]

The new institution—if "institution" is the right word to describe an informally linked collection of individuals of widely differing types performing widely different functions—introduced during the lifetime of the CPRS was the network of "special" or "policy" advisers. One or two ministers in the Heath cabinet of 1970–74 had such advisers, relatively young people, often on secondment from within the Conservative party organization. Brought into government on short-term contracts, they were virtually the only exception to the monopoly held by the career civil service on positions within departments. Even so, their positions were strictly advisory; they had no authority within the line hierarchy.

Uncertainty about the appropriate title for these people (in what sense were they "special"? on what kind of "policy" should they advise?) reflected the fundamental ambiguity of their role. Were they extensions of their ministers' general capability, or were they additional experts on subjects with which their ministers were concerned? Examples of both types can be identified, as well as a much larger number who do not obviously fall into either category.

When Wilson's Labour government succeeded Heath in 1974, advisers—apparently with little previous thought or selection—were brought in on a much larger scale. Virtually every minister in the 1974–79 administrations had an adviser, and some had more than one. As the new prime minister in 1979, Mrs. Thatcher was initially unenthusiastic about advisers, allegedly arguing that her cabinet colleagues should be capable of providing their own policy advice. However, over time she relaxed this attitude: today most ministers have an adviser.

In addition, Mrs. Thatcher herself came to rely heavily on personal advisers for reinforcement in her dealings with three departments which, for different reasons, she mistrusted. Like some of her predecessors, she felt that the Department of Education and Science lacked zeal in promoting educational reform and was too passive toward unresponsive local educational authorities. Her views were based partly on her own experience as head of the department in the Heath administration of the early 1970s. It was perhaps this experience that made her feel, when prime minister, that she could not rely even on the colleagues whom she had now appointed to head the department. In the late 1980s there were signs that she was using the then head of her Policy Unit (Brian Griffiths), a university academic on leave, as a countervailing force against the department. "It is a grim joke in the Department of Education and Science that Griffiths . . . is more in charge of education policy than the Secretary of State [for Education and Science]," noted a newspaper story.[21]

Mrs. Thatcher's attitude toward the Foreign and Commonwealth Office was rather different. She mistrusted it not because it was too passive but because it was too active in directions of which she disapproved. Like other senior British politicians, she seemed to view the FCO as in general liable to accommodate foreigners regardless of the government's priorities and domestic obligations. In particular, it was too enthusiastic about British integration with the European Community, too unconcerned about maintaining Britain's "sovereignty." To strengthen her hand in dealings with the FCO, Mrs. Thatcher used career diplomats whom she evidently felt to be more reliable than their colleagues. She appointed two personal advisers on foreign affairs, both former members of the foreign service (Sir Anthony Parsons, 1982–83, then Sir Percy Cradock). There were no signs that either of them advised the prime minister differently from their former colleagues, or that they played an important part in the policy-making process.

Much more significant in foreign affairs was an originally relatively junior career diplomat who was nominated by the FCO to the regular foreign affairs post among the prime minister's official civil service secretariat. Appointed in 1984, Charles Powell stayed in No. 10 Downing Street much longer than the normal tour of duty. By 1988 he had become a trusted confidant closely allied with Mrs. Thatcher in her opposition to closer European integration. He was widely believed to be the author of the notorious speech given by Mrs. Thatcher at Bruges in September 1988, when she declared, among other things, "We have not successfully rolled back the frontiers of the state in Britain, only to see them reimposed at a European level, with a European super-state exercising a new dominance from Brussels."[22] This was not the language that would have been used by the FCO or by the prime minister's colleague, the foreign secretary.

Charles Powell—created Sir Charles after Mrs. Thatcher's resignation in late 1990—was kept on by her successor John Major. During the crisis and subsequent war in the Persian Gulf, Powell was said to be acting as the main link between No. 10 Downing Street and the White House.

The third department against which Mrs. Thatcher felt in need of countervailing advice was the Treasury, responsible for the government's economic policy. Professor Alan Walters was the prime minister's personal economic adviser from 1979 to 1983, and again in 1989. His role was clearly to give Mrs. Thatcher intellectual support to counter the advice reaching her from the Treasury via the chancellor of the exchequer, an effective combination of a well-resourced department and a normally powerful minister. The tension generated in this case led to political disaster. When in 1989 Walters returned from the United States for his second stint in No. 10, his disagreements with the chancellor of the exchequer (Nigel Lawson), over possible British entry into a European Monetary System, became increasingly public knowledge. Walters finally published an article in an academic journal deriding the EMS and British entry and thus, by open implication, challenging the advice given by Lawson and the Treasury. Lawson resigned, followed a few hours later by Walters. The departure of Lawson, among the ablest and longest serving of Mrs. Thatcher's colleagues, was one of the main shocks to her administration that finally brought it down a year later.

As at all times since 1974, the choice of advisers—including the choice whether or not to appoint an adviser at all—has been left to ministers. The use made of advisers, or the use made by advisers of their own time, has been a function of their own characteristics and experience, the clarity with which their ministers have perceived their own needs, the possible contribution of advisers to those needs, and the circumstances in which they have found themselves. The first systematic survey of special advisers, and how they have been used since 1970, has only recently been completed. Its findings are not yet available. Some preliminary points that emerge are, for example, the distinctions in professional backgrounds according to party. A large proportion of Conservative advisers (1974–79, 1979–88) had come from the party's official Research Department; few had been academics. There was a much higher proportion of academics among Labour advisers (1974–79). Common to both parties has been the wide range of uses to which advisers have been put—and, within those, the surprisingly small part that advisers have played in the processes of actually *making* policy. Their role has been very different from that of the *policy analyst* as described by Arnold Meltsner—and different, indeed, from that of an *adviser* as the term might be commonly understood.[23]

The Ministerial Cabinet

Beyond this limited repertoire of limited challenges to "career" advice—prime minister's policy units, the CPRS, special advisers—

one other device remains regularly advocated but never yet tried. This is the so-called ministerial *cabinet,* on lines familiar in continental Europe. Translated to Britain, cabinets would perform for departmental ministers many of the functions performed for prime ministers by their policy units—advising, commenting on advice originating in the career hierarchy, acting as an additional contact point between ministers and their departments, and progress-chasing. The introduction of cabinets into British government was advocated in 1986 by a former adviser to Mrs. Thatcher, Sir John Hoskyns.[24] At about the same time, a House of Commons committee recommended that the government should make "a limited experiment" with the cabinet system, perhaps trying it in a single department.[25] This proposal was ignored (rather than rejected) by the government, but there has been no sign of any action on these lines.

The Prime Minister's Efficiency Unit

One final form of countervailing advice, introduced by Mrs. Thatcher, was a Prime Minister's Efficiency Unit. Immediately after her 1979 general election victory, she appointed Sir Derek Rayner, then joint managing director of the retail firm Marks and Spencer, to advise her on ways of eliminating waste and increasing efficiency in central government. Rayner had himself already worked in government under the previous Conservative administration of Edward Heath. His chosen technique for achieving his aims was a series of rapid surveys (known as "scrutinies") that focused on specific programs. To help him in running scrutinies, Rayner set up a very small office staffed by civil servants seconded from line departments.

Rayner himself laid down, in some detail, the guidelines for carrying out scrutinies, which though supervised by his own unit were actually carried out by officials in the departments concerned. The essence of a scrutiny was three key questions: "What is it for, what does it cost, and what value does it add?" Opinions vary both about the short-run impact and about the wider significance of Rayner's efficiency unit (whose subsequent heads have been, first, another businessman working, like Rayner, part-time, and from the autumn of 1988, a recently retired senior civil servant). Its supporters point to the hundreds of millions of pounds in potential savings identified, and the (considerably fewer) savings agreed; they also argue that the unit's activities have helped change the civil service's attitudes to waste and to ways of reducing it. Its detractors point out that the savings actually made are fewer still, that the unit has not touched on the far larger sums involved in main program costs and—closely related to this—that it has had little or nothing to say about the effectiveness, as opposed to the efficiency, of government activities.

Conclusions: Some General Issues

When one considers British experience with the provision of countervailing analysis and advice over the past seventy years, one fact stands out. Throughout the whole period—save for the exceptional years of the Second World War—the principle has been maintained that the main stream of advice reaching ministers from the career civil service should be undiluted, untainted, by advice from any other source. Countervailing advice—to change the simile—has thus been "bolted on" to the main system in the form of small staffs or individuals, clearly identifiable and with functions clearly differentiated from those of career officials in line positions.

This prompts several questions. First, whether "bolting on" countervailing advice, rather than integrating it into the system, affords politicians in office a bureaucracy that is sufficiently sensitive to their views of the world and susceptible to control by them. Secondly, whether for politicians "bolting on" is an adequate substitute for either more direct manipulation or infiltration of the career bureaucracy—or whether it is effective only if it complements these approaches. Changing the perspective slightly, it can be asked whether providing countervailing advice in this form can, as it were, immunize the executive machine against pressures that seek to overturn or at least dilute the supremacy of the career bureaucracy.

In answering these questions, one must consider several important issues. These issues are, first, the nature of working relationships between "countervailers" and the career bureaucracy; second, the appropriate location of, and the identity of the main clientele for, such analysis and advice in a cabinet system; third, the nature of working relationships between different sources of countervailing advice.

An analyst trying to play a countervailing role must decide how far to distance himself from the line—and thus in Britain the career—bureaucracy. Some distance, and some tension, is inevitable. The analyst is by definition challenging the advice coming up the line. He is thus challenging line officials' competence and the interests they represent. He is also challenging the ministers whom those officials advise—as did Mrs. Thatcher's Powell and Walters. This is particularly important in Britain where the career service prides itself on its professionalism and its ability to advise impartially and to work zealously for governments of any party. Spared the tasks of having to implement the policies on which he advises, anyone offering countervailing advice may be regarded as "irresponsible" by those who have to deal with the consequences. Privileged to intervene at the top and, often, at a late stage in the decision-making process, he may well be regarded as disruptive by those who manage the policy timetable; they may envy the leverage which his position affords him and resent his influence in general. ("You don't seem to realize that you are making a lot of extra work for very busy people," said one of the cabinet secretariat to a member of the CPRS apropos of one of the latter's interventions in some ministerial discussion.)[26]

Within limits, the "countervailer" can control these responses by deciding just how far to operate openly, thus revealing the exact nature of his intentions. Responses are also a function of the adviser's own attitudes and operating style, and the current context and conventions. The acceptability of countervailing advice at the center has varied directly with the centralization of political power. Thus the "garden suburb" of 1916–18, though its relationships with line departments seem to have been fairly harmonious, vanished with the wartime emergency. By contrast, Lord Cherwell, it was said, "detested bureaucrats, who responded with fear and suspicion."[27] His interventions in the policy process, often only thinly disguised by the attachment of Churchill's signature, were deeply resented in Whitehall. But the extent of Churchill's authority, especially in his wartime administration, made such resentment of no significance. Nonetheless, Cherwell and his statistical section did not survive their patron, nor were thought appropriate models for imitation by the following prime minister. The senior "countervailer" in the Attlee years that followed, Sir Edwin Plowden, while making it clear that he was not a member of the career bureaucracy and that he had no long-term personal expectations within the career system, chose to work very much "with the grain" of the official machine. He contrived to make himself acceptable not only to career officials but also, like them, to politicians of both main governing parties.

The CPRS varied both in structure and in tactics and in the responses which its interventions provoked. Its first head, Lord Rothschild, was a man of great force of character. He built up with Edward Heath, the prime minister who had appointed him, a relationship not unlike that between Churchill and Cherwell thirty years before. (A major difference was that few of Rothschild's minutes were circulated over Heath's signature.) The blunt and sometimes polemical style of CPRS interventions under Rothschild was sometimes resented elsewhere in Whitehall. As long as Rothchild retained Heath's support, this did not matter. It did matter on the occasion that Rothschild overstepped the mark and offered the results of some countervailing analysis, and some advice, in public. In 1973 he allowed to be published the text of a lecture—reflecting some recent work by the Hudson Institute—in which he warned the world (and, in effect, the government) that Britain was well on the way to becoming a second- or third-class power and ought to behave appropriately.[28] Many observers believed that this episode, and the offical reprimand that followed, permanently damaged the working relationship between the two men, though both have since denied this.

Rothschild's style was more flamboyant and, occasionally, combative than that of his successors. But even he took advantage, like them, of his ability to intervene privately. This meant channeling his advice not to the cabinet as a whole—the ostensible client of CPRS—but to the prime minister alone. Personal advice of this kind had the advantage of passing unnoticed by other senior ministers whose own advice and policies it might challenge, and who might thus object to it. (Tony Benn, minister of energy in the Labour government of 1976–79, objected strongly and publicly to attempts to persuade the cabinet against his preferred choice of nuclear reactor for the United Kingdom's power-generating program. In Nigel Lawson's struggles with Alan Walters for Mrs.

Thatcher's ear on European monetary policy, the last straw was the open publication by Walters of an article ridiculing Lawson's views.

Advising covertly had the disadvantage that, since the CPRS's client was the cabinet, if the CPRS worked too much through the prime minister alone, it was open to the charge of not doing the task for which it had been created.

Some CPRS interventions were wholly public, such as its 1977 report on the cost and effectiveness of Britain's overseas representation.[29] This was published and subsequently debated in Parliament. Its conclusions—which, like Rothschild's remarks some years earlier, derived largely from the premise that Britain was no longer a first-class power—were greeted with great hostility in more traditionally minded circles, and by some of those who saw their interests threatened. A well-orchestrated campaign against the report influenced debates in Parliament, the media, and elsewhere.

This episode illustrated one dilemma faced by the adviser who wishes to challenge the status quo, particularly when the status quo is defended by powerful and well-entrenched interests. Should he challenge it publicly, in the hope of enlisting support on a wide front against policies and interests that may be deeply entrenched in the government machine? If so, he must be willing to use the same weapons—backstairs briefings, leaks, innuendo—that his opponents will certainly use against him, having the advantage of much greater resources. Or should he hope to use reasoning, persuasion, interdepartmental committees, and the conventional approaches of internal bureaucratic debate? The CPRS experienced the drawbacks of this approach in relation to its unpublished report (1974) on race relations policy. Unwelcome to an administration that did not want to divert scarce resources to a relatively unpopular and—at that time—problematic policy area, the report found little support within the government and was not available to the potential liberal constitutency outside it. No action followed from it.

By contrast, both past and present Prime Minister's Units have always had the double advantage of having a client who is usually relatively accessible—even if not necessarily willing to take advice offered—and in a position to initiate action, and of being able, if they wish, to advise that client privately. The bulk of the CPRS's output was seen by all or most cabinet ministers, and thus by their civil servants. But Whitehall has usually been left to infer from scraps of evidence whether a question or instruction from a prime minister has been based on briefing from the Prime Minister's Unit. The unit has not been obliged to show its hand openly. As long as it has had the confidence and support of the prime minister, it has not needed allies elsewhere in the machine. Under Mrs. Thatcher its heads had no previous experience of government and presented this fact, if anything, as a virtue.

The advantages of giving countervailing advice in private were highlighted by the one recent episode when the advice, and the fact that it had been offered, became all too public knowledge. As chancellor of the exchequer Nigel Lawson was, in theory, Mrs. Thatcher's principal adviser on economic policy. When it became known that Sir Alan Walters was offering advice directly opposed to his own, Lawson clearly felt that his authority was being undermined and his position made untenable. The result was his own resignation and that of Walters.

The undoubted success of Sir Derek Rayner's Efficiency Unit, at least in establishing the unit as a respected force in Whitehall, owed much to Mrs. Thatcher's backing but much, also, to Rayner's own diplomatic skills and his applied knowledge of the system—derived partly from his own previous experience in government. He also, though an outsider himself, chose to work with the grain in staffing both his central unit and the individual scrutiny teams with career officials (albeit relatively junior ones). The prime minister's known support for the cause of efficiency in general and for the unit in particular has meant that the unit has risked little in publishing its reports. It should, however, be added that its proposals for efficiency savings have been implemented only in part.

The preceding discussion has already touched on the issue of where best in a *cabinet* system to locate a central source of countervailing advice. Not much more can be said on this beyond the obvious point that if an analytical/advisory unit purports to be working for the cabinet collectively, it almost certainly has to be housed with whatever other institutions serve the cabinet. It in theory can be located in the Prime Minister's Office; but then the pretence that its services are generally available to all ministers becomes hard to support. Even if it is physically close to the cabinet secretariat, the two should be seen as independent of each other. The role of the secretariat, as it has developed in Britain since 1916, is very much that of disinterested broker and manager of the central business of government; its stylized records of cabinet and other ministerial discussions are almost invariably accepted as authoritative without challenge or amendment. (The one episode in recent history in which a cabinet member did challenge the cabinet minutes was a stage in an escalating row that culminated in his resignation.)[30] An advisory unit, by contrast, is bound to develop and periodically express particular points of view.

Finally, since countervailing advisers are almost by definition both outnumbered by the line bureaucracy and isolated in their positions within it, their relationships with each other can be critical in determining their effectiveness. Hugh Heclo's classic account of government in Washington, D.C., describes the weakness of a system in which a large number of outsiders brought in to support the president know neither Washington nor each other.[31] The problems of discontinuity and absence of institutional memory (or learning) are severe, and most severe at the top of the system. In Whitehall, continuity is assured by reserving virtually all the key positions for insiders, career professionals. Would-be "countervailers" need to be part of a network if they are not to be sidetracked or neutralized. The Official Secrets Act and the style of government to which it contributes seriously hinders objective networking across the ring-fence separating government from the outside world. Many government "secrets" may not be and are not shared even with the party organization of the administration's own party. Countervailing advisers therefore need to develop networks mainly within government.

The elements of several natural networks exist, though some are more easily activated than others. The political advisers are in one sense a natural network of people with common status and shared objectives, but communication among them is hindered by differences in age, experience, ideological fervor, professional orientation, and sheer competence. Specialist cadres such as economists or scientists are networks potentially open to outsiders, partly because their training inclines them to look critically at the assumptions and arguments used by politicians and their "generalist" advisers. In Whitehall an additional bond between such cadres and countervailing advisers is that the former are still mainly used in staff roles—that is to say, as special advisers. Many of them are familiar with the frustrations of advisers, commenting only by invitation on policy issues and often excluded, deliberately or not, from the implementation process.

This last point offers a clue to answering the question posed earlier about the adequacy of countervailing advice as an instrument of political control over a bureaucracy. Some senior British civil servants seem to have accepted "policy advisers" in particular, perhaps including the Prime Minister's Policy Unit in this, as an acceptable alternative to "politicizing" the line bureaucracy—indeed, perhaps as a preemptive move that may reduce pressures in favor of politicization. If ministers have access to personal advisers of their own, the argument seems to run, they do not need to intervene in the hallowed process of filling senior line posts by internal selection.

If this is the argument used, its main premise is false. Firm control over the policy process requires not only adequate advice but also the capacity to control the implementation of decisions once made. The latter may well require political influence over the selection of staff for line positions. Whether and how this might be done are questions outside the scope of this chapter. The point is that adequate countervailing analysis and advice are only part of the necessary contributions to effective management of the public policy process.

Notes

This chapter is based on a paper originally presented to a Conference on Executive Leadership and the Executive Establishment, Georgetown University, September 1988.

1. *Top Jobs in Whitehall,* report of a Royal Institute of Public Administration working party (London: RIPA, 1987).

2. Lord Hunt of Tanworth, in *Advising the Rulers,* ed. William Plowden (Oxford: Blackwell, 1987), p. 69.

3. John Turner, *Lloyd George's Secretariat* (Cambridge: Cambridge University Press, 1981).

4. Martin Gilbert, *Finest Hour: Winston S. Churchill 1939–41* (London: Heinemann, 1983), p. 48.

5. Ibid., p. 49.

6. G.D.A. MacDougall, "The Prime Minister's Statistical Section," in *Lessons of the British War Economy,* ed. D. N. Chester (Cambridge: Cambridge University Press, 1951), pp. 58–59.

7. Edwin Plowden, *An Industrialist in the Treasury* (London: Andre Deutsch, 1989), p. 9.

8. Ibid., p. 170.

9. Ibid.

10. Quoted in Tessa Blackstone and William Plowden, *Inside the Think Tank: Advising the Cabinet 1971–83* (London: Heinemann, 1988), p. 7.

11. Ibid.

12. Ibid., p. 8.

13. Ibid.

14. Cmnd. 4506, *The Reorganization of Central Government* (London: HMSO, 1970), p. 13.

15. Blackstone and Plowden, *Inside the Think Tank,* p. 56, emphasis added.

16. Author's recollection.

17. G. W. Jones, in *Advising the Rulers,* ed. Plowden, p. 54.

18. David Willetts, "The Role of the Prime Minister's Policy Unit," *Public Administration* 65 (Winter 1987), 450–51.

19. Ibid., p. 445.

20. Blackstone and Plowden, *Inside the Think Tank,* p. 56.

21. David Gow, "Round Brian Quiz," *The Guardian* (London), 19 July 1988, p. 13.

22. Quoted in Anthony Bevins, "Labour Takes Lead in Europe," *The Independent* (London), 9 May 1989.

23. Arnold Meltsner, *Policy Analysts in the Bureaucracy,* (Berkeley and Los Angeles: University of California Press, 1986).

24. Sir John Hoskyns et al, *Re-skilling Government* (London: Institute of Director, 1986, mimeographed), pp. 15–16.

25. *Civil Servants and Ministers: Duties and Responsibilities,* seventh report from the Treasury and Civil Service Committee, sess. 1985–86, HC 92-I, pars. 5.28–32.

26. Author's recollection.

27. Hans Daalder, *Cabinet Reform in Britain, 1914–63* (London: Oxford University Press, 1964), p. 212.

28. *The Times* (London), 26 September 1973, p. 1.

29. Central Policy Review Staff, *Review of Overseas Representation* (London: HMSO, August 1977).

30. Magnus Linklater and David Leigh, *Not with Honour: The Inside Story of the Westland Scandal* (London: Sphere Books, 1986), pp. 99–101.

31. Hugh Heclo, *A Government of Strangers* (Washington, D.C.: Brookings, 1977).

11

Executive Office Agencies and Advisory Policy Units

STUART E. EIZENSTAT

This chapter will discuss the roles within the Executive Office of the President of the Council of Economic Advisers (CEA), the Office of Management and Budget (OMB), and a new White House Secretariat. My observations are based on my experience in the Carter administration as assistant to the president for domestic affairs and policy, 1977–81.

The Council of Economic Advisers

The Council of Economic Advisers, created by President Truman in 1946, should continue to serve the role of an economic think tank for the president. But it cannot effectively serve the role of economic policy coordinator for the various agencies providing economic advice for the president. That role should be played by an assistant to the president for economic policy on the White House staff.

Very early in 1977 (the early days of the Carter administration), an issue which really bedeviled us—and I would say frankly was never resolved through the end of the administration—was the question of coordinating economic policy. There was no question that Zbigniew Brzezinski was in charge of coordinating national security policy. And there was no question about my authority to coordinate domestic internal policy, social policy. There really remained a question about the coordination of economic policy. I suggested to Charlie Schultze, chairman of the Council of Economic Advisers, the possibility of having him move over to the West Wing and serve as the economic coordinator—that is, to coordinate the different departmental recommendations on economic policy, to provide a synthesis, an analysis; to be a mediator, sometimes an arbitrator, so that the president got the same kind of synthesized and coordinated recommendations in economic policy as he did in foreign and domestic policy. Mr. Schultze—properly, in retrospect—demurred, feeling that if in fact he had taken on that role the uniqueness of the CEA as an independent source of economic advice and analysis would be compromised; that is, it would have then been not simply an educator and an advocate for economic efficiency, it would have inevitably gotten its fingernails dirty and become a political institution, brokering compromises. And yet, as a result of that decision, no one in our administration was an economic coordinator. Sometimes I ended up doing it. There was always a question of what was really economic and what was social policy. Is the minimum wage a social issue, or is it an economic issue? Obviously, almost every decision you make, from agricultural set-asides to minimum wage to regulatory decisions, has an economic impact. Sometimes the secretary of the treasury, as the chairman of our Economic Policy Group, served that function. But I am absolutely of the opinion, regardless of who the secretary is and what his relationship is to the president and what his skills are, that you cannot have economic policy coordinated by the secretary of the treasury. The treasury secretary should be the president's chief economic spokesman. He should chair a cabinet-level economic policy group. Every modern president has had one and should. However, the head of one sister department cannot coordinate and mediate among and between other sister agencies. You must have some White House involvement.

The Ford model was to use Bill Seidman as assistant to the president for economic policy. He was not on the Council of Economic Advisers; in fact, he is not a professional economist. He did not compete with the CEA. His job was to be the White House coordinator for the economic policy. He did not try to supplant President Ford's treasury secretary, Bill Simon. He tried to coordinate across departmental lines, which Simon could not do, given his role. My advice is that the CEA should not be something it is not. It has an important role to play in providing independent economic advice for the president from a White House, not an agency, perspective. But given its limitations, there is a need for somebody in the White House who is charged with coordinating economic policy. I could have done the job had I clearly been charged to do it, but I am not sure that it would have been a very good idea. My hands were more than full with other things. I think it is useful, knowing that there is going to be an overlap between economic and social policy, to have one person who serves solely in the economic coordinating role.

Yet, having said this, I should add that a good CEA chairman cannot simply remain on the sidelines of policy development providing economic advice from an ivory tower. There were a number of instances in which Charlie Schultze inevitably got wrapped up to some degree in the political process. Let me provide a few examples. During 1977–78, he got enmeshed, together with me, in negotiating with the Congress on a congressional initiative called the Humphrey-Hawkins bill. The creation of the CEA came in the Full Employment Act of 1946. Humphrey-Hawkins was to be the modernized, streamlined version of the Full Employment Act of 1946. It would define full employment as 4 percent unemployment. There would be requirements about the Federal Reserve and the president taking actions necessary to achieve 4 percent unemployment. It was very ambitious—we felt overly ambitious—public policy. Charlie Schultze got involved to a very great degree with me in negotiating with Senator Humphrey and Congressman Gus Hawkins in putting an inflation requirement in and making its targets more realistic and flexible. This was a situation in which the chairman of the Council of Economic Advisers was involved in the policy process in a very real and direct way.

A second example was the ill-fated fifty-dollar rebate, which was part of the Carter administration's 1977 economic stimulus package, and which the president early in his administration decided to drop. At a meeting in the Roosevelt Room, Bert Lance, the OMB director, and Treasury Secretary Mike Blumenthal both urged that it be dropped—Lance taking the traditional OMB view that it cost money, and Blumenthal because he was concerned about its inflationary aspects. Charlie Schultze argued very strongly, as did I, that it would be a mistake to drop it because the economy needed a stimulus, and, besides, it would be sign of inconstancy of economic policy if it were dropped so precipitously. The president rejected our advice and it was dropped. It was taken as a sign of inconstancy. Senator Muskie was angered because as the chairman of the Senate Budget Committee he had gone to the extraordinary length of developing a third concurrent resolution to fit in the rebate. And, without any advance notice that the rebate was being dropped, he read on the wire that the president had decided to drop it.

A third example of CEA's deep involvement in the policy process was the decision of whether or not to veto the 1978 Tax Reform Act. The president had sent up an ambitious loophole-closing reform bill that came back in a form which no one could quite distinguish. It had capital gains cuts and very few of our loophole closings. There was a question of whether it should be vetoed. The president was very close to vetoing it on policy grounds. The Council of Economic Advisers made a very strong argument, no so much on tax policy grounds but on macroeconomic grounds that it would be a mistake to veto it. Here again the CEA chairman did not just sit back and let things happen. He is not just an advocate for efficiency in some theoretical sense. He has to get involved in day-to-day decisions. But the CEA's involvement should be limited to economic, not political, arguments. In this case, the CEA won. The president did sign the bill.

The fourth and perhaps most interesting example is Charlie Schultze's chairmanship of the Regulatory Analysis Review Group (RARG). This was part of the Carter administration's effort to bring organization, coherence, coordination, as well as cost-effectiveness and cost-benefit analysis, to regulatory measures. It was in many ways the precursor to what the Reagan administration has done through the OMB process. Charlie Schultze chaired that group. It had the power of picking out proposed regulations from our Regulatory Council, chaired by Doug Costle of the Environmental Protection Agency (EPA), and subjecting some of the major proposed regulations to an independent cost-benefit analysis, separate from the analysis of the agency proposing it. This is enormously useful because it provided the president for the first time with an independent analysis of the regulation which the bureaucracy—always tending to understate the cost of its own regulation—was proposing. But it created problems for the CEA as well. Number one, it did get the CEA chairman involved in some difficult political decisions. For instance, in the EPA's cotton dust standards and new-source performance standards, Charlie Schultze had to go head-to-head with agency heads in ways that previous CEA chairmen had not done. It put us in a situation in which issues had to be taken to President Carter that were too detailed for presidential decisions.

These regulatory issues always involved the basic question of whether you turn the dial one more notch (for example, do you try with cotton dust standards to protect the asthmatics?). And that extra notch is always what costs at the margin a tremendous amount of additional money. Charlie Schultze and I talked on several occasions about how inappropriate it was to have President Carter making decisions about whether the emission standard should be one-tenth of one percent more or less than what the agency was presenting, even though there were very real costs in the economy in that decision. Frankly, there is no good answer to that. It is difficult to present to the president, and yet there is no one else to make those kinds of decisions. Indeed, the president was sued in a landmark case brought by environmentalists who contended that when the statute said that the administration of EPA shall promulgate regulations, it did not mean the president; that the president's sole authority in that situation was to fire the head of EPA if he did not like the result, not to get involved in the process itself. Thankfully, the court recognized that at least to some extent the president was the chief executive officer and had a right to get involved in these issues if he wished to do so.

Office of Management and Budget

With respect to OMB, it was always my procedure, when we had interagency meetings, to develop a policy matter for the president to make sure that at least one of the OMB assistant directors—that is, one of the political appointees—was present. Although we had battle after battle with OMB, we did not see OMB as an enemy per se. Nor did we simply bring them in at the very end of the process, presenting them with a fait accompli and only asking for the costs of the program we had developed. We involved OMB at every stage of the process, and we looked to them not just for budget advice, but to give us an historical memory, to provide policy analysis in a more rigorous way than we were capable of doing because my Domestic Policy Staff was composed, essentially, of policy generalists who combined policy with political skills. There were inevitable clashes with OMB. There were very few things on which we agreed. We wanted to spend more, and they wanted to spend less. That was understandable and inevitable and useful. I would contrast that, however, with the relationship between OMB and the domestic staff in the Reagan administration. At least while David Stockman was OMB director, and to some extent with Jim Miller, domestic policy *and* budget decisions were made by OMB. That is because there were very few purely policy-driven decisions in the domestic area under the Reagan administration. Their decisions were budget-driven. The imperative was to cut across-the-board. The Reagan Office of Policy Development tended to take a more secondary role to OMB than our Domestic Policy Staff took relative to OMB in the Carter administration, where we had a domestic policy agenda. We had campaign commitments that we wanted to fulfill. And while we involved OMB at every stage, we tended, I think, to be more the whip hand in driving that process, whereas I think OMB was more the whip hand in the Reagan administration. This indicates that the goals of the president have a major impact on the role OMB will play in an administration.

Another element with respect to OMB involves transitions between administrations, such as the one through which we have just come, with the inauguration of George Bush. Through no fault of OMB, it does not play the kind of role in transitions it should. That is because of the preposterous notion that the outgoing president should present a full-blown budget, even though he will have utterly nothing to do with passing it or implementing it. So Ronald Reagan in 1988–89, Jimmy Carter in 1980–81, and Gerald Ford in 1976–77 went through the process of budget appeals and preparation of a full-blown budget. All of those budgets are highly politicized since departing presidents use them as their parting statement to the world. When there is a change of parties, the outgoing budget becomes a way of embarrassing the incoming administration. It makes it more difficult for the incoming administration to present its budget. It makes it more difficult for the incoming administration to get its hands on the OMB data early enough to present an alternate budget by the end of February, because OMB is consumed with preparing the outgoing president's budget. The answer is to have the outgoing president present only a current services budget and to give the incoming administration almost immediate access to the budget examiners and to the OMB data. The transition is inherently chaotic. Hundreds of appointments must be made, legislative priorities chosen, foreign dignitaries met. There is precious little time to put together a new budget. The earlier a new president can get his hands on the data and the less he must compare his budget to the often unrealistic budget submitted by the outgoing president, the better.

Another point I wish to raise regarding OMB is its management role—the *M* in OMB, envisioned by President Nixon when he changed the Bureau of the Budget to OMB in 1971. I am skeptical that several hundred professionals in OMB can effectively manage the enormous and complex Executive Branch bureaucracy. The span of control, the ability to manage the bureaucracy from the White House is inherently limited. If we want to put another fifteen people in the management function and tell ourselves that that is going to really help, we are deluding ourselves. We have to recognize that there are limits to how far OMB can go in its management function.

One last point must be made about OMB. As David Stockman has admitted, OMB's economic forecasts and budget numbers were highly politicized in the early Reagan years. It is essential that OMB be viewed as an objective agency whose figures can be trusted by the president, the bureaucracy, the Congress, and the public.

White House Secretariat

I am deeply troubled by the absence of an institutional memory concerning the presidency. I believe we should establish a small White House Secretariat of high-level career civil servants to provide historical continuity to presidents. Let me just paint very quickly a picture of what an incoming president faces. He comes into the White House January 20, and the only institutional memory besides the career bureaucracy at OMB, at few holdovers from the low-level CEA staff, and maybe a few holdovers at the NSC are basically the navy waiters at the White House mess! The pictures are gone; the files are taken to the soon-to-be-built presidential library. There are virtually no career holdovers around the presidency. And so you get a Bay of Pigs because President Kennedy misunderstood what it was that Eisenhower was doing with the Cuban exiles, and there was no institutional memory to bring the new team up to speed. You get the kind of SALT II decision made in March 1977, departing from the Ford-Brezhnev Vladivostok formula. You get the inconsistencies because there is no historical memory orienting the presidency at all. Imagine a new CEO in a corporation coming in and having to decide whether to build a new widget plant. He turns to his vice-president in charge of widgets and asks for advice. And the vice-president says, "How do I know? I just came in with you." And so the president says, "Well, look at the files and let us see how our widgets are doing." And he goes to the file cabinet under "W" for "widgets" and it is empty because the outgoing president took them to his library. You can get them under a convoluted system only if you want to spend a couple of months trying. There is no data tracking. There is no way of pulling back studies that have been done. By establishing within the Executive Office of the President a small, professional White House Secretariat, similar to what exists around the British and Canadian prime ministers, there would be a career group that would provide some historical memory, that would do data tracking, that would allow you to pull past studies up, that would say, "Mr. President, if you make this decision, please recognize the past president already stepped on that land mine and it blew up" and that would serve as some degree of ballast for the entirely political staff in the other units of the White House. Such a secretariat would at least provide some degree of continuity and historical memory for an excessively politicized White House.

PART IV

Advice to Presidents and Prime Ministers on Foreign and Defense Policy

12

The National Security Adviser:
A Presidential Perspective

KEVIN V. MULCAHY AND
HAROLD F. KENDRICK

"The President needs help," said Louis Brownlow in 1937,[1] and over the past fifty years many commentators have agreed that he has gotten it—and then some. Although Brownlow's Report of the President's Committee on Administrative Management did not address directly the issue of national security policy making, it did speak forcefully about the need for presidential staff assistance in general.

His immediate staff assistance is entirely inadequate. He should be given a small number of executive assistants who would be his direct aides in dealing with the managerial agencies and administrative departments of the Government. . . .Their function would be . . . to assist him in obtaining quickly and without delay all pertinent information possessed by any of the executive departments so as to guide him in making his responsible decisions and then, when decision's have been made, to assist him in seeing that every administrative department and agency affected is promptly informed.[2]

A similar concern for assisting the president in the conduct of U.S. foreign affairs led to the creation of the National Security Council (NSC) and its staff in 1947.

In particular, the National Security Adviser (NSA) has, from a presidential perspective, been an invaluable ally in the realization of a White House–based foreign policy. However, as the Irangate affair demonstrated, the use of the national security assistant has not been without consequence for the policy making process. Indeed, the NSA and his staff have come to perform roles in the management of national security that would have surprised Brownlow and his committee colleagues.

This discussion is informed by concerns similar to those of the Committee on Administrative Management with how the president is best able to fulfill his duties as chief executive and, in this case, as chief architect of U.S. national security. Specifically, it analyzes the roles that assistants for national security affairs have played in the policy-making process, evaluates the utility of those roles for assisting the president in making his responsible decisions, and attempts to clarify the president's unique position as the manager of American national security.

The Structure of National Security Policymaking

Public Law 80-253, enacted on July 26, 1947, represents the first, and still the most important, statutory guideline for the organization of national security affairs. Interestingly, in retrospect, the least controversial element in the act was the creation of the National Security Council (NSC). By far, the greatest controversy concerned a unified national military establishment, with three constituent services (army, navy, air force) under a secretary of defense. The Joint Chiefs of Staff (JCS) and the Central Intelligence Agency (CIA) were also established after considerable debate about organizational structure and political accountability.[3] On the other hand, "The concept of a regular and permanent organization for the coordination of national security policy was as widely accepted in Congress as in the Executive."[4]

The function of the National Security Council, as defined in Title I, headed "Coordination for National Security," was "to advise the President with respect to the integration of domestic, foreign, and military policies relating to the national security." And "it shall, subject to the direction of the President, be the duty of the Council . . . to consider policies on matters of common interest to the departments and agencies concerned with the national security, and to make recommendations to the President, in connection therewith."[5] In the 1947 legislation, the NSC's membership was made up of the president, the secretaries of state, defense, army, navy, air force, and the chairman of the National Security Resources Board. Other officials were designated who could serve as members "from time to time," and the NSC was provided with a staff headed by a civilian executive secretary.

The officials comprising the NSC have varied over the years, although they have always included the secretaries of state and defense, and (since 1950) the vice-president, with the head of the CIA, in his capacity as director of central intelligence, as a statutory adviser. The deletion of the service secretaries was an important, early change recommended by the Hoover Commission in 1949, which also recommended improved liaison between the NSC and the JCS.[6] These recommendations were reflected in Public Law 81-216, passed on August 10, 1949, which excluded the service secretaries while designating the Joint Chiefs corporately as the "principal military advisers to the President." At the same time, Reorganization Plan No. 4 formally recognized the NSC as part of the Executive Office of the President (EOP). The Goldwater-Nichols Defense Reorganization Act of 1986 designated the chairman of the Joint Chiefs of Staff individually as the president's principal military adviser and a statutory adviser to the NSC.

The role of the NSA in the national security process has also evolved over time. The NSA under Truman (then known as the executive secretary of the NSC) was thought of as an anonymous servant of the council. He headed a small staff of permanent council employees and a larger body of officials seconded from the constituent agencies—especially from the State Department. In the pre–Korean War period, the NSC staff was organized into an Office of the Executive Secretary composed of the following: permanent NSC employees; the staff, which was made up entirely of member-agency employees detailed full-time to the NSC and supervised by a State Department coordinator; and the consultants to the executive secretary, who were the chief policy planners of each council agency (for example, the head of the State Department's Policy Planning Staff).

In 1950, Truman ordered a reshuffling of the staff. The staff and consultants were replaced by a senior staff and staff assistants, who, while still located in the agencies, were now under the direction of the NSC's executive secretary. As Stanley Falk has observed, "The position of the Executive Secretary, as chairman of the Senior Staff and also head of the permanent NSC staff in the White House, gave that official an intimate view of the President's opinions and desires that he could bring to bear quite early in the planning process."[7]

From this administrative foundation grew the Office of the Assistant to the President for National Security Affairs, which under subsequent presidents came to rival and eclipse the State Department for dominance in the conduct of American foreign policy. In recent years, presidents have increasingly turned to their assistants for national security affairs, rather than the secretaries of state or defense, for foreign policy advice. What seems to have become a permanent feature of foreign policy making may be explained in four ways: (1) the NSA shares the president's unique perspective, and his personal fate is closely tied to the president's political fortunes; (2) centralization of policy making in the White House permits a closer integration of foreign and domestic policy and puts the president's chief adviser for foreign affairs in a close working relationships with the president's domestic advisers; (3) as the focus of foreign policy has broadened to encompass many diverse activities, it has been revealed that the State Department simply lacks the expertise to challenge the other departments and the power to enforce its primacy;[8] and (4) a department secretary cannot match the advantage provided by the NSA's physical presence in the White House itself.[9]

The issues in the debate over organizing for national security have been fully detailed elsewhere.[10] However, to explain the subsequent development of the NSC, its staff, and the NSA, we should note some of the NSC's more prominent institutional characteristics.

First, the NSC was established as a civilian agency. Despite the arguments of former navy secretary, and first secretary of defense, James A. Forrestal, that the council and its staff be "housed as close as possible to the Secretary of Defense," the NSC was designated as a presidential staff agency. Despite the recent prominence of military personnel on the NSC staff, its director has functioned as an assistant to the president.

Second, the NSC staff, as distinct from the council itself, has emerged as an integral part of the Executive Office of the President. As the NSC staff organization has mirrored the major functional divisions of the departments of State and Defense as well as the Central Intelligence Agency, the occasions for frequent and ongoing interactions have certainly helped solidify the position of the NSC as an institutional actor in making foreign policy.

Third, the council and staff, whatever their institutional prominence in the EOP, have operated in an explicitly advisory capacity. As the NSC's chairman, the president would be no more bound by a council vote than a cabinet vote. In fact, the NSC was designed as an interdepartmental forum for the presentation, formulation, and supervision of policies to be implemented by the relevant line agencies. Presidents may or may not attend NSC debates, are free to accept or reject its recommendations, and have organized the NSC staff to suit their personal management styles. The Congressional Research Service's analysis of the NSC in 1977 observed, "The changeable nature of its organization and its designation as an advisory body to the President also meant that the NSC was a malleable organization, to be used as each President saw fit. Thus, its use, internal substructure and ultimate effect would be directly dependent on the style and wishes of the President."[11]

Fourth, although devised to enhance interdepartmental coordination, the NSC is more than a deliberative body to advise the president. In the person of the national security adviser, it is also a major, independent actor in the advisory process. Thus the NSA has become a significant actor in foreign policy making—a force to be reckoned with, often an equal to the secretary of state, sometimes more than an equal.[12] There are various explanations for the rise of the NSA, and these will be considered in the typology of national security assistant roles that follows.

The National Security Advisory System: A Typology

The administrative history of the national security adviser over the past forty years suggests the elements of a typology that will prove useful for better understanding national security policy making. In particular, certain designations are employed—*administrator, coordinator, counselor, agent*—to describe different roles that have been played by national security assistants in the past and that constitute the repertory of roles available to future assistants. The Irangate affair also suggests an aberrant role—the NSA as insurgent—that serves as a warning for what can happen with a national security policy–making process that is out of control.

It cannot be emphasized too strongly that the choice of a particular role from among those available is strictly determined by presidential preference. How the assistant for national security affairs is to be cast depends ultimately on what role the president has cast for himself in the management of U.S. foreign affairs. Similarly, an assistant's success will depend on adopting or adapting to whatever role best facilitates presidential preferences in managing national security. The personal resources that an NSA brings to his position will largely determine his success in fulfilling the president's policy-making and managerial expectations.

Figure 2 presents a typology, or classification according to characteristics exhibited, of the roles played by national security assistants over the past four decades. Before elaborating on the patterns represented, we should note two limitations about the use of such a typology. First, as with all such summary representations, there is a degree of over simplification. For example, the implication that only one role is being played by a particular assistant is incomplete; rather, a more accurate implication is that the categorization of each assistant reflected his dominant (but not exclusive) role.

Second, the two variables associated with the typology—*policy-making responsibility,* the formulation of new initiatives in foreign affairs that results from a close association with the president, and *implementation responsibility,* which refers to the NSA's involvement in hands-on direction of departmental programs as presidential surrogate—are very broad measures of a role definition that have been selected from among the many that may be applicable. Nonetheless, our formalized construct calls attention to certain identifiable patterns by which NSAs have performed their duties and which should persist as management options. Furthermore, as these roles are identified, the consequences of each for the policy-making process become clearer.

Figure 3 categorizes the sixteen national security advisers who have served between 1947 and 1988 according to the typology of

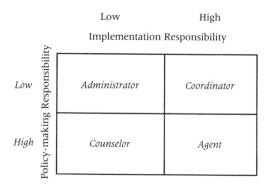

FIGURE 2. A Typology of National Security Assistants' Roles

Low   High

Implementation Responsibility

	Low		High	
Allen		Clark		
	Administrator		*Coordinator*	
			Cutler	
	Souers		Anderson	
	Lay		Gray	
	Powell			
	Carlucci Scowcroft		McFarlane	
	Bundy		Kissinger	
	Rostow			
	Counselor		*Agent*	
		Brzezinski		Poindexter

Left axis (bottom to top): Policy-making Responsibility — Low (top), High (bottom)

FIGURE 3. National Security Assistants and Their Roles
in the Policy-making Process, 1947–88

roles offered here. The ideal types come quickly to mind: Souers as *administrator*, Cutler as *coordinator*, Bundy as *counselor*, Kissinger as *agent*. While this classification generally accords with the historical record, there can be differences about the placement of particular NSAs on such a graph. Accordingly, the location of the NSAs within the matrix has been used to suggest mixed types. For example, Brzezinski, was a *counselor* who would be an *agent*, although he never acquired Kissinger's mastery over the policy-making process. Poindexter is classified as an *agent*, but he is essentially off the table. This deviant case of the NSA as insurgent will be discussed in greater detail after the following elaboration of our typology of roles.

Roles of National Security Assistants

Administrator

The national security adviser as *administrator* has both low implementation and low policy-making responsibilities. This NSA is essentially a servant of the NSC as a presidential institution, rather than a personal and political aide. The duties of this type of NSA include briefing the president on the international situation, representing departmental proposals and viewpoints, scheduling matters for presidential decisions, and monitoring NSC directives. The role of the administrator emphasizes the day-to-day business of the foreign policy–making process. This kind of management suggests an extremely reduced stature for the NSA and his staff. Consequently, neither the preeminence of the State Department, nor the position of the secretary of state as the "orchestra leader" and "first among equals" in national security policy making, would be threatened.[13]

The quintessential NSA administrator was Adm. Sidney W. Souers, President Truman's executive secretary of the NSC. Souers, a model of political rectitude and administrative restraint, was extremely sensitive, even deferential, to the position of the State Department. Understandably, he must have perceived President Truman's high personal regard for his secretaries of state and defense and realized that Truman preferred the "classical model" of State Department dominance of foreign affairs.[14] Souers's custodial role over the NSC advisory process was almost as highly circumscribed as his political role, which precluded attending White House staff meetings, despite efforts by some Truman aides to augment his political responsibilities. "The security assistant had little authority, staff capability or [often] desire to monitor the bureaucracy's implementation of the president's decisions; and his ability to coordinate defense and foreign policy were also constrained."[15] Essentially, Souers saw his role as that of a nonpolitical presidential official responsible for staffing the NSC's advisory process.[16]

Another NSA who falls in the category of administrator was Gen. Brent Scowcroft under President Gerald Ford. General Scowcroft's operating style was completely opposite to that of the preceding NSA, Henry Kissinger, who, even when serving as secretary of state, continued to dominate the national security policy–making process. Scowcroft, who had served as Kissinger's deputy, realized that the situation required an NSA with a more self-effacing style, giving priority to organization and the faithful presentation of the views of NSC members. He did not act independently or negotiate for the president, but functioned instead as a senior administrative aide and staff assistant. The qualities attributed to Scowcroft—"cool, hardworking, straight forward, a good administrator"—were precisely the qualities that appealed to Ford.[17] Scowcroft never appeared on a national interview show, and his name was rarely mentioned in the press.[18] Despite playing a more limited role for the NSA when compared to Kissinger, Scowcroft has often been singled out as one of the most successful NSAs because he did not make himself into a public spokesman or diplomatic conduit.[19]

President Ronald Reagan's first NSA, Richard Allen, was also an administrator. Allen consistently endorsed a low-profile conception of his job and asserted that he had no interest in making policy. As he put it, "The policy formulation function of the national security adviser should be off-loaded to the Secretary of State."[20] Concurrently, Allen's status was diminished by having to report to White House Counsel Edwin Meese instead of directly to Reagan. This arrangement thus weakened his capacity to serve as an adviser who could compensate for the president's admitted deficiencies in foreign affairs.

Coordinator

The role of the NSA as *coordinator* involves the recognition of two enduring characteristics of national security policy making: (1) that, even with a strong secretary of state, most decisions involve more than just diplomacy and cannot remain the exclusive preserve of the State Department; and (2) that the management of interdepartmental policies and programs will be neither self-executing nor without conflict among the principals involved. The overall coordination of this process is necessarily a presidential task, and the NSA becomes the chosen presidential taskmaster.

The NSA as coordinator facilitates policy making but is not an initiator of policy. He is, instead, responsible for defining policy options for NSC consideration. He manages the flow of ideas, information, policies, and programs involved in the national security process. Although the NSA may exercise considerable influence, it is as a presidential staff assistant, not as an independent actor. The NSA's role entails policy review and program management, while the principals (particularly the president and the secretary of state) make and implement the decisions.

Robert Cutler, President Eisenhower's special assistant for national security affairs, served as a coordinator of the policy-making process. Eisenhower's national security system was characterized as a "policy hill": the NSC Planning Board considered policy recommendations to be submitted to the council where they were debated prior to presidential approval. The approved policy went "down the other side of the policy hill to departments and agencies responsible for its execution,"[21] and the Operations Control Board (OCB) monitored implementation. The NSC was the apex of this formalized and highly structured system, and Cutler was responsible for its direction.

Even though Cutler chaired the two interdepartmental committees that buttressed the NSC (the Planning Board and OCB) and initiated discussions at council meetings, his primary responsiblity was to ensure that all points of view were considered and to summarize these findings at NSC meetings—"maintaining the quality and character of advising as a process, not simply . . . expressing those views he and his staff favored."[22] Cutler was concerned with ensuring an orderly policy-making process by relating current and past NSC decisions, seeing that NSC discussion remained on track, and specifying the implications of all options involved with a decision.[23] Cutler, as well as his successors Dillon Anderson and Gordon Gray, saw themselves as servants of the NSC rather than as independent actors in the policy-making process. On the other hand, they institutionalized presidential staff involvement in the evolution and evaluation of national security policy.

Two of President Reagan's NSAs were coordinators: William P. Clark and Robert McFarlane. McFarlane, in particular, acted as an "honest broker" in the national security policy–making process. His ability to work as a "team player" allowed Secretary of State George Shultz to become the administration's premier foreign policy maker, while ensuring the White House support that was the prerequisite for such preeminence. For a two-year period (1983–85), the Shultz-McFarlane axis imparted a measure of coherence to the Reagan administration's foreign policy, where disarray seemed to have previously been the order of the day.

Counselor

The NSA as *counselor* functions in a largely personal relationship to the president: evaluating, rather than simply presenting policy alternatives; intervening in the departments to get information or other points of view; not merely articulating, but also advocating the presidential perspective on a proposed policy—generally by seeking "to pinpoint and balance others' biases rather than to press his own."[24] The NSA counselor does not preside over a structured advisory system, but rather is a major participant in the informal advisory process. Consequently, he is allowed to spend more time on ad hoc policy making and serving immediate presidential needs.

The increased operational orientation of the NSC staff under a counselor is designed to introduce the widest range of alternative actions from which the president might choose. While the NSA might respect the secretary of state and his "formal prerogatives,"[25] he and his staff can venture deeply into State Department business: clearing and drafting cables, monitoring the communications system. Moreover, as the NSC staff assumes operational responsibilities, the likelihood increases of conflict between "the president's prime agent of coordination" and the State Department over questions of which policies will meet presidential expectations.[26]

President Kennedy's NSA, McGeorge Bundy, created the role of presidential counselor. Bundy saw his job as clarifying alternatives set before the president, recording decisions, and monitoring follow-through. However, his work was not so innocent of competition with the State Department as he may have thought. As Kennedy's frustrations with the State Department's bureaucratic routine mounted, the role of Bundy—"a crisp, terse, intellectual operator"—grew.[27] Most important, Bundy, as well as his successor Walt W. Rostow, was close to "an aggressive, pragmatic President whose style meshed well with his own."[28]

Bundy's service as NSA points up an aspect of White House staffing that has not been lost on future advisers, or secretaries of state, that physical proximity to the president creates special relationships. When Bundy maneuvered his office from the Executive Office Building to the West Wing of the White House and established the Situation Room, he engineered a major administrative coup. He was now "at the end of the buzzer," at the president's immediate call, ensconced within the political staff, capable of access to the Oval Office without necessarily having a specified appointment or a specific agenda. No other national security policy maker enjoys such a potential advantage.

President Carter wanted Secretary of State Cyrus Vance to be his principal foreign policy adviser and NSA Zbigneiw Brzezinski to serve as a personal counselor. To Secretary Vance's disadvantage,

Brzezinski proved to be aggressive in gaining both the president's confidence and access to his presence. Brzezinski realized that, as the president's assistant, the NSA was the guardian of the "presidential perspective" in decision making. As time passed, Brzezinski acted more and more as Carter's foreign policy spokesman and became increasingly involved in diplomatic operations. By mid-1978, Brzezinski had transformed his role as presidential counselor into that of vigorous public advocate for important foreign policy decisions.[29] Although Brzezinski never realized the policy-making preeminence of Kissinger, this was not for want of aspiration or effort.

Agent

The NSA as *agent* combines the duties of a coordinator (directing a planning process) with those of a counselor (serving as a personal presidential adviser and advocate). As agent, the NSA dominates the process for formulating national security policy—making many decisions himself, advocating others—and acts as the primary presidential spokesman for foreign affairs. This virtually eliminates and distinction between the duties of the national security adviser and the secretary of state. Thus, the NSA becomes "the key line operator in every important respect."[30] The overall purpose of this type of system is to strengthen the intellectual and bureaucratic resources of the White House in order to ensure direct presidential control over national security policy making.[31] Administratively, the State Department is displaced to the periphery, and the NSC staff, in effect, becomes a "rival State Department."

Henry Kissinger, national security adviser under Richard Nixon, was, like McGeorge Bundy, an intellectual who was disposed to advance his own ideas. However, what distinguished Kissinger from other NSAs before or since was the degree to which he transformed the scope of his office. Before the end of Nixon's first term, Kissinger was unquestionably the prime presidential adviser on foreign affairs. "If Bundy had intruded on the role of the Secretary of State, Kissinger obliterated it."[32] The actual secretary of state, William P. Rogers, was virtually eclipsed by Kissinger, who would eventually combine both positions in an unprecedented consolidation of policy-making powers.

As a presidential agent, Kissinger not only briefed Nixon daily on the nation's security, but also increasingly spoke on behalf of the president and finally served as the prime negotiator for matters relating to Vietnam, China, and SALT. These were the principal items on the Nixon foreign policy agenda, and Kissinger was the focal point for both their conceptual and operational realization. The Situation Room provided the "back channels" by which foreign policy could be conducted from the White House. Kissinger ultimately acquired decisive control over both the formulation and conduct of foreign affairs. By doing so, he acquired de facto powers greater than the de jure authority of the secretaries of state and defense.

After his tenure at the State Department, Kissinger declared his conviction, while admitting that he had not held it when in the White House, that the secretary of state should be every administration's chief foreign policy spokesman. The NSA, in contrast, should play only a coordinating role in ensuring that all points of view on a proposed policy are heard. "If the security adviser becomes active in the development and articulation of policy, he must inevitably diminish the Secretary of State and reduce his effectiveness."[33] This, of course, was exactly Secretary Rogers's experience. While successive presidents and national security assistants have announced themselves opposed to a Kissinger-type approach to national security policy making, the allures and successes of the agent role remain undeniable. Indeed, Admiral John Poindexter pushed the agent role one step further by acting on the basis of his personal assessment of the president's intentions rather than upon explicit presidential policies.

The Irangate episode revealed a dramatic perversion of the legitimate role of the NSC staff in the policy-making process as defined both by statue and customary usages.[34] It was not just that the arms-for-hostages deal with Iran was "an inept policy, poorly implemented,"[35] or that the NSC system failed; rather, the advisory process was ignored or not used.[36] During the Poindexter insurgency, the NSC became a "shadowy parallel government," operating with little or no supervision and without the limitations on executive actions that are normally assumed in a democratic system.[37] Accountability was further undermined by cabals within the executive branch to keep major public officials (such as the secretaries of state and defense) from knowing the details of Iran-contra activities.[38] Admiral Poindexter testified that he deliberately withheld knowledge of the details from President Reagan so as to

provide him with "plausible deniability."[39] Constitutional accountability was thus sacrificed to political convenience.

Irrespective of the particular national security advisory processes that a president may use, the record of Irangate suggests the
need for following a series of steps or established procedures in the
decision-making process if further incidents of insurgency are to
be avoided. These include: (1) clear and accurate identification of
problems; (2) comprehensive and objective intelligence gathering;
(3) consultation with experts; (4) solicitation of views about proposed policies by all major participants; (5) full evaluation of policy proposals at the highest levels; (6) clear identification of the
consequences of policy options; (7) decision by the president and
wide communication of his decision at all levels of government;
(8) observance of all legal restraints upon proposed action; (9)
careful monitoring of policy implementation; and (10) periodic
policy evaluation and program review.

As should be clear from the record of the Iran-contra affair, few
of these guidelines were observed or acknowledged during the
latter part of the Reagan administration. While the insurgency of
Poindexter and North was an aberration in the history of national
security advisory models, it was the inevitable consequence of
President Reagan's administrative style. Whatever the ultimate
legal judgments on his subordinates, President Reagan must necessarily bear the ultimate responsibility for the insurgency within his
administration.

Presidents and the Management of National Security

Constitutional provisions, administrative precedents, and electoral promises collectively dictate that a newly elected president
must approach the organization of government from a personal
perspective. Defining the president's perspective is a central White
House responsibility; the management of national security is
hardly an exception to this rule. Indeed, given the centrality of
presidential decision making for the conduct of foreign affairs,
how a president defines his responsibility for national security is
one of his most crucial decisions. It should also be abundantly
clear that it is both impossible and inadvisable to mandate a particular mode of presidential decision making that must be followed by all chief executives. Nevertheless, the evidence from our

review of the historical record does suggest certain conclusions that can be drawn—and a few recommendations that might be proposed—that would better inform the management of national security affairs.

The most obvious conclusion is that the NSA has been institutionalized as part of the national security policy–making process on a level with the secretaries of state and defense and the CIA director. At the same time, we have observed rather dramatic oscillations in the ways in which presidents have used their national security assistants and the NSC staff. In what has been almost a rule of "reactive reorganization," successive administrations have discovered the wisdom of structuring their national security advisory process in a manner that presumably corrects the defects of their predecessors.[40] For example, Kennedy dismantled the Eisenhower machinery in the light of the Jackson Subcommittee's criticisms; Nixon reversed this collegiality and reconstructed a hierarchial NSC staff.

To some extent these shifts in organizational structure reflect the conventional political wisdom of the day. As we have observed, national security policy making involves the exercise of presidential responsibilities in ways that are largely unfettered by constitutional or institutional constraints.[41] Consequently, the fair degree of variability in the NSA's political and administrative role is because the nature of this role "is primarily determined by the man it serves."[42] In this situation, presidents are faced with the crucial, initial task of designating a role for the NSA as part of the overall management of national security affairs. Accomplishing this task requires the president to determine certain managerial policies.

First, a president would be advised to define a role for his NSA consistent with his preferences for the general management of the government. For example, if a president were committed to the principle of "cabinet government"—in this case, the predominance of the State Department—the appointment of a NSA with strong policy positions and personal ambitions would invite the bureaucratic warfare that debilitated the Carter foreign policy. If President Carter really wished to have Secretary Vance direct the policy process, he should have appointed someone more like Brent Scowcroft rather than Zbigniew Brzezinski as his NSA.

Second, the history of the NSC over the past forty years does suggest that neither the *agent* nor the *administrator* roles of presidential management are to be recommended. The machinations of Admiral Poindexter, a self-appointed presidential agent, indicate how easily the exigencies of national security can provide a veil for insurgent operations, that is, those without presidential authorization and uninformed by departmental expertise. In any case, the agent's intrusion upon the function of the departments will cause problems in the operation of foreign policy. On the other hand, the administrator role may easily prove too weak in providing the advice that the president needs to make transdepartmental decisions. Increasingly, national security decision making requires White House adjudication of competing bureaucratic claims. Indeed, as General Scowcroft reemerged in the Bush administration, it has been as a more visible coordinator to compensate for the absence of a commanding cabinet secretary.

Third, whether a president chooses to manage national security policy with a coordinator or counselor is largely a matter of background and temperament. Yet, it needs to be noted that both of these models have costs as well as benefits. Not every president will be knowledgeable about the international situation, confident in actively voicing his opinion, nor comfortable with the give-and-take of collegial decision making. Although a counselor can assist the president in husbanding these resources, he will be inevitably tempted to do more than this. In contrast, the structured character of formalized national security management may prove exasperating to presidents who prefer a more flexible and free-wheeling approach. The benefits of procedural regularity, predictability, and accountability may be perceived as stultifying and wheel-spinning.

Fourth, a president should decide whether or not to have a confirmed NSA. Zbigniew Brzezinski argues that there are two overall approaches to presidential management of national security affairs: the secretarial and the presidential. In the former case, the president would designate a strong secretary of state to be his surrogate for international relations and a NSA who "would facilitate the flow upward to the President of information upon which he is to base his decisions and the flow downward from the President of decisions once taken for execution by the department or departments affected."[43] Since the secretary of state would be the administration's chief foreign policy maker, and, as he is accountable to Congress, there would be no need for confirmation of the NSA. In the latter case, where responsibility for the direction and coordination of national security policy is vested in the NSA, accountability may demand the congressional oversight associated with the confirmation process. Brzezinski, for his part, argues for both an expanded NSA role and statutory confirmation.

Lastly, the administrative record of the national security advisory process suggests a restrained NSA role—at most that of a counselor, more likely of a coordinator; an agent would be too formidable, and an administrator lacking structural support would not be formidable enough. Worse than the risks associated with an NSA as administrator or agent, however, is a situation where a president vacillates over the designation of a given role or chooses a national security assistant with personality traits inconsistent with the demands of the designated role. It is hard to disagree with what Alexander George has concluded: "The experience of every president from Truman to Reagan makes one conclusion inescapable: a president must first define his own role in the national security policymaking system before he can design and manage the roles and relationships of the major participants."[44]

Conclusion

In the light of Irangate and the more general "rise of the assistant," several of Louis Brownlow's observations about presidential policy management have a currency equal to when they were presented fifty years ago. The most frequently noted is the absence of the "passion for anonymity" that was to be a distinguishing characteristic of a presidential assistant. NSAs have often possessed the qualities of "high competence" and "great physical vigor" that Brownlow also noted, but they have rarely been anonymous.[45] Less frequently noted is Brownlow's observation regarding the proper characteristic of White House staffers:

Their effectiveness in assisting the President will, we think, be directly proportional to their ability to discharge their functions with restraint. They would remain in the background, issue no orders, make no decisions, emit no public statements. . . . They should be men in whom the President has personal confidence and whose character and attitude is such that they would not attempt to exercise power on their own account.[46]

As has been often observed, the administrative history of national security policy making evidences quite contrary behavior by

NSAs—not only by Poindexter, but also by Brzezinski, Kissinger, and to some extent McFarlane, Rostow, and Bundy. These aides have had power to make decisions and issue instructions in their own right. They have been interposed between the president and department heads and, in many ways, have acted as assistant presidents. All of this runs counter to the specific warnings of the Brownlow Committee Report.[47]

While warning against a "palace guard" in the White House, Brownlow recognized that the "loneliness and complexity" of presidential governance required presidents to have "intimates and experts" immediately about him.[48] The relationship between Kennedy and Bundy, Nixon and Kissinger, Carter and Brzezinski, Reagan and Clark testify to this predilection. Presidents *do* need help, which explains why the assistant for national security affairs will always be a force to be reckoned with in the policy-making arena. Again, Brownlow addresses this general problem. "The structure of the Government throws an impossible task upon the Chief Executive. No President can possibly give adequate supervision to the multitude of agencies which have been set up to carry on the work of the Government, nor can he coordinate their activities and policies."[49] Nowhere is this situation more apparent than with the administration of national security policy. Indeed, the case for the NSA and his staff can be made in Brownlow's words.

Expand the White House staff so that the President may have a sufficient group of able assistants in his own office to keep him in closer and easier touch with the widespread affairs of administration and to make a speedier clearance of knowledge needed for executive decision.[50]

The difficulty has been how to strike a balance between the president's need for help and the requirements of democratic governance. The Irangate affair may have been the deviant case in the administration of national security affairs. However, the roles played by several NSAs in the past twenty-five years documents many examples of behavior that transcended the restraint, rectitude, and reticence called for by the Brownlow Committee Report. Consequently, it may be time to reexamine the issue of the "role and accountability" of the national security adviser especially as regards Senate confirmation.

As the *New York Times* editorialized in 1988, "The Reagan national security operation has been beset by repeated shortcomings and failures, and some, like Iran-Contra, were catastrophic. These have to do with the President's own lassitude and failure to make clear policy decisions."[51] This judgment reaffirms what has been argued throughout—that the structure and successful management of national security policy making is fundamentally a presidential responsibility. When Brownlow's Committee on Administrative Management argued for enhanced staff assistance, it was to allow the president to better execute the powers of his office. No staff agency of the presidency, however, can relieve the chief executive officer of the United States of the admittedly heavy personal burden entailed by his constitutional responsibilities.

Notes

1. *Administrative Management in the Government of the United States*, report of the President's Committee on Administrative Management (Washington, D.C.: GPO, 1937), p. 5 (hereafter referred to as the *Brownlow Committee Report*).

2. Ibid.

3. See Demetrius Caraley, *The Politics of Defense Unification* (New York: Columbia University Press, 1966).

4. Mark M. Lowenthal, *The National Security Council: Organizational History* (Washington, D.C.: Congressional Research Service, 1978), p. 11 (hereafter referred to as *Congressional Research Service Report*).

5. Public Law 80-253, Title I, secs. 101 (a), (b).

6. Commission on the Organization of the Executive Branch of the Government, *National Security Organization* (Washington, D.C.: GPO, 1949), pp. 15–16, 74–76.

7. Stanley L. Falk, "The National Security Council Under Truman, Eisenhower, and Kennedy," *Political Science Quarterly* 79 (September 1964), 415.

8. Zbigniew Brzezinski, *Power and Principle: Memoirs of the National Security Adviser, 1977–1981* (New York: Farrar, Straus, and Giroux, 1983), pp. 534–35.

9. Cecil V. Crabb and Kevin V. Mulcahy, *Presidents and Foreign Policy Making: From FDR to Reagan* (Baton Rouge: Louisiana State University Press, 1986), pp. 334–35.

10. Anna Kasten Nelson, "National Security I: Inventing a Process," in *The Illusion of Presidential Government*, ed. Hugh Heclo and Lester M. Salamon (Boulder, Colo.: Westview, 1981), pp. 229–31; Harry S. Truman, *Memoirs: Years of Trial and Hope* (Garden City, N.Y.: Doubleday, 1955), pp. 46–60; Paul Y. Hammond, "The National Security Council as a Device for Interdepartmental Coordination: An Interpretation and Appraisal," *American Political Science Review* 54 (December 1960), 899–901.

11. *Congressional Research Service Report*, p. 13.

12. Falk, "The National Security Council," p. 414.

13. U.S. Senate Subcommittee on National Policy Machinery of the Committee on Government Operations, *Organizing for National Security* (Washington, D.C., GPO, 1961), 1:564, 561.

14. Crabb and Mulcahy, *Presidents and Foreign Policy Making*, pp. 122–55.

15. Joseph G. Bock and Duncan L. Clarke, "The National Security Assistant and the White House Staff: National Security Policy Decisionmaking and Domestic Political Considerations, 1947–84," *Presidential Studies Quarterly* 16 (Spring 1986), 259.

16. Sidney W. Souers, "Policy Formulation for National Security," *American Political Science Review* 43 (Spring 1949), 537.

17. *New York Times*, Nov. 4, 1975; Gerald Ford, *A Time to Heal* (New York: Harper and Row, 1979), p. 326.

18. I. M. Destler, "A Job That Doesn't Work," *Foreign Policy* 38 (Spring 1980), 89.

19. *New York Times*, Feb. 3, 1989.

20. Ibid., Mar. 8, 1981.

21. Robert Cutler, "The Department of the National Security Council," *Foreign Affairs* 34 (April 1956), 448.

22. Fred I. Greenstein and John P. Burke, "Comparative Models of Presidential Decisionmaking: Eisenhower and Johnson," presented at the annual meeting of the American Political Science Association, 1985, pp. 13–14.

23. Ibid., p. 14.

24. I. M. Destler, "National Security II: The Rise of the Assistant," in *The Illusion of Presidential Government*, ed. Hugh Heclo and Lester M. Salamon (Boulder, Colo.: Westview Press, 1981), p. 268.

25. I. M. Destler, Leslie Gelb, and Anthony Lake, *Our Own Worst Enemy: The Unmaking of American Foreign Policy* (New York: Simon and Schuster, 1984), p. 194.

26. I. M. Destler, *Presidents, Bureaucrats and Foreign Policy* (Princeton, N.J.: Princeton University Press, 1972), pp. 102–03.

27. Destler et al., *Our Own Worst Enemy*, p. 184.

28. Ibid.

29. Alexander George, *Presidential Decision Making in Foreign Policy* (Boulder, Colo.: Westview Press, 1980), p. 200.

30. Destler, "National Security II," p. 271.

31. George, *Presidential Decision Making*, p. 177.

32. Destler et al., *Our Own Worst Enemy*, p. 208.

33. Henry Kissinger, *The White House Years* (Boston: Little, Brown, 1979), pp. 11–12.

34. *Report of the Congressional Committee Investigating the Iran-Contra Affair*. Joint Hearings before the Select Committee on Secret Military Assistance to Iran and the Nicaraguan Opposition, U.S. Senate, and the Select Committee to Investigate Covert Arms Transactions with Iran (Washington, D.C.: GPO, 1987), p. 13 (hereafter referred to as the *Iran-Contra Report*).

35. *The Tower Commission Report: The Full Text of the President's Special Review Board* (New York: Times Books and Bantam Books, 1987), p. 70 (hereafter referred to as the *Tower Commission Report*).

36. Ibid., p. 80.

37. Ibid., p. xv.

38. *Iran-Contra Report*, pp. 14–16.

39. Ibid., p. 17.

40. Destler et al., *Our Own Worst Enemy*, p. 168; Nelson, "National Security I," p. 259; Destler, "National Security II," pp. 263, 272.

41. Bock and Clarke, "The National Security Assistant," p. 258.

42. John E. Endicott, "The National Security Council," in *American Defense Policy,* ed. Endicott and Roy W. Strafford, Jr. (Baltimore: Johns Hopkins University Press, 1981), p. 314.

43. Brzezinski, *Power and Principle,* pp. 533–35.

44. George, *Presidential Decision Making,* p. 146.

45. *Brownlow Committee Report,* p. 5; see also Louis Brownlow, *A Passion for Anonymity* (Chicago: University of Chicago Press, 1958), pp. 381, 469; and *The President and the Presidency* (Chicago: Public Administration Service, 1949), p. 195.

46. *Brownlow Committee Report,* p. 5.

47. Ibid.

48. Brownlow, *President and Presidency,* p. 109.

49. Ibid., p. 32.

50. Ibid., p. 52.

51. *New York Times,* July 19, 1988.

13

National Security Affairs:
A Defense Department Perspective

LAWRENCE J. KORB

Some fifty years ago, the Brownlow Committee argued that the whole of the executive branch of the federal government should be overhauled and that the 100 agencies reporting to the president should be reorganized under a few large departments in which every executive authority should find its place. The committee suggested a dozen great departments. Included among these were two departments dealing with defense matters, viz., War and Navy.[1]

Some forty years ago, in light of the experiences of World War II, the Eberstadt Committee recommended the creation of a national military establishment headed by a single secretary of defense. Based upon the work of this committee, as well as several other groups, Congress passed the National Security Act (NSA) 1947, which among other things established a single Department of Defense (DOD).

Over the past four decades, sixteen men have occupied the position of secretary of defense for eight different presidents, four from each party. During these same forty years, the NSA of 1947 has been modified in a major way on four occasions: 1949, 1953, 1958, and 1986. Each of these so-called reorganizations has enhanced the formal powers of the secretary of defense at the expense of the separate military departments (army, navy, and air force) within DOD. In 1949, the secretaries of the separate military departments or service secretaries lost their cabinet status. In 1953, the service secretaries were removed from the military chain of command. The 1958 Reorganization Act gave the secretary of defense the authority to establish defense agencies to carry out functions, like supply, intelligence and communication, that cut across service lines. The

Defense Reorganization Act of 1986 gave the secretary of defense control over the acquisition process through the establishment of the position of an undersecretary of defense for acquisition, with power to bypass the service secretaries.

Nonetheless all during this period, the secretary of defense has had two main roles in the national security decision-making process: as principal military adviser to the president and manager of the world's largest bureaucracy.

Yet in carrying out these functions, the secretary of defense has many potential rivals both inside and outside DOD. Within DOD, the secretary's main adversaries are the professional military, whose leaders, the Joint Chiefs of Staff (JCS), possess military expertise as well as the legal right of direct access to the president and concurrent membership on the National Security Council (NSC). Outside of DOD, the secretary's primary rivals for influence are the National Security Adviser as well as the secretary of state.

During these past four decades, the formal powers of the chairman of the JCS were also enhanced considerably. The position evolved from that of first among equals in 1949 to that of the senior military officer of the United States by 1986. As originally conceived, the chairman was to be coordinator of JCS activities who would have no separate staff or take independent positions. With the passage of the 1986 Reorganization Act, the chairman was given his own staff, command authority, and the right to make decisions and to take positions without getting a consensus from the other members of the JCS.

The formal powers of the secretary of defense's outside rivals, the secretary of state and the national security adviser, were not changed very much during this period. However, the role of the national security adviser increased dramatically as presidents began to draw more and more power away from the agencies and into the White House.

The manner in which secretaries of defense have carried out their main responsibilities depends on various factors. First is their own background and experience. Some secretaries have brought to their post many years of experience in defense matters and politics and government. Others have been neophytes in both defense and government. For example, Charles Wilson and Neil McElroy came directly to DOD from General Motors and Procter and Gamble, respectively, into the Eisenhower administration. On the other hand, James Schlesinger headed the AEC and CIA before coming to DOD and had written extensively on national security issues before joining the Nixon cabinet. Second, their tenure in office. Only five of the sixteen secretaries have served as long as four years. Another ten have served less than two years, hardly enough time to make a significant impact. Third, the expectations of and their relationship with the presidents they have served. Some presidents, like Ronald Reagan, favored cabinet government while others, like Richard Nixon, were distrustful of agency heads being "captured by the natives." Some secretaries, like Caspar Weinberger, knew the president before taking office; others, like Robert McNamara, developed a close relationship with him only after assuming the post. Weinberger had worked on Reagan's campaign for governor of California in 1966, served as his state budget director for three years, and had been adviser to Reagan in his 1976 and 1980 presidential campaigns. McNamara, despite never having met Kennedy before his 1960 election, developed a strong professional and personal relationship with the president and his family. Even today, McNamara is close to the Kennedys. Fourth, the quality of the other key appointees. Strong national security advisers, secretaries of state, or the JCS, can make it difficult for the secretary of defense to have the influence he wishes.

Obviously, the most effective secretary of defense should bring to the office a knowledge of defense issues and a background in government, should remain in office for an extended period, and should have or should develop a good relationship with the president. Moreover, if the president is willing to delegate power to the cabinet agencies and the secretary of state is comparatively weak, the secretary of defense should be even more effective. The least effective defense chief would be a neophyte in defense and government, lack a strong relationship with the president, leave office after a brief stay, and be forced to compete with both a strong national security adviser and secretary of state.

None of the first sixteen secretaries has possessed all of the favorable assets, nor has anyone displayed every single negative attribute. Nor are these characteristics the sole determinant of their effectiveness. We need also to look at the roles that defense secretaries have attempted to play within DOD and the national security structure. If this role selection is congruent with their environment and backgrounds, their effectiveness will be enhanced.

Internal Role Theories

One way of comparing secretaries of defense in relation to their internal environment is to categorize their internal management style as active or passive. An active secretary of defense provides strong aggressive leadership in running DOD. This leadership extends not only to managing the department, that is, to the budget and acquisition process, but also to formulating the policy of the department on such critical issues as employment of nuclear weapons or arms control. A passive secretary of defense allows the military services to run the department while he merely maintains the appearance of civilian control; that is, he reigns rather than rules, with the result that the interests of the individual services or the military are served rather than the larger interests of national defense or national security.

As indicated in table 12, the overwhelming majority of secretaries, eleven, have more or less opted for an active role. Indeed, this is not surprising; presidents normally expect their secretaries of defense to ensure that the whole of DOD is greater than the sum of its individual parts and that their secretaries of defense will exert strong civilian control. Indeed, every administration has at one time or another had to face charges of waste and mismanagement in DOD.

However, of those eleven activists, seven did not serve in office long enough to see if they could sustain that active posture in areas like the design of the defense budget or arms control processes vis-à-vis the uniformed military for an extended period. Elliot Richardson was in office only three months in early 1973 when the unfolding Watergate crisis forced President Nixon to move him from defense to justice. Robert Lovett (1951–53), Thomas Gates (1959–61), Donald Rumsfeld (1975–77), and Frank Carlucci (1987–89) were all appointed by lame duck presidents less than a year before the next election. Similarly, James Forrestal (1947–49) and Louis Johnson (1949–50) were both fired by President Truman after just over a year in office. Thus, only four men, Robert McNamara (1961–68), Melvin Laird

TABLE 12. Internal Roles of the Secretary of
Defense

Active	Passive
Forrestal (1947–49)	Marshall (1950–51)
Johnson (1949–50)	Wilson (1953–57)
Lovett (1951–53)	McElroy (1957–59)
Gates (1959–61)	Clifford (1968–69)
McNamara (1961–68)	Weinberger (1981–87)
Laird (1969–73)	
Richardson (1973)	
Schlesinger (1973–75)	
Rumsfeld (1975–77)	
Brown (1977–81)	
Carlucci (1987–89)	

Sources: Derived from Stanley Falk and Harold Bauer, *The National Security Structure* (Washington, D.C.: Industrial College of the Armed Forces, 1976); and James Roherty, *Decisions of Robert McNamara* (Coral Gables, Fla.: University of Miami Press, 1979).

(1969–73), James Schlesinger (1973–75), and Harold Brown (1977–81) were able to exert active influence within DOD for a prolonged period of time.

There are three obvious reasons why Laird, Schlesinger, and Brown were all able to exert such control over the Pentagon. First, each had significant governmental experience prior to coming to the Pentagon. Laird had been an eight-term congressman from Wisconsin. Schlesinger, as mentioned above, had been the head of AEC and CIA and an associate director of OMB; and Brown had been an undersecretary of defense and secretary of the air force. Second, each understood the issues that affect national security policy. Laird was a leading member of the Defense Appropriations Subcommittee in the House for over a decade. Schlesinger and Brown were both defense intellectuals from their earliest days in the academy.[2] Both could debate even the most arcane defense issue with military and civilian experts. Third, by the 1970s the power and prestige of the JCS waned as the World War II heroes passed from the scene and the Vietnam commanders came to power without a great deal of prestige. For example, Forrestal and Johnson dealt with military leaders like Eisenhower, Bradley, Collins, and Vandenberg.

McNamara had neither the background nor the experience of

the other activist managers. Moreover, he had a more prestigious JCS than his colleagues who ran DOD in the 1970s. McNamara had to contend with such powerful military figures as Curtis Lemay and Arleigh Burke. Yet he was the most active and dominating secretary of defense in the forty-year history of DOD. There were five main reasons for McNamara's success. First, he demanded and received from Presidents Kennedy and Johnson full authority over defense matters, including the power to hire and fire his military and civilian staff.[3] He exercised this power with great effect, firing both the chairman of the JCS (Lyman Lemnitzer) and the chief of naval operations (George Anderson) as well as the secretary of the army (Elvis Stahr) during his first two years in office. More important, he refused to place people in key positions if they were not qualified, even if they had strong political connections. McNamara refused to appoint Franklin Roosevelt, Jr., as secretary of the navy despite a personal request from President Kennedy. Second, he assembled a high-quality staff in the Office of the Secretary of Defense. Some of McNamara's whiz kids were people like Paul Nitze, Charles Hitch, Paul Warnke, Cyrus Vance and Paul Ignatius. Third, he imposed a decision-making system, PPBS, on the Pentagon that allowed decisions to be made on terms with which he was familiar and negated the role of pure military experience. Nearly three decades after he imposed PPBS upon DOD, McNamara's decision-making framework still stands. Fourth, he was a brilliant man with seemingly inexhaustible energy. Within days after taking over DOD, he was conversant with the most recondite defense issues and familiar with even the smallest detail in the defense program. Fifth, McNamara gained the confidence, respect, and even the friendship of his presidents and became part of their inner circle.

Five of the sixteen secretaries have chosen to play a less active role in managing DOD and thus essentially ceded running of the department to the military services. They were George Marshall (1950–51), Charles Wilson (1953–57), Neil McElroy (1957–59), Clark Clifford (1968–69), and Caspar Weinberger (1981–87). The passivity of Marshall and Clifford was somewhat understandable. Marshall, a career army officer who had served as secretary of state and army chief of staff and was not in the best of health when he took the post, had stipulated in advance that he would serve for only a year. Because of the crisis created by the North Korean invasion, President Truman appointed him as much for what he represented as for what he wished him to do. While Marshall's appointment did succeed in helping the country absorb the shock of the North Korean attack on South Korea, his failure to reign in General MacArthur cost the country dearly. In the fall of 1950, Marshall allowed MacArthur to violate the letter and spirit of Pentagon directives about sending U.S. troops toward the Chinese border. This lead to the massive Chinese entry into the conflict in November 1950 and to the heavy casualties that American troops suffered immediately after the Chinese attack. Clifford focused almost all his energies in his ten months in office on getting President Johnson to begin the peace process in Vietnam, a substantial accomplishment. Wilson, McElroy, and Weinberger were the only secretaries to play a passive role for a significant period: McElroy for two years, Wilson four and a half, and Weinberger almost seven years.

Wilson's and McElroy's passivity in office regarding internal defense matters was caused by a combination of three factors. First, as noted above, each lacked defense knowledge and previous government experience. Both came to DOD indirectly from corporate America: Wilson from General Motors and McElroy from Procter and Gamble. Second, they both served a president who in effect wanted to carry the defense portfolio himself. Career military officer, World War II supreme allied commander and army chief of staff, President Dwight Eisenhower often relied on his own military judgment or dealt directly with his World War II comrades serving on the JCS.[4] Third, the military leaders serving under Wilson and McElroy were household names because of their World War II exploits. Men like Matthew Ridgway, Maxwell Taylor, and Arleigh Burke were among the senior military advisors to Wilson and McElroy.

Weinberger's passive management style is much harder to comprehend. President Reagan was a close personal friend of his and was willing to delegate considerable authority to his former California budget director. Weinberger came to DOD with broad government experience at both the state and federal level, and his military chiefs were more managers than warriors. Finally, he showered DOD with more funds than the military services had ever dreamed possible. There is no doubt that he could have controlled the Pentagon from top to bottom had he wished.

He appears to have allowed the military services to dominate the process for three reasons.[5] First, because of his experience at HEW and OMB in the 1970s, Weinberger had concluded that there was too much centralization within federal agencies. He even fought the Congress in the mid-1980s when the legislature wanted to increase his formal powers vis-à-vis the services through the passage of the 1986 Defense Reorganization Act. Second, he wanted to focus his energies on increasing the amount of funds made available to DOD rather than on how the funds were spent. He often commented that the state of our defenses was so bad when he took office in 1981 that it did not matter where the funds were spent. Third, Weinberger's service on MacArthur's staff in World War II seemed to place him somewhat in awe of bemedaled military chieftans. In his acceptance speech at the Democratic National Convention in July 1988, Democratic candidate Governor Michael Dukakis implicitly criticized Weinberger's passive stewardship of the Pentagon when he stated that if elected, he would appoint a secretary of defense who would manage the Pentagon rather than be managed by the Pentagon.

External Roles

In addition to managing the budget and acquisition processes within DOD, secretaries of defense, as statutory members of the NSC and as the president's principal defense adviser, have an opportunity to have a substantial impact on governmentwide national security policy. Those who take an activist role in national security policy formulation can be classified as *generalists*, while those who are unable or unwilling to play such a role can be classified as *functionalists*. The latter normally focus their efforts on improving the efficiency of defense management rather than concerning themselves with overall national security policy. These categories are not mutually exclusive; an individual secretary may choose to emphasize *both*.

Table 13 displays the sixteen secretaries in these three categories. As the table indicates, the great majority of the secretaries have chosen to take an activist role in the formulation of national security policy. In the Truman administration, all of the defense secretaries except Louis Johnson took the generalist role. This is not surprising, since Truman chose his defense chiefs as much for their experience in and familiarity with military matters as for their managerial ability.[6] Forrestal, Lovett, and Marshall had all held high posts in the defense establishment in World War II, and Lovett and Marshall had held high-level positions in the State Department in the immediate post–World War II period. Forrestal's efforts to warn his colleagues about Soviet belligerency laid the foundation for the containment policy and NSC-68, while Marshall and Lovett worked closely with President Truman and their old colleague, Secretary of State Acheson, on the implementation of containment and the conduct of the Korean War. Moreover, during the Truman administration, the assistant to the president for national security affairs was much more of an executive secretary than a policy maker. The NSC adviser made the trains run on time and did not focus on how to build the railroad.

Only Louis Johnson was a functionalist. At Truman's direction, he focused his energies almost exclusively on cutting out waste, duplication, and unnecessary weapon systems. In his eighteen months in office, Johnson succeed in slashing the defense budget by 20 percent, leaving us woefully unprepared for the Korean conflict and forcing his secretary of the navy to resign in protest. For his efforts in carrying out Truman's directive to cut defense spending, Johnson was made a scapegoat for the poor state of our defense in June 1950 and was fired by President Truman soon after the North Korean invasion.

The Eisenhower secretaries focused primarily on achieving efficiencies in DOD. This is not surprising, given the backgrounds of his first two secretaries, Wilson and McElroy; Eisenhower's own military background; and the preeminence of Secretary of State John Foster Dulles, a man Eisenhower considered without peer in politico-military affairs.[7] In the waning days of the Eisenhower administration, Thomas Gates, taking advantage of the 1958 Reorganization Act, did inject himself into the military planning process, preparing the way for future secretaries to participate actively and constructively in the security policy process whenever given the opportunity by the president.[8]

National security policy in the Kennedy-Johnson years was dominated by Secretary of Defense Robert McNamara. He served at the helm of the Pentagon for all but ten months of those turbulent eight years. Not only did he play an activist or generalist role throughout the government, he simultaneously carried on a func-

TABLE 13. External Roles of the
Secretary of Defense

Generalist	Both	Functionalist
Forrestal	McNamara	Johnson
Marshall	Brown	Wilson
Lovett		McElroy
Gates		Richardson
Clifford		
Laird		
Schlesinger		
Rumsfeld		
Weinberger		
Carlucci		

Sources: See table 1.

tionalist role by revolutionizing the management of DOD. With a weak secretary of state in Dean Rusk, a still unstructured NSC process, and a close personal relationship with the president, McNamara was able to have a large impact on national security policy. So great was McNamara's impact that National Security Adviser McGeorge Bundy and Budget Director Kermit Gordon came to the Pentagon to review the annual defense budget rather than McNamara going to the White House to defend his proposal.[9] Within DOD, McNamara revolutionized defense management by creating large defense agencies to absorb common service functions, like supply and communication, and by establishing program categories to analyze defense programs across, rather than within, service boundaries.

McNamara's clout within the Johnson administration began to wane after 1966 as his doubts about the war in Vietnam increased. In early 1968, Johnson "kicked him upstairs" to the World Bank because of this. Ironically, his replacement, Clark Clifford, was much more skeptical about Vietnam and almost singlehandedly succeeded in convincing President Johnson of the folly of his Vietnam policies.

Just as McNamara dominated the Kennedy-Johnson years, national security decision making in the Nixon-Ford years was dominated by Henry Kissinger, serving first as NSC adviser and then as secretary of state. Kissinger, with the support of President Nixon, truly revolutionized the role of the NSC adviser. He increased the size of the staff to over 100 people and organized it into groups that paralleled the functional and regional organizations in the Departments of State and Defense. In addition, Kissinger organized an elaborate set of committees and subcommittees, controlled by himself, to present options to the president. Finally, Kissinger also controlled the issues that the president would consider.

Melvin Laird, Nixon's first secretary of defense, tried to play the activist role but with only a modicum of success. Indeed, Laird was so often in conflict with Kissinger and Nixon over ending U.S. involvement in Vietnam that he occasionally carried out sensitive dealings and negotiations without coordinating them with the White House to preclude Kissinger's or Nixon's disapproval.[10] Moreover, Laird actually refused to carry out some of Nixon's instructions concerning the conduct of the war, thus forcing Kissinger to by-pass him and send the president's instructions directly to the chairman of the JCS.[11]

Laird's successor, Elliot Richardson, was able to accomplish only one thing in his short term in office: he closed or realigned some 100 military bases. Since this was one of the greatest efficiencies accomplished in the post–World War II period in DOD, Richardson clearly deserves his place as a functionalist.

During his first year in office, James Schlesinger had exceptional freedom in defense matters because of the preoccupation of the Nixon White House with the unfolding Watergate crisis. In the Ford administration, with his background in national security strategy, Schlesinger potentially could have had a great impact on national security policy because President Ford restored a sense of purpose to the cabinet and lowered the profile of the NSC by replacing Kissinger as national security adviser with the low-key Brent Scowcroft, who was more a facilitator than a policy maker. However, Schlesinger's poor personal relations with the president and influential congressmen who were former colleagues of President Ford and his policy differences with Secretary of State Kissinger led to his dismissal. Donald Rumsfeld, who had none of these liabilities, could have played a large role if Gerald Ford had been reelected.

Like his mentor, Robert McNamara, Harold Brown attempted to play both a functionalist and generalist role. However, he was not very effective in either. His plans for an overhaul of the defense management structure were thwarted by the Congress. Moreover,

President Carter, who was inexperienced in defense matters despite the fact that he graduated from the Naval Academy, personally made both large and small defense decisions—for example, the B1 bomber or the MX missile and military pay raises. Nor did the president give Brown the support he needed with the Congress or the services.[12]

Within the administration, Brown was overshadowed by Brzezinski, who was a strong NSC adviser, and Secretary of State Cyrus Vance. Brown's impact came primarily from aligning himself with the hard-line positions of Brzezinski. Brown's relative impotence may be traced primarily to his lack of personal rapport with Carter. He had the background and expertise, but never seemed to break into the president's inner circle, as McNamara did with Kennedy, and as Brzezinski and (for a time) Vance did with Carter.

One who came to office with a strong personal relationship with the president was Caspar Weinberger, who served Ronald Reagan for almost seven years. Weinberger attempted to play an activist role and initially had a great impact on the process, particularly in areas of strategic policy, export controls, and arms reduction. This was not only because of his close relationship with the president and his own extensive background in bureaucratic politics, but also because of the feuds between Secretary of State Haig and the White House staff and the weakness of Reagan's first NSC advisers. However, during Reagan's second term, Weinberger's influence declined rapidly because of his intractable policy positions, his poor management of DOD, and his stubbornness with the Congress. This, coupled with the emergence of capable figures like Robert McFarlane and Frank Carlucci at the NSC, and George Shultz at State, led to Weinberger being on the losing side of many major national security decisions in the second Reagan administration and his resignation in late 1987.

Frank Carlucci did not have the personal rapport with the president that Weinberger did. However, his wide government experience and the rapport and respect he enjoyed in Congress and the State Department more than made up for this deficiency and allowed him to play a significant activist role on such issues as the Intermediate Nuclear Forces (INF) Agreement and on U.S. military intervention in the Persian Gulf in the waning days of the Reagan administration. Moreover, had President Bush not ruled out reappointing him so early into his tenure, the arms procurement scandals that broke out in the summer of 1987 may have allowed Carlucci to become a strong functionalist as well.

Conclusion

The secretary of defense can choose to play an active or passive role both in relation to his department and the national security policy process. As is indicated in figure 4, more than half (nine) have chosen to actively manage DOD and to participate fully in the NSC process.

The president and the nation are clearly better served when the defense secretary can play this active role in both spheres. Secretaries who adopt a passive style of defense management allow the military services to waste money by duplicating weapons systems and jeopardize national security by neglecting critical functions like air and sea lift. For example, Wilson and McElroy allowed the armed services to develop a dozen ballistic missile systems, while Weinberger allowed the navy to build carriers at the expense of necessities like minesweepers. Moreover, he permitted the procurement process to spin so wildly out of control that President

| | EXTERNAL | |
	Generalists	Functionalists
INTERNAL — Active	Forrestal Lovett Gates McNamara Laird Schlesinger Rumsfeld Brown Carlucci	Johnson Richardson
INTERNAL — Passive	Marshall Clifford Weinberger	Wilson McElroy

FIGURE 4. Internal and External Roles of the Secretary of Defense

Sources: See table 12.

Reagan had to appoint a blue-ribbon commission on defense management, the Packard Commission, to deal with the mess. Similarly, secretaries who focus only on defense efficiency and ignore national security policy formulation can leave the president without the input he needs to make informed decisions and allow him to become a captive of his NSC. The Iran-contra scandal shows the dénouement of such a situation.

Therefore, it is important that the secretary of defense have the potential to provide active leadership within DOD and to play a meaningful role in national security decision making. This means that the individual appointed to lead the Pentagon must have the knowledge and experience, as well as rapport with the president, necessary to perform both those roles. As the above discussion shows, lacking all or some of these attributes can render a secretary impotent.

How active a role the secretary of defense should play will depend upon how the president chooses to exercise his own constitutional prerogatives. The Brownlow Committee argued for superdepartments and staff assistance. The NSA of 1947 and its amendments consolidated the three military departments into one and established the NSC. But ultimately the president can use or abuse these instruments.

Notes

1. *Administrative Management in the Government of the United States* (Washington, D.C.: GPO, 1937), p. 32.

2. Schlesinger's field of expertise was in defense economics, while Brown was a physicist who worked in nuclear weapons laboratories.

3. Richard Stubbing, *The Defense Game* (New York: Harper and Row, 1986), pp. 264–65.

4. Stanley Falk and Harold Bauer, *The National Security Structure* (Washington, D.C.: Industrial College of the Armed Forces, 1976), pp. 106–07.

5. These insights are derived from conversations I had with Weinberger during the five years I worked for him as assistant secretary of defense (Manpower, Reserve Affairs, and Logistics).

6. Falk and Bauer, *The National Security Structure,* pp. 106–07.

7. Carl Borklund, *Men of the Pentagon* (New York: Praeger, 1966), p. 145.

8. Falk and Bauer, *The National Security Structure,* pp. 106–07.

9. Stubbing, *The Defense Game,* p. 285.

10. Richard Nixon, *RN* (New York: Harper, 1977), p. 433.

11. John Erlichman, *Witness to Power: The Nixon Years* (New York: Simon and Schuster, 1982), p. 94.

12. Stubbing, *The Defense Game,* pp. 344, 366.

14

The Whitehall Model: Career Staff Support for Cabinet in Foreign Affairs

PETER HENNESSY

In Washington Lord Halifax
Once whispered to Lord Keynes,
"It's true *they* have money bags,
But *we* have all the brains."
  —*Anonymous verse in British papers dealing with negotiation of the
  American Loan, 1945*

What you have got to do in foreign affairs is not to create a situation.
  —*Ernest Bevin, late 1940s*

I know nothing about diplomacy, but I just know and believe that I
want certain things for Britain.
  —*Margaret Thatcher, 1979*[1]

Paul Gore-Booth was a singular man with a strong dash of the unorthodox. Occasionally, he took time off as permanent secretary at the Foreign Office to don deerstalker and tweeds before traveling to Switzerland where, as president of the Sherlock Holmes Society, he reenacted the great sleuth's battle with Professor Moriarty at the Reischenbach Falls.[2] Also, he spoke truth unto power. It was Gore-Booth who drafted a memo to protest the folly of the Suez incident in 1956 and presented it to his chief, Sir Ivone Kirkpatrick, one of the few officials who knew what was happening.[3]

In retirement Gore-Booth revealed a considerable gift for capturing and expressing the purpose of postwar British foreign policy. The function of the Foreign Office, he wrote, was "keeping the nation's nerve." This, he added; was "a real task for some institution thinking in world terms to keep cool and to devise and execute, within the limits of knowledge, money and power, progressive but realistic policies to advance long-term interests rather

than to satisfy immediate emotions. There is no great glamour
about this. But we tried to do it, and not without success."[4] Satisfying, no doubt, the modern requirement of management by objectives, Gore-Booth moved from the vague to the specific: "The
object of policy had to be to ensure that a great nation could stop
half-way down and establish itself as a second-level power with
real tasks to perform and obligations to fulfull."[5] This was not the
self-image of the heroic period of postwar British foreign policy
making in the late 1940s when the scaffolding of its bureaucratic
support structure was put in place. Ernest Bevin was not a man to
think in terms of the orderly management of decline. He could not
bear the idea of a "scuttle out of [India] without the dignity or
plan" in 1947.[6] A year later he took comfort from the notion that
by developing the British Empire in Africa: "We could have the
United States dependent on us, and eating out of our hand in four
or five years. . . . The United States is very barren of essential
minerals, and in Africa we have them all."[7] The motivation behind Bevin's foreign policy was his conviction that, in time, the
British economy could return the nation to the status of a great
power. It was not for him, therefore, to permanently close important options for those who came after him in the foreign secretary's chair. This was precisely the argument which led him to
push hard for an independent British nuclear weapons capability
with "the bloody Union Jack on top of it."[8]

Heroic it may have been, but not sustainable. Occasionally, the
occupant of Bevin's old chair could be as despondent as he had
been optimistic. During a strategy session in November 1974 at
Chequers, the prime minister's country seat, with the economy at
a discouragingly low ebb and OPEC prices rising rapidly, James
Callaghan told members of Harold Wilson's last cabinet (according to Mrs. Barbara Castle's diary):

If we ever got to a siege economy, he, Jim, dreaded the effect on our
democracy. He didn't think that the US would do a Suez in the Middle
East. The more likely prospect was our declining influence. "Our prospect is that we shall lose our seat on the Security Council." Jim concluded
gloomily that in his view, we should go on sliding downhill for the next
few years.[9]

Between British foreign secretaries at their most bullish and
bearish, there is a place for the permanent, professional nerve-

stiffener. Indeed, the delicate handling needed to sustain morale and keep up the self-image of professionals in the Foreign Office, other departments of state, the clandestine agencies, and at all levels of policy making up through cabinet and standing committees on overseas and defense policy is still very much in demand.

The argument put forth by Britain's managers of orderly decline (aptly described by Sir William Armstrong, former permanent secretary to the treasury)[10] in their own defense should be presented because *all* the important players, except temporary ministers, are career officials enjoying permanent tenure and a job-for-life. Their argument runs something like the following:

Since 1945 the art of the British foreign policy adviser has been that of a seasoned gambler under duress obliged to make the best of an ever poorer hand. Though the public's perception always lagged behind ours, we insiders recognized and coped with the benchmarks of Britain's decline as we crossed them—our ceasing to be a global superpower with withdrawal from Greece and India in 1947; our simultaneous recognition that we could no longer fight a major war without material assistance from the United States; our recognition after Suez that we could no longer fight a minor war without, at least, the acquiescence of the United States; our recognition after the Kruschev-Kennedy meeting in Vienna in 1961 that we could no longer expect an automatic place at the "top table"; our recognition at Nassau in 1962 that a modern British nuclear force was no longer possible without American equipment and know-how; our recognition with the final withdrawals from East of Suez in 1968–71 that we could no longer be a global power; our recognition since 1973 that we are a medium-sized regional power within the larger group of the EEC; our skillful acceptance (hiccups like Rhodesia apart) of the right moment to withdraw gracefully from the territories acquired in the past; at every point our mix of diplomacy and defense has been enhanced by top-rate staff work processed by a policy-making machine refined by long years of experience to a level of performance that excites envy from others; even from some superpowers.

In the penultimate section of this chapter, I will criticize this reassuring self-image held for so long by most British players of the Great Game, as the Kipling generation labeled it. First, I will look at its mechanical underpinnings, the advice machine and the decision-taking control rooms served by the machine. Because it is part of the conventional wisdom of decline managers that first-class intelligence and staff work are invaluable "force-multipliers" for those whose real forces grow ever thinner on the ground.

The Advice Machine

Our Cabinet committee system is, generally speaking, admired abroad and envied by others.
   —*Lord Greenhill, former head of the diplomatic service, 1988*

The National Security Council, created in 1947, [was] modelled on the British War Cabinet.
   —*Zara Steiner, 1987*

For a British civil servant there is no problem so acute that it won't yield to a careful piece of drafting.
   —*Senior Australian civil servant, 1984*

If you ask the FO to write you a paper, you add up the paragraphs with odd numbers, and you get one opinion, add up the paragraphs with even numbers and you get another: and no conclusion.
   —*Winston Churchill, 1943*[11]

Mrs. Thatcher's Cabinet Committee on Oversea and Defence Policy, known as OD, traced its origin to the Committee of Imperial Defence created by her Conservative predecessor, A. J. Balfour, in 1902. The CID was a prototype NSC intended to modernize Whitehall's capability to meet the growing threat of European instability with the rise of the Kaiser's Germany.[12] Apart from World War I, when it was superseded by the War Council, the CID and its elaborate subcommittee system remained *the* forum the handling of foreign and defense issues of both high policy and detailed application until the outbreak of the Second World War in 1939. Since 1904 the prime minister has held the chair.

In machinery of government terms, Churchill ran a very personal war between 1940 and 1945. In effect, he split the cabinet in two: he waged war and designed strategy with the chiefs of staff while the Lord President's Committee functioned as a domestic cabinet dealing with everything else.[13] In 1945–46, the tidy-minded Attlee reviewed this arrangement and, with the help of Sir Edward Bridges, former secretary of the War Cabinet, and two soldier/administrators, generals Sir Hastings Ismay and Sir Ian Jacob, Attlee created a new Cabinet Defence Committee in January 1947.[14] What emerged was the old CID minus its imperial component.

However, the new Cabinet Defence Committee did not include foreign affairs. A striking lacuna in Attlee's elaborate cabinet structure was that no committee was assigned foreign affairs. In practice, Attlee and Bevin disposed of it themselves.[15] In fact, no formal foreign affairs committee was created until 1962, after another review undertaken for Harold Macmillan again by the old firm of Whitehall warriors, Ismay and Jacob.[16]

This organization instituted under Macmillan has held, with few minor modifications, ever since. At the apex of foreign and defense policy making, tightly brigaded together since 1962, has been the Defence and Oversea Policy Committee of the Cabinet, chaired by the Prime Minister (its name changes from administration to administration and its initials involve a combination of the same letters—DOPC, OPD, OD, etc.). Every Whitehall department making an input in foreign policy has its inputs processed by a free standing Oversea and Defence Secretariat in the Cabinet Office. In return, the secretariat briefs the ministers on OD (current usage), briefs its subcommittees or *ad hoc* groups occasionally spawned to tackle specific issues. It is the summit of Whitehall's foreign, defense, and intelligence machines.

The quality and range of advice were transformed by World War II, the great divide between the CID machinery bequeathed by the Edwardians and the modern machinery fashioned for total war and adapted after 1945 for cold war. Interdepartmental and interservice rivalry are perpetual problems in any bureaucracy, regardless of the strength of the central decision-making agency. The five decades since the founding of the Joint Intelligence Committee[17] are replete with attempts to gain clarity and consistency by subduing the turf fights that arise on the periphery. The British tend to think Whitehall still has a long way to go to achieve the desired level of coordination. Washington insiders would give an arm and a leg to reach Whitehall's present state of the art. The Whitehall foreign and defense policy system obliges every prime minister, even one as strong as Mrs. Thatcher, to work through the consultative process. In the British context, an Iran-contra affair would be even more of an anomaly than the Suez affair in 1956.

The centripetal thrust has been most marked on the defense side. During the war years, Churchill took the title of minister of defense as well as prime minister and busied himself with devices such as countermanding the tendencies of the chiefs toward dark blue, khaki, or light blue, and chaired about a tenth of the chiefs-of-staff meetings himself.[18] In an aside to Harold Macmillan he once observed, "you may take the most gallant sailor, the most intrepid airman or the most audacious soldier, put them at a table together—what do you get? The sum of their fears."[19]

Attlee created what was intended to be a strong, coordinating central department in 1947 to counteract the institutionalized pressure-grouping of the War Office, the Air Ministry, and the Admiralty. Ismay's and Jacob's recall to the colors showed the how the prototype Ministry of Defence was ignored. The abolition of the service ministries and the creation of a single Defence Ministry in 1964, with a new chief of defense staff in charge of the Chiefs of Staff Committee, took the process a step further. In 1981, Mrs. Thatcher removed the individual service chiefs from their seats at OD meetings, leaving only the chief of defense staff to represent their views. Finally, in 1984, Mr. Michael Heseltine diminished the power of the individual armed services still further by pushing through a plan that he literally outlined on the back of an envelope on a flight home from Kuwait.[20]

Given the powerful traditions and loyalties of the uniformed services, each burst of reorganization provoked resistance and outcries. In contrast, the equivalent of rejigging on the overseas policy side has been smooth and decorous. There, too, since 1945 concentration has gone forward through the gradual mutation or disappearance of old departments: beginning with the expiration of the India Office in 1947 and the transmogrification of the Dominions Office to the Commonwealth Office that same year; the merger of the Colonial and Commonwealth Offices in 1966 to the creation of the unified Foreign and Commonwealth Office in 1968 under single political and administrative chiefs merged in the foreign and commonwealth secretary and the head of the diplomatic service. A parallel process of modernizing the FO has occurred under the goad of ministers (the Eden-Bevin reforms of 1943)[21] and the pressure of external inquiries (Plowden 1946; Duncan 1968; Berrill 1977).[22]

The intelligence side has undergone some reorganization, although, as one expected, it received the least attention of all. Given the nature of the Soviet threat as perceived as early as the Tehran Conference in 1943 and the crucial significance of signals intelligence once Bletchley Park got into its code-breaking stride in 1940–41, there was no danger of British intelligence services being reduced to a care-and-maintenance level of funds or personnel as they had been after 1919. All the key agencies remained in full operation: M16, the Secret Intelligence Service (under the Foreign Office); the Government Code and Cipher School, later renamed the Government Communications Headquarters (Foreign Office); M15, the Security Service (Home Office); Naval Intelligence Department (Admiralty); Military Intelligence (War Office); and Air Intelligence (Air Ministry). Only the Special Operations Executive (behind the lines activities) and the Political Warfare Executive (black propaganda) were closed down after 1945.

The special intelligence connection developed between Britain and the United States during the war was formalized and extended after peace through the secret U.K.-U.S. agreement of 1947.[23] Its continued vitality and utility is confirmed every week when representatives of the U.S. intelligence community meet with their British counterparts in the Cabinet Office in London before the weekly meeting of the JIC.[24]

The intelligence section of the advice machine has been reorganized intermittently since 1945. In 1957, the JIC moved from being a satrapy of the chiefs of staff to integration in the Cabinet Office.[25] In 1964, the service intelligence departments were fused into a single Defence Intelligence Staff under a chief of defense intelligence.[26] In the early 1970s, Mr. Edward Heath moved toward improved performance at the center by appointing a coordinator of security and intelligence in the Cabinet Office. Also, he stepped up the collection of economic intelligence.[27] After the Falklands War, the JIC and its assessments staff in the Cabinet Office were reviewed; the chairmanship of the JIC was removed from the Foreign Office in 1983; and direct access to the prime minister herself was given to the man-in-place on an ad hominem basis.[28] Mrs. Thatcher, in keeping with the trend, also emphasized the importance of economic intelligence.[29]

It is easy but erroneous to forget the economic input into the cabinet's foreign policy advice machine. The external economic dimension is ignored at its peril by any postwar British government as even the well-organized Attlee administration discovered, thus prompting the creation of its Economic Policy Cabinet Committee in 1947.[30] The Treasury's Overseas Finance Sector is the institutionalization of an untinted window through which to view the outside world of international economy in its various guises. It has existed since the first days of peace when Keynes warned the Attlee cabinet of a forthcoming "financial Dunkirk."[31] The problems that Gore-Booth labeled "a thinly lined Exchequer,"[32] have never, in fact, been far from ministers' minds. Forty years before Paul Kennedy's great synthesis became required reading in the foreign ministries of the world,[33] Bevin told the miners that if *they* gave him another million tons of coal, *he* could give the country a new foreign policy.[34]

The economic input into cabinet foreign policy making has changed little in terms of Whitehall departments. The Treasury has been crucial throughout, and the chancellor of the exchequer has been a constant member of whichever cabinet committee mattered in foreign policy terms. The industrial departments have gone through a series of baffling mutations,[35] although some form of a Board or Department of Trade has almost always been visible; and, intoning its litany of "export or die," has occupied a less than glamorous seat at the cabinet committee table.

Occasionally, there has been a bureaucratic outrider in Whitehall wielding his somewhat transient influence on the economic front. In the early postwar years, Sir Edwin Plowden, then head of the Central Economic Planning Staff, took the lead in several of the burden-sharing negotiations on Western rearmament and thus had noticeable input to the financial management of the Korean War.[36] Lord Cherwell, paymaster-general and head of Churchill's revived Statistical Section (a wartime invention to keep tabs on Whitehall), played a crucial role in killing the Treasury/Bank of England plan to float the pound in 1952.[37]

More recently, Lord Rothschild's central policy review staff surpassed the rest of Whitehall with a prediction, well before the Yom Kippur War of 1973, of a rise in oil prices if the OPEC cartel were to flex its muscles.[38] In the Thatcher era, there was a one-man equivalent of Plowden's CEPS, Cherwell's Statistical Section, and Rothschild's CPRS in the person of Sir Alan Walters—Mrs. Thatcher's part-time economic adviser. He was also influential in obstructing Britain's entry to the European Monetary System despite the wishes of the Foreign Office and Treasury.[39]

Mrs. Thatcher preferred individual advice over institutional advice and was moved to abolish the CPRS in 1983. Since the Falklands crisis of 1982, she made use of an equivalent of Walters on the foreign side. Her first foreign affairs adviser was Sir Anthony Parsons, an unorthodox and slightly dashing career diplomat and ambassador to the United Nations. He had won her admiration during a Chequers meeting on the Falklands War when he told her to stop interrupting him.[40] Parsons was succeeded after the 1983 election by the leading FCO sinologist of his generation, Sir Percy Cradock, who negotiated the treaty that will transfer Hong Kong to the People's Republic of China. Cradock and Parsons served as the prime minister's eyes and ears on the JIC[41] and were a continuous source of advice on foreign policy and defense issues. Another individual source of advice and, reputedly, strong influence on Mrs. Thatcher was her private secretary, Charles Powell.

The foreign policy-making cadre insofar as I have described it, is noticeably lacking a European adviser. Although the FCO is in the lead for the U.K.'s representation to the Community both in London and Brussels, the U.K.'s policy toward the EEC addresses the whole spectrum of economic, industrial, and social issues. And the pile of EEC directives grows higher as the trade and professional barriers fall.

No simple description of European policy making is possible. It has a European secretariat in the Cabinet Office entirely distinct from its equivalent for overseas and defense policy. Unlike the Callaghan administration, which was neater in this respect, European business these days can be tackled in a variety of ways at the top of the cabinet committee structure. For example, many of the most important EEC issues, such as Britain's share of the budget, are handled in EA, the Cabinet Committee on Economic Strategy that was chaired by Mrs. Thatcher.[42] Other issues are resolved in OD(E), Oversea and Defence (Europe), presided over by Foreign Secretary Sir Geoffrey Howe.[43] Ironically, the untidiness of European policy making reflects the "half-in, half-out" attitude of several members of recent Thatcher cabinets.[44] Whitehall's advice machine, apart from the brief Heath premiership, has always had difficulties in nudging ministerial committees into a more *communitaire* frame of mind. Despite being latecomers to the notion of a post-imperial Britain within the EEC (Treasury and the Foreign Office were not converted until circa 1960), the foreign and economic policy-making bureaucracy has advised with a zeal and consistency which has infuriated more than one foreign minister.[45] The decision-making cycle, however, is supposed to forestall such disruptions. In Whitehall the democratic theory is that elected officers (ministers) shall always prevail over appointed officers (diplomats, civil servants, and intelligence officers) and the decision-making machine is designed to carry the theory into practice.

The Decision Cycle

> He told his colleagues about his great aunt's Daimler, which had travelled at the "sensible speed of thirty miles an hour," and was sufficiently spacious to enable one to descend from it without removing one's top hat. Nowadays, alas! people have a mania for dashing around. But that being so, Britain ought to "cater for this profitable modern eccentricity"! He thought they all readily agreed. It was all over in a few minutes.
> —*Nigel Lawson and Jock Bruce-Gardyne on the meeting of the Macmillan cabinet in 1962 at which it was decided to collaborate with the French in making the Concorde.*

> Jim [Callaghan] wanted it [Polaris] down to three, just to save money, of course. But George Brown wanted it down to three on the grounds that, with three boats, we couldn't be sure always of having one on patrol, and, therefore, it couldn't be regarded as capable of being used independently. And I remember Michael Stewart saying . . . it reminded him very much of when he was on the committee of the Fulham Co-op and they were discussing the 1930s, being good Methodists all, whether for the first time they should stock wine. And they finally decided they would stock wine but only very poor wine.
> —*Denis Healey recalling the cabinet meeting at Chequers in 1964 where it was decided to go ahead with the Polaris nuclear force for the Royal Navy.*

> Geoffrey, I know what you're going to recommend and the answer is "No!"
> —*Mrs. Thatcher to the foreign secretary, Sir Geoffrey Howe, at a meeting of the Oversea and Defence Committee of the cabinet in January 1984 to discuss the possibility of exploratory talks with the Alfonsín government in Buenos Aires.*[46]

Historians, the archive-mongers in particular, suffer from an occupational hazard. It is easy to be persuaded by the minutes of meetings that calm, reason, and the Socratic method prevailed where they patently did not. Harold Macmillan, himself a great stylist in the cabinet room, recognized this misconception and, as minister of housing and local government in the early 1950s, addressed a member of the cabinet secretariat, Sir George Mallaby, about it:

Historians reading this [set of cabinet minutes] 50 or 100 years hence will get a totally false picture. They will be filled with admiration and surprise to find that the Cabinet were so intellectually disciplined that they argued each issue methodically and logically through to a neat set of precise conclusions. It isn't like that at all, you know.[47]

At some times and on certain issues it is difficult for outsiders to appreciate fully just how spotty the quality of ministerial decision taking can be. Take the Falkland Islands—a "front burner" issue for the cabinet's OD Committee since 1982. It was not always so. When official papers for 1954 were released at the Public Record Office in 1985 under the Thirty-Year Rule, Admiralty files dealing with the response to a possible assault on the islands by General Perón were declassified. They prompted one senior Admiralty civil servant to recollect a ministerial meeting where the First Lord (i.e., navy minister) J.P.L. Thomas was asked by a colleague just exactly where the Falklands were. With supreme self-assurance, Thomas drew a ring around St. Helena and tossed the map across the table.[48] Matters had improved a bit by the early 1980s but not enough for OD to prevent Galtieri from carrying out what Perón had only ruminated about.

Despite the disturbing description given above, on the positive side, there is a general regularity to the foreign policy-making process at the highest level in Whitehall, a smoothness of operation that justifies Lord Greenhill's belief that the British way is widely admired abroad. The operational smoothness derives from the continuity of official personnel and the efficiency of the Cabinet Office machinery. When the government in Whitehall changes, there is none of the uprooting and overhauling that occurs on the Washington scene. The second person to call upon a new prime minister (the first is the Downing Street principal private secretary, a career person) is the secretary of the cabinet. He outlines the most urgent business requiring a collective, as opposed to prime ministerial, decision and suggests an embryonic committee structure to tackle it. His suggestion is invariably accepted, and the result always bears the genetic traces of the system established by Lloyd George and the first cabinet secretary, Sir Maurice Hankey, in 1916. As for procedures, the meetings are called, the substance recorded, and the minutes circulated to those who "need to know" without breaking stride.

The chemistry of the meetings is another matter, as Macmillan made plain in his aside to Mallaby. The system as a whole has to cope with issues of all kinds—the routine, the *ad hoc,* and the unexpected. The routine, in the sense of the forseeable rather than the prosaic or trivial, is tackled by OD which meets once a week when Parliament is sitting. The background briefing provided for it is impressive. Prime Minister Thatcher had a "steering brief" in her role as chairman delivered by the cabinet offices' Oversea and Defence Secretariat. Her Downing Street foreign affairs adviser, Sir Percy Cradock, often put in a personal brief in as well. Each departmental minister attending (membership fluctuates, but always includes the foreign secretary, the chancellor of the exchequer, and the defense secretary or ministers standing-in in their absence) has in hand a cabinet office paper and a brief from his own ministry. In addition, ministers receive the weekly "Red Book" of intelligence assessments and summaries produced by the Joint Intelligence Committee after myriad inputs from open and closed sources are processed by its regionally focused current intelligence groups.

Grand-scale, time-consuming issues, foreseeable and foreseen, are usually taken in a sub/group of OD especially commissioned for the task. For example, OD (HK) dealt with the protracted and delicate negotiations covering the transfer of the sovereignty of Hong Kong from the United Kingdom to the People's Republic of China due in 1997.[49] An unforeseen emergency, like the Falklands crisis of April–June 1982, was handled by OD (SA)—that is, Oversea and Defence, South Atlantic—which became popularly known as the War Cabinet.[50]

Slightly less grand issues are often processed through a third layer of cabinet committees in the MISC, or miscellaneous series. For example, an official, as opposed to a ministerial group, MISC 32, was active in the early eighties on the logistics of deploying the British armed forces outside the NATO area. It was chaired by the then head of the Oversea and Defence Secretariat, Sir Robert Wade-Gery.[51] In 1983 the prime minister herself took the chair at MISC 91, a committee convened for the purpose of choosing a new antiradar missile for the Royal Air Force.[52] In many ways the full cabinet is a ratifying body for decisions processed and taken in the network of cabinet committees. However, it takes up two fixed items at every weekly cabinet meeting on Thursday morning which are the report on foreign affairs by the foreign secretary and the forthcoming business in Parliament. Under Mrs. Thatcher, these meetings were not necessarily a gathering for enlightenment or for decision taking. Grand-scale issues requiring a decision are treated as separate items of business and, most often, the prime minister decides what decisions will be taken at this level. It is not always easy for a minister to force an issue onto the cabinet agenda as Michael Heseltine discovered during the Westland affair. At whatever level these committees operate, they are the beneficiaries of what Michael Heseltine, former defense secretary, called the "Rolls Royce" service from "a machine of supreme quality."[53] The question remains, is the outcome up to Rolls Royce standards?

Performance Assessment

We, my dear Crossman, are Greeks in this American empire. You will find the Americans much as the Greeks found the Romans—great big, vulgar, bustling people, more virtuous than we are and also more idle, with more unspoiled virtues but also more corrupt. We must run AFHQ [Allied Forces Headquarters] as the Greek slaves ran the operations of the Emperor Claudius.
   —*Harold Macmillan to Richard Crossman, Algiers, 1943*

It was an extraordinary relationship because it rested on no legal claim; it was formalised by no document; it was carried forward by succeeding British governments as if no alternative was conceivable. Britain's influence was great precisely because it never insisted on it; the "special relationship" demonstrated the value of intangibles.
   —*Henry Kissinger, 1979*

In our foreign policy 1945–70, could our governments have done better? My answer is, "I doubt it." But I can hear you saying in the immortal words of Mandy Rice Davies, "he would say that, wouldn't he?"
   —*Lord Greenhill, 1988*[54]

On the grand strategy level, Lord Greenhill's verdict on his profession and his times is quite creditable. Such advantages as Britain possessed—an experienced political and official class, a high degree of political bipartisanship in the postwar period, an intangible like the "special relationship" milked for all it was worth (particularly on the nuclear weapons side after the restoration of collaboration in 1958) and freedom from internal faction and external pressure groups[55]—were used to the full. In the context of the great debate stimulated by Paul Kennedy's *The Rise and Fall of the Great Powers*, the Greenhills and Gore-Booths are exemplars of the cool and seasoned realists easing their political chiefs into an appreciation that the world has changed and suggesting a series of timely and prudent adjustments to fit into the new mode.

This would wash as welcome balm to British sensibilities and wise warning to those who might follow us down the superpower path if it were shown to be deliberate and planned to meet anticipated events. It was not. That other great figure of postwar British diplomacy, Sir Roger Makins, now Lord Sherfield—at the heart of the special relationship for over twenty years—has admitted as much. In an interview with the BBC's Michael Charlton for *The Price of Victory* (a program about Britain's missed opportunities), Lord Sherfield's remarks reminded us of the danger of feeding back Whitehall's preoccupations of the 1970s and 1980s into the heroic and spartan period of foreign policy making immediately after the war when Bevin was buying time for his successors. Sherfield told Charlton:

Two things we were not to foresee. The first was de Gaulle and what that meant in terms of European defence, European political organization, and so on; and the second thing, which I certainly never foresaw and would not, I think, perhaps have credited at the time we are talking about—1950—was the economic and industrial failure in the United Kingdom in the 1960s. It was perhaps to be foreseen, but I certainly did not foresee it.[56]

Whatever the shortcomings then, one must still ask: were the readjustments made smoothly and on time? Such things are very difficult to measure. However, there is one revealing test: how many times since 1945 has the cabinet, its advice machine, and its committees had to undertake the painful labor of a defense review when resources no longer tallied with aspirations? The answer is no less than eight: 1949–50, 1953–54, 1957, 1964–65, 1965–68, 1974–75, 1981, and 1990.[57] Four of these instances fall under Labour and four fall under Conservative governments—though to be fair, the 1990 "Options for Change" review was in response to the ending of the cold war, not a cash crisis.[58] Whatever conclusions one may draw from this record, timely and orderly management of decline is not one of them. Understandably, ministers are reluctant to ask themselves profound and disturbing questions such as "Are we trying to do too much?" unless events force them to that point.

It is the job of the adviser and the diplomat to put the best

possible face on reality. "When you need credit, you usually wear
your best suit," was how Lord Greenhill put it.[59] I recall an interview with Sir Antony Acland, then head of the diplomatic service,
in which he compared Bevin's time to the 1980s; he emphasized
that the United Kingdom still had an Atlantic, a Commonwealth,
and a European role as in the late 1940s.[60] Sir Antony's successor,
Sir Patrick Wright, updated the Gore-Booth version of the purpose
of the FO. Sir Patrick told me:

> For much of my career, for post-imperial and other reasons, we have
> been in the business of managing decline and adjusting to Britain's posi-
> tion after the war. What encourages me, and I tell this to the new en-
> trants to the [Diplomatic] Service, it seems to me that we are out of that
> period of managing decline. This is not a party-political point. Our job is
> to promote the development of British interests in an era in which Britain
> has a new political and economic strength and respect in the world. This
> opens new opportunities.[61]

Will this sound hubristic to early twenty-first-century ears? I hope
not, but it may.

It's the job of the intelligence services to bring reality forcefully
to bear in the counsels of their customers. It's no easy task when
their customers, ministers on OD, are also their political chiefs and
their paymasters and quartermasters as well. Assessment here is
all but impossible. Without an official history for the years since
1945 similar to Sir Harry Hinsley's for World War II, the answer to
several key questions (the quality of advice just before the Chinese
intervention in Korea in 1950; the concern about who would
replace Nasser in Cairo in 1956) is unknowable until peacetime
intelligence archives are released under the Thirty-Year Rule.

The only evidence one has is anecdotal. For example, after President Nyerere sought British military assistance to quell internal
unrest in Tanzania in 1963, the then foreign secretary, Lord Home,
asked the then first sea lord, Lord Mountbatten, "On how many
occasions have we had to send out military expeditions of this
kind since the war and on how many occasions was the trouble
foreseen?" His answer was, "Forty-eight and none."[62] The exception, where we can refer to chapter and verse is the Falklands War.
In this instance the conclusion of the Franks inquiry was far from
reassuring on both the intelligence side (a shakeup of the organization of the JIC followed) and on the OD side. The criticism, though
couched in typical British understatement, was unmistakable:

Government policy towards Argentina and the Falkland Islands was never formally discussed outside the Foreign and Commonwealth Office after January 1981. Thereafter the time was never judged to be ripe although we were told in oral evidence that, *subject to the availability of minister* [emphasis added], a Defence Committee [i.e., OD] meeting could have been called at any time, if necessary at short notice. There was no meeting of the Defence Committee to discuss the Falklands in Cabinet, even after the New York talks of 26 and 27 February [with the Argentine government] until Lord Carrington [the foreign secretary] reported on events in South Georgia on 25 March, 1982.[63]

Lord Franks (a former ambassador to Washington) and his fellow privy counselors concluded:

We cannot say what the outcome of a meeting of the Defence Committee might have been, or whether the course of events would have been altered if it had met in September 1981; but, in our view, it could have been advantageous, and fully in line with Whitehall practice, for ministers to have reviewed collectively at that time, or in the months immediately ahead, the current negotiating position; the implications of the conflict between the attitudes of the Islanders and the aims of the [Argentine] Junta; and the longer-term policy options in relation to the dispute.[64]

The Franks Report raised questions about the competence of OD to handle what, rightly or wrongly, are seen as second- or third-order problems. While busy ministers are often in the air on a round of international meetings, the tendency of departments is to keep to themselves with little attention or time available for collective decisions at meetings of cabinet committees or to ignore the sometimes leaden performance of intelligence services when coping with "running-sore" problems such as the Falklands.

Bearing in mind that disasters are written up while triumphs are ignored and routine is not mentioned at all, what improvements could be made to the British foreign policy Rolls Royce which, in its original design, is almost as venerable as the real thing?

A New Specification

It was a devastating experience, and one that I found it difficult to talk about for about two years afterwards.
    —*David Young, MOD assistant secretary, on the Think Tank's attempt to refashion Britain's overseas representation.*

The Foreign Office . . . less of an oak than a willow.
    —*Lord Gore-Booth, 1974*[65]

To certain tough Whitehall operators, David Young included, those who try to reform it may find the FCO more of a rod than an oak or a willow. It has a tough and ancient tradition that makes it a formidable first line of defense. As Sir Edward Bridges put it during a lecture at the Imperial Defence College in 1952, "With some of the older departments—Treasury and Foreign Office are examples—there is no comprehensive statutory definition of duties. . . . the older and more fundamental powers . . . are inferred from custom and long practice."[66]

Anyone who calls for a review of the foreign side of Whitehall is referred to the long trail of inquiries since Eden/Bevin and warned of the horticultural cost of uprooting a delicate plant too often. But the machinery of government aspects have not been properly examined by an official inquiry since the Haldane Report of 1918,[67] a long time ago even by Foreign Office standards. What is needed is a specific examination of the *central* machinery of foreign and defense policy (including its intelligence back-up) rather than look at the hyperscrutinized overseas representation side.

Support for this notion has come from influential and knowledgeable quarters in recent years. For example, the late David Watt, while director-general of the Royal Institute of International Affairs in London, noticed the shortcomings exposed by Britain's membership in the EEC. In a lecture at Chatham House marking the bicentenary of the Foreign Office in 1982, he said:

There will have to be a much more elaborate form of interdepartmental liaison than now exists to co-ordinate our foreign policy interests. The Cabinet and its sub-committees work reasonably well where traditional fuctional issues like defence interact with foreign relations; less well on geographical areas, such as the European Community, where large numbers of departments are concerned; and often not at all where the ministries are as ill-assorted as, say, the Foreign and Commonwealth Office, the Department of Education and Science, and the Department of Health and Social Security, handling various aspects of the overseas students [payment of fees] question.[68]

In the 1980s on the intelligence side, there has been the megacriticism in the Franks Report of the JIC and its machinery and the occasional criticism of the quality of personnel, their pay, prospects, and conditions, engaged in military intelligence assessment of the Soviet Union and the Warsaw Pact.[69]

On the megalevel, Sir Frank Cooper, a former permanent secretary at the Ministry of Defence, has raised the question of whether Britain needs "some kind of National Security Council with, supporting it, a properly qualified military and civil secretariat or planning staff?"[70] An intriguing reflection, given that the NSC was modeled on British practice in two world wars. Recently, Sir Frank has pursued this notion further.

The United States experience of a National Security Council has not been altogether happy, for example, the relationship between the NSC Adviser and both the State Department and the Pentagon—particularly the former—has had its ups and downs and sometimes, far from producing co-ordination, has seemed to produce alienation.

Nevertheless, the British tend to be at the other end of the spectrum, though it is perhaps significant that the Cabinet Office plays a far more prominent role in co-ordinating intelligence and nuclear policies than it does in many other fields, both in a national sense, and, of course, in an international sense.

It is also perhaps true that at times of major crisis the British Cabinet Office has played a very active role in co-ordination: I suppose the classic examples recently are at a time of a Defence Review, Cuba, or in a major change of policy such as the withdrawal East of Suez.

Historically the British were at the forefront of co-ordinating advice within Government and seeking to bring together foreign and defence policy. This goes back to the days of the Imperial Committee right up—and continuously—to the present day Defence and Oversea Policy Committee which is serviced by the Cabinet Office. Yet the Cabinet Office has very little experience of defence and the Secretariat is basically provided by people temporarily on loan (for a couple of years) from the FCO and the MOD. The question is, ought it to have a rather stronger persona?

One of the difficulties is that we are hung up by our past. Any heightened activity by the Cabinet Office tends to be regarded as a precursor of a defence review. Yet, there is evidence of growing concern, that we are not able and have never been able in the recent past, to bring together our forces and or commitments and to enunciate policy. Some will argue that to have the Cabinet Office play a larger role gives undue power to people without responsibility (perhaps even without sufficient knowledge), that it is a disruptive element, and that it simply tends to bring about change for change's sake.

My own view is that we would benefit as a nation from having a somewhat higher profile in the Cabinet Office with an identifiable team acting as a Defence and Oversea Policy Advisory Group. Could such a group have improved the handling of the Falklands crisis? Would it move policy along toward the decision-making point? Do we need an ongoing group to support and advise the decision-makers? Would the MOD and FCO benefit from more external scrutiny, as there are few genuine practitioners in the field outside comparable to the fields of economics and social affairs?

I think there is a good argument for a small team that does not operate competitively or aggressively vis-à-vis the two main Departments of State. It would be a difficult feat to install such a team and avoid friction. Nevertheless the style and practice of British Government, particularly from the centre, lends itself to this possibility and, the true safeguard is that ministers are on the Defence and Oversea Policy Committee and the team would work for them.[71]

It should be seriously considered on a preliminary agenda for a "Haldane on foreign and defence policy-making." It would be reassuring if it could be implemented without the customary stimulus of a crisis to bring the idea to ministerial attention. Crises are rarely conducive to calm and careful planning, as Harold Macmillan reminded us when he pinned a note to the cabinet room door during the Suez crisis. "Quiet, calm deliberation disentangles every knot."[72]

Notes

1. The anonymous verse is found in Richard N. Gardner, *Sterling-Dollar Diplomacy,* exp. ed. (McGraw-Hill, 1969), p. xvii; the Bevin quotation is found in Roy Jenkins, *Nine Men of Power* (Hamish Hamilton, 1974), p. 77; the Thatcher quotation comes from Kenneth Harris, *Thatcher* (Weidenfeld and Nicolson, 1988), p. 99.

2. Paul Gore-Booth, *With Great Truth and Respect* (Constable, 1974), pp. 397–98.

3. Memo, dated 2 November 1945, in Peter Hennesy and Mark Laity, "Suez—What the Papers Say," *Contemporary Record* 1 (Spring 1987), 5; the original is in the Gore-Booth MS, Bodleian Library, Oxford.

4. Gore-Booth, *With Great Truth and Respect,* pp. 424–25.

5. Ibid., p. 424.

6. Public Record Office (PRO), FO 800/470/IND/47/1.

7. John Gallagher, *The Decline, Revival and Fall of the British Empire* (Cambridge University Press, 1982), p. 146.

8. Peter Hennessy, *Cabinet* (Blackwell, 1986), pp. 126–27.

9. Barbara Castle, *The Castle Diaries, 1974–76* (Weidenfeld, 1980), pp. 219–24.

10. Peter Hennessy, *Whitehall* (Free Press, 1990), p. 76.

11. Lord Greenhill, "British Foreign Policy, 1945–70: Could We Have Done Better?" Address to the Institute of Contemporary British History, London School of Economics Summer School on British History, 8 July 1988; Zara Steiner, "Decison-Making in American and British Foreign Policy: An Open and Shut Case," *Review of International Studies* 13 (1987), 7; the Australian civil servant made this statement to me; Churchill is quoted in Alistair Horne, *Macmillan, 1894–1956: The Making of a Prime Minister* (Macmillan, 1988).

12. On the genesis of the CID, see Stephen Roskill, *Hankey, Man of Secrets,* vol. 1: *1877–1918* (Collins, 1970), pp. 90–91.

13. For an account of Whitehall under Churchhill-as-war-maker, see J. M. Lee, *The Churchill Coalition, 1940–1945* (Batsford, 1980), pp. 52–81.

14. Franklyn A. Johnson, *Defence by Ministry* (Duckworth, 1980), pp. 18–21.

15. Alan Bullock, *Ernest Bevin, Foreign Secretary* (Heinemann, 1983), pp. 56–

57; Peter Hennessy and Andrew Arends, *Mr Attlee's Engine Room: Cabinet Committee Structure and the Labour Government 1945–51*, Strathclyde Papers on Government and Politics No. 26, 1983, p. 10.

16. *Central Organisation for Defence*, Cmnd. 2097 (HMSO, 1963), pp. 2–3.

17. For the origins of the JIC, see F. H. Hinsley, *British Intelligence in the Second World War* (HMSO, 1979), pp. 3–44.

18. Johnson, *Defence by Ministry*, p. 16.

19. Alistair Horne, *Macmillan: Politician, 1894–1956* (Penguin, 1989).

20. The envelope is reproduced in Michael Heseltine, *Where There's a Will* (Hutchinson, 1987), p. 29.

21. See Geoffrey Moorhouse, *The Diplomats: The Foreign Office Today* (Cape, 1987), pp. 24, 28, 53, 325.

22. *Report of the Committee on Representational Services Overseas* (HMSO, 1964); *Report of the Review Committee on Overseas Representation, 1968–69* (HMSO, 1969); *Report of Overseas Representation, Report by the Central Policy Review Staff* (HMSO, 1977).

23. Christopher Andrew, *Secret Service: The Making of the British Intelligence Community* (Heinemann, 1985), pp. 421–92.

24. Hennessy, *Cabinet*, pp. 25–26.

25. Private information.

26. Cmnd. 2097.

27. Private information.

28. Private information.

29. Private information.

30. Alec Cairncross, *Years of Recovery: British Economic Policy 1945–51* (Methuen, 1985), pp. 51–53.

31. Public Record Office, CAB 129/1, CP(45)112; "Our Overseas Financial Prospects," 14 August 1945.

32. Gore-Booth, *With Great Truth and Respect*, p. 232.

33. Paul Kennedy, *The Rise and Fall of the Great Powers* (Unwin Hyman, 1988).

34. Recalled by Bevin's private secretary, Sir Nicholas Henderson, in his farewell dispatch from the Paris embassy, 31 March 1979; published in *The Economist*, 2 June 1979, pp. 29–40.

35. See Brian Hogwood, "The Rise and Fall and Rise of the Department of Trade and Industry," in *Organizing Governance, Governing Organizations*, ed. Colin Campbell, S.J., and B. Guy Peters (Pittsburgh, Pa.: University of Pittsburgh Press, 1988), pp. 209–32.

36. Sir Edward Bridges as head of the civil service wrote privately to a leading Conservative shortly before Labour fell outlining Plowden's contribution in an attempt to allay the impression that he was a socialist appointee who should be removed if Churchill returned to office. Churchill was returned and Plowden stayed, building up a fruitful relationship with the new chancellor, R. A. Butler.

37. The plan, code-named "Robot," and Cherwell's role in its destruction, are described in Samuel Brittan, *Steering the Economy* (Secker and Warburg, 1970) and Anthony Seldon, *Churchill's Indian Summer* (Hodder, 1981), pp. 162, 165, 168, 171–73.

38. See Tessa Blackstone and William Plowden, *Inside the Think Tank: Advising the Cabinet 1971–1983* (Heinemann, 1988).

39. Sir Alan was a rather full-time adviser between 1980 and 1983. In the summer of 1988, it became clear that the frequency of his visits to No. 10 and his

contributions to the PM were about to increase once more (William Keegan, "Walters' Return a Snub to Lawson," *The Observer,* 17 July 1988).

40. See Hennessy, *Whitehall,* pp. 646–67.

41. Private information.

42. Hennessy, *Cabinet,* p. 27.

43. Ibid.

44. A recent example is the conversation between two cabinet ministers who left office after the 1987 general election. John Biffen declared to an *Independent* journalist that one country within the EEC would have to stand its ground to counteract the enthusiasms of the Community's trade commissioner, Lord Cockfield. Norman Tebbit chipped in, "I'm a Gaullist, too. . . . The creation of Euro-regulation and, in effect, a Euro-government, is bound to end in tears" (Andrew Gimson, "Who's a Tory?" *The Spectator,* 9 July 1988).

45. As foreign secretary, 1977–79, David Owen took the view that in European matters "Foreign Office civil servants had been acting almost as politicians, making political concessions and judgements" (*Personally Speaking* [Weidenfeld, 1987], p. 110).

46. Jock Bruce-Gardyne and Nigel Lawson, *The Power Game* (Macmillan, 1976), p. 28; Healey told this story on *A Bloody Union Jack on Top of It. Programme 2: From Polaris to Trident,* BBC Radio 4, 12 May 1988; Mrs. Thatcher is quoted in Hennessy, *Cabinet,* p. 99.

47. Sir George Mallaby, *From My Level* (Hutchinson, 1965), pp. 16–17.

48. David Walker, "Churchill advised to leave Falklands unguarded," *The Times,* 12 January 1985.

49. Hennessy, *Cabinet,* p. 28.

50. Lawrence Freedman, *Britain and the Falklands War* (Institute of Contemporary History/Blackwell, 1988), pp. 11–12, 76–77, 122.

51. Hennessy, *Cabinet,* p. 29.

52. Ibid., p. 30.

53. Evidence before the all-party Treasury and Civil Service Committee of the House of Commons, 22 June 1988.

54. Richard Crossman, "The Making of Macmillan," *The Sunday Telegraph,* 9 February 1964; Henry Kissinger, *The White House Years* (Little, Brown, 1979), p. 90; Greenhill, "British Foreign Policy, 1945–70."

55. See Zara Steiner's comparison of the climate in which the Foreign Office and the State Department work ("Decision-Making in American and British Foreign Policy," p. 14).

56. Michael Charlton, *The Price of Victory* (BBC, 1983), p. 117.

57. See Peter Hennessy, "Permanent Government: Waiting for Defence Review No. 8," *New Statesman,* 17 July 1987.

58. They include Paul Kennedy himself (Kennedy, *The Rise and Fall of the Great Powers,* pp. 482–83).

59. Greenhill, "British Foreign Policy 1945–70."

60. Peter Hennessy, "Whitehall Brief: Timely reminder of a bulldog presence," *The Times,* 1 November 1983.

61. Peter Hennessy, "Whitehall Watch: Sober message for defence chiefs," *The Independent,* 18 March 1988.

62. Lord Home, interview for Brook Productions' Channel 4 programme, *All the Prime Minister's Men,* BBC television, April 1986.

63. *Falkland Islands Review. Report of a Committee of Privy Counsellors,* Cmnd. 8787 (HMSO, 1983), p. 79.

64. Ibid.

65. David Young, quoted in Peter Hennessy, Susan Morrison, and Richard Townsend, *Routine Punctuated by Orgies: The Central Policy Review Staff, 1970–83,* Strathclyde Papers on Government and Politics No. 31, 1985, p. 57; Gore-Booth, *With Great Truth and Respect,* p. 405.

66. Quoted in Hennessy, *Whitehall,* p. 17.

67. Ministry of Reconstruction, *Report of the Machinery of Government Committee,* Cmnd. 9230, HMSO, 1918.

68. Ferdinand Mount, ed., *The Inquiring Eye: A Selection of the Writings of David Watt* (Penguin, 1988), pp. 39–40.

69. See Michael Herman, "Reflections on the study of Soviet military literature," *RUSI Journal,* Summer 1988, pp. 78–84.

70. Sir Frank Cooper, "Affordable Defence: In Search of a Strategy," lecture to the Royal United Services Institute, 9 October 1985.

71. Letter to the author, 11 July 1988.

72. From Gilbert and Sullivan, *The Gondoliers,* quoted in Alan Thompson, *The Day Before Yesterday: An Illustrated History of Britain from Attlee to Macmillan* (Sidgwick and Jackson, 1971), p. 163.

PART V

Personal Staff for Presidents and Prime Ministers

15

White House Staffing:
Salvation, Damnation, and Uncertainty

JOSEPH A. PIKA

Since its creation in 1939, the Executive Office of the President (EOP) has been the object of hope, despair, and intense curiosity for both members of the media and the academic community. Hope rested on the anticipation that presidents provided with adequate staff resources could provide the strong central leadership that many believe the country so desperately needs. Despair arose later as it was realized that staffs could be a liability as well as an asset both to the president and to the nation. Curiosity has remained throughout as the press pursues White House intrigues and academics seek to unravel the complex variables that influence staff behavior and operation. Regardless of whether one regarded staffing as salvation, damnation, or a problem of uncertainty, few have hesitated to offer prescriptions. Unfortunately, built-in pressures for prescription may be so powerful that they ultimately inhibit our ability to improve staffing to any substantial degree.

The White House Office is only one part of the larger problem of staffing the American presidency.[1] But White House staffing has become the central issue over the past two decades; the size, structure, influence, role, and accountability of the staff have been major topics of public discussion. Indeed, John Hart argues that the White House staff has come to play the dominant role in a new institution of American government, the presidential branch.[2] Although all presidents have enjoyed some form of assistance, presidents since Franklin D. Roosevelt have come to rely ever more heavily on a growing cadre of "personal" White House aides while eroding the distinction with "institutional" assistants serving in other units of the Executive Office of the President. These developments are decried by the heirs of Louis Brownlow and the Committee on Administrative Management, whose 1937 report sought to redirect staff growth from "political" (White House) advisers to "expert" (institutional) units. Despite the best efforts of numerous reformers and the public fallout from occasional scandals, successive presidents have continued to rely primarily on their personal staffs. As Hart notes, reformers have never recognized that "what is good for the presidency is not necessarily good for the president."[3]

What exists, therefore, is an advisory structure that has grown significantly in size, is subject to virtually no statutory controls, and is heavily shaped by the needs of the current incumbent. A variety of external pressures and informal norms that constitute a White House "lore" also shape the staff's operation, but these can be readily violated and consequently serve as weak constraints, at best.

From its origins as a modest group of generalists, the modern White House has evolved into a collection of specialized staffs working in three broad areas of responsibility: politics, policy, and internal administration. Liaison is maintained with a range of outside forces including Congress, the media, political parties, and interest groups; public relations has increasingly become a generalized staff concern. These "political" assignments antedate the Brownlow Report, while policy roles are largely a post-Brownlow development. As presidential responsibilities expanded in economic, foreign, and domestic policy areas, so too did White House staff units emerge with the charge to oversee policy portfolios and the corresponding executive branch officials. Ironically, by legitimizing presidential staffing, the Brownlow committee may actually have stimulated the proliferation of political advisers rather than blunted their influence as originally intended.

One finds considerable continuity across administrations in fundamental features of White House staffing that can be attributed to similar external pressures ("deep structure"), shared "creeds," and common internal needs.[4] Recent administrations have also had to contend with common management problems resulting from staff proliferation and increased specialization: more frequent and more intense turf battles, growth in the number of voices claiming to speak for the president, reduced interaction between the president and all but a small circle of his most senior confidants, and internal advocacy of outside, nonpresidential interests. Despite such continuity, the White House advisory system is more often viewed in terms of change with analysts concentrating on variations in advice-giving and advice-taking that reflect differences in presidential style and managerial techniques. Each new administration offers the opportunity to derive lessons for its successors, but the effort is not always successful; one critic described the resulting "policy-relevant" literature as "prescriptions for appropriate organizational forms and sensibilities [that] are wondrously diverse and ultimately proverbial."[5]

Over the past fifty years, presidential staffing has been viewed as either a source of salvation or damnation for presidents. Researchers operating within both of these evaluative frameworks consider staff a significant determinant of administration performance and hope to generate advice on refined management techniques and better operating models as a means to improve results or avoid the most damaging advisory pathologies. After reviewing these perspectives, I will turn to the larger problems of generating prescriptions and developing a common analytic framework.

Salvation by Staff

Aaron Wildavsky's insightful essay entitled "Salvation by Staff" offers a sophisticated argument that identifies the negative as well as positive consequences of presidential staffing,[6] but the basic thrust of Wildavsky's argument was consistent with the overwhelmingly favorable consensus on the vital contribution made by presidential staff. From the time of Brownlow's famous assertion that "the President needs help," staffing had been regarded as the answer to a fundamental problem besetting U.S. presidents: administrative overload. Problems of management and politics flowed from the enormous and continuously multiplying demands for presidential leadership. The prescription constituted an "organizational fix" in two meanings of the term.

First, presidential problems, it was believed, can be remedied by an infusion of help, providing the resources needed to conduct the job. In Brownlow's view, the new assistance should be provided by experts whose help would be available to successive presidents. This stood in marked contrast to the direction of institutional development to that time which had emphasized provision of political aides to handle liaison with the press, party leaders and Congress.[7] But those more sympathetic to the president's political needs (including FDR) were no less convinced of the need for help to multiply and extend the president's eyes, ears, antennae, and bargaining reach. Increasingly, Brownlow's commitment to help presidents manage routine executive functions of budgeting, personnel, and planning gave way to the needs of performing the increasingly nonroutine activities of policy development, a process inherently political in its attempt to identify and address national needs as well as to promote presidential proposals.[8]

There was also a second sense of "organizational fix," the confidence that presidential structures and decision making are, if not perfectible, at least improvable. Thus, there was a search for lessons that had survived the test of usage. This policy-relevant literature continued to grow even after optimism on salvation by staff had begun to wane.

Not everyone, of course, endorsed the organizational fix. Richard Neustadt, although an important figure in the search for lessons, had enunciated a model of presidential leadership that rested on a "personalist solution," finding leaders with the right blend of experience, political sensitivity, and character to overcome the enormous systemic obstacles to centralized power. Resting heavily on a critique of Eisenhower's performance in office, Neustadt urged presidents to place minimal reliance on staff and to become fully engaged in the job. In this view, improving White House operations was no more than an adjunct to the more central problem.[9]

There were remarkably few expressions of disquiet regarding the staffing solution in the twenty years following Brownlow's reforms. Stephen K. Bailey, who as a member of the first Hoover Commission staff had studied managerial problems of the presidency, suggested in the mid-fifties that the rise of "superdepartmental power and structures" centered in the White House (which he termed "topside elephantiasis") was less benign than it appeared and identified several possible problems.[10] Bailey suggested presidents might be denied competitive advice; White House aides would reduce the status and prestige (and therefore effectiveness) of political appointees in departments and agencies whose quality might also decline; generating paper might be a more likely product than effective coordination; EOP units might create their own centers of power and alliances not likely to serve the president's best interests. These misgivings, running counter to the consensus, were expressed gently; as Bailey put it, "surely the evidence is insufficient to deny that these dangers exist."[11] A partial reversal would soon occur: the dangers of presidential staffing dominated concern, though hard evidence would remain meager.

Damnation by Staff

The new consensus that emerged early in the 1970s emphasized the negative impact of presidential staffs, particularly those in the White House. Staff members had not been unfailing sources of help to the presidents they served, but most problems involved personal indiscretions (or allegations thereof) that offered a readier target for administration critics than the chief executive himself. Both Franklin Roosevelt and Harry Truman endured charges that their staffs harbored communists. Several of Truman's initial circle of cronies lacked qualifications to provide advice to the leader of the Western world, deserved criticism and changes followed. Eisenhower endured the political (and to some extent personal) costs of the Sherman Adams affair, and most of his successors experienced similar embarrassments. Walter Jenkins's long association with Johnson had to be jettisoned; Bert Lance's private affairs became a public embarrassment for Carter; Reagan's difficulties with Richard Allen, Oliver North, and John Poindexter, as well as Bush's with John Sununu, are merely the latest in a long line of such incidents.[12]

Those concerned about damnation by staff, however, focused on problems that were *systemic* in nature and therefore much greater sources of worry. Similar misgivings had lain at the center of Bailey's predictions and were also evident in Wildavsky's exploration of staffing's dark side. Wildavsky's warning, actually targeted on reform proposals, could be read as recognition of a broader threat posed by staff members, themselves: "The overwhelming expectations surrounding the presidency naturally have led many people to suggest that the President needs help and they have devised means ostensibly for helping him. Presidents, however, sometimes need to be more wary of their friends than their enemies."[13] The list of problems posed by staff growth has now

become quite familiar: advisers may not share the president's preferences and may decide to act on their own initiative; overseeing
advisers has itself become a major task so that providing presidents with additional staff "just multiplies his managerial problems";[14] staff may overwhelm the president with information, assume operational responsibilities more appropriately handled in
the departments, and seek to shield the president by intercepting
or screening the flow of information or people out of an urge to be
protective or to preserve their own influence.

One year after Wildavsky's essay appeared, George Reedy's *Twi-
light of the Presidency* was published, an insider's account that popu-
larized concerns about the White House staff. On its heels came
the Watergate scandal and what seemed like daily revelations of
presidential venality, isolation, and unreality—produced, we were
told, by an overzealous "palace guard." Wildavsky's warning
seemed to have been fulfilled; "The President is not only served by
his staff; he must also constantly guard against becoming its victim."[15] Nixon, however, may not only have let down his guard but
also have been a willing accomplice in staff excesses.

Nixon's successors confronted a broad array of actions and recommendations focused on presidential staffing. Congress pursued
several paths: a push was undertaken to develop sources of information independent of the executive resulting in creation of the
Congressional Budget Office and the Office of Technology Assessment; investigations were launched into both White House growth
and violations of civil service guidelines; a traditional oversight
power, confirmation, was dusted off and applied to the director of
OMB. More specific advice addressed a broad range of presidential
activities. Observers seemed unanimous in urging a reduction in
the size of White House staff; cabinet government was urged as an
alternative to presidential government.[16] Maintaining an open
White House became a publicly announced presidential goal that
both Ford and Carter assumed could best be met through a so-
called spokes-in-a-wheel White House structure. To avoid serious
organizational pathologies, presidents were urged to make decisions through multiple-advocacy techniques;[17] institutional staffs
were held up as important repositories of assistance;[18] and presidents were urged to do less, or at least to promise less and to think
of themselves "not as the ultimate decision maker but as the preeminent 'national highlighter.' "[19]

The Reagan Experience:
Adding to Management "Lore"

When Ronald Reagan departed from office in January 1989, he left one of the richest records of White House management associated with any modern president. But that record also stands second only to Richard Nixon's in its controversial character, and analysts have been quick to identify both strengths and deficiencies. Early in the administration, serious questions were raised about Mr. Reagan's detached, nonengaged style; his "minimalist, chairman of the board" approach[20] violated many widely accepted canons of conduct enunciated by advocates of a strong presidency and suggested that the job really was not as burdensome as most observers had come to believe. Only the embarrassment of the Iran-contra affair prevented Reagan's "clean desk style" from becoming even more fashionable.[21]

Beyond Reagan's management style, however, the administration undertook a number of innovations in structure and technique that have attracted wide comment. Departing from the hierarchical White House structure common to Eisenhower and Nixon, the Reagan group adopted a variant of the customarily Democratic spokes-in-a-wheel model originated under FDR.[22] The troika of Meese-Baker-Deaver (comprising Reagan I) seemed to combine the efficiency of coordination provided by a chief of staff with the benefit of contending opinions voiced by multiple advisers. Edwin Meese, as counselor to the president, initially oversaw both domestic and foreign policy; William Clark gained access to the inner circle in 1982 (making it a quadrumvirate) and assumed primacy in foreign policy matters. James Baker III, as befits a chief of staff, managed day-to-day White House operations and oversaw the political staffs, while Michael Deaver, deputy chief of staff, specialized in the president's schedule and image. This group, combining diverse backgrounds and skills, has garnered much of the credit for administration victories gained during 1981, excelling in the ability to achieve a level of "strategic management" that had been largely absent in the two preceding administrations.[23] As is typical in much of the literature about staffing, successful outcomes were attributed to an effective structure and process which, in turn, prompted prescriptions based on the Reagan experience.[24]

Lending even greater credence to advice drawn from the Rea-

gan administration's first year was the dismal record associated
with the second White House structure (Reagan II) documented
in studies of the Iran-contra affair. With the departure of all three
members of the troika, Donald Regan, the first-term secretary of
the treasury, became chief of staff in a very different White House
that lacked the collaboration forced by the tripartite division of
labor found in Reagan I. Although many of the details remain
unknown, there is a growing consensus that Regan's appearance
of control encouraged the president to provide less than aggressive
oversight of policy and process, thereby indulging his natural proclivities to remain withdrawn. He felt confident in depending on
Regan without recognizing that chiefs of staff are no more able to
oversee everything than are presidents.[25]

Lessons drawn from Reagan praxis go far beyond White House
structure. Several potentially important departures involved the
cabinet and its relationship to the presidential branch. The system
of cabinet councils established during the first term (when they also
were most active) has been favorably viewed as an important stage
in the institutionalization of president–executive branch collaboration, but has also drawn less favorable reviews.[26] Within the first
Reagan White House and in working with the cabinet, the administration aggressively employed group-interaction techniques credited with building a sense of teamwork among major actors.
"Round-tabling" invited broad discussion of policy problems,
though carefully contained within boundaries of the Reagan
agenda, and senior White House aides met frequently among themselves, with the president, and with departmental officials. These
activities may have contributed heavily to the sense of internal
focus that characterized the administration during its most successful periods.[27] Moreover, a highly self-conscious effort to recruit
Reagan loyalists ("Reaganauts") is credited with extending presidential support throughout the bureaucracy and could account for
the remarkably high levels of agreement found among White
House aides as well.[28]

Critics contend that Reagan heightened the long-term trend toward politicization of institutional staff resources within the presidency. David Stockman's admission that as director of OMB he
had the agency's economic forecasts altered to provide figures
more favorable to the administration's preferred strategy removed
any remaining semblance of the bureau's "neutral competence,"

although some argue this represents less of a loss than is often claimed.[29] Early in the second term, the administration seriously considered dismantling the Council of Economic Advisers, another of the core group of institutional units whose survival hinged on its statutory authorization. As we now know, the administration shifted operational intelligence activities into the National Security Council, thereby ensuring unquestioned commitment to the president's foreign policy goals and avoidance of congressional scrutiny but sacrificing the expertise and internal checks that career staff can provide.

Staffing the presidency was far from smooth in the Reagan administration. There was apparently an inordinately heavy turnover in a number of key staff positions. There were four White House chiefs of staff (James Baker, Donald Regan, Howard Baker, Kenneth Duberstein), six national security advisers (Richard Allen, William Clark, Robert McFarland, John Poindexter, Frank Carlucci, and Colin Powell), and the Office of Policy Development had three heads in the administration's first three years, perhaps partly explaining its lack of influence.[30] Commentators have also questioned the wisdom of relying so heavily on military officials to staff the National Security Council.

This most recent White House experience has prompted some observers to suggest that the Reagan presidency, more than any of its modern predecessors, needs to be examined less in terms of the president's behavior and personal characteristics than those of his staff. As James David Barber has posed the issue, the key question for understanding the Reagan presidency is "Who was around him?"[31] This flows from concerns about the president's low level of activity, his noninvolvement in policy issues, and his detached style of operation. In many respects, Barber's suggestion raises the fundamental issue faced by students of the White House staff: just how important are they, and under what circumstances?[32] Efforts to develop a more thorough understanding of White House operations, as well as those designed to improve operations, encounter a number of difficulties.

Prescriptions Without Paradigms?

By examining how presidents have organized and employed their advisers, one hopes to glean lessons for the future. But evaluations of White House operations and resulting prescriptions should rest upon a firm analytic base; advice must be developed within a larger analytic framework that accurately reflects the nature of the executive advisory system as well as the complex interactions among numerous variables. Unfortunately, achieving this level of sophistication has proved far more difficult than is assumed. All too often one finds prescriptions without paradigms.

Alexander George has most fully explicated the case for developing a policy-relevant theory, and his work on presidential decision making serves as a model for those hoping to link theory and practical experience. George identifies the need for "contingent generalizations" and a "differentiated theory" designed "to provide guidance for action" to decision makers in coping with specific problems. Such a task can be viewed as distinct from the effort "to identify regularities and patterns and to develop propositions, sometimes probabilistic in form, describing and/or explaining them."[33] In the study of White House staffing, an exclusive focus on either effort is likely to entail substantial costs. A narrow emphasis on relevance will produce a lurching reaction to the perceived problems of today (and, more likely, yesterday), an unflattering but sometimes accurate characterization of the prescriptive literature. But an effort targeted exclusively on creating valid generalizations is likely to proceed at a snail's pace and miss the opportunity to serve a larger social purpose. The two efforts need to proceed simultaneously but they face a set of difficult analytic problems. Central among these are difficulties in characterizing White House operations, contending with the forces of academic fashion and partisanship, and assuming causation and intentionality. Each of these is discussed below with special attention to the Reagan experience.

As a focus of study, the White House reveals enormous variability. Not only is there substantial turnover in personnel both across and within administrations, but also one encounters far greater variation in operations during single administrations than has commonly been recognized. While the literature has focused heavily on formal structures, it is clear that informal structures of influence are likely to change rapidly. Moreover, decision-making processes probably vary more than is usually acknowledged.

Roger Porter argues that under Gerald Ford decision making varied by issue area; national security was handled through centralized management, domestic policy through a system of "adhoc-racy" and economic policy approximated a multiple-advocacy sys-tem.[34] Ben W. Heineman, Jr., reflecting on his experience in the Carter administration, suggests that presidential involvement var-ies by issue priority: on "first-order issues," presidents make virtu-ally all decisions; they set broad directions for second-order issues but leave details to EOP personnel; on third-order issues, presi-dents signify interest but delegate decision making.[35] Decision pro-cesses will also vary according to the dynamics of coalition forma-tion within the White House. Thus, it appears that during much of Reagan's first term, Michael Deaver aligned himself with James Baker on many issues, providing a basis for administration prag-matism (although they were not always successful in persuading the president to follow their advice as with the staff-supported effort to call for increased taxes in the FY 1983 budget). Had Deaver been aligned more often with Edwin Meese, social issues might have occupied a more prominent position on the administra-tion's agenda.[36]

All of this illustrates the difficulty of characterizing the White House; as a "natural system" it refuses to hold still, so that most of our characterizations are simplifications of the real complexity. Not only did the White House system of Reagan I differ in 1981 from that of 1983 (much as Carter I operated differently by the end of 1978 than it did in 1977), but also the systems are likely to change from month to month, if not week to week or problem to problem. How can one be certain that analytic constructs cap-ture significant dimensions of variation? Several innovative ap-proaches have been tried, but there is a pronounced tendency for observers to place too much emphasis on formal structure espe-cially in developing prescriptions.

Views of the White House are highly sensitive to several short-run analytic biases, particularly academic fashion and partisan-ship. The contemporary portrait of the immediately preceding White House, largely developed by the media, colors debate by defining the research agenda and, in some cases, identifying con-sensus solutions. Such "reactions" or "backlashes" to a predeces-sor's methods gives rise to the unusual pattern identified by Bert Rockman: "Presidents tend to beget their opposites."[37] This seems to occur through adjustments initiated from both outside and in-side the White House. Thus, we find Congress reacting to Roosevelt's personal adventurism by creating the Council of Economic Advisers and the National Security Council in an effort to constrain presidential choice; Kennedy rejecting most of Eisenhower's formal policy-making machinery for more informal devices; Ford and Carter consciously seeking more open decision-making structures to contrast with Nixon's closed apparatus; Reagan's people adopting agenda-limiting techniques and direction-setting priorities in contrast to Carter's celebrated lack of focus and direction. Given complaints about Reagan's relaxed style, it is not suprising to find George Bush projecting a "hands-on" presidential image, even if that were not his natural tendency.

Academic fashion plays a role, as well. Close scrutiny of the Kennedy administration's performance during the Bay of Pigs and Cuban Missile crises has left us with one of the most widely accepted prescriptions for presidential conduct: employ multiple advocacy as a means to avoid "groupthink" and other decision-making pathologies. Ford's Economic Policy Board has been widely embraced as a concrete example of multiple advocacy in action and therefore worthy of emulation.[38] Lessons drawn from Carter's experience concentrated more on the negative consequences of presidents immersing themselves in detail. Analysts of the Reagan experience have reached a consensus on the need for a chief of staff, which in turn has given rise to discussions on the appropriate role a chief of staff should play.[39]

Academic fashion may also have a partisan overlay. Eisenhower's foreign policy machinery was examined closely in the late 1950s by Senator Henry Jackson's subcommittee as a means to generate electorally useful criticism as well as guide the next administration. In the wake of Watergate, Ford probably had little choice but to adopt popular solutions to presidential isolation if he hoped to project an image of competency.[40] And one finds a pattern of partisan "modeling" in the design of White House staffs with Republicans focusing more on structure (the hierarchical staff model) and Democrats on people (the spokes model).[41]

There is a natural tendency among White House observers to draw a linkage between staff structure or decision process and outcomes. When one reviews the literature, however, it is clear that analysts sometimes draw contradictory conclusions about the consequences of similar structures[42] and that fail-safe systems do not exist. Sound processes can produce "normal failures"[43] just as unsound processes can produce "serendipitous successes." Nor can we hope to have much confidence in our ability to establish the link between process and outcomes. For example, it has been impossible to determine the importance of the much heralded procedures followed by the Kennedy administration during the Cuban Missile Crisis. The world may well have been saved by the Soviet decision to withdraw its missiles, but only recently has there been an opportunity to learn more about the Kremlin's decision-making process during this crisis. Nonetheless, we have operated for a quarter century with a widely held consensus on how U.S. actions induced the Soviet decision. In the absence of causal certainty, difficult to establish in virtually every case, there is a tendency to praise processes associated with outcomes considered successes and to urge avoidance of those associated with perceived failures.[44]

In similar fashion, most analysts view the White House as a planned, rational system rather than a natural, emergent system. Both elements are present in all organizations—a reconciliation of the classic argument between closed and open systems approaches—but efforts to impose rational design are not necessarily more powerful.[45] In addition, design decisions are not always the product of careful calculation. For example, it has been suggested that the Reagan staff apparatus was consciously designed to moderate the president's "vulnerability to facts," a recognized weakness.[46] On the other hand, there are numerous accounts suggesting that the Reagan staff setup was the product of a power struggle between Edwin Meese and James Baker over the division of responsibilities.[47] No doubt, there were efforts at conscious design: Reagan's occasional campaign problems with the media were vividly recalled, there was a Sacramento model available for use, and Meese was interested in organizational issues.[48] But the staff design that emerged may, like the product of any other bureaucratic politics struggle, have been unintended by any actor. Moreover, it was modified by use.

At best, then, the study of White House staffing is likely to be imperfect. But confronted with hopes of salvation or fear of damnation, observers and presidents alike seem to regard staff studies as urgent. White House actors seek help with current problems and have little interest in academic equivocations. In such a setting, it is easy to believe that prescriptions cannot await the development of paradigms.

Toward a Contingency Theory of White House Staffing

Developing a common analytic paradigm promises to be the most important step toward generating the kinds of advice presidents need. Efforts are best invested in the conduct of disciplined configurative case studies of staff operations, but without a commonly accepted set of concepts and formulations even acknowledged masters of multiple case studies, practicing the sophisticated skill of comparing and contrasting different administration experiences, fall into the pattern of idiographic case analysis—a natural tendency, given the wide range of possibly significant variables. In studying staffs, our arsenal of analytic concepts remains underdeveloped and other factors never remain equal.[49]

Within the literature on staffing, it is possible to discern the outlines of a "contingency theory" of White House organization and operations that recognizes the multiple factors that comprise that White House advisory system. Moreover, this approach does not assume there is "one best way" for presidents to organize and operate their staffs, an implicit element in many prescriptions. Approaching the problem in this way requires a shift in perspective: staffing must be viewed as a complex phenomenon to be explored through systematic research that will eventually establish just how valuable and significant White House assistants really are. In other words, staffing is a problem of uncertainty rather than a source of salvation or damnation whose improvement drives the research agenda. Ultimately, this effort should be able to provide advice that is firmly grounded on empirical research, even if it hedges advice by concentrating on probabilistic statements.

Students of the White House have generated an impressive list of variables that are potentially significant in shaping staff organization and operations. What has slowly emerged is a pretheoretical map that identifies factors important to understanding this phenomenon and to developing a sense of how they interact. Full development of such a framework lies beyond the scope of this chapter, but suggesting its outlines should contribute to the development of a shared analytic framework. I organize the discussion according to three distinct levels of analysis: presidential variables, collective features of the staff, and environmental influences.[50]

Sophisticated analysts of the White House have noted for some time that staffing practices vary with the situation being confronted and the president's qualities of leadership. We now have several effective statements of the "unique virtues and deficiencies" each incumbent brings to the office and the need for staff to complement the president's personal skills and compensate for his deficiencies.[51] This formulation represents significant progress beyond the far less sophisticated view of White House staff that was dominant for many years: staffs vary with the president in question since they inevitably "reflect" the president's views, skills, and tone.[52] By emphasizing presidential variables so heavily, this widely used version of a contingency theory is insufficiently complex and remains wholly inattentive to a wide range of other potentially significant variables.

Presidents should remain, of course, the starting point for studies of the White House, although their personal characteristics may have less impact on staff operations than is generally assumed. Particularly significant to the kinds of structures and processes adopted are presidents' *work habits* derived from previous experience (particularly their preferences in dealing with information and people), relevant skills (particularly political and analytic), and aspirations for their administration. The discussions of Alexander George and Bert Rockman are especially rich in this area.

Concentrating on discrete presidential characteristics is preferable to the generally less discriminating but more widely used concept of *presidential style,* which has almost endless variations. The most valuable treatments of style concentrate on a specific dimension of how presidents approach their job. For example, Fred Greenstein examines "leadership style," defined as the president's "operational code," the "distinctive ensemble of tactics" available for his use.[53] But there are many ways of conceptualizing *style.* Other versions deal with presidents' organizational style, management style, cognitive style, or decision-making style; there is even a strategic style that has been suggested for administrations, thereby moving the term from an individual to a collective level of analysis.[54] Although analysts frequently draw comparisons between presidents, there has been a strong tendency to regard each president as unique rather than concentrating on the analytic variable in question. Sorting through this conceptual jumble is essential if progess is to be made in developing a base of disciplined configurative case studies.

Collective characteristics of presidential staffs are important in their own right and not merely as an extension of the president. As noted above, it is now recognized that staffs complement and compensate for the mix of presidential skills and deficiencies, but staffs also constitute an *organizational matrix* that filters the president's influence on performance and probably has substantial independent impact. The matrix consists of both informal and formal characteristics.[55]

John Kessel's research on staff attitudes as well as communication and influence structures is especially innovative and valuable in this regard. By using identical research techniques and conceptualizations to study these dimensions of the Carter and Reagan staffs, he has been able to draw illuminating comparisons. Additional aspects of informal White House structures deserve systematic examination, as well. For example, many observers have suggested that staff members' collegiality and the quality of their collective knowledge and skills are important for presidential success, but our understanding of these features remains impressionistic.

Formal structural characteristics of the White House have drawn considerable attention and may even have been overemphasized in our desire to suggest avenues for improvement, but they remain a potentially critical feature of the staff system. Beyond the concern with how advisers are arrayed and how many enjoy access to the president, it would be useful to explore several other dimensions of formal White House structures. As noted above, presidents do not create the White House anew with each succeeding administration; deep structures are thrust upon the presidency by outside actors and tradition. We still do not fully understand how this process operates or how much independence presidents really enjoy in undertaking new departures in staffing. With the growth of White House staff specialization, local loyalties to the goals of particularized staff units have emerged, a pattern typical of all complex organizations. This development and its impact on the staff's internal coalitional dynamics remains largely unexplored.

Outside the White House, an impressive array of environmental conditions are potentially significant in influencing activities within the White House.[56] Clearly, levels of political support from Congress and the public are potentially important, as are public "moods" about the need for leadership, a point made by Rockman. However, more general types of conditions are likely to induce crisis behavior or a siege mentality among White House actors, two patterns frequently associated with errors in judgment. In this connection, Colin Campbell and Bert Rockman have suggested several regularities (or rhythms) in White House staffing patterns that seem to emerge from interaction with the environment. Following an initial shakedown period in each new administration characterized by enthusiasm for change and pursuit of a common agenda accompanied by attempts to build cabinet and staff collegiality, one finds structural and personnel adjustments being made in the face of increasing media scrutiny and congressional criticism; a "circle the wagons" mentality appears, as well as an associated centralizing of policy-making processes as first-term electoral campaigns approach.[57] No doubt, other environmental impacts exist, but we must be attuned to their potential effects before we can identify and study them systematically.

Pretheoretical frameworks presumably establish the ground work for generating research hypotheses and systematic research efforts. Even in the preliminary form sketched above, the full range of interactions among variables is daunting, particularly given the research difficulties already enumerated and the well-known problem of working with a small universe of cases. These limitations notwithstanding, it seems worthwhile to suggest that a more self-consciously rigorous effort is both possible and desirable. Far from diverging from the development of "policy-relevant theory," it is likely to produce advice of higher quality on an even wider array of problems.

The task of meshing "pure" and "applied" research is substantial; the work of some researchers, however, suggests that it can be accomplished, or at least approximated. The hope, of course, is that the research will pay dividends to a public that has come to expect so much of its presidents. Perhaps one of the greatest dividends will be a more realistic appraisal of what presidents can, in fact, hope to accomplish. Presidential staffing has proved to be no more the answer to the nation's problems than it has to the president's. But staffing has become a major force in American political life that is unlikely to disappear and needs to be more fully understood.

Notes

1. As Edward S. Corwin put it, "The 'Institutionalized Presidency' pivots, so to speak, on two hinges—the Executive Office of the President and the White House Office" (*The President: Offices and Powers, 1787–1984*, 5th ed. [New York: New York University Press, 1984], p. 340).

2. John Hart, *The Presidential Branch* (New York: Pergamon Press, 1987). Hart (pp. 3–4) credits Nelson Polsby with the term "presidential branch" (see Polsby, "Some Landmarks in Modern Presidential-Congressional Relations," in *Both Ends of the Avenue*, ed. Anthony King [Washington, D.C.: American Enterprise Institute, 1983], p. 20).

3. Hart, *The Presidential Branch*, pp. xii, 201; see also Aaron Wildavsky, "Salvation by Staff: Reform of the Presidential Office," in *The Presidency*, ed. Wildavsky (Boston: Little, Brown, 1969), pp. 694–700. See also Terry M. Moe, "The Politicized Presidency," in *The New Direction in American Politics*, ed. John E. Chubb and Paul E. Peterson (Washington, D.C.: Brookings, 1985); Margaret J. Wyszomirski, "The Deinstitutionalization of Presidential Staff Agencies," *Public Administration Review* 42 (1982): 448–58.

4. See Samuel Kernell, "The Creed and Reality of Modern White House Management," in *Chief of Staff: Twenty-five years of Managing the Presidency*, ed. Kernell and Samuel Popkin (Berkeley and Los Angeles: University of California Press, 1986), pp. 193–232; see also Hugh Heclo, "The Changing Presidential Office," in *Politics and the Oval Office*, ed. Arnold Meltsner (San Francisco: Institute for Contemporary Politics, 1981).

5. Bert Rockman, *The Leadership Question: The Presidency and the American System* (New York: Praeger, 1984), p. 204; on policy-relevant theory, see Alexander L. George and Richard Smoke, *Deterrence in American Foreign Policy* (New York: Columbia University Press, 1974), appendix; A. L. George, *Presidential Decisionmaking in Foreign Policy* (Boulder, Colo.: Westview, 1980), chap. 14; Norman Thomas, "Case Studies," in *Studying the Presidency*, ed. George C. Edwards and Stephen J. Wayne (Knoxville: University of Tennessee Press, 1983), esp. pp. 58–64.

6. Wildavsky, "Salvation by Staff"; Hart, *The Presidential Branch* (p. 4), notes that George Graham used the term "salvation by staff" in a 1950 essay.

7. Hart, *The Presidential Branch*, presents this argument persuasively (p. 27ff.).

8. Hugh Heclo refers to presidential aides as a "veritable political technocracy" and notes Michael McGeary's indentification of three management doctrines: president as business manager (Taft Commission), as administrative leader (Brownlow Committee), and as policy manager (Heineman Task Force, Ash Council). See Introduction to *The Illusion of Presidential Government*, ed. Heclo and Lester Salamon (Boulder, Colo.: Westview Press, 1981), pp. 11–13.

9. Richard Neustadt, *Presidential Power: The Politics of Leadership* (New York: Wiley, 1960); "Approaches to Staffing the Presidency: Notes on FDR and JFK," *American Political Science Review* 57 (1963): 855–64.

10. Stephen K. Bailey, "The President and His Political Executives," *Annals* 307 (September 1956): 30–32; Hart, *The Presidential Branch*, makes much the same argument (p. 4).

11. Bailey, "The President and His Political Executives," p. 32.

12. The problems of Lyn Nofziger and Michael Deaver in the Reagan years followed their departure from the White House staff.

13. Wildavsky, "Salvation by Staff," p. 694.

14. Ibid., p. 697.

15. Ibid.

16. Stephen Hess, *Organizing the Presidency* (Washington, D.C.: Brookings, 1976).

17. Alexander L. George, "The Case of Multiple Advocacy in Making Foreign Policy," *American Political Science Review* 66 (1972).

18. Hugh Heclo, "OMB and the Presidency: The Problems of Neutral Competence," *Public Interest* 38 (1975): 80–98.

19. Lester M. Salamon, "Conclusion: Beyond the Presidential Illusion— Toward a Constitutional Presidency," in *The Illusion of Presidential Government*, ed. Heclo and Salamon, pp. 287–95.

20. Paul J. Quirk, "What Must a President Know?" *Society* 20 (January– February 1983), and "Presidential Competence," in *The Presidency and the Political System*, ed. Michael Nelson (Washington, D.C.: C.Q. Press, 1984), pp. 133–55.

21. Richard Neustadt, comments at conference on "The Legacy of the Reagan Presidency," University of California, Davis, 1988.

22. See Colin Campbell, S.J., *Managing the Presidency: Carter, Reagan, and the Search for Executive Harmony* (Pittsburgh, Pa.: University of Pittsburgh Press, 1986), chap. 4; for more general discussion, see Fred I. Greenstein, "A President Is Forced to Resign: Watergate, White House Organization, and Nixon's Personality," in *America in the Seventies*, ed. Allan P. Sindler (Boston: Little, Brown, 1970); George, *Presidential Decisionmaking*.

23. Hugh Heclo and Rudolph G. Penner, "Fiscal and Political Strategy in the Reagan Administration," in *The Reagan Presidency: An Early Assessment*, ed. Fred I. Greenstein (Baltimore: Johns Hopkins University Press, 1983).

24. Campbell, *Managing the Presidency*, pp. 94, 11; however, Campbell hedges his prescription somewhat by making it dependent on the strategy adopted by an administration. Other support for Reagan's techniques has been more unrestrained; see Bruce Buchanan, "Constrained Diversity: The Organization Theory of the Presidency," presented at the annual meeting of the American Political Science Association, Chicago, 1987.

25. Letter from Richard Neustadt to Bruce Buchanan, published as "Does the White House Need a Strong Chief of Staff?" *Presidency Research* 10 (Fall 1987): 7–10; see also James Pfiffner, *The Strategic Presidency* (Chicago: Dorsey, 1988), chap. 2.

26. For the favorable view, see Campbell, *Managing the Presidency*. But see Chester A. Newland, "Executive Office Policy Apparatus: Enforcing the Reagan Agenda," in *The Reagan Presidency and the Governing of America*, ed. Lester M. Salamon and Michael S. Lund (Washington, D.C.: Urban Institute, 1984).

27. Campbell, *Managing the Presidency*, pp. 71–75, 101–05. Heclo and Penner, "Fiscal and Political Strategy in the Reagan Administration," make a similar point (p. 40). Also see Newland, "Executive Office Policy Apparatus," where he describes the Legislative Strategy Group and Budget Review Group as "collegial linking pins" for the White House and EOP (p. 148).

28. See John Kessel, "The Structures of the Carter White House," *American Journal of Political Science* 27 (1983): 431–63; Kessel "The Structures of the Reagan White House," *American Journal of Political Science* 28 (1984): 231–58; see also Kessel, *Presidential Parties* (Homewood, Ill.: Dorsey, 1984).

29. See Terry Moe, "The Politicized Presidency," for a discussion of "responsive competence" as no less important than "neutral competence."

30. Unfortunately, we have no baseline with which to compare these figures. Emmette S. Redford and Richard T. McCulley, *White House Operations: The Johnson Presidency* (Austin: University of Texas Press, 1986), argue that the Johnson White House suffered far less turnover than is generally supposed (chap. 2).

31. James David Barber, address at conference on "The Legacy of the Reagan Presidency," University of California, Davis, 1988; this interpretation accords with Barber's analysis: "At the heart of it all was a President continually in search of directors to tell him what to do" (*Presidential Character: Predicting Performance in the White House*, 3d ed. [Englewood Cliffs, N.J.: Prentice-Hall, 1985], p. 498).

32. George Edwards, "The Quantitative Study of the Presidency," *Presidential Studies Quarterly* 11 (1981): 148, notes that it has not yet been proved "that the organization of the White House staff has any influence on presidential decisions"; the argument could be extended to influence on any aspect of a president's behavior. See John P. Burke and Fred I. Greenstein *How President's Test Reality: Decisions on Vietnam 1954 and 1965* (New York: Russell Sage, 1989) for an effort to link structures and outcomes.

33. George and Smoke, *Deterrence in American Foreign Policy*, pp. 636, 617–18.

34. Roger Porter, "Gerald R. Ford: A Healing Presidency," in *Leadership in the Modern Presidency*, ed. Fred I. Greenstein (Cambridge, Mass.: Harvard University Press, 1988), p. 218.

35. Ben W. Heineman, "Comments," in *The Reagan Presidency and the Governing of America*, ed. Salamon and Lund; Heineman, of course, suggests this prescription as a way to structure presidential activity more effectively than it was under Carter. He suggests a "span of competence" for presidential attention by recommending that an administration tackle no more than five first-order issues and twenty-five second-order. This approach is like that of Robert Art, in "Bureaucratic Politics and American Foreign Policy: A Critique," *Policy Sciences* 4 (1973): 467–90. See also Heineman and Curtis A. Hessler, *Memorandum for the President* (New York: Random House, 1980).

36. On the effectiveness of the troika, note that social scientists consider three-member groups especially unstable (see Theodore Caplow, *Two Against One* [Englewood Cliffs, N.J.: Prentice-Hall, 1968]); but Richard Neustadt has noted, "Threesomes, for some reason, seem to work" ("Presidential Management," in *Improving the Accountability and Performance of Government* [Washington, D.C.: Brookings, 1982], p. 94).

37. Rockman, *The Leadership Question*, p. 123; on reactions and backlashes, see Pfiffner, *The Strategic Presidency*, p. 27ff., and Campbell, *Managing the Presidency*, p. 57.

38. See Roger Porter, *Presidential Decision-Making: The Economic Policy Board* (Cambridge, Mass.: Harvard University Press, 1980). In 1980, the National Academy of Public Administration, in *A Presidency for the 1980s*, endorsed the EPB model and suggested its adoption for both the NSC and domestic policy structures (Neustadt, "Presidential Management," p. 95).

39. Neustadt ("Does the White House Need a Strong Chief of Staff?") recommends that the chief of staff be less powerful than Sherman Adams, less assertive than H. R. Haldeman, less pretentious than Donald Regan; above all, he must not

usurp the president's role as primus inter pares. See also James Pfiffner, *the Strategic Presidency*, pp. 38–39.

40. Rockman (*The Leadership Question*, pp. 205–06) suggests that administrations seek to project an image of organizational competence. This is especially important, given the customary view that organization "reflects" the president.

41. Paradoxically, Campbell (*Managing the Presidency*, p. 266) notes that Republican administrations have been more attentive to group integrative techniques than Democratic ones, which may have needed them more.

42. Joseph A. Pika, "Management Style and the Organizational Matrix: Studying White House Operations," *Administration and Society* 20 (May 1988): 3–29.

43. Bert Rockman, "The Style and Organization of the Reagan Presidency," in *The Reagan Legacy: Promise and Performance*, ed. Charles O. Jones (Chatham, N.J.: Chatham House, 1988).

44. See Rockman, *The Leadership Question*, p. 194, for a similar conclusion.

45. See Phillip Selznick, "Foundations of the Theory of Organization, *American Sociological Review* 13 (February 1948).

46. For an example, see Rockman, "The Style and Organization of the Reagan Presidency," p. 7.

47. Newland, "Executive Office Policy Apparatus," pp. 142–43; Pfiffner, *The Strategic Presidency*, pp. 30–32; Laurence I. Barrett, *Gambling with History: Reagan in the White House* (New York: Penguin, 1983), pp. 76–77.

48. Chester A. Newland ("Executive Office Policy Apparatus," p. 143), who had access to internal Reagan administration memos, credits Roger Porter's transition memo with creating the Office of Policy Development and system of cabinet councils, a conscious decision that mediated a struggle over design.

49. See Thomas, "Case Studies"; see also Neustadt's reading of cases in *Presidential Power*, and Neustadt and Ernest R. May, *Thinking in Time: The Uses of History for Decision Makers* (New York: Free Press, 1986). For a notably self-conscious "controlled comparison" that also employs "plausible counterfactual reasoning," see Burke and Greenstein, *How Presidents Test Reality.*

50. See Joseph Pika, "Moving Beyond the Oval Office: Problems in Studying the Presidency," *Congress and the Presidency* 9 (1981–82): 17–36. A similar approach is found in: Karen M. Hult, "Advising the President: Changes and Continuities in Presidential Advisory Networks"; but see also Terry M. Moe, "Presidential Style and Presidential Theory," both presented at the NSF Conference, Research on the American Presidency, Pittsburgh, Pa., 1990.

51. See Greenstein, ed., *Leadership in the Modern Presidency*, pp. 81, 373, n. 16. See also Rockman, *The Leadership Question*, pp. 194–211, and "The Style and Organization of the Reagan Presidency," p. 5.

52. See, for example, Porter's discussion ("Gerald R. Ford," pp. 204–06) of Ford's own patient, measured approach to the presidency which led him to select people who were competent, compatible, team players; see also Richard Neustadt's description of Reagan's senior staff as "calm, cool, collected, neither paranoid nor nasty, with some saving humor and seemingly no taste for pulling wings off flies. . . . They presumably reflected their boss (which the others did too, of course)" (*Presidential Management*, p. 94).

53. Greenstein, *Leadership in the Modern Presidency*, p. 78; see also *The Hidden-Hand Presidency: Eisenhower as Leader* (New York: Basic Books, 1982).

54. See esp. George, *Presidential Decisionmaking*, and Campbell, *Managing the Presidency*, pp. 80–81, which employs the strategic conceptualization. Similar problems can be found in discussions of "institutionalization."

55. Pika, "Management Style and the Organizational Matrix."

56. Analysts must examine both real and *perceived* environmental conditions.

57. Rockman, "The Style and Organization of the Reagan Presidency," pp. 23–24; Colin Campbell, *Governments Under Stress* (Toronto: University of Toronto, 1983), and *Managing the Presidency.*

16

New and Old Lessons on
White House Management

SAMUEL KERNELL

By the time the Tower Review Board, investigating charges raised by the Iran-contra scandal, released its report in late February 1987, Donald Regan had become so controversial that only a mild rebuke by the commission was required to push him out of office. Agreeing with the general view in Washington that Regan, "more than almost any Chief of Staff of recent history . . . asserted personal control over the White House staff and sought to extend this control to the National Security Advisor," the report proceeded to chastise him for not being adequately informed about the National Security Council's dealings with Iran and for failing to orchestrate public disclosures once the operation became known.[1] It was probably inevitable that this, as with any, outside inspection of the natural tangle of interpersonal relations in the White House would have found room for improvement in a more "orderly process." The Tower Commission can be fairly read, in effect, as taking Regan to task for failing to measure up to his own aspiration to be a strong chief—for, if nothing else, Regan sought order. This is the wrong lesson to learn from Donald Regan's stewardship as chief of staff.

Donald Regan's downfall did not result from failing to be a strong enough chief, as the Tower Report implies, but from being a naive one. Simply said, he failed to appreciate the political character of his office. Assuming a faulty model of organization and control learned from years of running a major corporation, he acted in ways that insidiously undermined his position, even as his blunt, imperious manner gave the appearance of mastery. Once the revelations of the Iran-contra scandal began pouring forth, he became the easiest mark in Washington. In the end, all it took was the Tower Commission's nudge to return him to private life.

The moral of Don Regan's stewardship for students of the presidency is not to be found in the Tower Commission's criticisms, which stack up to little more than a list of peccadilloes when compared to the charges leveled against many of the other principals. Instead, the moral is to be found in the significant ways he acted on his naive conception of the institutional presidency.

Regan's Conception of the Staff and the Chief's Role

By his own assessment, Donald Regan's political skills were acquired during his career at Merrill Lynch. Joining the firm as a salesman after World War II, he advanced steadily up the organization; in 1970 he became its chairman of the board. Regan entered public service for the first time in 1981 at the age of sixty-two when he was appointed Reagan's treasury secretary. He did not see this lack of political experience as a deficiency as he tackled one of the biggest jobs in Washington, organizing the president's staff. He expected simply to recreate the corporate model of staff, which had served him so well on Wall Street.

And what is the Merrill Lynch model of organization that he was so eager to install in the White House? Above all, it emphasizes the leader's primacy in directing the organization's affairs and the staff's strictly subordinate position as implementer. At some level, this prescription is unarguable. What is a leader without authority? But the corporate model elevates hierarchy as the chief principle upon which the staff organization is founded. It requires a highly vertical organization with well-established lines of authority and clearly defined roles. Influence flows from the formal prerogatives of rank and office, rather than through the free exchange of ideas and the play of talent. Such arrangements place a premium upon loyalty, while initiative and self-reliance go unrewarded and sometimes are actively discouraged.

At Merrill Lynch, Regan had prided himself on his openness to advice from subordinates; staffs, after all, are supposed to help the CEO identify problems and possible solutions. But the decision is the leader's to make, and once made, everyone is immediately to "get on board." The fact that few among the White House staff, much less Congress, conformed to these expectations would be a constant source of irritation for Regan.

Inculcated in the corporate creed, Regan saw serious management problems with Reagan's first-term staff from his nearby perch at Treasury. Too often the president's aides lacked a unified strategy. Worse, at times, they worked at cross purposes. With the James Baker–Edwin Meese–Mike Deaver governing troika and National Security Adviser Robert McFarlane controlling their own bailiwicks and with each having direct access to President Reagan, no one individual held sufficient authority to coordinate White House operations. Also grating to Regan's sensibilities, some members of the staff appeared more sensitive to the positions of others outside the White House than to President Reagan's preferences. After listing instances in his memoirs, Regan complained: "Reagan was continuously being pressured to compromise in ways that preserved the influence and the policies of the defeated opposition."[2]

Most distasteful of all, Regan discovered that these senior aides enjoyed friendly relations with various Washingtonians who normally were numbered among the president's adversaries; these included liberal Democrats and White House correspondents. As a result, Regan noted with disapproval, the White House leaked like a sieve. Shortly after moving over to the White House, he discovered that the senior staff had actually been engaged in a strategy of systematic leaks in an effort to coopt the press. That they largely accomplished their purposes did little to endear Regan to these practices.

All of these features of the first-term staff added up to a White House that was highly responsive to the Washington community, where presumably the president should have been the staff's only client. This Donald Regan set out to change. "Let Reagan be Reagan," would be the motto of the second term, and the White House Office would be Regan's command post. What President Reagan needed was a top-down staff organization run by a strong chief. Donald Regan was just the man for the job. When he learned that Baker was eager to leave the White House, Regan jumped at the opportunity.

A Strong Chief Enters the White House

For a senior aide, Donald Regan enjoyed an unparalleled opportunity to implement his vision of the White House Office. President Reagan gave him carte blanche to do whatever he liked with staffing arrangements. Moreover, the inner circle of first-term aides was in the process of departing. Baker had moved over to Treasury, taking with him a number of his White House staff. Deaver already had announced plans to return to public relations consulting. Meese was awaiting confirmation as attorney general. The only potential sources of resistance to Regan's reorganization were the second-tier aides who would be demoted and have their autonomy curtailed.

In order to give the staff the order and direction Regan believed was lacking in the first term, he consolidated the various responsibilities of Baker, Deaver, and Meese into his office. The Domestic Council, for example was brought under his own direct supervision; by summer, John Svahn's role as its head had been eclipsed by one of Regan's assistants in the chief of staff's office.[3] The number of cabinet councils which had been staffed by the Domestic Council was reduced from seven to two. Only McFarlane at NSC and Nancy Reagan would retain an autonomous staff.

Other presidential offices that had enjoyed a reasonably free hand and easy access to the president were similarly downgraded. During the preceding four years, the presidential personnel office had occupied prestigious West Wing space under Assistant to the President Pendleton James. Under Regan the office was moved over to the Executive Office Building and its head, Robert Tuttle, was downgraded a rung to deputy assistant. When questioned whether as a result the office had lost much of its influence with the departments on personnel matters, Tuttle denied it, saying, "I have direct access to Don [Regan]."[4] Other offices were similarly demoted a rung or so down the organizational ladder, while still others were consolidated.

One staff activity that bucked the trend was communications. Here too, however, the purpose was to unify the White House, in this instance, to have it speak with one voice. Regan brought in a new director of communications, Patrick Buchanan, a conservative syndicated columnist and former Nixon speech writer, to bring coherence to Reagan's message. To accomplish this, the speech writers' group and the office of public liaison were brought under Buchanan's control. And after a turf battle with Ed Rollins for control of the political affairs office, Rollins left and Buchanan took over that office as well. While Buchanan consolidated his control of the communications apparatus and his position with the chief as "No. 1's No. 1," Regan sought to ensure that the president's coordinated messages would not be diluted by in-house leaks.[5] He ordered that all contacts with the press, including the networks, be cleared by the White House Press office.

Streamlining the organization meant that the number of senior-level aide positions could be reduced. Accordingly, the number of assistants to the president fell from nineteen to eleven.[6] Hierarchy brought a degree of discipline to the organization. By summer, many of the first-term lieutenants had either made peace with their new, reduced status, or had departed. Regan's pyramid was in place. Internal communication was to flow mostly down the organization in an orderly fashion with minimal leakage. Messages for external consumption, conversely, were to go up the ladder to selected senior aides for dissemination to the press. That was the plan.

But these formal arrangements never guaranteed Regan the control he sought. Some key actors—particularly, Nancy Reagan and National Security Adviser McFarlane and their staffs—remained insulated from Regan's control. Both were resourceful, with sizable staffs and good relations with important opinion leaders in the press. Almost from the beginning, disagreements erupted between these individuals and the new chief of staff.

Formal authority largely proved insufficient even in dealing with subordinates. Those personal staff members who moved over with Regan from Treasury behaved themselves well—too well for the press, who soon tagged them "the mice." But others were seldom so compliant. Within six months of Regan's arrival, rivalries and self-directed initiatives were surfacing throughout the organization. One senior aide reminisced, "The friction was so intense, it destroyed the ability and trust necessary to discuss issues in the open."[7] Buchanan and McFarlane tussled repeatedly over the substance and tenor of President Reagan's foreign policy addresses. McFarlane usually prevailed, but not without making compromises and having to fend off poaching on his jurisdiction. Moreover, he was convinced that Regan was cutting off his access to the president and was rumor-mongering. Frustrated, by late summer McFarlane had called it quits.

Lesser skirmishes of this kind pervaded the White House Office as first-term staff resisted the incursions of Regan's appointees. Eventually, even Buchanan departed after Regan's veto of his selection of an archconservative to head the corps of speech writers.[8]

These pressures could not be brokered within the organization and were soon vented in more virulent form to the news media. According to one account, "All quarters of the administration leaked regularly in an effort to . . . tip internal debates, and aggrandize their own roles."[9] In his memoirs, Regan laments that he was the only one observing his embargo on leaks.[10]

In the end, Regan failed in his effort to remake the president's staff in the image of Merrill Lynch. He could not even keep his speech writers in line, much less the actions of lower-level NSC staff, which despite his best efforts remained beyond the chief's sphere of influence.[11] The formal mechanisms of control were in place, but they, and ultimately their architect, were overrun by the reality of the office. That reality is the pluralism of the modern presidency.

Even with the perspicacity of hindsight, Don Regan fails to grasp why his successful management strategy at Merrill Lynch could not be duplicated at the White House. Throughout his memoirs, he draws unflattering comparisons between Washington politics and corporate practices. For him, the breaches of confidence, the disagreements over enunciated goals, and personality conflicts represented insubordination, pure and simple.

To some extent he is right. The White House has all the makings of an unruly organization. Many of its members are drawn to the job as much by their interest in advancing a particular policy agenda as by their desire to serve the president. And, unlike their corporate counterparts, White House aides do not view their positions as anything more than a way-station to another career. Turnover, consequently, is rapid—to such an extent that by the end of a four-year term, the membership has largely been reconstituted. Within such an organization, members may be expected to have a greater stake in the outcomes of an organization's decisions than in the integrity of its procedures. The competition of interests will frequently run afoul of the requirements of orderly administration. In these circumstances, traditional methods of supervision may fall short. Regan could not appreciate this; he had never worked in a setting where the organization's goals were continuously at issue. So he failed to recognize that contentious relations among the president's staff may only thinly shroud a competition of ideas over which his enforcement powers have limited value. Consequently, with the "mentality of a chief executive officer rather than of a politician," as one colleague described him, Regan tried "to get his way by bringing things under his control rather than working out deals."[12]

Regan's misperception of the basis of staff competition led to his misunderstanding his position as the president's most senior aide. The superficial similarities between the corporate chief executive officer and the president's chief of staff conceal profound differences. In the former case, abundant authority is vested in the position. The board of directors may decide to replace the incumbent, but only rarely will it act to diminish the CEO's status as the officer with the authority over and responsibility for the organization's performance. The board, after all, is bound to the CEO's role by its inability to run the corporation in the absence of other agents.

The chief of staff's position, in contrast, enjoys no such formal authority conferred by the by-laws of the organization. Some presidents, albeit fewer nowadays, have opted not to have a chief and to act as their own staff managers. Lyndon Johnson was the last to forgo a chief of staff throughout his term; Jimmy Carter began without a chief, but halfway through his term he became frustrated by coordinating staff work and delegated to aide Hamilton Jordan significant control over the daily operation of the White House. Others have sought to distribute the chief's duties among a cadre of senior aides. However configured, the chief's authority is in fact whatever the president extends to him; it remains personal, uncodified, easily reversible, and hence unstable.

The president's own welfare, after all, requires that he act so as to attract credit and avoid blame.[13] This fact makes poignant the chief of staff's ambivalent status, for at the least opportune moment from the chief's vantage point, his and the president's interests will tend to diverge. Presidents have been known to become attached to their assistants to such an extent that they forget the Machiavellian virtue of cutting off those aides who become so mired in controversy as to be a chronic liability to the president.

Senior aides must remain vigilant of this, for it implies that circumstances can arise that will bring the president's interests into conflict with their own.[14] When they most need the president's support, he can least afford to extend it. Brownlow's famous admonition to presidential assistants to cultivate a "passion for anonymity" is a good formula for survival. Adversaries will frequently find it easier to take on the chief than the president. Musing in his memoirs about the way reporters ferretted out scandal in the unauthorized sale of arms to Iran, Regan reveals a grim, belated appreciation of the chief of staff's peculiar vulnerability: "Because of my position, and because in a sense I was the only game in town, I was sought after by these excited men and women. The President was inaccessible on his mountaintop."[15] The modern White House Office requires coordination lest the centrifugal forces of pluralism prevent coherent presidential action. But it has to be coordination through politics rather than authority. This is the moral of Donal Regan's experience as chief of staff.

The Pluralism of the White House

Why is the White House a pluralistic organization? After all, loyalty to the president is a prerequisite of employment. Subordination of the staff members' personal and political goals to the president's ends would seem to be assured by their total dependency on him for their power and legitimacy. With formal authority concentrated at the top, what organization can one imagine better suited than the president's staff to act single-mindedly?

Despite the clear locus of formal authority at the top of the organization, the way the presidency has evolved during the past half century guarantees that pluralism will be well entrenched in the White House. The expansion of the staff's role to act as the president's agents, the growing division of labor, and the continuing efforts of presidents to centralize leadership have contributed to the emergence of an organization that houses a variety of interests that will frequently compete for the president's favor.

In large measure, the value of a staff member to the president lies in his or her serving as the president's agent. By *agent*, I mean an aide must at times make decisions on the president's behalf. Some critics of modern developments in the presidency would prefer that this not be so, but it is. The volume and diversity of demands placed on the modern office insist on the president's reliance on staff in ways that would have been inadvisable half a century ago. An aide's value to the president is directly proportional to the degree to which the aide's actions correspond to what the president would do were he making the decision. Otherwise—

that is, if the staff were merely Brownlow's anonymous, circum-ambient messengers—it would not relieve the president of the burdens of what Richard Neustadt has described as his modern clerkship.[16]

Staff discretion opens the organization to pluralism. Interests will not enter the White House randomly, reflecting merely the personal preferences of its members. Rather, they will be distributed predictably across the organization because the president recruits aides to staff positions with particular technical skills and political credentials. The press secretary will likely come from the ranks of journalism; the director of congressional liaison must already be welcome on Captiol Hill; the head of the political affairs office needs to have good rapport with the national party apparatus.

Even without selective recruitment, the division of labor within the modern White House Office alone suffices to guarantee the emergence of a large dose of pluralism. As the number and variety of external tasks increase, layers of specialized subunits proliferate to handle them. With the president's agents engaging different segments of the political environment, these cadres of experts on the staff will tend to adopt parochial views of the president's interests and priorities. At times, these will differ dramatically and bring the aides into conflict. The larger, more complex the president's staff, the stronger these forces of pluralism will be.

To these organizational dynamics should be added the political pressures for representation. The story of the postwar presidency is, in part, one of a continuing centralization within the White House of tasks for which presidents once depended upon the performance of other Washingtonians.[17] This readily can be seen in how present-day presidents approach personnel recruitment compared with their counterparts half a century ago. During the Roosevelt and Truman era, nominations for major political appointments frequently originated outside the White House and were routinely cleared first with the interested parties: the Democratic National Committee, key members of Congress, and those groups in the governing coalition whose interests were affected. In the Reagan White House, by contrast, nominees were typically identified by the presidential personnel office. Clearance took the form of an internal vetting among those senior aides who headed the relevant White House units, such as the congressional liaison and the political affairs offices.[18]

The reasons for this comprehensive, secular trend toward presidential centralization have been addressed elsewhere.[19] As decisions have been internalized, the payoff of insinuating one's preferences into the White House Office has increased commensurately. The proximity of the president's power has always made the White House staff an attractive group with whom to do business. From FDR's Tommy Corcoran to Mike Deaver, influence peddling has been a favorite sideline of favored presidential assistants. The circumstances that occasionally give rise to unethical practices are at work throughout the Washington community, as every interest seeks influence with the White House.

With presidential centralization, the need and hence efforts to infiltrate the White House staff have intensified. And because his leadership remains coalitional, the president will frequently welcome the overtures of groups seeking entry. Every president has found it prudent to balance the composition of his administration according to the ideological divisions within his party. Coalition building once took place almost exclusively through the cabinet appointments. Today, staff appointments are equally valuable in assembling an administration team from the disparate elements of the party.

The ways constituencies seek representation in the White House are too numerous to consider in detail here. A couple of examples will suffice to illustrate how they promote pluralism within the organization. One approach is to seek formal representation among the staff. Such practices began informally at least as far back as FDR. Today, it is assumed that a White House public liaison office will assign sympathetic staff to work with the major constituency groups. The Carter White House consolidated and institutionalized constituency services in Ann Wexler's public affairs office. Each of her assistants was assigned responsibilty for maintaining friendly relations with a particular constituency. Dramatically reflecting the pluralism that results from these arrangements, in 1978 an aide siding with his Jewish constituency's opposition to the sale of airplanes to Saudi Arabia resigned in protest.[20] A recent example had various scientists' groups trying to pin down commitments from presidential candidates Bush and Dukakis that their White House would have a science advisor.[21] "Everyone in the White House has a constituency," rued Michael Deaver during his service as presidential assistant.[22]

A more prevalent and milder strain of White Housitis takes the form of seeking access. Every agency, reporter, group, and member of Congress seeks someone on the staff from whom they can expect to receive sympathetic treatment. The division of labor of the modern presidential staff facilitates and largely legitimizes personal relationships of this sort. Influence is, after all, a two-way street. The president will occasionally need an entree with these constituencies.

When Donald Regan encountered this pluralism, he was incapable of seeing beyond its manifestation in personal rivalries to the structural sources of competing notions of the president's interest. To this chief of staff, Nancy Reagan was simply a meddling wife under the spell of some California astrologer, rather than a presidential adviser who at times proved herself more aware than anyone else (including her husband) of the president's political needs.

Against this pluralism-inducing array of organizational attributes and external pressures, Donald Regan constructed his pyramid. It failed. Suppressing conflict is probably impossible when it is rooted in the structure of the organization. In any event, it is undesirable to try. Presidents benefit from the competition, and stringent efforts to induce conformity only guarantee that the competition of ideas will be transmuted into some virulent form through public airing, which eventually will redound to the president's disadvantage. This is a lesson of Regan's stewardship.

But what is to be done? Presidents must be able to take concerted action. As President Carter discovered, even the appearance of confusion among the staff becomes a distinct liability. A paradox of the modern office is that the centralization of tasks within the White House and the resulting internal division of labor demand coordination, but they spawn forces that resist it.

Some have proposed to resolve this dilemma by turning back the clock. Sustained by the venerable creed that the president's staff should be no more than his personal entourage, they argue that if the president's staff were sharply pared back, the political community's many competing interests would be unable to take up residence in the White House.[23] Besides, aides have no business serving as agents, for only the president commands a sufficiently broad view of the political landscape to make wise decisions. "Rigorous efforts should be made to keep . . . staff small," intoned the National Academy of Public Administration in its first of a dozen or

so recommendations to the Reagan transition team. The proposal
went on to recommend that a scalpel be applied to those staff
positions that allow the representation of outside interests.[24] But
this prescription begs the question. The large, specialized staff is in
place because it serves the president's strategic interests. Surgery
on the organization would only succeed in leaving the president
an invalid, as self-reliant as ever, yet incapacitated.

This proposal misses the point for another reason. Staff pluralism is not peculiar to recent presidents. And while today's size and
complexity do accentuate the centrifugal forces within the White
House, competition has always been present. Indeed, the small
staffs of yesteryear occasionally experienced serious moments of
internal competition for influence with the president. At times,
those presidents found in the competition of aides a valuable
source of ideas and political intelligence. Regan reports in his
memoirs that President Reagan stipulated only one requirement
for his staff reorganization: that he receive all points of view. There
is no evidence in either man's actions that they appreciated what
this requires. President Reagan could have learned a lot on this
score from the man whose portrait he had hung in the Oval Office.
Thirty-five years earlier, Truman largely solved the organizational
puzzle of balancing order and creativity.

Pluralism in the Truman White House

Harry Truman's practices offer a poignant lesson because many
who would cut back the size and activities of the modern staff look
to his presidency as a model. His was arguably the first presidential
staff that sufficiently resembles the modern office to allow comparison. Presidents had historically called upon detailees from the
departments to perform clerical duties. In 1939, FDR first formally
designated presidential assistants. But until Truman no White
House Office functioned as a corporate unit.[25] He consolidated the
staff in the East and West Wings of the White House, worked with
them closely, and assigned them more or less routine work. All of
these familiar features of the modern staff represented innovations
over Roosevelt's practices.

Truman's experience is also an useful case for exploring pluralism, because no other president appears to have worked as inti-
mately or as harmoniously with his staff as did Truman. He met

with a dozen or so of his senior aides every morning, took them with him during his vacations in Key West, Florida, invited many to cruise aboard the presidential yacht, and included several among his small, select circle of poker partners. In Truman, then, we have a president who presided personally over a comparatively small White House Office comprised of staff who were both loyal to and fond of their boss. It is an ideal setting for testing the thesis of the inherent pluralism of presidential staff. If it shows up here, we should expect to find it everywhere.

President Truman ran his own White House, largely through daily morning meetings with a dozen or more aides.[26] At these hour-long sessions, he would hear reports on continuing activities, schedule individual meetings as needed later in the day, and give out new assignments. All of Truman's former aides are quick to point out that they were generalists or "troubleshooters," but when pressed, they acknowledge that Truman did tend to routinize some work with certain individuals. Matthew Connelly took care of the president's appointment calendar and scheduling; Donald Dawson ran political clearance of presidential appointments; David Niles maintained close relations with black and Jewish leaders. Others similarly were designated to handle regular tasks.

In addition to routines, one begins to find early signs of tiering and partitioning of staff relations. Some of the morning group had assistants who would see the president only when he needed their report on something they had been working on. Moreover, among the regular attendees at the morning briefings, two were clearly more senior than others. John Steelman, who had retained about a half dozen of his staff from the Office of War Mobilization and Reconversion as a condition for moving over full-time to the president's staff, was principally charged with fielding the president's day-to-day business.[27] He also handled Truman's troubled relations with the labor movement. The other primus inter pares was Clark Clifford, who as special counsel was responsible for overseeing speech writing and working with the cabinet, particularly in the realm of foreign and defense policy. Each worked with sizable junior staffs directly under his supervision.[28]

As a result, one finds coteries of like-minded staff working together informally to promote their policy preferences with the president. The most famous of these was the Wardman Park (also known as the "Monday night") group, assembled privately by

DNC official Oscar Ewing after the disastrous 1946 midterm congressional elections, to identify policies that would prepare the president for the 1948 election.[29] The group was comprised of less than a dozen liberals, mostly at the subcabinet level in the departments, and importantly, Clark Clifford. Conspicuously missing were New Deal Democrats whose loyalty to the president might be suspect and individuals who were otherwise appropriate but who were suspected of being too cozy with the press. With Clifford the conduit, many of Truman's initiatives originated over this group's dinner table conversations. Among the historically prominent initiatives to result from this exercise were the creation of the Fair Employment Practices Commission, national health care for the elderly, and recognition of Israel. Before amending and penning his name to James Rowe's famous campaign strategy memo and forwarding it to Truman, Clifford cleared it with this group.

Most who participated had no recollection that they or anyone else ever revealed its existence to the president. But others in the White House who opposed particular policies or were concerned that Clifford was pushing the president in too liberal a direction are on record as complaining about the group directly to the president. According to John Snyder, treasury secretary and the president's close personal friend, President Truman assuaged his misgivings about the group by telling him that he was well aware of what was going on and not to worry. No one would ever succeed in insinuating policies he did not desire.[30]

Pressures for representation from the outside may have been less prevalent then than today, but the division of labor and the clear importance of the staff in policy making behooved groups to look for a sympathetic ear among the staff. Early on, it became increasingly evident that the president was becoming dissatisfied with Secretary of Labor Schwellenbach's performance. Despite control of the second rungs of the Labor Department by their own number, the major unions began to lobby for representation on the president's senior staff. It may have contributed in fact to John Steelman's effectiveness in mediating labor disputes that involved the president. At times, Clifford, intent in buttressing the president's image in the country, urged forceful actions against organized labor, while Steelman argued for conciliation.

Perhaps former aide David Bell best summed up the pluralism of the White House reflected in the Steelman-Clifford competition and Truman's management of it: "It would be hard to tell what was the exact situation. There were times in the White House when it looked as though there was a constant, continuous and rather disturbing jockeying for position in influence between Steelman and Clifford. . . . In other times, the relationship did not appear to be that of a contest, but one of the effective, strong and useful cooperation between two members of the president's staff, and their respective assistants." He concluded as an afterthought, "The relationship was curious."[31] Rather than targeting it a feature to be suppressed, Truman cultivated staff pluralism. By personally managing the staff, he was able to cool off smouldering conflicts while maintaining diversity.[32] Invited to compare Truman's management style with his successors', William Hopkins, who served as executive clerk of the White House for every president from Truman through Nixon, judged Truman's the best.[33]

Conclusion: Lessons for the Modern White House

The president's staff neither is the kind of organization Donald Regan thought it was, nor should be. This chief of staff worked from the naive notion that the president would best be served by a staff structure that maximized responsiveness to orders from above and minimized initiative from below. Missing from Regan's concept of staff was an appreciation of its role in informing presidential decisions. So, being ill-conceived, the effort was doomed.

Regan's staff system failed the president. The Iran-contra scandal identified a number of imprudent presidential decisions—foremost among them, President's Reagan's decision to exchange missiles for hostages—that good staff work would have prevented. Equally instructive, Regan's staff reorganization failed to achieve the orderly, subordinate relations he sought. Initially, his efforts met with resistance from those aides who saw their roles diminished and subsequently from those who found administrative procedures stifling their opportunity to influence presidential decisions. With avenues of partisan discussion and resolution closed off, those assistants who disagreed with a policy either had to challenge Regan's prescribed procedures in order to make their case or had to go outside the organization to the press. To the chief, both were signs of disloyalty, indicating the need for yet stronger enforcement mechanisms. In the end, of course, his authority was insufficient to impose the unquestioning compliance he found desirable. He only succeeded in creating an organization that gave rise to precisely those pathologies of staff behavior he sought to avoid.

The challenge facing modern presidents is to create staff structures that supervise without stultifying. Platitudes are easy; practice promises to be more difficult, for the task involves nothing less than balancing order and creativity. Procedures designed to keep the president's agents well tethered are apt to be enlisted by senior aides to suppress dissent from below. Conversely, the competition of political interests rarely conforms to the requirements of orderly administration. Both order and creativity should be cultivated, but they can be only when the president and his senior managers appreciate that these virtues exist in a structural tension with one another.

In Truman's day, the challenge was easier. The staff was smaller, permitting his direct coordination. His was generally the only authority enlisted to regulate internal affairs. Moreover, the pressures of internal pluralism were less pronounced. Presidential centralization had not reached its current advanced stage and aides mainly served the president as generalists. Moreover, the president retained close, daily contacts with other political leaders whose differing vantage points enriched his own.

The modern president is not so well positioned. More self-reliant vis-à-vis the outside political community, the president is more dependent upon his staff both for implementing his policies and discerning the correct course of action. But this heightened dependency creates contradictions and renders precarious the balance between order and creativity.

There is no simple solution. No one best design springs forward to resolve this peculiarly modern dilemma. Various approaches have been tried, some more successful than others. President Carter installed Truman's spokes-of-the-wheel system, but soon found himself inundated by the details of policy, which one of his senior advisers offered as the reason he was unable to sort out his legislative priorities.[34] On the other end of the hierarchy continuum are Haldeman's and Regan's strong chief systems. These experiences suggest that the solution is to be found in moderation between these two extreme approaches. Gerald Ford had better luck with his two weak chiefs, Donald Rumsfeld and Dick Cheney, whose position was made somewhat stronger.

And there is the success of Reagan's first-term triumvirate, and later the quadrumvirate when William Clark joined the White House staff as national security adviser. But whether the diversity of priorities among Reagan's senior staff could be replicated in future administrations with equal success remains an open question. Some members of the first-term staff have attributed its cohesiveness in the face of sometimes sharp disagreements to a close personal bond that formed in the aftermath of the assassination attempt early in the first term.

Recognition of staff pluralism and the need for coordination pose constraints on organizational design. But there remains latitude for presidents to mold staff organizations with which they feel most comfortable. The lesson offered by recent experience, however, is that the answer does not lie in denying White House pluralism either through hierarchy or in vainly trying to return the White House staff to a status presidents abandoned long ago.

Notes

1. *Report of the President's Special Review Board*, February 26, 1987, pp. IV-2, V-3. The report also discloses a conversation between Col. Oliver North and National Security Adviser John Poindexter that Regan knew almost nothing about the operation and that it should be kept that way.

2. Donald Regan, *For the Record* (New York: Harcourt Brace Jovanovich, 1988), p. 245.

3. Dick Kirtschten, "Younger Aides, Outside Voices . . . Help Polish Donald Regan's Image," *National Journal*, October 26, 1985, pp. 2432–33.

4. Ronald Brownstein, "White House Personnel Office Struggles with More Vacancies, Less Influence," *National Journal*, June 15, 1985, p. 1408.

5. Dick Kirtschten, "Deaver's Departure in May Paves the Way . . . for Buchanan to Speak Loud and Clear," *National Journal*, May 4, 1985, p. 974.

6. Dick Kirtschten, "It's Crowded at the Top of Regan's Command . . . Causing a Case of the West Wing Job Jitters," *National Journal*, February 23, 1985, pp. 434–35.

7. Jane Mayer and Doyle McManus, *Landslide* (Boston: Houghton Mifflin, 1988), p. 186.

8. On the disagreement between Regan and Buchanan, see "Reagan's Speechwriter Says He Was Dismissed in Dispute," *New York Times*, June 10, 1986; Robert W. Merry, "Buchanan Seeks a New Speech Chief to Shape Hard-Line Rhetoric for Rest of Reagan's Term," *Wall Street Journal*, April 28, 1986. Buchanan's resignation a consideration of a run for the presidency is reported in James R. Dickenson, "White House Communications Aide Buchanan Resigns," *Washington Post*, February 4, 1987.

9. Mayer and McManus, *Landslide*, p. 186.

10. Regan, *For the Record*, p. 257. Others have questioned whether he too was not privately engaged in press relations (ibid., pp. 132–33.).

11. *Report of the President's Special Review Board*, p. IV-11.

12. The informant is William Niskanen in Bernard Weinraub, "How Donald Regan Runs the White House," *New York Times Magazine*, January 5, 1986.

13. Regan, in retrospection on his last days as chief of staff: "I was going down fast and the President's friends were afraid I would drag him down with me. If his popularity was destroyed, his ability to govern would be destroyed too. . . . Ronald Reagan had to get rid of me."

14. An example of this can be found in Regan's and Reagan's differing views on the president's involvement with the pending Tower Commission report. Sensing that the report would criticize his role, Regan insisted that the president be given an advance copy and that the White House respond quickly. President Reagan and some of his senior aides, on the other hand, feared that obtaining an advance copy would expose them to the press's suspicion of tampering, and they wanted ample time to evaluate the report and prepare a response to its proposals.

15. In his memoirs, Regan reveals a belated appreciation of his peculiar vulnerability. Writing about the incentives of reporters looking for scandal in the Iran arms sale, he observes, "Because of my position, and because in a sense I was the only game in town, I was sought after by these excited men and women. The President was inaccessible on his mountaintop" (*For the Record*, p. 45).

16. Peter Sperlich raised this issue in his early review essay of Richard Neustadt's *Presidential Power* (Sperlich, "Bargaining and Overload," in *The Presidency*, ed. Aaron Wildavsky [Boston: Little, Brown, 1975], pp. 406–35).

17. This theme is best developed in Terry M. Moe, "The Politicized Presidency," in *The New Direction in American Politics*, ed. John E. Chubb and Paul E. Peterson (Washington, D.C.: Brookings, 1985), pp. 235–72.

18. Samuel Kernell, "Evolution of the White House Staff," in *Can the Government Govern?* ed. John E. Chubb and Paul E. Peterson (Washington, D.C.: Brookings, 1989), pp. 192–97.

19. On this development within national security policy, see Margaret J. Wyszomirski, "The De-Institutionalization of Presidential Staff Agencies," *Public Administration* (1982): 448–59. On executive management, see Hugh Heclo, *A Government of Strangers* (Brookings, 1985). See also Moe, "The Politicized Presidency" and Kernell, "Evolution of the White House Staff."

20. Terence Smith, "Carter Liaison Aide with Jews to Quit White House," *New York Times*, March 9, 1978.

21. "Science Aide Stressed," *Los Angeles Times*, August 26, 1988.

22. Colin Campbell, interview with Michael Deaver, May 3, 1983, Washington, D.C.

23. See Samuel Kernell, "The Creed and Reality of Modern White House Management," in *Chief of Staff*, ed. Kernell and Samuel Popkin (University of California Press, 1986), pp. 192–232.

24. *A Presidency for the 1980s* (National Academy of Public Administration, 1980), p. 17.

25. The new assistants to the president were stationed in what was then the State Department building, and would occasionally be left out, or cut out, of West Wing activities. This reflects the fact that some of Roosevelt's most trusted advisers were men such as Thomas Corcoran and Harry Hopkins, who were never members of the staff.

26. The observations about the management of the Truman staff apply for late 1946 on.

27. Memo from James Webb to John Steelman, December 6, 1946 (Papers of James Webb, Harry S. Truman Library).

28. A telltale sign of an incipient division of labor and specialization can be found in the general inability of aides to recall much about the daily activities of those staff persons who worked elsewhere in the White House. "I don't know what Steelman did with all his staff," and "Connelly ran patronage and political travel and we stayed out of it" characterize recollections of prominent aides in oral history interview.

29. The best accounts of this little-known group can be found in the oral histories of Gerard Davidson and Oscar Ewing at the HST Library.

30. Transcript, John W. Snyder, Oral history interview, November 8, 1967, Truman Library.

31. Transcript, David E. Bell, oral history interview, August–October 1968, Truman Library.

32. Such a strategy necessitated a small staff. This had another benefit as well. By keeping important staff work farmed out to other presidential agencies— among them, the Bureau of the Budget, the Council of Economic Advisers, the National Security Council, and early on the Office of War Mobilization and Reconversion—Truman gained flexibility in picking and choosing his advice. Writing in 1956 on BOB's role in planning the president's legislative program, Richard E. Neustadt concluded that by having other presidential agencies closely involved in advising the president, Truman avoided the potential "suffocation" that might arise from performing all presidential work within the White House Office.

33. Interview with William Hopkins, April 1, 1988, Silver Spring, Md.

34. Senior Carter adviser Jack Watson has argued that this management system more than anything else pulled "the president into too much; he's involved in too many things. . . . Many of our problems . . . would have been solved had we started from the very beginning with a strong chief of staff system. . . . There were simply too many initiatives of too high a level of controversy and complexity that he wanted to do all at once" (*Chief of Staff*, ed. Kernell and Popkin, pp. 72–73).

17

Support for Prime Ministers:
A Comparative Perspective

PATRICK WELLER

Like presidents, prime ministers need help. But the form of that help is often disputed. While all agree that they require assistance in their role as head of government, their need for support as an individual is not so readily accepted. Constitutionally their chief advisers are meant to be their ministers. Parlimentary government is collective; ministers are supposed to be responible for the development and implementation of policy; cabinet is regarded as the proper forum of crucial decisions. Yet as prime ministers become active in more areas of policy, so the need for support for the individual, rather than the collectivity in cabinet, has become more obvious and its wisdom more strongly debated. Proposed forms of support for a prime minister are controversial because they incorporate a view of the processes of government. A decision of what support a prime minister should have will depend on perceptions of what that prime minister should do.[1]

This debate is most readily understood in the context of British government where there is greater credence given to constitutional norms—primarily because there is no written constitution to anchor the argument. One exchange of views will act as an exemplar of the broader issue. George Jones has argued that those who want to introduce a prime minister's department

wish to reshape government to meet the needs of prime ministers who want to intervene in detail in the policy process. Thus the implication is to shift responsibility from ministers and the cabinet to the prime minister. . . . The prime minister's *task*. . . . is to help colleagues reach agreement, to promote collegiality and a collective strategy. From time to time prime ministers may try to push their own particular line. . . . but such personal initiatives come up against the constraints of cabinet government. The urging of the prime minister's own policy may hinder the achievement of a united cabinet. The *logic* of the British constitution is that prime ministers do no intervene in the policy responsibilities of specific ministers in order to advance prime ministerial objectives. This intervention makes *constitutional sense* only if it is to enhance collective cabinet government.[2]

Jones argues that a skeptical prime minister *"should* not intervene" and take over that policy area. Too much promotion of a personal policy will frustrate the *"primary"* motive of engineering a consensus. The emphases are added because they indicate a clear normative view of what prime ministers should or should not do, starting from a discussion of what type of support they need. The wrong support, argues Jones, will encourage them to do what they shouldn't—interfere in policy—rather than design a consensus.

Lord Hunt of Tamworth, a former secretary of cabinet, responded to the above paper by Jones by arguing that reality had overtaken neat constitutional norms. He pointed out that the *role* of the prime minister had evolved from earlier days. The prime minister's role

now involves a need to be kept informed, not waiting for trouble to come along; a need to initiate and to call others in for collective discussion; a need to act as the guardian of the strategy, although not necessarily as the architect of it. . . . The prime minister must steer, but in a direction that the cabinet as a whole supports. I do not think it possible—regrettable as it may be—to think of the prime minister in this country simply as holding the ring as neutral chairman.[3]

Hunt believed that as the role had changed, so the existing system of support was inadequate; he saw a need to increase the support and agreed with the proposition that the best solution probably was "a prime minister's department, so long as it is still called the Cabinet Office."

Jones's assumptions were constitutional—what should the prime minister do and what support does he or she need to do that proper role? Hunt's concern was operational; the role has changed and the prime minister needs support in the roles he *is* now playing. Richard French, in a discussion of the role played by the Privy Council Office in Canada, has categorized those who adopted the Jones approach as theorists, and the second school as pragmatists.[4] Theorists complain that prime ministers no longer fulfill their classic functions and that their support should be designed only to allow them to fill those traditional roles; pragmatists ask what prime ministers do and ask how best they can be supported.

The approach of the theorists—deriving supporting structures from constitutional assumptions—has two basic problems. The most glaring is that many prime ministers do not accept their implicit job descriptions. *All* prime ministers have policy interests. The more powerful—Thatcher, Fraser, and Trudeau are clear examples from different countries—will become personally involved in a range of crucial issues and will often be the driving force behind that policy development. They know what they want to do and require support to assist them in that role; their powers exist, are used, and will continue to be used. The second problem is that, with the growing emphasis on the leader in the media, formulas designed to reduce or restrict their power seem unrealistic. As Dror has claimed, the growing importance of leaders

limits the usefulness of reducing the importance of leaders as a main strategy for reducing the impact of their inbuilt defects. Rather, it increases the importance of upgrading the performance of advisers to rulers as a means of improving the production functions of rulership in respect of expanding essential and desirable functions.[5]

If prime ministers have chosen to expand their influence, and if their ministerial colleagues individually or collectively in cabinet have neither the wish nor the capacity to limit them, it serves little purpose to complain they should not be acting in this way.

The pragmatist approach asks instead: how well do the supporting structures serve what the prime minister is doing, and can they be improved? How can the supporting structure assist in managing the political process and establishing the agenda? If a prime minister's activities are regarded as too extensive, intruding too much on the prerogatives of his or her colleagues, then the remedy lies in the hands of those colleagues. Prime ministers may well be as powerful as their colleagues allow them to be. That power is a function of personality and position; it is not caused by the support they get. The concern of the pragmatists is operational: allowing prime ministers to do what they choose to do, and to do it better.

The Roles

There are many ways of characterizing the prime minister's job. For the purposes of analysis here it can be conveniently divided into three parts: managing the administrative process, managing the political processes, influencing and/or controlling the policy content. The first concerns those traditional functions that see prime ministers chairing the cabinet, acting as head of the civil service, determining the administrative arrangements of departments: "holding the ring as neutral chairman," to adopt Lord Hunt's terms, or "the prime minister's prerogatives," to use a PCO expression.

The second part of the job can be regarded as managing the political agenda, that is, the relationship with bodies outside the government. Some of these are obviously part of the partisan arena, such as dealing with the party and the media. But not all of the political agenda can be seen as partisan in that party sense. In a federal system prime ministers must constantly negotiate with state or provincial premiers who regard themselves as equals, as heads of government in their own right. So too must prime ministers as national leaders deal with foreign heads of state and international conferences.

The final category is perhaps, as the discussion so far indicates, the most controversial. It concerns the choice of prime ministers to become involved with the details of policy in as many areas as they desire and the impact they have on policy outcomes. One point needs to be made clearly: detailed policy briefing of prime ministers does not mean that they have *necessarily* taken control of that policy area or are running the policy. They still may be working through the minister because they do not have the time to do anything else. But obviously they can and do take over the running of, or maintain a controlling interest in, some policies. Policy advice *can* augment the prime minister's power. Whichever style is adopted, prime ministers need the information to estimate whether the minister's proposals are acceptable and, if required, how they can be improved. They may indeed need the assistance in order to keep up with the growing complexity of government. Greater assistance or better focused information may be essential for prime ministers to sustain their power, not increase it. It will depend on the use they make of that information. The PCO in Canada has called these functions the prime minister's "priorities" or "interests."

In each category the prime ministers will need a different sort of advice, requiring a variety of skills and backgrounds from their advisers. Since all prime ministers have to some extent become involved in all three categories, the question to ask is how are their supporting services organized, what assistance do they provide, and how effectively are they seen to work? Those questions direct attention to some inevitable dilemmas that must be faced in the organization of that support. To each of these dilemmas there are a variety of solutions, each compatible with cabinet and parliamentary government, adopted by different countries.

First, who are the structures to serve: the prime minister as an individual or the cabinet as a collectivity? The assumption has often been that, if the prime minister's primary responsibility has been to facilitate cabinet processes, then the support should be designed to assist all ministers so that a cabinet view can be developed. Cabinets have always faced what might be termed the collective problem. How best can information be arranged and problems analyzed so that all the cabinet members may make an informed and constructive contribution to the decision? Collective briefs have been considered for those ministers who are not otherwise given advice by their departments. Yet all the attempts to assist the cabinet as a group may have had occasional successes, but have never been regarded as a continuous success. By contrast, as the role of the prime ministers has developed and as the pressures for government solutions have grown, so their need as individuals for advice that approaches problems from their unique perspective has become more apparent.

Second, who is best equipped to provide that service: the neutral, career bureaucrats or personally appointed partisans who share the political priorities of the prime ministers? The former traditionally bring subject expertise and long experience in the processes of administration and of making the machines of government work; they regard themselves as professionals in making the machinery of government work smoothly. The latter are passionate, committed, and dedicated to the survival of the government, but will have less experience of government and administration. Both groups will bring different skills and perspectives to their advice.

Third, should that advice be reactive or designed to examine longer-term and strategic issues? As prime ministers are often regarded as guardians of the strategy, as the protectors of priorities, their supporting structures could be designed to that end. Indeed, many observers regard the prime minister as the only possible person who can retain a broad overview, a perspective that can relate the separate policies to the general thrust of government policy. Most ministers are too involved with the narrow horizons of their portfolio; even if as a treasurer they have a broader perspective, it is economic or specialized. Prime ministers can retain the political oversight and sense of direction. But, as much of their responsibility is to solve problems, to settle crisis, to manage the unmanageable, so their attention is often on the immediate. A balance may be needed, but how can it be devised?

Each of these dilemmas provides an analytical focus with which to ask how prime ministers in Britain, Canada, and Australia—all with similar systems of parlimentary government and basically similar assumptions about the processes of cabinet decision making—have organized their support for each of the three roles mentioned.

Managing the Administrative Machinery

Cabinet government can work smoothly only if the prime minister chooses. Attention to the operations of cabinet is a necessary, but not sufficient, condition for effective governing. Prime ministers determine agenda, allocate items to suitable committees, chair meetings, and where necessary authorize the final shape of decisions. They need to ensure that cabinet reaches a decision, or at least some clear conclusion. Their role is to make the process of collective decision making work by emphasizing the need for a collective result.

In every country these procedures are supported by career civil servants: in Britain through the Cabinet Office, in Canada the Privy Council Office (PCO), and in Australia the Department of the Prime Minister and Cabinet (PMC). Gradually the processes of cabinet decision making have become more formalized. Starting under the pressure of wartime administration (1914–18 for Britain, 1939–45 for Canada and Australia), the cabinet secretariat has brought routine and procedure to the system.

Governing has changed. Cabinets have to make decisions on a wider range of interrelated issues; economic management, with its broad implications, is now the principal criterion of success. The age when ministers could even partly act as independent agents within their portfolio has disappeared. Media pressures require a united front. Therefore there is a constant demand for more and more items to be considered by cabinet. The old, often casual, system whereby there was no coordination between ministers and departments before a submission was discussed still existed in Canada under Person. Trudeau's concern with the careful management of process brought organization to the Canada cabinet system. In Australia the process has gradually evolved in the last twenty years, with the rules regulating cabinet now made explicit and even published.[6]

As a consequence, the prime minister requires the cabinet secretariat to insist that the proper procedures are followed. Ministers in all three countries are now required to forecast the cabinet submissions likely to be presented in the next few months. Those submissions are required to follow a prescribed format and the secretariats have the ability to send them back, either because the format is not correct or because the proper consultations or coordination has not been completed. That is, they have the delegated authority of the prime minister and can use it as long as the prime minister supports them. The secretariats would not delay any issue, however badly documented, that the prime minister wanted discussed; they might think carefully about asking for a document prepared by a powerful minister to be rewritten.

In all three systems, submissions have to be lodged some days in advance, so that they can be circulated as widely as is required and ministers can be briefed. In Australia, for instance, they need to be sent to the cabinet office ten days before the cabinet meeting. That requirement for notice can be waived by ministers appealing to the prime minister, who will determine whether the item should be listed, always acting with the advantage of official advice. The decision will depend on the urgency of the issue.

Cabinet agendas are determined by the prime minister, on the advice of the cabinet secretariat. Prime ministers will decide not only what will be discussed but also where it will be decided—or, at times, whether it will be decided at all, as some issues have been deliberately kept off the agenda. Cabinet committees are always established by the writ of the prime minister, who determines their terms of reference, their membership, and their capacity to make final decisions. Prime ministers have always used these powers extensively. Thatcher held many of the important economics discussions in the "E" committee on Future Economic Policy because she could be assured of a majority there. Trudeau used the Priorities and Planning Committee as a de facto inner cabinet because the

Canadian cabinet was far too large—up to forty people under Mulroney—for effective policy discussion. Mulroney has used the Operations Committee, chaired by his deputy, as the most important forum. Fraser often took politically sensitive issues to the Coordination Committee and economic issues to the Monetary Policy Committee. In all these cases, the prime ministers were advised by the cabinet secretariat who would constantly mind the machine, bringing forward proposals for improving or expediting the processes. Many of the changes to the cabinet system—the "envelope" budgetary procedures in Canada, a decision by the Hawke government to consider "under-the-line" items (that is, items without a written submission) at the end, not the beginning, of the agenda—were initiated in cabinet secretariats in an effort to expedite decisions or concentrate the minds of ministers on necessary information. Their advice was both strategic and political, explaining how best to get results and what problems might make it difficult.

The cabinet secretariat was also responsible for recording the decisions made in cabinet meetings, no small task when cabinet or one of its committees could meet so often (over 400 meetings, for instance, in 1969 and 1970 in Canada, and in 1979 in Australia) and made so many decisions (over 19,000 in the seven years of the Fraser government). Many decisions are simple to record, extracted from the clear recommendations of submissions; but others need to draw skilfully from the discussion. Most decisions are circulated without prime ministers' approval, although if they consider it sensitive or important, they can examine a draft. Otherwise, again, these functions are primarily the responsibility of the cabinet secretariat.

Agenda, scheduling, committee structures, decisions—all these are arranged by the cabinet secretariat—and have been with a growing degree of routine. But all these services are exercised with the approval of the prime minister or, when more difficult, the decisions are taken by the prime minister on the advice of officials. Prime ministers are never likely to give up controls over the cabinet agenda or allow other ministers to chair cabinet meetings; those roles are too important as a means of controlling the processes of government. The cabinet secretariats therefore deal with the routine, and they naturally seek guidance on other politically sensitive questions from the prime ministers.

In much of the theory, the secretariats are seen to be responsible for serving the collectivity. But the practice belies that confident assertion. They may indeed implore a prime minister to take issues to cabinet; they may advise that further consultation is needed; they may warn of difficulties of too speedy a decision. One function of the secretariat is to allow collective judgments to be better informed and considered. But the cabinet secretariats do that by working through the prime minister. Their influence can be effective only if the prime minister chooses to make it work, because the impact of the secretariats depends in all important issues on persuading the prime minister. A British prime minister has declared that the cabinet secretary is secretary *of* cabinet, but *to* the prime minister. Cabinet secretariats all try to make the collective systems work by servicing cabinet through the prime minister. But they will all eventually accept the decisions of the prime minister, even if those decisions do not assist collective decision making. It is the prime minister's responsiblity to make the system work.

This relationship is consolidated by other factors. The cabinet secretariats traditionally provide a brief to the prime minister on any issue coming before cabinet. That brief may be procedural in its approach, pointing to the areas of dispute to be considered. In Australia and Canada it may also include a recommendation about a desirable result. The advice will be provided only to the prime minister or, as appropriate, to the chair of any committee. It will let the prime minister start with the decided advantage that the brief provides. Prime ministers who wish to steer cabinet in a direction they regard as acceptable may use that advantage. The cabinet offices also provide a brief or other information on any subject that the prime ministers regard as important, whether or not it is coming to cabinet. Prime ministers may choose to deal individually with ministers; they need advice before they act.

Prime ministers are effecitvely responsible for senior civil service appointments, particularly to positions as head of department, and for decisions on the machinery of government. The PCO, PMC, and the Cabinet Office are the principal advisers to the prime ministers in each of these functions. Onetime rivals—the Civil Service department in Britain and the Public Service Board in Australia—have been abolished. Some machinery of government changes, such as the creation of giant departments by Heath in 1970 or Hawke in 1987, may be driven by demands of efficiency and economy. The establishment of the ministers of state by Trudeau can be interpreted as part of a search for better coordination. In these cases the original impetus may be political, as in Heath's plans, or administrative, as in Australia in 1987. But changes are frequently made to meet the political requirements caused by ministerial failure or political embarrassment, too. In each country the decisions are those of the prime ministers, acting as head of government. The heads of the Cabinet Office, the PCO, and PMC are also the chief advisers on senior appointments—advisers to the prime minister, not to cabinet.

Cabinet secretariats have become institutionalized. They are staffed with career officials who develop the expertise to manage the system and are concerned to make the process of cabinet government work. That is unchallenged. But the style, the vigor, the direction of that system at the margins—in the use of agenda, committee structures, and processes of consultation—will depend on the prime minister. There is a difference between the style of Fraser and Hawke, of Callaghan and Thatcher, and the way in which they have used the support of the cabinet secretariat. A range of issues must come to cabinet; cabinet cannot be ignored; the constraints on the prime minister in the manipulation of cabinet are great. But the advantages of controlling the system are considerable too. The cabinet secretariats assist the prime ministers in making the collective system of decision making work.

Managing the Political Agenda

Prime ministers are seen as head of their political parties and have to deal with the media. They are responsible for the allocation of patronage and, in federal systems, for dealing with state and provincial premiers. In each of these roles they need advice and assistance.

Some of these functions are clearly regarded as the proper responsibility of political appointees, members of the prime ministers' personal offices, rather than of the career public servants. Media staff have become more crucial. As the media expects prime ministers to have a view on everything important, so the urgency of briefings and meetings has grown. In their own way, prime ministers too want to influence the image of the governments. Prime ministers such as Hawke and Mulroney are always conscious of their public reputation and the perception of their performance.

Party involvement will depend on the structure of the parties. In Canada the machinery of the party is confederal. In many provinces the federal and local parties maintain different organizations, even if with an overlapping membership. The federal Liberal party barely existed between elections when Trudeau was in power; it acted more as an electoral machine than an ideological or organizational body. Partly as a consequence, the prime minister's office (PMO) in Canada has retained an important role in running the party and maintaining the links with the regions. Under Trudeau, as the Liberal party's fortunes declined in the provinces, much of the electoral strategy was determined in the PMO. It explains in part the size of the PMO; it assists organizing far more than the routine that is the staple of other offices.

Australian parties are federal. The Liberal and Labor party secretariats have regular contact with the prime minister and help to direct the political agenda. They provide assistance in the briefing for question time, strategic advice on issue management, and information about electoral reactions to government policy. Yet much of the direct influence is vested in the state branches; they select candidates, maintain branches, and through the state parliaments have direct policy interests. Prime ministers in both parties may persuade the power brokers to cooperate; they cannot command. The PMO may act as a personal arm of the prime minster in links with the branches; as much as a month each year of the prime minister's time may be taken up by attendance at party councils, executive meetings, and conferences. Speeches need to be written, plans coordinated. Further, the growth of the factional system within the Labor party has required Hawke to have members of his private staff negotiate with the factional leaders in the parliamentary party and the branches to ensure cooperation and support for government policies.

By contrast, in Britain a Conservative prime minister appoints the chairman of the party, often choosing a strong cabinet colleague for the position. The party headquarters retains a research staff. The chief whip lives two doors away. There is no need for his or her own staff to play the roles. In the Labor party, a prime minister has a more difficult relationship with the party machinery, but has not appointed staff specifically to maintain a liaison with the party.

On the fringes of direct party politics are areas where the locus of the advice differs. In the provision of patronage, appointments in Britain and Australia are scrutinized by civil servants. A member of the No. 10 staff, often with long tenure as a career civil servant, routinely provides support to the prime minister for honors and appointments, from bishops to knights. The Ceremonial and Hospitality branch of PMC fulfills a similar role at the center of Australian government. Of course, in both countries many jobs are the gift of ministers; recommendations for appointments may be brought to cabinet, after being approved by the prime minister and, in Australia, usually cleared by the senior minister from the state they live in.

In Canada patronage plays a far more public role. Both Trudeau and Mulroney have been criticized for the range and the partisanship of their appointments. An officer within the PMO, usually a senior and close adviser of the prime minister, has generally been responsible for maintaining lists of suitable appointees. Traditionally the responsibility for patronage has been the prerogative of the senior minister from each province. An effort to centralize patronage in the prime minister's office under Trudeau was regarded as less than successful. It is notable that the Canadian PMO has a high profile in the provision of patronage and general acceptance that it is a proper partisan role. Patronage was accepted as a matter for the office, not the bureaucracy.

In Canada and Australia, the federal structure adds to the pressure on the prime ministers. Negotiating with the premiers, whether individually or collectively at premiers' conferences, is time-consuming because the state or provincial leaders regard themselves as heads of state. They claim the right to speak on behalf of their locality, even though they may be arguing against a prime minister for the same party. In both countries the PCO, through the Federal Provincial Relations Office, or the PMC must provide continuing support for these activities.

Policy Advice and Management

The area of policy advice and management has traditionally been the most controversial, both in terms of how much support is needed, who should provide it, and with what time horizons. What is important to realize is that prime ministers are interested in policy detail; the only matters of dispute are to what extent they are involved and what support they should get. If not properly informed, their involvement is likely to be ineffective or even dangerous. The question then must be: if they demand advice, how should it be organized?

In Britain the impact of the Cabinet Office on policy has often been greater than it appears. Lord Hunt has commented that he was struck "by the relative increase in the proportion of the time [he] had to give to the prime minister as compared to the time [he] could give to running the ordinary business of the Cabinet office."[7] Cabinet officials may participate in official committees, but more important they may be required to provide specific advice to a prime minister who wants an answer or an analysis of a policy. British prime ministers can also receive direct advice from the Treasury. At No. 10 Downing Street the prime minister is further served by a small cadre of officials. They are always on secondment from the civil service, with the position and principal private secretary being a stepping stone to a departmental secretaryship. The group is flexible, skillful, and nonpartisan.

But in the last two decades prime ministers have also appointed other partisan policy advisers.[8] Prime ministers have often had one or two personal advisers—Macmillan had John Wyndham and Heath Douglas Hurd. But in 1974 Wilson appointed a Policy Unit, headed by Bernard Donoghue. The unit has been described as "the most significant, though as yet relatively small, institutional change in the political direction of government in Britain since 1945."[9] It contained around seven people with specialist skills and could range across government activity—as far, that is, as such a small group could effectively go.

Thatcher initially abolished the Policy Unit, but appointed a small group of advisers, including specialists on economic and foreign policy matters; the appointments "reflected the more directive and interventionist style of the prime minister. She felt a personal responsibility for the policy of the government." In 1984 the unit became well defined, with nine members with specific responsibilities; they therefore had the ability to comment selectively on any area of government activity. They constituted one of a flexible mixture of partisan and nonpartisan advisers at No. 10, "a place of distinct entities but not rigid demarcations."[10]

In Canada the demarcation between the PCO and PMO is strictly on partisan-nonpartisan lines, but where the policy advice is given, the distinctions are not so clear. Both are housed in the Langevin Block and may combine to discuss the potential agenda. Under Trudeau the PCO was divided into an Operations Section that serviced cabinet, and a Plans Division that was designed to support the prime minister's interests, to provide briefing and advice in those areas where the prime minister chose to participate.

PMO too had a policy capacity that has varied according to political priorities, the prime minister's demands, and the interests of its principal members. Lalonde and Axworthy under Trudeau, Roy and Burney (a career civil servant) under Mulroney, were not exclusively concerned with shuffling the paper but with getting the policy directions right. By contrast, Coutts emphasized the switchboard role, understanding the need to keep Trudeau in contact with the party and the electorate. The contrast between the PCO and PMO was, according to one participant, that the former was nonpartisan, operationally active, and politically sensitive, while the latter was partisan, politically active, and operationally sensitive.[11] There was no clear distinction about the territory the two units could cover in policy areas; their responsibility was to inform the prime minister.

In Australia similar complementary roles are played by PMC and the PMO. The degree of their policy involvement depends on the interest of the prime minister. Since 1973 PMC has developed a capacity to provide policy advice on any area of government activity. Fraser used it extensively; he could ask advice on anything that was happening in government. He had a wide range of interests, was the source of innumerable ideas that he wanted ministers to pursue, and always wanted to be well informed on any policy that his ministers might pursue. He never wanted to be the hostage of a single source of advice and therefore sought both alternative views and comments on other people's analysis. PMC had to be ready to provide any or all of these services, almost in an instant. As its secretary said, "We do not feel inhibited in what some might interpret as the role of second opinion."[12] The department could not be inhibited because the prime minister demanded it. Hawke is less interested in the details of policy and leaves far more to his ministers; the policy divisions therefore play a less substantial role. But the department has created divisions such as the Office of the Status of Women and the Office of Multicultural Affairs that maintain an overview of government policy in areas of political priority or symbolic importance and provide the prime minister with a brief that is separate from that offered by other sections of the department. PMC is also politically aware in its advice, far more explicitly so than the Canadian PCO, according to officers seconded from the latter to work in the former.

The Australian PMO also maintains a policy role, if the prime minister chooses. Its business is to support whatever the prime minister chooses to do. Under Whitlam and Fraser, its small policy area inevitably became involved, usually in close cooperation with the department, in debating outcomes and proposing alternatives. Some important decisions had their origin there. Its function, according to the leading exponent in Fraser's office, Professor David Kemp, is to provide the "political" input to understand issues from the unique perspective of the prime minister. The PMO was designed to do those things that the prime minister would do if he had more time.[13]

Policy advising is therefore provided by a combination of partisan and career officials. Yet most of it is essentially short-term. There have been efforts at strategic planning. The CPRS was initially supposed to develop a strategy. The Priorities exercise in Canada in 1974–75 was designed to establish clearly the government's priorities. Yet the first became more concerned with solving pressing problems, and the second was overtaken by the change of circumstances. In Australia the creation of an Economic Planning Advisory Committee was a symbol of the Hawke government's commitment to planning, but it has been used more to legitimate government policies than to influence them, and has been marginalized by being shifted away from the centre of the machine.[14]

Nor have attempts to advise cabinet as a collectivity appear to have been any more successful. Weekends at Chequers or Meach Lake are regarded as desirable in theory (and the principle of a cabinet meeting without submissions to examine strategy was espoused in principle by the incoming Hawke government in 1983), but they do not appear to have been successful in practice, often leading to impatience in ministers who wanted to return to solving immediate problems.[15] The collective advice of the CPRS to ministers was regarded as of limited value.

In part these failures may be an inevitable consequence of the political process. Prime ministers may know where they want to go; they need advice on how to get there. Or they may be obsessed with solving immediate problems. If they fit the first category, they do not need long-term units; if the second they can't use them. Besides, powerful ministers may object to a central unit imposing a view of governmental directions. If planning units are to survive, they need to be isolated from immediate pressures; that is unlikely to occur in any prime minister's office. But, second, many important changes are not planned, but are developed as part of the art of the possible. Most of Trudeau's changes of policy occurred outside the official planning framework. Privatization in Britain was a policy that worked and was expanded, rather than a grand strategy. Electoral pressures drive change.

Advice to prime ministers has therefore tended to be short-term, policy-oriented, and individual. Cabinet, it appears, works better if the prime ministers are sufficiently well informed to be able either to mold a consensus or to manipulate the processes in such a way that they can get their own way.

Do they get enough policy advice? There is no doubt they get enough advice; the real question is whether the material they get is necessarily appropriate. In Australia the flexibility of PMC means the department can be reoriented to meet the demands and style of a new prime minister. In Canada the PCO and PMO can combine to provide an extensive service. In neither country have the leaders complained about the inadequacy of the advisory machine or, too often, the quality of the advice, although former officials have debated its effectiveness in Canada.[16] Prime ministers have chosen to use the combination of career and noncareer advisers in different ways to meet their needs. Both countries have flexible systems. In Britain, by contrast, those closest to the leader doubt whether the advice has the depth necessary to allow prime ministers to intervene *effectively* in policy, although they acknowledge that they constantly will become involved. Sir Kenneth Berrill thought the advice was patchy and the prime minister needed support "in some depth across the width of government department."[17] Sir John Hoskyns wanted a small department.[18] Lord Hunt thought the advice was "thin."[19] All recommended some greater capacity to provide policy advice, because "practice shows that [prime ministers] want advice from someone they regard as their own."[20]

Policy advice to the prime minister needs special qualities. It has to relate the specific to the broader picture. It has to allow the prime minister to concentrate on the disputed points. These may be part of developing a government view that has support. It may also let the prime minister intervene in an informed and effective way in whatever area he or she chooses. There may be an inevitable problem in that a small secretariat or office, however skilled, cannot match the depth of knowledge of the operational department. But, equally important, it brings a different perspective, the view of the prime minister, to that analysis. The prime minister's perspective may be distinct from the collective view, at least initially.

What Support Is Best?

Cultures and history have brought their own style to the Westminster system of governments. As federations, Canada and Australia make demands on the prime minister that no British prime minister has. Dealing with state or provincial premiers, and with colleagues who "represent" their regions, creates problems that are never duplicated in a unitary system. Notions of propriety—"what should public servants do"—may differ. So too does the sheer weight of civil service tradition, so much greater in Britain than in the postwar machines that constitute the Canadian and Australian public services.

But prime ministers need support to do what they choose to do. If they are to be limited or restricted to what may be regarded as a proper role—and that is a political decision—then the appropriate forum is the cabinet, where the collective weight of ministers may restrict and restrain a leader. If cabinet has not the will or the capacity, it is illogical to assume that an ill-informed leader is preferable to one that is well briefed.

The lessons that emerge from these descriptions are that a range of alternatives are possible. There is an accepted need for a nonpolitically based support for cabinet, although as that becomes more complex, so the serivce is provided more for a prime minister than for cabinet collectively. There is a need for partisan assistance in party and media matters. In policy concerns—usually short-term and crisis-management—a combination of career and partisan advisers can work together to provide the support prime ministers need. Prime ministers have all ensured that they receive advice from several channels. Ministers are not prevented from being their chief's main advisers, if they have the ability. Supporting institutions may be as flexible and responsive as the leaders require. The name of the support services is not too important: the functions delivered by No. 10 and the Cabinet Office in Britain, by the PCO and the PMO in Canada, by PMC and PMO in Australia are beginning to look increasingly similar. They are all compatible with collective cabinet decision making and with parliamentary government.

It is fallacious to argue that the existence of a prime minister's department indicates that a prime minister is as a consequence more presidential than a prime minister serviced only by a cabinet office. The power of a prime minister is determined primarily by political constraints, above all by the capacity or will of ministers to assert their own authority and independence. The structure of support will have only a limited impact. The development of those structures, in their different forms, have been a response to, not a cause of, the new pressures that have developed in modern government. As a result they are all servicing, more or less explicitly, the prime minister as an individual and through the prime minister assisting the cabinet. They provide the help necessary to keep the prime ministers informed and to give them some opportunity to act in reality as heads of government.

Notes

1. For a broader comparative discussion, see Patrick Weller, *First Among Equals: Prime Ministers in Westminster Systems* (Sydney: Allen & Unwin, 1985). See also Colin Campbell, *Governments Under Stress* (Toronto: University of Toronto Press, 1983).

2. George W. Jones, "The United Kingdom," in *Advising the Rulers,* ed. William Plowden (Oxford: Basil Blackwell, 1987), p. 64.

3. Lord Hunt of Tamworth, "The United Kingdom," in ibid., p. 68.

4. Richard French, "The Privy Council Office: Support for Cabinet Decision-Making," in *The Canadian Political Process,* 3d ed., ed. Richard Schultz et al. (Toronto: Holt, Rinehart and Winston, 1979), p. 388.

5. Yehezkel Dror, "Conclusions," in ibid., p. 188.

6. *The Cabinet Handbook,* 2d ed. (Canberra: Australian Government Printing Service, 1988).

7. Lord Hunt of Tamworth, "The United Kingdom," p. 68.

8. See Jones, "The United Kingdom," and "The Prime Minister's Aides," in *The British Prime Minister,* 2d ed., ed. Anthony King (London: Macmillan, 1985).

9. Richard Rose, "British Government: The Job at the Top," in *Presidents and Prime Ministers,* ed. R. Rose and Ezra Suleiman (Washington, D.C.: American Enterprise Institute, 1980), p. 45.

10. Jones, "The United Kingdom," p. 59.

11. Marc Lalonde, "The Changing Role of the Prime Minister's Office," *Canadian Public Administration* 14 (1971).

12. G.J. Yeend, "The Department of the Prime Minister and Cabinet in Perspective," *Australian Journal of Public Administration* 38 (1979); 143.

13. James Walter, *The Ministers' Minders* (Melbourne: Oxford University Press, 1986), pp. 76–98.

14. Richard French, *How Ottawa Decides* (Toronto: James Lorimer, 1980); Gwynneth Singleton, "The Economic Planning Advisory Committee: The Reality of Consensus," *Politics* 20 (May 1985).

15. Edmund Dell, "Collective Responsibility: Fact, Fiction or Facade?" in *Policy and Practice: The Experience of Government* (London: Royal Institute of Public Administration, 1980).

16. See the exchange of views by Douglas Hartle, Richard Van Loan, and Richard French in *Canadian Public Administration,* Spring 1983.

17. Sir Kenneth Berrill, *Strength at the Centre: The Case for a Prime Minister's Department* (London: University of London Press, 1980), pp. 3, 14.

18. Sir John Hoskyns, "Whitehall and Westminster: An Outsider's View," *Parliamentary Affairs* 36 (1983): 147.

19. Lord Hunt of Tamworth, "The United Kingdom," p. 68.

20. Ibid., p. 69.

18

The Role of Press Secretaries on Chief Executive Staffs in Anglo-American Systems

COLIN SEYMOUR-URE

News is the atmosphere of politics, claimed Woodrow Wilson. Journalism and politics have often been overlapping occupations, and news media are essential to the rituals of electoral politics and to the everyday conduct of government. It is therefore natural to find a press secretary in the entourage of a president or prime minister, frequently as one of the earliest appointments. What is important and distinctive about the job, and what may we expect to learn by analyzing its use under different chief executives? This chapter outlines a general model of the development of the press secretary's role, mainly since 1945, in the United States and three parlimentary regimes—Australia, Canada, and the United Kingdom—and discusses some issues, first, about the role of the press secretary himself (only once *her*self, in Canada) and, second, about its implications for the office of president or prime minister.

Such a study may be fruitful on several grounds. The press secretary necessarily works closely with the chief executive. Individual appointments are a good guide to chief executives' personal styles and their attitudes to public communication. The secretary's job, further, reflects the changes produced in the political environment by the growth of television and the speed of electronic communications. It can thus provide insights into how these changes may have affected the chief executive's job.

The press secretary's office is especially distinctive for two reasons. Unlike the members of a chief executive's immediate entourage—a prime minister's private office or the senior White House staff—he has a certain "apartness," occasionally likened to that of a court jester. (One of Robert Menzies's secretaries was indeed given that nickname.) His primary duty is to the chief executive: yet he cannot effectively fulfill it without a commitment also to the different, and potentially conflicting, goals of his news media clientele. He is a man in the middle. The tension is constructive, in that the interests of each side are served by the secretary taking account of the other. It is best exemplified in the fundamental importance of his credibility. A secretary is little use to his boss without the confidence of the press, nor to the press without the confidence of his boss. In rare cases of extreme opposition between chief executive and the press, such as during the Watergate scandal, the job becomes virtually impossible. Even in ordinary times, credibility, once lost, has proved very difficult for a secretary to regain.

The second reason why the secretary is distinctive follows from the conundrum faced by all governments about managing their public communication. Public communication is not only an end in itself, linked to the processes of political choice and legitimacy. It is an important aspect too of the whole range of government policy areas. Wherever government depends upon popular consent, the substance and public presentation of policies become entangled. When governments decide what to do, they presumably choose options they think will succeed. To the extent that success depends on effective presentation, then presentation becomes one of the substantive criteria of choice. Put crudely, governments need to decide first what share of resources to devote to substance and what to presentation; next, how far presentation should be hived off and given to a special organization; and third, whether such offices are best run by communication specialists or by policy specialists.

Obviously, governments do not actually go through that chain of decisions. The point is that there is no compelling logic that justifies giving communications management a higher rather than a lower priority. At any given level of policy success, it can probably be argued that more resources for communication would produce more success. As a specific example of communications management, the office of press secretary is thus inherently flexible, having central influence with one chief executive and functionary status with another.

Last, the press secretary is a promising case for comparisons—

not only across time and among different parliamentary regimes, but also between prime ministers and presidents. Despite the differences of constitutional context, the press corps of Westminster, Ottawa, and Canberra focus on their chief executives in much the same way as the White House press corps does, sharing many of the same beliefs about the nature of politics and news and of their own "Fourth Estate" responsibilities. They work also with the same technology; and television has made comparable voracious demands in each capital. The rise of the press secretary has accompanied also the rise of "big government," in which factors of scale and specialization may have had more impact on the office than whether the growth took place in a presidential or a parlimentary system. The importance of temperament must also again be stressed: within obvious constraints, the press secretary's role is determined more by the chief executive's temperament than by constitutional forms.

Chief Executives and Press Secretaries: A General Model

The flexible nature of the work is shown by the fact that few press secretaries have had a formal job description. Some have felt that if they needed to ask what the job entailed, this would have shown they were not right for it. Table 14 lists those who have held the post. In all four countries, the work has come to include, in varying proportions, four roles: that of *spokesman, adviser on media relations, agent,* and *manager.* As spokesman, the secretary provides a channel from the chief executive to the news media and back—a role that enables him, of course, to block contact as well as to facilitate it. As adviser, he may help with anything from grooming the chief executive for TV performances to strategy about media use. As agent he deals with news executives and journalists, representing their interests and those of the chief executive to each other. As manager, he runs an office and manages its relations with other parts of the chief executive's entourage.

Until World War II (later, in Canada), these roles were rudimentary. The "office" of press secretary could refer to a post but hardly an institution. With growth it has become in turn specialized, institutionalized, intensified, and diverse. The development can be presented diagrammatically as a circle (see figure 1). Starting from

TABLE 14. Presidents' and Prime Ministers' Press Secretaries
in the United States, Australia, Canada, and the United Kingdom

President/ Prime Minister	Date of Taking Office (month/year)	Press Secretaries (month/year of succession)
United States		
F. D. Roosevelt	1/1933	S. Early
H. S. Truman	4/1945	C. Ross, J. Short (12/1950), R. Tubby (9/1952)
D. D. Eisenhower	1/1953	J. Hagerty
J. F. Kennedy	1/1961	P. Salinger
L. B. Johnson	11/1963	P. Salinger, G. Reedy (3/1964), W. Moyers (7/1965), G. Christian (1/1967)
R. M. Nixon	1/1969	R. Ziegler
G. Ford	8/1974	J. ter Horst, R. Nessen (9/1974)
J. Carter	1/1977	J. Powell
R. Reagan	1/1981	J. Brady, L. Speakes (4/1981), M. Fitzwater (1/1987)
G. Bush	1/1989	M. Fitzwater
Australia		
J. A. Lyons	12/1931	I. Douglas (?/1934)
J. J. Curtin	10/1941	D. Rodgers
J. B. Chifley	7/1945	D. Rodgers
R. G. Menzies	12/1949	S. Cockburn, H. Dash (?/1953), R. Maley (1/1961), T. Eggleton (6/1965)
H. H. Holt[a]	1/1966	T. Eggleton
J. G. Gorton	1/1968	T. Eggleton
W. McMahon	3/1971	R. MacDonald
E. G. Whitlam	12/1972	E. Walsh, D. Solomon (12/1974)
J. M. Fraser	11/1975	D. Barnett, J. Bonner (?/1982), E. Dean (?/1982)
R. J. L. Hawke	3/1983	G. Walsh, P. Ellercamp (?/1986), B. Cassidy (11/1986)
Canada		
J. G. Diefenbaker	6/1957	J. Nelson, J. Fisher (7/1961)
L. B. Pearson	4/1963	R. O'Hagan, R. LeBlanc (?/1967)
P. E. Trudeau	4/1968	R. LeBlanc, P. Roberts (3/1971), P. O'Neil (2/1973), C. Tower (6/1975), R. O'Hagan (?/1976)
J. Clark	5/1979	J. Osler
P. E. Trudeau	3/1980	P. Gossage, N. Senecal (5/1982), R. Coleman (12/1983)
J. Turner	6/1984	R. Coleman
B. Mulroney	9/1984	B. Fox,[b] M. Gratton (9/1985), M. Lortie (3/1987)
United Kingdom		
C. R. Attlee	7/1945	F. Williams, P. Jordan (12/1947), R. Bacon (6/1951)

President/ Prime Minister	Date of Taking Office (month/year)	Press Secretaries (month/year of succession)
W. S. Churchill	10/1951	F. Clark (?/1952)
A. Eden	4/1955	(F. Clark), W. Clark (10/1955), A. Richardson (11/1956)
H. Macmillan	1/1957	H. Evans
A. Douglas-Home	10/1963	J. Groves
H. Wilson	10/1964	T. Lloyd-Hughes, J. Haines (6/1969)
E. G. Heath	6/1970	D. Maitland, R. Haydon (4/1973)
H. Wilson	3/1974	J. Haines
J. Callaghan	4/1976	T. McCaffrey
M. Thatcher	5/1979	H. James, B. Ingham (11/1979)
J. Major	11/1990	G. O'Donnell (11/1990)

a. After Holt's drowning in December 1967, J. McEwen served as interim prime minister for three weeks before Gorton's election.

b. Fox became "communications director" in 9/1985 and was succeeded as such by B. Phillips in 3/1987.

a historical position where the president or prime minister was historically his own press secretary, each stage represents a new development in the use of surrogates. The path returns to the chief executive, rather than being linear, because the logical conclusion of the development is to place the chief executive personally at the center of public communication again, as performer, media strategist, and manager. The historical tendency has been to move round the circle; but this should not be taken to mean that now all chief executives necessarily conduct news operations personally and at a high pitch. On the contrary, the lack of a clear logic for determining the priority for public communication has enabled particular chief executives who value it low to adopt the practice of some earlier stage of the development (making allowance for changes in technology). Equally, some chief executives already adopted a maximalist view of the importance of public communication before the process of specialization had gone very far. The journalist Richard Strout, for instance, recalling Stephen Early, Franklin Roosevelt's press secretary in the New Deal years, could comment: "The whole admininstration was a public relations effort, and Early was right in the middle of it."[1] What is new since then is not the capacity of chief executives to stress the importance of public relations but the institutional apparatus and techniques available for their use.

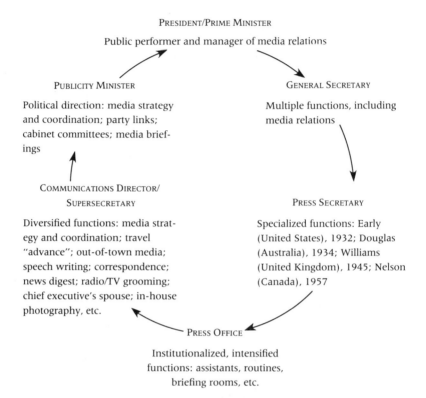

PRESIDENT/PRIME MINISTER
Public performer and manager of media relations

PUBLICITY MINISTER
Political direction: media strategy
and coordination; party links;
cabinet committees; media briefings

GENERAL SECRETARY
Multiple functions, including
media relations

COMMUNICATIONS DIRECTOR/
SUPERSECRETARY
Diversified functions: media strategy and coordination; travel
"advance"; out-of-town media;
speech writing; correspondence;
news digest; radio/TV grooming;
chief executive's spouse; in-house
photography, etc.

PRESS SECRETARY
Specialized functions: Early
(United States), 1932; Douglas
(Australia), 1934; Williams
(United Kingdom), 1945; Nelson
(Canada), 1957

PRESS OFFICE
Institutionalized, intensified
functions: assistants, routines,
briefing rooms, etc.

FIGURE 5. Presidents' and Prime Ministers' Media Relations:
A Cycle of Development

Press work in all the countries considered here was first done as
one of several responsibilities of a general aide or secretary. Until
Hoover's time the president was permitted only two White House
assistants at a professional level. Franklin Roosevelt acquired four,
but even Stephen Early, appointed in 1933 and generally acknowledged as the first specialist press secretary, spread his activities
beyond press relations.[2] In the United Kingdom, the first press
officer at No. 10 Downing Street, George Steward, was appointed
during the financial crisis of 1931 and stayed till the Second World
War. But he was a peripheral figure, and most Downing Street
news came through parliamentary political sources.[3] The first
press secretary with functions spanning the range specified above
was Francis Williams, appointed by incoming Prime Minister
Clement Attlee in 1945. In Australia the first was appointed in
1934. In Ottawa the old practice of a prime minister brushing up

against journalists on Parliament Hill and relying on a private secretary to gloss information for the press continued late into the 1950s. In the 1957 election campaign which ended the years of Liberal ascendancy, the populist John Diefenbaker promised the press corps to appoint a press secretary. Having won, he did— selecting the president of the Ottawa Press Gallery, Jim Nelson, and then not knowing quite what to do with him. The idea of a press secretary, one might say, was still more important than the fact.

The novelty of a specialized press secretary was reflected in an uncertainty of title. Early was styled secretary to the president; Nelson, news secretary; Williams, cumbersomely, adviser on public relations. Nor, in the parliamentary systems, did the post become immediately entrenched. Williams's successor in 1947, Philip Jordan, did not carry the same weight either in or out of Downing Street. Churchill did away with the post altogether in 1951 and had to be persuaded to reinstate it.[4] Menzies was similarly unenthusiastic on taking office in 1949; and Nelson's successors under Diefenbaker lacked a clear-cut specialist role. It is tempting to see in this faltering start the distaste of three prime ministers, each a dedicated parliamentarian and skilled performer, for an intermediary who might complicate their publicity.

Having survived more than one chief executive, the press secretaryship became institutionalized and the work progressively more intense. Between the early Eisenhower and the Nixon administrations, the White House press staff grew from ten to more than thirty.[5] Elsewhere the scale was much smaller, but the trend was the same. The secretary acquired one or more deputies and assistants, with an element of subject specialization (for example, in foreign affairs). Routines developed—for distributing handouts, making a record of briefings, coordinating with departments, providing a daily news digest, managing the chief executive's press conferences (and preparing him for them). Details vary greatly— in the extent to which chief executives hold press conferences at all, for instance, or in whether they have a morning staff meeting (which, if they do, the press secretary in most cases attends).

Even at the most mundane level there is a marked lack of continuity between one administration and another, a reflection in part again of the personal nature of the secretary's appointment. Between a defeated administration and an electoral victor, such as Fraser and Hawke in 1983, this is broadly understandable; but it means that much of the collective memory lies with the journalists and that each new press secretary takes some months to settle down. This happens even when he has himself been a member of the press corps, as is common in Canada and Australia and was Harold Wilson's practice in the U.K.

These developments have been gradual. The secretaries who made the greatest mark, in this administrative sense, have chiefly been those longest if office. For example, in the White House Hagerty (1953–60) is noted for a pioneering attention to logistical detail.[6] In Canberra Eggleton (1965–71) built up and streamlined the office at the end of the Menzies era. In Downing Street Maitland (1970–73), though not long serving, secured extra resources and introduced new methods of news coordination; and Ingham (1979–90) developed career management for the Whitehall information officers who form the core of the Downing Street Press Office on secondment from the departments.

The next stage of development was diversification. The growth of TV made new demands, first affecting politics in the United States and Canada during the 1950s, in the U.K. in the 1960s, and Australia in the 1970s. Chief executives increasingly needed advice not only on what to say but on what programs, how often, and in what tone of voice. Their spouses needed help, too. Press officers also found themselves in the travel agency business, as jet transport made it practical and often expedient to take the press on the chief executive's trips. Press secretaries took on the responsibility for "advancing" these visits and went over the ground beforehand to plan media coverage. Advice on media relations became more complex. The growth of polling added a further dimension. Meanwhile, activities such as speech writing, correspondence with the public, and even such details as the work of an in-house photographer all became more elaborate.

The result of this diversity was a proliferation of offices and of sometimes ill-defined advisory functions that extended beyond the press secretary's reach. The areas staying within his responsibility varied—as much within the different countries as between them. Thus speech writing, for instance, was initially a press office responsibility under Carter but was not under Reagan. Institutionalized diversification has been greatest, as one would expect, in the White House. Since Nixon created an Office of Communications under the San Diego newspaper editor Herb Klein in 1969, there has always been a director of communications and a group of offices generally within his responsibility.[7] In their Reagan form, these included Media Relations, dealing with specialist and out-of-town media, Public Liaison, Public Affairs and Communications Planning, Speech Writing, and TV Production. This was in addition to the Press Office. The relative status of the communications director and the press secretary has changed, formally and informally, during successive administrations. The existence of a director certainly need not entail reduced influence for the secretary, as the example of Jody Powell showed in the Carter administration.[8]

Institutional ramifications have been fewer in prime ministerial regimes. There, communications directors have in effect been supersecretaries and still sometimes styled press secretary. Early examples such as Dick O'Hagan (Pearson and Trudeau) have been partisan figures, close counselors to the prime minister, at arm's length from day-to-day press work and more concerned with general media implications of the government's program and strategy.[9] Bernard Ingham, clearly, was a supersecretary for Mrs. Thatcher, though the unique Downing Street system of unattributable twice-daily collective briefings kept him in regular contact with reporters. An alternative, which appears to be the Australian custom, is for the strategic and coordination aspects of communications direction to be a function of the prime minister's private office—whether or not the press secretary himself is an intimate (like Hawke's secretary Barrie Cassidy) or less close (like Fraser's secretary David Barnett).

The last stage in the media relations cycle, hypothetical more than common in practice, is reached when communications management acquires such political priority that, in cabinet systems, it achieves explicit ministerial oversight. This may involve a cabinet committee, as in Australia and Canada for brief periods under Fraser and Trudeau. More recently, Brian Mulroney gave the responsibility to his deputy prime minister, Dan Mazankowski. There is normally a minister responsible at Westminster for answering parliamentary questions about government information services. Sometimes a minister has also dealt with the media more generally on behalf of the prime minister and cabinet;[10] but this practice fell away in the Wilson administration and has not been revived on the same scale. The prime minister tends to be his or her own publicity minister. The pressures of cabinet government probably work in that direction.

In the sections that follow, some of the issues raised by this model are explored in more detail.

Aspects of the Press Secretary's Role

Journalists, Partisans, Public Servants: Who Is Right for the Job?

The requirement that a press secretary has credibility with the press skews a chief executive's choice toward people with experience in news work. The skew is least evident in Washington, where a previous close association with the president, on the campaign trail for instance, may be more important than press experience. Thus Ziegler had been in advertising, Powell a graduate student in political science, Brady a lobbyist and legislative assistant. Presidents who succeeded in mid-term have taken over their predecessor's secretary (Johnson and Salinger), called on a long-term associate (Truman and Ross), or chosen an experienced Washington correspondent (Ford and ter Horst/Nessen). Salinger and Ross were both in fact former journalists. Where secretaries themselves have needed replacing, presidents have sometimes gone outside the administration and have chosen journalists (Truman and Short: Johnson and Christian); or they have chosen an insider even if he had no press experience (Johnson and Reedy/ Moyers; Reagan and Fitzwater). Altogether, five U.S. presidential press secretaries out of sixteen have served without previous experience in press work. In Australia, by contrast, there have been none; in Canada four out of eighteen; and in the U.K. four out of sixteen. Nearly all the exceptions outside Washington have been career civil servants, except for Coleman (Trudeau and Turner), who had been in the army.

The choices open to an incoming chief executive may be visualized in the form of a decision path with several sets of alternatives. First, does the chief executive want a communications specialist or not? If a specialist, should it be a working journalist or a civil service information officer? If a journalist, should he come from print or broadcasting and from the press corps or outside? If not a civil servant, should he be a partisan or a nonpartisan?

Few press secretaries, as we have just seen, have had no "information work" experience at all. In Ottawa and Canberra, an appointment directly from the press corps is not uncommon. In the U.K. the only examples are the appointments by Eden (William Clark, not strictly a member of the Downing Street "lobby correspondents" group) and Wilson (Lloyd-Hughes, 1964–69; Haines 1969–70 and 1974–76). Only three of the Washington secretaries came actually direct from the White House press corps (Short, ter Horst, and Nessen), and ter Horst resigned after a month because of the Nixon pardon.

Apart from the wider range of nonjournalistic experience among Washington press secretaries than elsewhere, the main exception to the general pattern is the regular use in Downing Street of civil service information officers. These are typically people who started work as journalists and then entered the civil service as information officers (for example, Fife Clark, Evans, Groves, James, Ingham). Two others, who worked for Ted Heath, make a unique pair. Heath wished to model his press secretary on the example of Chancellor Brandt's secretary in Bonn, Konrad Ahlers, and appointed first Donald Maitland, ambassador in Tripoli, and later Robin Haydon, high commissioner in Malawi. Both were career diplomats and both had experience as head of the Foreign Office News Department. This, unusual for Whitehall, is almost never run by an information officer. (The one exception, Tom McCaffrey, was appointed when Jim Callaghan was foreign secretary and moved with him to Downing Street in 1976.)

From the Downing Street side there seems no doubt that Maitland in particular was a great success.[11] He was close to Heath and widely experienced in European matters that were at the heart of Heath's program. He and Haydon certainly had credibility with the press corps; but there may have been less "understanding," viewed from the press side, than comes with an ex-journalist secretary.

Canadian prime ministers have occasionally adopted this practice too. Twice under Trudeau and once under Mulroney (up to 1987), a foreign service officer has been seconded initially as deputy and has then succeeded as press secretary. The first, Peter Roberts, was offered the opportunity to move onto the prime minister's political staff after two years but chose to return to the department. The second, Nicole Senecal, is the only woman to have been press secretary in any of the four countries. Marc Lartie, the third, had had Washington experience and succeeded a journalist, Michel

Gratton, when Mulroney reorganized his private office in the spring of 1987. The Department of External Affairs has found the practice useful in helping to ensure efficient foreign policy briefing and—under Trudeau, whose attitude to the department was lukewarm—in having a presence close to the prime minister. In the White House it has become normal for one of the deputy press secretaries to be on secondment from the State Department.

The problem with civil service press secretaries, in the parliamentary system but not in Washington, is with partisanship. Most—probably all— have formally been civil servants while in post, though at least once in Ottawa the governing party has apparently paid half the secretary's salary (for O'Hagan, under Pearson); and a similar arrangement was mooted in the Conservative party for Eden's secretary William Clark. But whatever his background, the rule is strictly maintained in the U.K., and perhaps less so in Autralia and Canada, that while the press secretary is a public employee he should not contribute to the prime minister's party work. In small things and where activities are clearly labeled, the rule is practical. For instance, the Downing Street Press Office would not distribute speeches made by Mrs. Thatcher to Conservative party meetings. A press officer might even accompany her to the hall but would dutifully leave her at the door. Bernard Ingham stayed away from the Conservative party's annual conference. The Press Office plays no part at all in election campaigns.

All this suits the career appointees well, in Canada as in the U.K. It suits the nonpartisan outside appointees too. William Clark was not a Conservative anyway, so he certainly did not relish the prospect of party links. Wilson's first press secretary, Lloyd-Hughes, appointed direct from the press corps, played the role of a career appointee to such an extent that Wilson had to draft in a "parliamentary press liaison officer," Gerald Kaufman, to handle political press relations from Downing Street—though paid by the Labour party. When Lloyd-Hughes moved to a different job in the government information service, Wilson appointed a partisan, Joe Haines, to succeed him. Haines ran Wilson's office in opposition from 1970–74 and came back as press secretary again from 1974–76. Despite his party background he claims not to have been troubled by line-drawing problems while a temporary civil servant. Australian secretaries are typically in the same position. It now seems taken for granted in Canberra by politicians and the press alike that the press secretary will be a partisan appointment. During the long Liberal ascendancy of the 1950s and 1960s, Menzies and his immediate successors could feign indifference, but this changed with Whitlam's Labour administration elected in 1972.

One needs to keep clear, however, the distinction between a partisan appointment and partisan behavior in office. The latter may be easily avoided for explicit party activities but far less so in the general conduct of government business. The triennial system of elections in Australia, with the polling and marketing techniques developed in recent years, has strengthened the idea of a "permanent campaign."[12] The effect of sure exclusion from any activity with a party tinge would be to make the press secretary a functionary and reduce his usefulness to the press. In practice, the secretaries serving both master and clients best have probably blurred the nonpartisan line, whether or not they were partisan appointments. Bernard Ingham, for instance, was very close to Mrs. Thatcher and was sometimes criticized on the grounds that his ought to be a partisan—indeed, a ministerial—appointment. Haines, though unpopular with some of the press corps, was certainly an intimate of Wilson.

If these arguments are right, why are civil service appointees the rule in Downing Street? The answer seems to lie in two unique features of the Downing Street system—the secretary's role as coordinator of information services in the departments and his off-the-record spokesman routine. He can win the confidence of the departments better if he is an insider; and the press corps like a spokesman with an element of detachment (arguably lost in the case of a long-serving appointee like Ingham), who is unlikely to parrot a party line and make knee-jerk reactions to events, nor to persist in comments too much at odds with plausible versions of the truth. He can behave in this way partly because his career base outside the prime minister's circle gives him protection. It also means that he knows his way around Whitehall better than an outside appointee.

The differences reduce to this. An outside appointee, especially if partisan, will trade on his strengths of political connection and privy advice. Civil servants will more likely trade on political sobriety and knowledge of the machine. Outsiders will tend to mute their opinions; civil servants, to take on the government's color. At the extremes, the outsider will join the career civil service (Lloyd-Hughes) and the insider will leave it (Evans, McCaffrey).

What matters most to a prime minister—and to a president—is his secretary's commitment. This, again, is an index of credibility, and it matters therefore also to the secretary and his clients. More than anything the press corps need to know where they stand with the secretary. The example of William Clark makes the point. Anguished by Eden's Suez policy in 1956, his doubts became plain to Eden and confused the press, and his term ended quickly with honorable resignation.[13]

The Press Secretary's Tenure: How Long to Stay?

Few press secretaries work for more than one chief executive— another indication again of the personal nature of the appointment. A few in London and Washington have worked as a deputy in one administration and secretary in another. (These include Speakes, Groves, and James. The latter were both civil servants.) In every case the reason has been, initially at least, to help with a transition. This can be an emergency—Salinger staying on board after Kennedy's assassination, Eggleton after Holt's drowning, and Groves after Macmillan's resignation through illness. In the other cases it is deliberately planned—Fitzwater to smooth Bush's transition from vice-president to president; Coleman to ease Turner in at the end of the Trudeau era; James (after a period away from Downing Street) to get the Thatcher Press Office going in 1979. The exceptional case is O'Hagan, who served Pearson from 1963– 66 and did not come back to work for Trudeau until 1976.

Viewed the other way round, few prime ministers have had only one press secretary. Secretaries almost uniformly quote two years as optimum for the job. To some extent that is an aspiration, reflecting the strains of being man-in-the-middle and maintaining credibility on both sides. Sometimes an election or resignation may tip them out earlier; and one or two have proved mistaken appointments. Their commitment and the engrossing nature of the job—seven days a week, all hours of the day, at the call of their clients and their boss—tend to lock them in. The pattern is thus of a large number serving about two years or less, and a few who soldier on. These last, notably O'Hagan and Gossage (including time as deputy) in Canada, Eggleton and Barnett in Australia, Evans and Ingham in the U.K., risk becoming "contaminated" by association with one prime minister or party. Eggleton took the logical step of becoming a senior party official. Others have left journalism or (like Barnett) had rather to "work their way back."

The fixed-term presidency means that Washington secretaries implicitly sign on for the duration, at least of the first term. Early served throughout Roosevelt's presidency (and is still the record holder). Only Hagerty has since served two full terms. But death and accidents have increased the number of presidents with more than one secretary. Johnson remains the only one to fall out with his secretaries: he was on his fourth by 1968.

The lesson appears to be that for the needs of the chief executive and the press corps, a secretary who remains in post as long as his boss is most desirable—provided his credibility stays high. The arguments for a shorter term are all based in the self-interest and career goals of the secretary. Staying on could be a boon if he wished to use the office as a pathway to politics. But, perhaps oddly, few do: Eggleton apart, LeBlanc, who became a minister with Trudeau, is the chief example. Otherwise he takes a risk in not getting out.

The Press Secretary as Intermediary: The Scope of the Job

Chief executives' contacts with the media take three forms. First, they communicate direct to an audience, without a journalistic filter, through television and radio addresses, broadcasts from legislatures, conferences, and conventions. Less frequently, they put their names to articles in the press. Second, they meet, or are reported by, journalists acting as a filter to the media. This may be at times and in locations arranged for that purpose, such as press conferences and TV interviews; or as a by-product of some activity that journalists witness, and where their contact with the chief executive may be peripheral, unexpected, possibly intrusive. Third is the contact, or both these kinds, by persons speaking in the chief executive's name—sometimes authorized, like a press secretary or colleague, sometimes unauthorized. There are many variations, including the paradoxical, as when a chief executive talks to journalists but insists they attribute his remarks elsewhere. (An Australian prime minister in the early 1900s, Alfred Deakin, used to speculate anonymously on the affairs of his own government in weekly articles for the London *Morning Post*.)[14]

In each form a key issue is that of control, over the time, place and duration of contact, its content and the use made of it (including attribution). In helping to determine how far control is exercised in practice by the media and how far by the chief executive, the press secretary may act as an *adviser* on the chief executive's performances; as *intermediary/moderator* of contacts with journalists; and as *spokesman* in the chief executive's name.

Adviser on Performance. Chief executives are almost by definition accomplished performers by the time they reach office. They are likely to need major advice thereafter chiefly about adaptation to new developments in media. Since the rise of the press secretary, TV has been the great innovation. The impetus to learn its tricks came largely from party managers, because of its importance in election campaigns and the connections between parties and the worlds of advertising and PR. Few secretaries, even now, have had experience as TV producers and performers, so they have not been well equipped to give advice. Gossage, who was, briefed Trudeau about behavior before the cameras. Such advice has generally been at a trivial level. For instance, Ingham's deputy in 1988, Terry Perks, "got Mrs. Thatcher out of hats" when she was minister of education, because her face became invisible when she bent to speak to children.

Press secretaries have frequently been involved, on the other hand, in advice about the tactics of performance—such as where and how often to appear on television. The scale of potential media demands makes this a major operation in Washington, a preoccupation of the Office of Media Relations and the Office of Public Affairs. But there is much of the seamless web about it, since media performance—in Washington and elsewhere—is likely to be part of a broader political strategy ultimately controlled by the chief executive's most senior advisers. The secretary will be one of many voices raised. For prime ministers there is again a strong party dimension; and in Australia an election is never far away. But on a day-to-day basis the press secretary will keep track of the chief executive's broadcast appearances and press interviews and modulate them according to a balance that seeks to satisfy the media clientele and his own interests. Hawke's secretary, Barrie Cassidy, did this very systematically, matching program appearances with particular target audiences. In comparison, Ingham's calculations appeared rather more approximate.

Manager of Chief Executives' Contact with Journalists.

1. Churchill, taxed with complaints about lack of press contact in his postwar premiership, reeled off a list of press barons among his friends. At that level, his contact was good; among the working press it was virtually nonexistent.[15] Press secretaries have little to do with their chief executives' media contacts on high or intimate levels and may not even have a clear idea how extensive these are—particuarly by telephone. Some, such as Eden and Prime Minister Billy McMahon of Australia, have been notorious for their use of the phone, usually for complaining.

Chief executives do have friends among the working press—presidents with columnists, for instance. But many of these private contacts are about high policy, to do with electoral support or media legislation, and not directly about the kind of news routines that concern the press secretary. Much of the time the secretary tends to operate at a more mundane level, with routine the key. Thus it has always been a Press Office responsibility to process requests from journalists for interviews with the chief executive. Discretion in granting them varies greatly: it would be a good index of a secretary's place in the pecking order, and an index too of his credibility with the press.

Equally variable is the secretary's contribution to speech writing. This is always a collaborative effort. Some secretaries, particularly in the early days of the office, have spent a lot of time and energy on it. In Washington they now spend little, even when they have had formal responsibility for the speech-writing team. Typically, a secretary elsewhere will have a chance to look at a speech and suggest ideas and phrases but will work more closely only with speeches that are about the media.

2. The rise of the press secretary has coincided with the eclipse of railway travel. Jet transport and electronic news technology have institutionalized the traveling press corps and increased the amount of travel abroad. Descriptions of Menzies, Diefenbaker, and Macmillan traveling by air in the 1950s and 1960s sound like Victorian safaris. In addition to the tiny official party, one or at most two jounalists would make up the entourage along with a

Mountie (in Canada) as "security" and a stray relative or two. Now, as Ingham puts it, press offices are one-man travel agencies. Secretaries talk in zoological terms of "care and feeding" of a large number of reporters. The reporters come to take such care for granted, despite (or perhaps because of) their being made to pay for it. At summits or in outlandish places—Moscow and Beijing before they opened up; Vietnam during the war—there is prestige for the press (reflected in hats and T-shirts with appropriate insignia displayed back home), but a tendency to "pack journalsim" with everyone writing the same story.[16] Journalists are close to the chief executive for longer periods than usual. Even on less glamorous trips, air travel finds them locked together for long periods, a compartment away from the chief executive.

All this gives the press secretary leverage. The type of airplane, the seats available for the press, and whether there will be a separate press plane, are not his decisions (though his success in battling for press places may affect his reputation). But typically he makes the rules for allocating places, and sometimes the actual choice of people to fill them. In flight, the nuances of news exchange are subtle. The press know the chief executive may have work to do. Equally, it is difficult for him or her to ignore them altogether without seeming to make a statement comparable to the ambiguities of a spoken "No comment." The furnishings of an airplane make for informality. News exchange thus tends to be on a shirtsleeves basis—chatty, informal, inconsequential. Though physically confined, the contact is unstructured. For the journalist, it is an occasion to pick up the chance remark; for the chief executive, to socialize and show a human side.

These intrinsic uncertainties are managed or contained by "joking relationships." Trying on the suggestion of an inflight press conference, Canadian journalists "petitioned" Trudeau and received a reply in Latin.[17] Press secretaries may benefit from playing the fool, and certainly from identifying themselves as much as possible with the mood of their clientele and meeting its needs. Ralph Coleman built a reputation in Ottawa as the master of the logistics of media travel and was rewarded by promotion from assistant to full press secretary. Many of the same uncertainties about the terms of news exchange, and the influence they give the press secretary, apply when the chief executive is on holiday or receives the press at home. Where there is a misunderstanding, on the other hand, they have been the occasion for recrimination.

3. "Doorstopping," which the Canadians call "scrumming," involves comparable nuances of news exchange but on a much smaller scale, and it poses greater problems of control for the press secretary as manager. Doorstops are impromptu question-and-answer sessions. They are generally held on the move or in ill-defined locations, but they sometimes develop a routine.

Geography is an important factor in whether the chief executive is obliged, reluctantly or not, to cooperate. In Ottawa it is difficult not to. The prime minister cannot easily sneak anywhere from the Parliament buildings. He is beset by corridors and staircases. He has one office in the building and another across the street, with more doors and staircases. Scrumming started there at tense moments in the Suez crisis in 1956, when Prime Minister St. Laurent was accosted on his way to and from the Cabinet Room (also in the Parliament buildings).[18] With tape recorders and hand-held cameras, the practice grew. It became routine for the prime minister and perhaps his colleagues to be quizzed by journalists as they emerged from cabinet. Until television was allowed into the Commons Chamber itself, Trudeau used to speak impromptu to the cameras in the lobby outside too.

A similar practice developed somewhat later in Australia, where, as in Ottawa, the Cabinet Room and the prime minister's office are in the Parliament House. The geography of the old building (replaced in 1988) made the outside entrances the best places for an encounter. Scrums were cultivated especially by Malcolm Fraser in the 1970s, so as to exploit the growing radio and TV press corps of Canberra. At Westminster, by contrast, the prime minister can more easily arrive unnoticed; and the famous Commons lobby, which gives its name to the elite political press corps (the lobby correspondents), is not one which the prime minister needs frequent. Even if he does, the rule for journalists is that they must not importune nor dally in groups. Journalists sometimes doorstop at Downing Street, and the practice may grow. One of Mrs. Thatcher's best remembered Falklands War comments, calling excitedly on viewers to rejoice at the recapture of South Georgia, was a doorstop interview, and John Major gave a press conference outside No. 10 Downing Street on the morning in January

1991 when war began in the Persian Gulf. But the Downing Street doorstop is not in fact a convenient place for political correspondents. Apart from anything else, they may get a better comment from the press secretary inside.

The geography of the White House, in the same way, makes it fairly easy for the president to dodge reporters—as witness the hopeful recourse to questions shouted at President Reagan against the whir of helicopter blades on the White House lawn. Until some deliberate reconstruction in Nixon's time, the press could indeed waylay the president and his visitors. The origins of the press corps' occupancy of space in the White House was precisely Theodore Roosevelt's invitation to reporters loitering on the doorstep to come in out of the cold.[19]

Press secretaries and their bosses find doorstopping useful for the apt, up-to-the-minute comment, especially on camera, but immensely tiresome when they want to be left alone. New incumbents find it difficult to avoid and are often well disposed anyway. Press secretaries become involved in negotiations with press corps officers about terms and conditions.

There are practical difficulties, too, especially indoors at Ottawa. Journalists trip over cables. Prime ministers want somewhere to put their glasses or something to hold, and they may be bad at extricating themselves (like Trudeau). In their efforts to keep the initiative, secretaries have tried to regularize doorstops by moving them to special briefing rooms or, in Hawke's case, his office. Mulroney has sometimes used a collapsible podium with an imposing coat of arms. Even when a deal is made like Hawke's (and a similar Trudeau expedient in the early 1970s), to swap doorstops for a short daily meeting, the practice never quite dies out. For the secretary and the chief executive it is a fluid situation, and one fraught with the risk of making an unguarded remark.

4. Press conferences are a kind of large-scale, organized doorstop with a similar need for control but without the risks of spontaneity. Press secretaries are involved as intermediaries, agents, and managers. They deal with negotiations about the frequency and format of conferences and the preparation and briefing of the chief executive. In Canada and Australia they sometimes conduct the conference and decide when to end it; and they mop up afterwards, fielding queries and issuing clarifications.

The disadvantage of a regular press conference to the chief executive as news manager has always been that sooner or later he will have to face questions he would rather avoid—like Reagan, obviously, about Irangate. At other times the press will be uninterested in what he wants to say. Trudeau, in this situation, once put a question to himself, telling the press corps it was more interesting than theirs (and embarrassing his press secretary, who had prepared him to expect the press to ask it). To the press, the disadvantage is that a regular conference may indeed be an empty ritual or an occasion for government propaganda that cannot be entirely set aside. Yet without a regular conference they risk losing leverage over the chief executive when they do want one.

Arrangements about press conferences tend therefore not to be in equilibrium. Partly because some people handle them better than others, practice has varied widely among chief executives and within particular incumbencies. Candidates sometimes make a commitment to a regular conference which, once in office, they implicitly regret. "Regular" becomes "infrequent" or "occasional," and press secretaries find themselves caught uncomfortably between a reluctant executive and an impatient press corps. Some prime ministers, like Joe Clark in his short incumbency, and Gough Whitlam, do stick quite closely to their promise. Fraser introduced a new twist in Australia for a time by holding separate conferences for print and electronic media. Trudeau's practice fluctuated, like that of several American presidents. The interval between presidential press conferences is one measure of the president's confidence in his standing with the press and public.[20]

The chief executive's press conference was transformed by the intrusion of TV. Washington, again, made the running, first with Eisenhower and then when Kennedy went on television live. Ottawa and Canberra followed in the 1960s. The lineage runs from the twice-weekly round-the-desk exchanges between Franklin Roosevelt and a small band of regulars, reporting on or off the record at the president's will, to the present stylized conferences in the East Room of the White House, where leading reporters wear makeup because they are as much a part of the show as the president. For these conferences, the appropriate image is the medieval joust or ordeal. Will the president be unhorsed? Can he stand the test of burning coals?

Prime ministers in the United Kingdom have, uniquely, refused to give regular press conferences. Ted Heath gave three large televised conferences in 1973 but abandoned the experiment in the face of media skepticism about their value for genuine news exchange. For many years the Leader of the Commons has met the lobby journalists collectively once a week to discuss parlimentary business (sometimes an elastic term). Other ministers have also sometimes been deputized to brief on the cabinet's behalf. Most prime ministers have met the lobby from time to time—as little as once or twice a year, in the case of Eden or Macmillan, and almost weekly in the case of Wilson's first administration.[21] These have been off-the-record occasions, certainly not open to the cameras. Prime ministers have preferred instead, as did Mrs. Thatcher, the carefully chosen broadcast interview. Otherwise they have held conferences only during election campaigns (since 1959) and occasionally for some specific purpose such as the launch of a new policy initiative.

Spokesman or Surrogate for the Chief Executive. The main reason, probably, why British prime ministers have been able to get away with not having press conferences is that a major role of their press secretaries has always been to hold them—off the record—on their behalf. (The other reasons, which prime ministers elsewhere might pray in aid if it suited them, and which presidents of course cannot, have to do with the interlocutory role of Parliament.)

All press secretaries brief on behalf of the chief executive, though not all have been able to speak with equal confidence in his name. Briefings can range from the routine, open, collective briefing to the one-off, private, individual briefing in person or by phone. On his use of, and performance in, all of these, much of a secretary's credibility depends; and briefings occupy much of his time.

Collective briefings are dominated by routine. In Washington and London, where the secretary has traditionally briefed the press corps in the morning (and the afternoon too, in London), the early part of the day involves calls to departments and agencies to gather and coordinate information for active or reactive use at the briefing. With the growth of the TV networks as news priority setters, there is some effort in the White House (though less, apparently, at Downing Street) to determine a "story of the day." Depending on their degree of access and their chief executive's administrative style, secretaries may also have attended an early morning meeting of senior executive staff, chaired either by a chief of staff or the executive himself (sometimes in informal surroundings, such as a Downing Street breakfast room). The secretary plays a feedback role at such meetings, but they are primarily useful to him for gathering information and possibly getting a "steer" on the latest news.

These preparations provide a structure and a rhythm for the secretary's office as a collective organization. With the briefings that follow, they give order and coherence to an official version—mostly public in Washington; filtered through the confidentiality rules in Downing Street—of the affairs of the president and the prime minister. They are an important means of trying to keep the news initiative. For the press corps, collective briefings are an efficient way of receiving routine, noncompetitive news (for example, of appointments, or the chief executive's engagements); but, being shared, they have limited value in the search for distinctive or exclusive news. Mostly, to judge by the games played between secretary and press corps in White House briefings, they are an occasion to test the secretary's credibility and competence, gauge the state of his relationship with the chief executive, and maintain their own status in their peer group and more widely in their news organization.

In Australia and Canada, collective briefings by the press secretary have rarely happened in private and almost never in public. The exceptions have been isolated briefings at airports or, in more recent years, during summits. Why the reluctance? Canadian secretaries admit to occasional pressure from journalists, due partly to awareness of practices in Washington; and they claim the press secretary is more often quoted by name than ten or fifteen years ago. But in both countries secretaries invoke almost piously the principles of parliamentary government: if the prime minister has something to say he should say it himself, preferably on the floor of the legislature, where he can be held accountable (with the television cameras watching, in Ottawa if not quite yet in Canberra). Moreover, since Australian and Canadian prime ministers are so much more accessible personally to the press corps, there is less of an argument for a routine spokesman. But this situation could change with a reclusive prime minister.

The most frequently challenged feature of the Downing Street briefings is their confidentiality.[22] Secretaries prepared to accept attribution (at least sometimes), such as Maitland under Heath, faced resistance from lobby journalists to whom the confidential quality of the briefings was their basic value. In the Thatcher administration, the decisive resistance came rather from the press secretary. Journalists refusing to accept the rules were excluded from the briefings (but could of course use agency copy). The complaint was that briefing off the record gave too much discretion to the prime minister and press secretary—for kite-flying and attaching "deniability" to a story, for instance.

The same objections are not raised to the press secretary's briefings of individuals or groups. The pattern doubtless differs from capital to capital, but the dynamics of the secretary/journalist relationship are similar and the definitions of "off the record," "background," nonattributability and the like seem indistinguishable. Press secretaries almost all describe the relationship as an unending struggle to convey the understanding of events that they would wish. Journalists have an equal tendency to see themselves as the hapless instruments of archmanipulators. These attitudes, of course, reflect common themes in the political cultures of the four countries. They epitomize the secretary's predicament of trying to serve two masters with potentially conflicting interests.

The Lone Voice or the Loudest Voice: How Many Masters Does the Press Secretary Serve?

Analysis of these intermediary roles begs the question of how many masters the press secretary serves. The answer is generally complex and adds to the difficulties of the job.

The formal position is simple. In Washington the secretary serves the president; and in cabinet systems the principle of collective responsibility means that serving the cabinet and serving the prime minister amount to the same thing. The first clue to the practical complications is that the secretary has always been located in the prime minister's office, not in the cabinet secretariat or its Australian and Canadian equivalents. (The single exception, due to Churchill's antipathy to the post, seems to have been Fife Clark). This gives him a direct orientation toward the prime minister and no doubt reinforces the personal nature of the appointment.

The complexity of the secretary's position depends on how far the cabinet does behave as an entity. To the extent that it does not, he risks being caught up in the tensions and in the inevitable rival leaks. A civil service appointee may distance himself from these, but they will not necessarily have derived entirely from party considerations. A cabinet may simply take time to reach a collective view or may be seriously split on a question of policy. There will occasionally be messy resignations and controversial reconstructions. The secretary can never aspire to be an exclusive news source, but if he turns aside too many leading questions, he jeopardizes his authority and his capacity to influence the news agenda. The alternative risks, if he does not hesitate to enter the fray, are of losing his prime minister's confidence or—more likely—of being seen too uncompromisingly as the prime minister's man.

These dilemmas are greatest in the United Kingdom, for the British press secretary has much the biggest coordinating role. He is explicitly secretary for the government as a whole, chairing a weekly meeting of departmental information officers and helping discreetly to orchestrate ministerial radio and TV broadcasts. The role is administrative: as a spokesman, the Downing Street secretary could not possibly cover in detail the whole range of departments. The object, in essence, is that the government should speak with one voice—but not entirely with the voice of No. 10.

In Australia and Canada, the same general principle of collective responsibility governs the cabinet, but local conditions (federalism, French Canada) have given the prime minister and his colleagues a different relationship. Coordination at press secretary level has been attempted in Canada from time to time, but mainly on a simple basis of trying to prevent the government from scooping itself. A prime minister's press secretary who threw his weight around in other ministers' offices would soon run into difficulties. In Canberra, the proliferation of ministerial press secretaries in the Whitlam government created if anything disharmony. Under Hawke, a "ministerial media group" undertook a certain amount of coordination, but not from within the Press office. In both countries there have been spasmodic ministerial attempts at coordination.

Because the presidency too is in practice collective, notwithstanding the president's individual constitutional responsibility, the question, "How many masters?" also arises in Washington. It was confronted explicitly in 1969 when Herb Klein, director of communications, was charged with coordinating communications for the administration as a whole. The Press Office has an important role in trying to ensure that the White House collectively, and the White House and individual departments such as State and Defense, are in step day by day. When the press secretary is caught up in internal tensions, however, these are likely to be between persons all of whom are theoretically responsible to the president. Secretaries whose line to the president has been most direct (Early, Hagerty, Powell) have had fewer problems than others whose line of responsibility has passed through a director of communications or chief of staff. The main problems have been either of access—getting (and staying) on the inside track—or of formal lines of responsibility failing to match realities.[23] Like the parliamentary press secretaries, the secretary in Washington must also temper loyalty to the president with a recognition of the plausibility of some alternative versions of the truth emerging from different sources in the White House. The price of excessive loyalty can be the loss of credibility.

Political Back-up for the Press Secretary?

The tendency for the institutionalized press secretary to develop into the role of a "supersecretary" or director of communications raises issues about political backup in the parliamentary models.

One part a minister can play, where the secretary has a comparatively weak coordinating function, is to orchestrate government publicity on a political level. These efforts have been spasmodic in Australia and Canada, depending mainly on the random enthusiasms of particular ministers or influential backbenchers and the willingness of the prime minister to play along. They illustrate well the point, made in the introduction, that a case can always be argued for spending more efforts on improved communications. Lester Pearson was faced with precisely such a claim and was happy to let the Liberal M.P. who argued it take publicity initiatives that resulted for a while in the establishment of a Cabinet Committee. Similar moves in the early 1970s under Trudeau produced a committee supervising a so-called weekly blurb a publicity handout for Liberal parliamentarians in their constituencies. In Fraser's time, a cabinet publicity committee sat for a while in Canberra, but no one, Fraser included, seems to have attached importance to it.

Efforts have also been made in Australia and Canada, within

the official cabinet machinery, to attach statements about public presentation to proposals put up by departments to the cabinet. This practice was introduced in the U.K., too, on the initiative of Heath's press secretary, Donald Maitland, but it has evidently not survived.

There has been no equivalent elsewhere to the occasional appointment in the U.K. of a "minister of public relations." The best examples were Charles Hill and Bill Deedes, during the years 1956–64. Such a minister has generally substituted for the prime minister as a private briefer and performer, sometimes on a weekly basis. He has chaired the weekly coordination meeting of departmental information officers, instead of the press secretary. He has managed relations with news executives and broadcasters and helped to orchestrate ministerial performances. He has boosted the press secretary's authority in crises such as Suez and the Falklands; and he has been responsible for advising the prime minister on public relations and information services strategy.

Hill and Deedes were particularly important because, after Churchill's inertia, Eden wanted the whole subject reviewed and upgraded; because the political potential of TV was becoming rapidly apparent; and because the transitions from Eden to Macmillan and Macmillan to Home were in different ways precipitate, so that a minister with a specific portfolio and publicity experience (Hill as a broadcaster, Deedes as a journalist) was a useful support for the prime minister—and for the press secretary.

Other ministers, before and since, have performed some of those roles, and they do indeed roughly parallel the press secretary's, but with a partisan flavor and ministerial clout. The combination can work very smoothly, particularly with a civil service press secretary. But when there is no minister, it is easy to see that the secretaries themselves can slip into a quasi-ministerial role. Only on the rarest occasions have they actually been called into a cabinet meeting, but their attendance with ministers at cabinet committees and ad hoc ministerial meetings is as common as that of other senior civil servants. Attlee's press secretary, Francis Williams, a pioneer and in some ways a role model, "seemed to have the status almost of a minister."[24] Under Mrs. Thatcher, Bernard Ingham was depicted in the same way—and criticized for it. Undeniably, the ministerial and civil service roles can in practice be blurred.

The Press Secretary and Policy: How Much Say?

Are press secretaries getting drawn into decisions about the merits of policy because of their advisory role in its presentation? The question applies especially to the partisan press secretaries and to the White House press secretary—the latter because of the fluid decision-making patterns in the institutional presidency.

Certainly a few press secretaries, starting with Early himself, have become substantive policy advisers. The types of policy to which their situation enables them to contribute are the highly generalized—policy as general goal or attitude ("Our policy on nuclear weapons/foreign aid/the environment is . . .")—and the highly specific—particular items of legislation or administrative action. Some have had a special interest—Reedy in labor relations, William Clark in economic development. Haines has described in detail how, with Wilson's encouragement, he promoted public housing reforms.[25] Barnett pressed foreign exchange and social welfare advice on Malcolm Fraser. More often, the contribution has probably come because of a press secretary's closeness to the chief executive at critical moments.

There is little evidence, however, that secretaries are getting drawn into substantive policy more and more. The "functionary" press secretaries are by definition excluded, and there have still been some of these in recent years. For the others, their advice remains limited to policy on presentation, no doubt partly because that is how the job should be and they are too busy with their own routines; and because they are involved with most issues too late or, obviously, at too great a distance from the departments concerned. It remains arguable, on the other hand, for reasons elaborated earlier, that the indirect influence exerted over substantive policy by the secretary's advice on presentation is likely to be greater than it used to be before the growth of television.

Conclusions:
The Press Secretary and the Chief Executive's Role

What, in conclusion, may the development of the office of press secretary suggest about the role of the chief executive?

Gone are the days, first, when a chief executive could hope, as did Truman or Eisenhower, to "let the facts speak for themselves."[26] Eisenhower was fortunate to have an ingeniously activist press secretary, Hagerty; and chief executives (Mrs. Thatcher among them) may still afford to be uninterested in the nuances of media relations if they are as well served. But any chief executive who does not include people with communications experience among his or her immediate advisers and provide material support and status for the press secretary risks losing the initiative in the battle for public opinion.

The complexity of the media environment, further, makes it probable that prime ministers will now always be their own publicity minister. Specific tasks may be delegated, such as oversight of the departmental information services in the United Kingdom. But the links between electoral strategy, attitude surveys, the targeting of social groups, policy development, and media management all mean that full responsibility cannot in practice be delegated. The same developments probably mean that communications management would prove to be taking up more of a prime minister's resources of time and energy than they did forty years ago, if these things could be measured. In the Nixon and Reagan White Houses, too, several key figures around the president have had backgrounds in some branch of communication; and Carter strengthened such advice as his administration progressed. Communications management has long been a preoccupation of the presidency, and it appears to permeate the work of the office more widely than ever.

The entrenchment of the press secretary and the heightened priority of communications management by prime ministers tempt one to look for a broader convergence of presidential and prime ministerial styles. Television in particular can be shown to help a prime minister dominate his or her colleagues as a performer and to provide an informal base of popular authority independent of the legislature. It arguably increases the prime minister's role as a mobilizer of opinion; and in Australia and Canada it seems more and more to portray the prime minister as a quasi–head of state, as the ties with the British crown decline without a corresponding elevation of the governor-generalship.

All these tendencies are broadly presidential—applying the word both to the modes of public communication by prime ministers and to the implications these have for their various managerial, policy, and symbolic roles. All follow from the prime minis-

ter's performance on TV, and with all of them therefore the press
secretary is directly or indirectly involved.

The fact that prime ministers have the power to dominate the
screen does not mean that they will. They do in election campaigns; but at other times their "dominance" may paradoxically
be used to keep themselves off the screen and to push colleagues
on (if that seems to the prime minister's advantage). The point is
that, in the management of the cabinet, TV gives prime ministers
influence which, up to the point when a colleague resigns, they
can probably use against their colleagues better than colleagues
can against them.

By opening up a wide range of news locations, television has
forced prime ministers to make choices, as U.S. presidents have
already had to do, about the best location for putting out a particular message. For presidents, TV has forced, by comparison, a quantitative change. For prime ministers it has been qualitative, tending to draw them away from their parliamentary base—whether
to "scrums" in the lobbies just outside, or to the distant arenas of
TV summitry. When press secretaries started, the prime minister's
publicity was largely a matter of putting a gloss on his parliamentary performace (party occasions aside). This is still a time-
consuming routine, but strategically it has shrunk. Parliament of
course remains the prime minister's constitutional base, for which
he or she can never substitute a media mandate; but political
authority even there depends in part on peer group estimates of
the prime minister's performance on TV. Nor does the constitutional imperative prevent the development of a presidential style
of governing by prime ministers with a dominant public image
among their colleagues.

The "opinion-mobilizing role," traditionally weaker among
prime ministers than presidents, is linked more speculatively to TV
than are these other characteristics. It is linked also to intricate
questions about the role of ideology in policy making and to trends
in the party systems of parliamentary regimes. Policy making, arguably, is now driven less strongly than in the thirty years or so after
1945 both by ideology and by party. Prime ministers such as Mrs.
Thatcher may still have very strongly stated general beliefs. But
these are expressed in expediential actions reflecting more than
previously the claims of interest groups than of parties. Compare,
for instance, the dogma of Attlee's postwar nationalization pro-

gram, rooted deep in the class-based ideology of the Labour party, with the expediency of Mrs. Thatcher's privatization program—which did not feature in the rhetoric of her bid for power in 1979. Prime ministers who are not tied tightly to a party ideology perhaps have greater scope for setting the political agenda through media management. This is partly, again, a matter of trying to keep the media initiative.

As to the press secretaryship itself, this chapter has generalized a good deal. The reason is partly the limitations of space; but generalization is justified by the substantial similarities of the office between one country and another. Form and scale have changed over time. But chief executives work in a world where the common features of mass media, especially TV and radio, demand common types of response—certainly in the four countries considered here. All social institutions are to some extent conditioned by the media of communication. The behavior of chief executives and of those who work for them is no exception.

Notes

Much of the material for this chapter has been obtained by interviews, on or off the record, with present and former press secretaries and other members of presidents' and prime ministers' staffs. Citations have been limited to documentary sources. The research was carried out with the support of the Economic and Social Research Council of the U.K. (award no. E00232197), the Woodrow Wilson International Center, Washington, D.C., the Canadian High Commission, London, and the Australian National University, Canberra. This support is gratefully acknowledged.

1. M.B. Grossman and M.J. Kumar, *Portraying the President* (Baltimore: Johns Hopkins University Press, 1981), p. 23.

2. See, e.g., P. Anderson, *The President's Men* (New York, Doubleday, 1969).

3. Michael Cockerell, Peter Hennessy, and David Walker, *Sources Close to the Prime Minister* (London: Macmillan, 1984), p. 37.

4. Anthony Seldon, *Churchill's Indian Summer* (London: Hodder and Stoughton, 1981), p. 60.

5. Grossman and Kumar, *Portraying the President,* p. 23.

6. Elmer E. Cornwell, Jr., *Presidential Leadership of Public Opinion* (Bloomington: Indiana Unversity Press, 1965), pp. 218–20.

7. Stephen Hess, *The Government/Press Connection* (Washington, D.C.: Brookings, 1984), p. 8.

8. Jody Powell, *The Other Side of the Story* (New York: William Morrow, 1984).

9. Christina McCall-Newman, *Grits* (Toronto: Macmillan of Canada, 1982).

10. Charles Hill, *Both Sides of the Hill* (London: Heinemann, 1964).

11. Douglas Hurd, *An End to Promises* (London: Collins, 1979), pp. 73–74.

12. Stephen Mills, *The New Machine Men* (Ringwood, Victoria: Penguin Books, 1986).

13. William Clark, *From Three Worlds* (London: Sidgwick and Jackson, 1986).

14. A. Deakin, *Federated Australia* (Melbourne: Melbourne University Press, 1968).

15. J. Margach, *The Abuse of Power* (London: W. H. Allen, 1978), pp. 64–70.

16. James Deakin, *Straight Stuff* (New York: William Morrow, 1984).

17. Patrick Gossage, *Close to the Charisma* (Toronto: McClelland and Stewart, 1986), p. 192.

18. Dale C. Thomson, *Louis St. Laurent* (Toronto: Macmillan of Canada, 1967), pp. 469–71.

19. Hess, *The Government/Press Connection*, p. 1.

20. Samuel Kernell, *Going Public* (Washington, D.C.: CQ Press, 1986), chap. 3.

21. Colin Seymour-Ure, *The Press, Politics and the Public* (London: Methuen, 1968), p. 240.

22. For example, Cockerell et al., *Sources Close to the Prime Minister,* chap. 3.

23. Hess, *The Government/Press Connection,* p. 58.

24. *Manchester Guardian,* 14 October 1954.

25. Joe Haines, *The Politics of Power* (London: Jonathan Cape, 1977), chap. 5.

26. Colin Seymour-Ure, *The American President: Power and Communication* (New York: St. Martin's Press, 1982), chap. 3.

Notes on Contributors

Peter Aucoin is professor of political science and public administration at Dalhousie University and until recently was director of research for the Canadian Royal Commission on Electoral Reform and Party Financing. His many publications include books and articles on public administration and political institutions in Canada. He is the editor of *The Politics and Management of Restraint in Government* and coauthor of *The Centralization-Decentralization Conundrum: Organization Design and Management in Canadian Government*.

Colin Campbell, S.J. is University Professor in the Isabelle A. and Henry D. Martin Chair in Philosophy and Politics at Georgetown University and also directs the Graduate Public Policy Program. He is the author or coauthor of *The Canadian Senate, The Superbureaucrats, Governments under Stress, Managing the Presidency,* and *Politics and Government in Europe Today.* His coedited books include *Organizing Governance, Governing Organizations* and *The Bush Presidency: First Appraisals.* He is also editor of the international journal *Governance,* published by Basil Blackwell of Oxford.

Stuart Eizenstat was assistant to the president for domestic affairs and policy and executive director of the White House Domestic Policy Staff during the Carter administration. He is now a partner in the Washington law firm of Powell, Goldstein, Frazer, and Murphy and has been an adjunct lecturer at the John F. Kennedy School of Government at Harvard University since 1982.

Peter Hennessy is a visiting professor of government at Strathclyde University and cofounder of the Institute of Contemporary British History. He is "Whitehall Watch" columnist of *The Independent* and a regular presenter of the BBC Radio 4 "Analysis" program. He reported on Whitehall for ten years, mainly for *The Times,* the *Financial Times,* and *The Economist.* He is the author of *Cabinet* and *Whitehall* and coauthor of *Ruling Performance: British Governments from Attlee to Thatcher.*

Tom Hockin is a member of the Canadian Parliament for London West, Ontario, and the minister of state (small businesses and tourism), in which capacity he established the National Entrepreneurship Development Institute. He was formerly Canada's minister of state (finance). He is the author of several books on Canadian government and politics and has taught at York University and the University of Western Ontario.

George W. Jones is professor of government at the London School of Economics at the University of London. He has written extensively about the British prime minister, the cabinet, and their advisory networks, as well as on British local government, central-local relations, and local government finance. He recently completed a study for the Italian National Research Council on the prime minister's office in Britain since 1979 and is editor of *West European Prime Ministers*.

Harold F. Kendrick was a graduate student in political science at Louisiana State University, Baton Rouge, and research assistant for Kevin V. Mulcahy in writing *American National Security: A Presidential Perspective*.

Samuel Kernell is professor of political science and coordinator of the American Political Institutions Project at the University of California, San Diego. He has authored and edited numerous works, most recently, *Going Public: New Strategies of Presidential Leadership* and *Parallel Politics: Economic Policymaking in Japan and the United States*.

Lawrence J. Korb is director of the Center for Public Policy Education and senior fellow at the Brookings Institution. He has served as dean of the Graduate School of Public and International Affairs at the University of Pittsburgh, vice-president of the Raytheon Company, assistant secretary of defense under the Reagan administration, and on the faculty of the U.S. Naval War College. He is the author of *The Joint Chiefs of Staff: The First Twenty-Five Years* and *The Rise and Fall of the Pentagon*.

Kevin V. Mulcahy is associate professor of political science at Louisiana State University, Baton Rouge. Among his publications are: *America Votes, Public Policy and the Arts, Presidents and the Administration of Foreign Policy: FDR to Reagan, American National Secu-*

rity: A Presidential Perspective. He is currently at work on *America's Commitment to Culture* as well as a book on George Bush's presidential management style and a study of Walt W. Rostow as national security adviser.

B. Guy Peters is Maurice Falk Professor of American Government and chair of the Department of Political Science at the University of Pittsburgh. He is coeditor of *Governance* and formerly cochair of the International Political Science Association Research Committee on the Structure and Organization of Government. He has written many books and articles on public policy and administration, including *the Politics of Bureaucracy, Comparing Public Bureaucracies,* and *Public Administration: Challenges, Choices, Consequences.*

James P. Pfiffner is professor of government and politics at George Mason University. He was formerly on the faculty at the University of California, Riverside, and California State University, Fullerton. He is the author of *The Strategic Presidency* and *The President, the Budget, and Congress: Impoundment and the 1974 Budget Act,* editor of *The President and Economic Policy* and *The Managerial Presidency,* and coeditor of *The Presidency in Transition.*

Joseph A. Pika is associate professor of political science and international relations at the University of Delaware. He has published widely on the presidency, focusing on White House staffing and relations between the White House and outside constituencies, especially interest groups and Congress. He is currently at work on a study of presidential relations with interest groups from Roosevelt to Reagan, as well as texts on presidential elections and the presidency in general.

William Plowden is research associate, Institute of Policy Research, London. He was executive director of the U.K. Harkness Fellowships at the Commonwealth Fund, 1988–1991. He was director-general of the Royal Institute of Public Administration, London, 1978–1988. Before that time he was a policy analyst in the Central Policy Review Staff, Cabinet Office, lecturer in government at the London School of Economics, and an official on the U.K. Board of Trade. He is the author of *The Motor Car and Politics in Britain* and coauthor of *Inside the Think Tank: Advising the Cabinet 1971–83.*

Roger B. Porter is assistant to the president for economic and domestic policy. He is on leave from the Kennedy School of Government at Harvard University, where he is the IBM Professor of Business and Government. During the Reagan and Ford administrations, he was deputy assistant to the president and director of the Office of Policy Development and special assistant to the president and executive secretary of the Economic Policy Board. He is the author of *Presidential Decision Making* and *The U.S.-U.S.S.R. Grain Agreement.*

Bert A. Rockman is a senior fellow in the Governmental Studies Program of the Brookings Institution and professor of political science and research professor in the University Center for International Studies at the University of Pittsburgh. He is the author of *The Leadership Question: The Presidency and the American System,* coauthor of *Bureaucrats and Politicians in Western Democracies.* He is also coeditor of *Elite Studies and Communist Politics* and *The Bush Presidency: First Appraisals.* He is currently working as coinvestigator on a twenty-year time-series study of senior executives in the U.S. federal government.

Colin Seymour-Ure is professor of government at the University of Kent. He has published widely in many aspects of the relations between government and mass communication, from political rumors to press partisanship. His books include *The American President: Power and Communication* and *The British Press and Broadcasting since 1945.*

Patrick Weller is professor of politics and public policy and director of the Centre for Australian Public Sector Management in the Division of Commerce and Administration at Griffith University. He is the author or coauthor of *Treasury Control in Australia, Politics and Policy in Australia, Can Ministers Cope?, First Among Equals,* and *Malcolm Fraser PM.*

Margaret Jane Wyszomirski is director of the Office of Policy, Planning, and Research at the National Endowment for the Arts and formerly director of the graduate public policy program at Georgetown University. She has published widely on the presidency, American public policy, and arts policy, and is on the editorial board of *Governance* and the *Journal of Arts Management and the Law.* Her co-edited books include *Art, Ideology, and Politics* and *The Cost of Culture;* she edited *Congress and the Arts.*

Pitt Series in Policy and Institutional Studies
Bert A. Rockman, Editor

The Acid Rain Controversy
James L. Regens and Robert W. Rycroft

Affirmative Action at Work: Law, Politics, and Ethics
Bron Raymond Taylor

Agency Merger and Bureaucratic Redesign
Karen M. Hult

The Aging: A Guide to Public Policy
Bennett M. Rich and Martha Baum

Arms for the Horn: U.S. Security Policy in Ethiopia and Somalia, 1953–1991
Jeffrey A. Lefebvre

The Atlantic Alliance and the Middle East
Joseph I. Coffey and Gianni Bonvicini, Editors

The Budget-Maximizing Bureaucrat: Appraisals and Evidence
André Blais and Stéphane Dion

Clean Air: The Policies and Politics of Pollution Control
Charles O. Jones

The Competitive City: The Political Economy of Suburbia
Mark Schneider

Conflict and Rhetoric in French Policymaking
Frank R. Baumgartner

Congress and Economic Policymaking
Darrell M. West

Congress Oversees the Bureaucracy: Studies in Legislative Supervision
Morris S. Ogul

Democracy in Japan
Takeshi Ishida and Ellis S. Krauss, Editors

Demographic Change and the American Future
R. Scott Fosler, William Alonso, Jack A. Meyer, and Rosemary Kern

Economic Decline and Political Change: Canada, Great Britain, and the United States
Harold D. Clarke, Marianne C. Stewart, and Gary Zuk, Editors

Executive Leadership in Anglo-American Systems
Colin Campbell, S.J., and Margaret Jane Wyszomirski, Editors

Extraordinary Measures: The Exercise of Prerogative Powers in the United States
Daniel P. Franklin

Foreign Policy Motivation: A General Theory and a Case Study
Richard W. Cottam

"He Shall Not Pass This Way Again": The Legacy of Justice William O. Douglas
Stephen L. Wasby, Editor

Homeward Bound: Explaining Changes in Congressional Behavior
Glenn Parker

How Does Social Science Work? Reflections on Practice
Paul Diesing

Imagery and Ideology in U.S. Policy Toward Libya, 1969–1982
Mahmoud G. ElWarfally

The Impact of Policy Analysis
James M. Rogers

Iran and the United States: A Cold War Case Study
Richard W. Cottam

Japanese Prefectures and Policymaking
Steven R. Reed

Making Regulatory Policy
Keith Hawkins and John M. Thomas, Editors

Managing the Presidency: Carter, Reagan, and the Search for Executive Harmony
Colin Campbell, S.J.

Organizing Governance, Governing Organizations
Colin Campbell, S.J., and B. Guy Peters, Editors

Party Organizations in American Politics
Cornelius P. Cotter et al.

Perceptions and Behavior in Soviet Foreign Policy
Richard K. Herrmann

Pesticides and Politics: The Life Cycle of a Public Issue
Christopher J. Bosso

Policy Analysis by Design
Davis B. Bobrow and John S. Dryzek

The Political Failure of Employment Policy, 1945–1982
Gary Mucciaroni

Political Leadership: A Source Book
Barbara Kellerman, Editor

The Politics of Public Utility Regulation
William T. Gormley, Jr.

The Politics of the U.S. Cabinet: Representation in the Executive Branch, 1789–1984
Jeffrey E. Cohen

Politics Within the State: Elite Bureaucrats and Industrial Policy in Authoritarian Brazil
Ben Ross Schneider

The Presidency and Public Policy Making
George C. Edwards III, Steven A. Shull, and Norman C. Thomas, Editors

Private Markets and Public Intervention: A Primer for Policy Designers
Harvey Averch

Public Policy in Latin America: A Comparative Survey
John W. Sloan

Reluctant Partners: Implementing Federal Policy
Robert P. Stoker

Roads to Reason: Transportation, Administration, and Rationality in Colombia
Richard E. Hartwig

Site Unseen: The Politics of Siting a Nuclear Waste Repository
Gerald Jacob

The Struggle for Social Security, 1900–1935
Roy Lubove

Tage Erlander: Serving the Welfare State, 1946–1969
Olof Ruin

Traffic Safety Reform in the United States and Great Britain
Jerome S. Legge, Jr.

Urban Alternatives: Public and Private Markets in the Provision of Local Services
Robert M. Stein

The U.S. Experiment in Social Medicine: The Community Health Center Program, 1965–1986
Alice Sardell